*Religion and Politics
in Europe and the United States*

Religion and Politics
in Europe and the United States

Transnational Historical Approaches

Edited by

Volker Depkat and Jürgen Martschukat

Woodrow Wilson Center Press
Washington, D.C.

The Johns Hopkins University Press
Baltimore

EDITORIAL OFFICES

Woodrow Wilson Center Press
Woodrow Wilson International Center for Scholars
One Woodrow Wilson Plaza
1300 Pennsylvania Avenue NW
Washington, D.C. 20004-3027
www.wilsoncenter.org

ORDER FROM

The Johns Hopkins University Press
Hampden Station
P.O. Box 50370
Baltimore, Maryland 20211
Telephone 1-800-527-5487
www.press.jhu.edu/books/

2 4 6 8 9 7 5 3 1

Library of Congress Cataloging-in-Publication Data Applied For

ISBN 978-1-4214-0810-1

Wilson Center

Woodrow Wilson International Center for Scholars

The Wilson Center, chartered by Congress as the official memorial to President Woodrow Wilson, is the nation's key non-partisan policy forum for tackling global issues through independent research and open dialogue to inform actionable ideas for Congress, the Administration, and the broader policy community.

Conclusions or opinions expressed in Center publications and programs are those of the authors and speakers and do not necessarily reflect the views of the Center staff, fellows, trustees, advisory groups, or any individuals or organizations that provide financial support to the Center.

The Center is the home of dialogue television and radio, *The WQ* digital magazine, and Woodrow Wilson Center Press. Please visit us on the web at www.wilsoncenter.org.

Jane Harman, Director, President, and CEO

Contents

Acknowledgments

The chapters in this book were originally presented at the Ninth Krefeld Historical Symposium in the City of Krefeld in May 2008. We want to thank the contributors for their interest, their enthusiastic participation, and their patience. We are grateful for the support and the financial funding provided by the City of Krefeld, the Gerda Henkel Foundation, and the Kuckartz Foundation. We thank Friedhelm Kutz, Mareen Herda, and our colleagues on the Academic Advisory Board of the City of Krefeld, Norbert Finzsch and Ursula Lehmkuhl, for their cooperation and assistance. Furthermore, we would like to thank Jedidiah Becker for his thorough job in editing the contributions by the native speakers of German in this volume. Finally, we want to use the opportunity to commemorate Jürgen Jacobs, who, as director of the Fachbereich Stadtmarketing, Medien, Büro des Rates, was a strong supporter of the Ninth and other Krefeld Historical Symposia. He died at age 51 in March 2009.

Religion and Politics
in Europe and the United States

Chapter 1

Introduction: Religion and Politics in Europe and the United States

Volker Depkat and Jürgen Martschukat

When Judith Butler, Jürgen Habermas, Charles Taylor, and Cornel West meet for a panel discussion, something fundamental must be at stake. On October 22, 2009, New York University invited four of the world's most renowned and influential intellectuals from Europe, Canada, and the United States to "rethink secularism" and consider "the power of religion in the public sphere." A large audience, eager to gain a deeper understanding of religion, secularism, and the modern world, waited to gain access to this intellectual marathon of four and one-half hours, which received a global audience through extensive international press coverage.[1]

The discussion site at Cooper Union's Great Hall in lower Manhattan is just a stone's throw away from Ground Zero, an epicenter of an event that made religion's unbroken significance in the modern world visible. At first glance, it seems obvious that 9/11 brought religion back to the agenda of politicians, intellectuals, and the larger public alike. As we argue in the final chapter of the book, an upsurge of sentiments, arguments, and actions driven by religion and religious convictions followed the attacks on the

1

Twin Towers and the Pentagon. A return of religion has been proclaimed in both Europe and America by philosophers such as Jürgen Habermas and Charles Taylor, referring to numerous interrelations and interactions among religious leaders, politicians, and the state.[2] Arguing from a historian's perspective, however, one also must stress that religion, understood by Frank Lambert "as a set of beliefs in a transcendent God, grounded in an authoritative sacred text, and expressed by a body of believers through the performance of certain rituals and adherence to a specific moral code," has never vanished from the modern age.[3]

For those primarily seeking to understand the concept of modernity, the powerful dynamics of Christian forces in the West after 9/11 was more stunning, requiring an explanation greater than the Islamic drive in Middle Eastern and West Asian societies, politics, and cultures. The eminence of religion and its influence on Western politics in recent years raises the question as to what extent our understanding of modernity, rationality, and secularism must be reconsidered. Let us stress here that in using the term *modernity* we refer neither to a teleological process nor to an ethical judgment, but rather to a historically specific social, cultural, and political configuration that emerged with the Enlightenment in the eighteenth century and is defined by shared values, practices, and structures of social organization. Our denotation of *the West* is also historically specific. Even though in regard to this book, the West can be vaguely determined in geographic categories as meaning both sides of the North Atlantic, the term is broader in its meaning. It is conclusively used, as defined by historians Dipesh Chakrabarty and Anselm Doering-Manteuffel, as a reference to a mutual tradition of thought and a shared system of cultural values and social organization emerging from multidirectional processes of cultural transfer over the Atlantic Ocean since the eighteenth century.[4] With the Enlightenment and the Age of Atlantic and Democratic Revolutions,[5] this cultural and political constellation called *Western modernity* began taking shape in Europe and America. One of the basic premises of its historical narrative was the creation of a secular and rational world, based on a separation of reason, politics, and the state in one sphere and religion, enchantment, and the churches in a separate domain. It is important to keep in mind that this grand historical narrative was shaped by a genuinely modern and Western historiography, unfolding precisely in those enlightened and post-revolutionary nineteenth-century Western cultures that were described by the narrative as approaching the ultimate stage of human development. In juxtaposition to Western modernity, on the basis of a gaze that perhaps is best described as following "orientalist" patterns, this narrative presented non-Western and premodern societies as interminably grounded in irrational religiosity.[6]

Therefore, reevaluating the ties and frictions between religion, secularism, and modernity and reconsidering the "power of religion" in the "public sphere," which Jürgen Habermas described in his highly influential study as the primary site of rational discourse in democratic societies,[7] also means questioning the basic premises of our history, culture, and society and crossing into the practices and prejudices of historians and sociologists themselves. Thus, critical reflections on the relationship of religion and politics in Europe and the United States also invite us to abandon any notion of our history as a teleological path to modernity and of the division of our world into secular centers and religious peripheries.

Yet the constellation is even more manifold than this. Without question, the frequently touted dichotomy between the "the West and the rest" or the "modern and the premodern parts of world" must be exposed as overly simplistic. Even the West itself is not as homogeneous as it initially might appear in a dichotomization of "the West and the rest."[8] After 9/11, frictions between Europe and the United States became more visible than before, as Europe and America diverged substantially in their political agendas and the meaning given to so-called moral values and religious beliefs in political culture, as well as in their political decision-making processes. The American response to the attacks on the Twin Towers and the Pentagon revitalized an old debate regarding the character, traditions, and specificities of U.S. foreign policy in comparison to Europe's former great powers and empire builders, thus igniting transatlantic arguments revolving around the notion of the United States as a "crusader state."[9] Without doubt, in the early twenty-first century, Europe also experienced an upsurge of political conservatism, yet the "old world" did not see the formation and rise of a religious right as powerful and politically influential as that in America. The frequent recourse to scripture by the George W. Bush administration for grounding or garnishing political positions puzzled most European observers. After the attacks on the World Trade Center, these differences in the role of religion in politics advanced to impede the dialogue between Europe and America. One might even write that in a post-9/11 world hardly any other issue seemed to exist that revealed transatlantic differences as clearly as the relationship of religion and politics.

These geopolitical jolts at the beginning of the twenty-first century have inspired political scientists and historians alike to intensify their scrutiny of religion, politics, and their history on both sides of the Atlantic more deeply. In this context, focusing on European–American relations and the meaning of religion requires the dissolution of the seeming unity of the West and a carving out of differences and marking of common points for both sides of the Atlantic. Second, and equally important, each analysis of the present requires an understanding of the past. Accordingly, political commentators have sought to explain transatlantic tensions in the twenty-first century by examining the divergence in religiosity in the Age of Atlantic Revolutions.[10] Likewise, political scientists and sociologists have compared the development of societies with extended social security systems, on the one hand, with societies strongly based on individualism, personal risk, and an accompanying larger socioeconomic vulnerability on the other. They stress that being exposed to personal risk drives religiosity. Also, historians of European–American relations joined this debate, leading many to rethink and revalue their findings and models, for instance, of an "American exceptionalism" or a "German *Sonderweg*."[11]

Scrutinizing the relationship of religion and politics in history quickly discloses the persistence and continued relevance of religion in the modern world. First of all, this relevance can be seen in scholarly research because historians, sociologists, and other scholars have never totally abandoned the study of religion and secularism; some have even suggested rethinking our historical and historiographical premises on the basis of notions of secularism and modernity prior to 2001. After all, powerful religious fundamentalism existed in early twentieth-century America, climaxing in 1925 in the Scopes Trial as a public battle between Darwinism and a literal reading of the Bible. Also, the contemporary rise of religious conservatism did not begin with 9/11 but rather in the 1970s, gaining ground with the so-called Reagan Revolution.[12] Second, since the Age of Democratic Revolutions, as a set of random historical examples indicate, the significance and power of religious premises never disappeared in Western societies, though they have not necessarily been fundamentalist or extremist in their expression. For instance, although the eighteenth century saw a transformation of power structures and the development of a new legitimation of political rule heading away from transcendental power toward contract theory, religious—and specifically Christian—influence was nevertheless deemed indispensable for the functioning and survival of a polity. During the American Revolution, politicians and philosophers excitedly discussed how their republican experiment for a state lacking divine authority and transcendentally legitimated power could continue to exist successfully. As a solution, they stressed that a good Christian incorporated all the particular qualities required to make a good republican citizen. As the Philadelphian Benjamin Rush explained in 1786:

> A Christian … cannot fail of being a republican, for every precept of the Gospel inculcates those degrees of humility, self-denial, and brotherly kindness, which are directly opposed to the pride of monarchy and the pageantry of a court. A Christian cannot fail of being useful to the republic, for his religion teacheth him, that no man 'liveth to himself.' And lastly, a Christian cannot fail of being wholly inoffensive, for his religion teacheth him, in all things to do to others what he would wish, in like circumstances, they should do to him.[13]

Let us, as a second example, look at European perspectives on the American democratic experiment. The U.S. constitution and democracy, with its faith in individualism, appeared to many an observer as not only the first but also the "purest" concretization of a world based on the ideas and values of the Enlightenment. In the 1830s, the French traveler Alexis de Tocqueville saw the United States as the land of Europe's future—that is, as the beacon of radical democracy and individualism indicating the direction toward which the process of world history would head. At the same time, Tocqueville presented a nuanced understanding of the relationship of religion and politics in modern history, in general, and in the United States, in particular. Although he praised a secular and individualized American society, Tocqueville also stressed the significant meaning of religion for the *polis*. Religion, Tocqueville wrote, was the means to teach the enterprising and profit-maximizing American citizen a spirit that was indispensable for the fruitful existence of the republic. Religion made the individual understand his "duties towards his kind and thus [drew] him at times from the contemplation of himself."[14] Also, Tocqueville was astounded by the very worldly way that religion was actually lived in America, through the here and now, as opposed to what he understood as the premodern alternative European version—namely, through medieval religious practices:

> In the Middle Ages the clergy spoke of nothing but a future state; they hardly cared to prove that a sincere Christian may be a happy man here below. But the American preachers are constantly referring to the earth, and it is only with great difficulty that they can divert their attention from it. To touch their congregations, they always show them how fa-

vorable religious opinions are to freedom and public tranquillity; and it is often difficult to ascertain from their discourses whether the principal object of religion is to procure eternal felicity in the other world or prosperity in this.[15]

As a third example, we would like to take a look at the *fin de siècle*. Both major issues raised by Benjamin Rush and Alexis de Tocqueville—that is, worldly prosperity and religion as a moral resource in a secular *polis*—reverberate in the writings of the great European theoreticians of modernity, rationalization, and individualization: Max Weber and Émile Durkheim. For Weber, denoting the "disenchantment of the world" and its rationalization did not necessarily imply an end of religion and its influence. After all, in his seminal and admittedly highly contested study, *The Protestant Ethic and the Spirit of Capitalism*, Weber traced the origins of modern capitalism to the Puritan mindset of colonial North America.[16] Émile Durkheim, another sociological godfather of modernity, stressed the significance of religion and religious rituals as a socially cohesive force. By understanding religion as social cement strengthening a polity and its collective moral, Durkheim did not maintain a dichotomy of the spiritual and the carnal but presented religion and the polity as closely intertwined.[17] Even though Durkheim did not base his findings on observations of American society, thoughts previously uttered by Rush and Tocqueville on the meaning of religion for the American republic resonated in Durkheim's writings.

As a fourth and final example, let us take a brief look at the institutional level of religion: the churches. In Europe, churches partnered extensively in state-building processes from the beginning, thereby producing strong alliances between crown and altar.[18] However, the emerging monarchic states and organized church apparatuses were anything but equal partners, because the authority of the state rested to a very large degree on the subjugation of the churches under the rule of the crown. As junior partners in the state-building process, the state churches served important functions in disciplining subjects and keeping democratic aspirations in check. The guarantee of religious freedom in the late eighteenth and early nineteenth centuries did not translate into European monarchies relinquishing their control over churches. On the contrary, with the authority and bureaucracies of the state now fully developed, the state's rule over the churches reached its climax in Europe around 1800. No longer in need of a junior partner, European state bureaucracies embarked on conflict-prone policies of aggressive secularization. After the revolutions of 1848 and 1849, state pressures on the churches lessened considerably. Yet particularly in Protestant states, the alliance between crown and altar remained largely intact. Even the downfall of powerful monarchies in the wake of World War I did not lead to the complete separation of church and state. Although the European democracies emerging from the carnage on the battlefields remained strictly neutral in religious matters, the separation of church and state remained incomplete. In Germany, some of the formerly established churches were legally defined as public institutions and not as private associations, thus explaining why the Catholic Church and several Protestant churches in Germany continue to collect taxes through the state to this very day. In Great Britain and throughout Scandinavia, mild forms of established churchdom persist.

In America, democracy did not develop against the churches and religious communities, but very much with and within them. The church stood not as an enemy to self-government, self-determination, and self-reliance, but rather as one of their strongest roots.[19] Against this backdrop, separation of church and state was not only a means to protect the state and politics from the dominating influence of the churches, but also an instrument to protect the churches from the desires of politics and politicians.[20] Furthermore, American democracy, economy, and liberalism unleashed unrelenting pressures on churches and religious communities to transform themselves to adapt to these specific circumstances within the contexts of America's sociopolitical systems. The specific forms of institutionalizing religion in the United States, the organizational setup of churches and religious communities, the methods of financing them, the innovative uses of modern media, and finally the specific forms of politicization of churches and religious communities in America's democracy—all cannot be understood without taking into account the constant pressure to innovate and adapt to American modernity.[21]

Driven by these contemporary debates, questions, and reevaluations, this book will contribute to the discussion on the relationship of religion and politics in modern Western societies, providing timely discussions and arguments with a historically deep perspective. In doing so, we will seek to carve out common grounds and differences between Europe and the United States in the Atlantic world. Our analyses and the concept of this book are provided with fertile ground by current and dynamic historiographic debates on "political history" and its reconceptualization as "history of the political" and of "the polity." At first glance, the difference between *politics* and *the political* might sound marginal, yet a closer look reveals it as seminal. Whereas a traditional approach defined *politics* as a set of institutions and governing practices of the state and by the state, more recent perspectives, speaking of *the political*, instead try to grasp a socially, culturally, intellectually, and also institutionally structured space in which human beings live and interact. This broader understanding of the political as the structures, strategies, means, and perceptions that organize the polity encompasses political cultures and the cultural foundations of the political, becoming manifest in the ensemble of values and practices that define individual and collective perspectives of the world and explain it as meaningful. If the realm of the political is understood as a multilayered field of interaction that structures the social and cultural organization of a *polis* and is simultaneously structured by it, then without doubt, analyzing the political requires also taking spiritual and religious forces into account. Vice versa, types of religious belief, as well as religious practices and interactions, are of utmost political significance. If politics is more than institutional regulations and governing practices by the state and for the state, an institutional separation of state and church does not necessarily lead to a disentanglement of politics and religion. The new history of the political provides us with concepts and perspectives to take this situation into account, thereby allowing us to understand historically how religious symbols and actions can become focal elements of political debate, as well as how they become crucial for institutionalizing and upholding a political order that is based on particular values.[22]

To put the contemporary debates about religion and politics, as well as the transatlantic convergences and divergences in the field, into a historical perspective, we will follow five trajectories. These paths will take us to major intersections of modernity, the polity, and religion and their historical formations. Each trajectory will provide observations on the United States and Europe, thereby opening up an Atlantic space full of demarcations, interactions, and interdependences. A first and most significant field is the legitimation of power and rule, moving through a period of essential transformation in the eighteenth century. Yet as contributions by both Frank Kelleter and Michael Broers will show as they scrutinize the problem of religion in the postrevolutionary state in part I of the book, religious rationales did not entirely disappear in Europe or America. Exposing the various alliances that religious and Enlightenment discourses entered into, Kelleter argues in chapter 2 that a specific language of reason that emerged in Revolutionary America supported a democratic consensus. As hinted earlier by Benjamin Rush's equating a good republican to a good Christian, we will learn how religion was very well deprived of its justifying function for legitimate rule. Yet the principles of enlightened politics were nevertheless implemented—not against, but within established Christian traditions. American revolutionaries claimed to be in agreement with the new nation's Christian heritage, seeing religion as a moral resource that could hold together a society organized solely on the basis of natural rights liberalism, while containing all sorts of radicalisms in check.

At the same time, the various Protestant churches perceived liberal democracy as the best guarantor of their own religious freedom as the condition of possibility for "true" Christianity to emerge henceforth. As we are told by Michael Broers in chapter 3, European societies also continued to use religion as a social, political, and cultural cement while in a secular world shaped by the French Revolution and Napoleonic reforms. However, Broers interprets the renaissance of a political culture centering on monarchy, the divine right of kings, and the public displays of piety in the first half of the nineteenth century as nostalgia, responding to the ruptures created by the bureaucracy-driven politics of secularism in post-Napoleonic Europe. Thus, in the legitimation of political power and rule on both sides of the Atlantic, reason and religion went hand in hand, yet the form of their arrangement varied substantially.

Part II of the book will zoom in on one of the major elements of statehood, describing how religious motivations and justifications of punishments were both abandoned and taken on from the eighteenth century until today. Here, the book will focus on the death penalty and the history of its (de)legitimation as one of the recent sites of major differences in the Atlantic realm. Daniel A. Cohen explores in chapter 4 the ways in which New Englanders interwove religious and secular ideologies in grappling with issues of crime and punishment from the 1670s through the 1820s. According to Cohen, Americans of the eighteenth and nineteenth centuries felt most comfortable when they could plausibly incorporate the multiple sanctions of Protestant belief, Enlightenment ideology, and revolutionary patriotism into the field of criminal justice.

In a similar vein, André Krischer shows in chapter 5 how, step by step, theological arguments lost importance in the early modern English criminal procedure between 1600 and 1800, whereas at the same time, theologians shifted the focus of their sermons to the punishment of the offender. Krischer describes this shift as "rearguard action ... of religion in the context of modernization." Again, rationalization and religion intermingled on both sides of the Atlantic, yet in different forms. Anthony Santoro takes up this argument with regard to contemporary penal politics in the United States in chapter 6, where he discusses the power of religious patterns of perception and action in Virginia's current death penalty system.

The complicated relationship of religion, science, and technology in the modern world is the subject of part III of the book. In chapter 7, James Gilbert unearths the complex constitutional relationships between the state, civil society, and religious institutions in the market-driven universe of U.S. culture, framing the development of sciences, technology, and religion in America. In chapter 8, Ronald E. Doel moves our attention to the crucial creationist–evolutionist debate, clearly exposing the idea of a war between science and religion as an integral part of modernity's mindset and a cultural construction emerging in the process of the formation of this mindset. Whereas Gilbert and Doel stress the strong influence of religious belief on scientific questions and findings in America, Monika Wohlrab-Sahr and Thomas Schmidt-Lux take us in chapter 9 to the history of the German Democratic Republic (GDR) and, therefore, of a state that pursued a strict policy of secularization, which turned the supposed antagonism between religion and science into a key element of GDR ideology and identity politics.

Ethnic diversity and racial discrimination are two sides of the same coin, both being immensely powerful in the creation of a modern order. Thus we arrive at the topic of part IV of our book. Often enough, ethnic and racial categorizations were driven by and attached to certain types of religious beliefs. Klaus Hödl and Michelle Mart show in their chapters how self-images and perceptions of Jews in both Europe and the United States in the late nineteenth and twentieth centuries corresponded with their opportunities for political and social participation. Both chapters 10 and 11 take the fluidity of religious identities in the modern world as their point of departure and discuss the practices of marginalization as well as Jewish counterstrategies. In doing so, they demonstrate how religious forces participated in the creation of a racially defined polity. They also show how religious attributes are racialized and to what extent they were used differently in the construction of citizenship and nationhood in Austria and the United States.

Finally, part V of the book addresses violence and warfare, taking us into the realm of international politics to critically assess the potential for conflict emerging from religious worldviews. Historian Michael Hochgeschwender explores in chapter 12 the basic constellations of the issue by asking what exactly defines violent acts as religious and under which historical conditions are religious worldviews prone to realize their potential for conflict. Political scientist Gerlinde Groitl utters a word of caution in chapter 13 not to overstate the role of religion in international conflicts and in global power structures after the end of the Cold War. Other forces that are not necessarily related to religion—such as globalization, the weakening of state structures, and the empowerment of nonstate actors—must also be taken into account.

Thus, the chapters by Michael Hochgeschwender and Gerlinde Groitl, as well as the concluding remarks from our perspective in the final chapter of the book, stress that after 9/11 and the recent end of secularism not every move is driven by religious forces. Yet they simultaneously remind us that rethinking secularism leads to the conclusion that religion is an immensely powerful player in the sphere of the political, precisely because of its interaction with so many other forces. Furthermore, the findings of this book suggest that processes of secularization are anything but linear and that the continuing struggle between the disenchantment and reenchantment of the world is a constitutive element of modernity itself. To describe the equally synergetic and troubled relationships between religion and politics in the modern age, a language of cycles, crosscurrents, ebbs and flows, ongoing tensions, and ideological synergies appears to be more appropriate than a language of linearity. This remains, as will be shown in the following pages, generally true for both Europe and America, yet with immense differences in detail, intensity, and context. Only historical, deep analyses can provide us with the insight needed to understand the differences, similarities, and interdependencies of religion and politics for both sides of the Atlantic.

Notes

1. See, for instance, Sebastian Moll, "Tagung in New York: Einsatz in Manhattan." *Frankfurter Rundschau*, October 24, 2010.

2. Charles Taylor, *A Secular Age* (Cambridge, MA: Harvard University Press, 2007); Jürgen Habermas, *Between Naturalism and Religion: Philosophical Essays*, trans. Ciaran Cronin (Cambridge, U.K.: Polity Press, 2008; first published 2005 in German); Hans Joas and Klaus Wiegandt, eds., *Säkularisierung und die Weltreligionen* (Frankfurt: Fischer, 2007). A sociological blind eye until the beginning of the 1980s with regard to religion as a significant factor in American public life and politics is, for instance, diagnosed by Allen D. Hertzke, "American Religion and Politics: A Review Essay," *Western Political Quarterly* 41, no. 4 (1988): 825–38.

3. Frank Lambert, *Religion in American Politics: A Short History* (Princeton, NJ: Princeton University Press, 2008), 11.

4. Dipesh Chakrabarty, *Provincializing Europe: Postcolonial Thought and Historical Difference* (Princeton, NJ: Princeton University Press, 2000); Anselm Doering-Manteuffel, *Wie westlich sind die Deutschen: Amerikanisierung und Westernisierung im 20. Jahrhundert* (Göttingen, Germany: Vandenhoeck & Ruprecht, 1999).

5. Jacques Godechot, *France and the Atlantic Revolution of the Eighteenth Century, 1770–1799* (New York: Free Press, 1965); Robert Palmer, *The Age of Democratic Revolutions*, 2 vols. (Princeton, NJ; Princeton University Press, 1959).

6. David Gary Shaw, "Modernity between Us and Them: The Place of Religion within History," *History and Theory* 45 (December 2006): 1–9, especially at 4–5; Talal Asad, *Formations of the Secular: Christianity, Islam, Modernity* (Stanford, CA: Stanford University Press, 2003); Shmuel N. Eisenstadt, "Multiple Modernities," *Daedalus* 129, no. 1 (Winter 2000): 1–29; Edward Said, *Orientalism* (New York: Vintage, 1979).

7. Jürgen Habermas, *The Structural Transformation of the Public Sphere: An Inquiry into a Category of Bourgeois Society* (Cambridge, MA: MIT Press, 1989; 1962 in German).

8. Stuart Hall, "The West and the Rest: Discourse and Power," in *Modernity: An Introduction to Modern Societies*, ed. Stuart Hall, David Held, Don Hubert, and Kenneth Thompson (Oxford, U.K.: Blackwell, 1996): 184–227.

9. See, for instance, Jochen Hils and Jürgen Wilzewski, eds., *Defekte Demokratie: Crusader State? Die Weltpolitik der USA in der Ära Bush* (Trier, Germany: Wissenschaftlicher Verlag, 2006); Carl P. Close and Robert Higgs, eds., *Opposing the Crusader State: Alternatives to Global Interventionism* (Oakland, CA: Independent Institute, 2007); Walter A. McDougall, *Promised Land, Crusader State: The American Encounter with the World Since 1776* (Boston: Houghton Mifflin, 1997); Michael Lind, *The American Way of Strategy* (Oxford, U.K.: Oxford University Press, 2006); Robert Kagan, *Of Paradise and Power: America and Europe in the New World Order* (New York: Knopf, 2003); Robert Kagan, *Dangerous Nation* (New York: Knopf, 2006); Gerlinde Groitl, *Evangelical Internationalism: The American Christian Right and Global Human Rights* (Hamburg, Germany: Kovač, 2007).

10. Brian C. Anderson, "Secular Europe, Religious America," *Public Interest* 155 (2004): 143–58.

11. Pippa Norris and Ronald Inglehart, *Sacred and Secular: Religion and Politics Worldwide* (Cambridge, U.K.: Cambridge University Press, 2004); Hartmut Lehmann, ed., *Transatlantische Religionsgeschichte: 18. bis 20. Jahrhundert* (Göttingen, Germany: Wallstein, 2006). See also Tobias Mörschel, ed., *Macht Glaube Politik? Religion und Politik in Europa und Amerika* (Göttingen, Germany: Vandenhoeck & Ruprecht, 2006); Dagmar Pruin, Rolf Schieder, and Johannes Zachhuber, eds., *Religion and Politics in the United States and Germany: Old Divisions and New Frontiers; Religion und Politik in den USA: Traditionelle Differenzen und neue Herausforderungen* (Berlin: LIT, 2008). The recent literature is analyzed by Uta Andrea Balbier, "'Sag: Wie hast Du's mit der Religion?' Das Verhältnis von Religion und Politik als Gretchenfrage der Zeitgeschichte," H-Soz-u-Kult, Berlin, November 10, 2009, http://hsozkult.geschichte. hu-berlin.de/forum/2009-11-001.

12. See, for instance, the intriguing discussion of the return of religion as opposed to religion as a persistent force and continuously used analytical tool between R. Stephen Warner, "Work in Progress toward a New Paradigm for the Sociological Study of Religion in the United States," *American Journal of Sociology* 98, no. 5 (1993): 1044–93, and Frank J. Lechner, "The 'New Paradigm' in the Sociology of Religion:

Comment on Warner," *American Journal of Sociology* 103, no. 1 (1997): 182–92. Numerous publications describe and analyze the rise of the religious right since the 1970s; see, for instance, Clyde Wilcox and Carin Larson, *Onward Christian Soldiers? The Religious Right in American Politics*, 3rd ed. (Boulder, CO: Westview Press, 2006).

13. Benjamin Rush, *A Plan for the Establishment of Public Schools and the Diffusion of Knowledge in Pennsylvania; to Which Are Added, Thoughts upon the Mode of Education, Proper in a Republic* (Philadelphia: Thomas Dobson, 1786), 16.

14. Alexis de Tocqueville, *Democracy in America*, trans. Henry Reeve (New York: Colonial Press, 1899; first published in 1835/1840), vol. 2, sec. 1, chap. 5, http://xroads. virginia.edu/~HYPER/DETOC/toc_indx.html.

15. Tocqueville, *Democracy in America*, vol. 2, sec. 2, chap. 9.

16. Max Weber, *The Protestant Ethic and the Spirit of Capitalism*, trans. Talcott Parsons (London: Routledge, 1992; first published 1904–05 in German).

17. Émile Durkheim, *The Elementary Forms of Religious Life* (New York: Free Press, 1995; first published 1912 in French). See also Émile Durkheim, *On Morality and Society: Selected Writings*, ed. Robert N. Bellah (Chicago: University of Chicago Press, 1973); Stuart Hall, David Held, Don Hubert, and Kenneth Thompson, eds., *Modernity: An Introduction to Modern Societies* (Oxford, U.K.: Blackwell, 1996), especially at 149–81; and Lise Ann Tole, "Durkheim on Religion and Moral Community in Modernity," *Sociological Inquiry* 61, no. 1 (1993): 1–29.

18. The latest, most thorough, and most admirable synthesis of the vast literature in the field is by Wolfgang Reinhard, *Geschichte der Staatsgewalt: Eine vergleichende Verfassungsgeschichte Europas von den Anfängen bis zur Gegenwart* (Munich, Germany: C. H. Beck, 1999), 259–81.

19. For more on the revolution, see Patricia U. Bonomi, "'Hippocrates' Twins': Religion and Politics in the American Revolution, *The History Teacher* 29, no. 2 (1996), 137–44.

20. As Robert Bellah has argued in a sideline of his famous essay on "civil religion," the emphasis on the clear-cut separation of state and church in the United States might have been corroborated by Christian groups' efforts to achieve an explicit recognition of the sovereignty of Christ in the American Constitution. Such recognition would have meant an intermingling of church and state and the identification of a specific type of religion as hegemonic. See Robert N. Bellah, "Civil Religion in America," *Daedalus* 96, no. 1 (1967): 19, footnote 1.

21. R. Laurence Moore, *Selling God: American Religion in the Marketplace of Culture* (New York: Oxford University Press, 1994). There is an immense body of literature on religion and popular culture in America. See, for instance, Lynn Schofield Clark, "Religion, American Style: Critical Cultural Analyses of Religion, Media, and Popular Culture," *American Quarterly* 58, no. 2 (2006): 523–33; David Morgan, *The Sacred Gaze: Religious Visual Culture in Theory and in Practice* (Berkeley: University of California Press, 2005); Sean McCloud, *Making the American Religious Fringe: Exotics, Subversives, and Journalists, 1955–1993* (Chapel Hill: University of North Carolina Press, 2004); Heather Hendershot, *Shaking the World for Jesus: Media and Conservative Evangelical Culture* (Chicago: University of Chicago Press, 2004); David Chidester, *Authentic Fakes: Religion and American Popular Culture* (Berkeley: University of California Press, 2005); Judith Weisenfeld, *Hollywood Be Thy Name: African American Religion in American Film, 1929–1949* (Berkeley: University of California Press, 2007).

22. On the cultural history of the political, see Achim Landwehr, "Diskurs–Macht–Wissen: Perspektiven einer Kulturgeschichte des Politischen," *Archiv für Kulturgeschichte* 85 (2003): 71–117; Ute Frevert and Heinz-Gerhard Haupt, eds., *Neue Politikgeschichte: Perspektiven einer historischen Politikforschung* (Frankfurt: Campus, 2005); Barbara Stollberg-Rilinger, ed., *Was heisst Kulturgeschichte des Politischen?* (Berlin: Duncker & Humblot, 2005); Frank Boesch and Norman Domeier, "Cultural History of Politics: Concepts and Debates," *European Review of History* 15, no. 6 (2008): 577–86; Steven Pincus and William Novak, "Political History after the Cultural Turn," *Perspectives on History* 49, no. 5 (2011): 19–21, http://www.historians.org/perspectives/issues/2011/1105/1105for3.cfm.

Part I

State Formation

Chapter 2

Commitment and Competition: A Religion Enlightenment in Revolutionary America

Frank Kelleter

This work investigates the relationship between religious and enlightened discourses in Revolutionary America. The first part traces the development of this relationship, from the taxation crisis to the Revolution (1760s and 1770s), when a new rhetoric of patriotic commitment coincided with the emergence of competing spheres of social action (religious and political). The second part of this chapter deals with the changed situation in the 1780s, when the constitutional role of religion in the new nation was under discussion. Most religious denominations were ready to accept and support the secular Constitution, but the language of modern constitutionalism put heavy pressures on their investment in metaphysical truth. Conversely, as political actors continued to draw on religious semantics to endow the new nation with metaphysical justification, their operations within a framework of secular procedures were in constant need of adjustment and explanation.

I wish to thank Christy Hosefelder and Daniel Stein for their assistance and critique.

1760s and 1770s

When Alexis de Tocqueville traveled through North America in 1831, he thought that he saw an exceptional society. Despite the lessons that the United States provided for European liberalism, this nation seemed to have found a relatively independent path into modernity. Repeatedly, Tocqueville hinted at the role of religion in this context: whereas the French Revolution had tried to de-Christianize the republic, the American revolutionary experiment had been mobilized in essential ways by religious convictions and institutions. In America, the principles of enlightened politics were implemented not against but within established Christian traditions. Liberty and faith, Tocqueville concluded, were inseparably connected in the United States.

Since Tocqueville came to this conclusion, the image of a Christian Enlightenment in America—and of a Christian Revolution—has appeared plausible to numerous U.S. historians, probably because Tocqueville's diagnosis is largely consistent with revolutionary self-descriptions. Already in the 1760s, colonial protesters legitimized their actions by recourse to the continued validity of established virtues and institutions. Even when the forces of resistance grew increasingly radical in the second half of the 1770s and began creating audaciously new visions of political organization, the importance of religion to an independent America was never seriously questioned, no matter how divided revolutionary interest groups were on other issues.[1] Later, in the 1790s, combat ensued between two different interpretations of the American Revolution, but no overt animosity concerning religion surfaced, because each party claimed to agree with America's Christian heritage. It seems reasonable to conclude that the close association of liberty and faith, and reason and religion, fulfilled a national—in fact, a nationalizing—function: whatever else was the content of political–religious associations in Revolutionary America, they always also provided continuity in a period of institutional upheaval and cultural self-doubt.

The popular image of the United States as a Christian nation is irresistible—and a myth. If we understand modernity as a social dynamic that is able to use destabilizations (innovations) as stabilizing factors of its own continuity, the process of modernization becomes visible as one that simultaneously delegitimizes and reintegrates cultural authority.[2] To understand the modernity of the American Revolution, therefore, means to turn away from questions of who believed what or which groups rallied around which philosophical causes.[3] Instead, we need to engage questions of a different type: What happens to cultural semantics (a society's conceptual map of the world) when historical actors find their self-made environments rapidly gaining in complexity and becoming increasingly unpredictable? What happens when people are confronted with increasingly discrete spheres of action that provoke distinctions previously meaningless to their social self-understanding?

As this chapter illustrates, religion and politics in Revolutionary America evolved as such spheres of action, while the contemporaries worked hard to conceptually reintegrate—and thus paradoxically stabilize—the attendant process of differentiation. Choosing between politics and religion would have made little sense to most revolutionaries (the same is true for the notion of secularization), and yet religious faith and modern politics in eighteenth-century America increasingly recognized themselves as competing epistemological and social forces, even and especially when they served each other.[4] In short, I propose to substitute questions such as "who believed what?" or "who represented which social order?" with questions about which (communicative) *practices* were possible and likely under different circumstances and how such practices allowed the emergence of self-aware groups with distinctive semantics.[5]

This approach does not deny that Christian doctrine, especially in its Protestant varieties, shaped the mental world of most revolutionaries. Hence, to understand the function of faith in the American political enlightenment, we need to acknowledge that semantic and practical homologies existed between principles of the Enlightenment and Christian principles— in particular, between the colonial type of Whig ideology and colonial Protestantism. In 1775, Edmund Burke reminded the English Parliament that American denominations were of an exceptionally militant cast:[6]

All Protestantism, even the most cold and passive, is a sort of dissent. But the religion most prevalent in our northern colonies is a refinement on the principle of resistance: it is the dissidence of dissent, and the protestantism of the Protestant religion. This religion, under a variety of denominations agreeing in nothing but in the communion of the spirit of liberty, is predominant in most of the northern provinces, where the Church of England, notwithstanding its legal rights, is in reality no more than a sort of private sect.

According to Burke, it would have been naïve to expect the American colonists to refrain on religious grounds from confronting English rule.

The opposite was true, he thought. But to say that northern Puritanism was compatible—indeed, historically interwoven—with specific strands of American revolutionary ideology is not to say that the colonies' resistance was religiously motivated or that it pursued primarily religious goals. Ultimately, the Revolution limited the institutional influence of the clergy to policy making. And while the Declaration of Independence still mentioned a "Creator"—although one without discernible Christian attributes—the Constitution was silent about any kind of God and proclaimed the separation of state and church institutions.[7]

More difficult than the question of why Christian politicians established a secular state is the question of why they were supported in this by leading representatives of the established churches. It is relatively easy to see why John Adams praised religious luminaries such as Charles Chauncy and Jonathan Mayhew as distinguished patriots, but it is less clear why the majority of colonial ministers welcomed the dissident attitude of political leaders, regardless of whether those ministers practiced and preached a more orthodox or a more evangelical kind of Protestantism.[8] Historical actors, of course, have interests, and the more materialistic those interests are, the more we tend to describe them as causes of social reality. Thus, historians can make short shrift of the questions asked earlier in this chapter by simply declaring that in most colonies (especially in New England) religious offices were elected offices. Hence, the ministers had no choice but to reflect the political climate of the day—had they done otherwise, they would have risked losing their positions.

Straightforward as this explanation is, it reduces modernization to individual intentions, decisions, and motivations. But how would it affect our understanding of the Revolution if we conceived of modernization as a process of making possible, in the first place, particular intentions, decisions, and motivations? What would it mean to acknowledge that individuals recognize themselves as being individuals in these actions rather than as acting the way they do *because* they are individuals?

American historiographies of the Revolution have largely resisted—or failed to recognize—observer positions that derive a concept of individual agency from its systemic conditions of possibility. More frequently than not, American historiographies of the Revolution reproduce competing self-definitions of the Revolution. As a result, the relationship between religion and politics is mostly theorized in terms of which convictions turned people into consequential actors. Evangelical Christians, in particular, are often described as natural allies of the Revolution. Ruth Bloch, for one, has stressed the importance of apocalyptic thought in the political rhetoric of the 1760s and 1770s; even Thomas Paine resorted to such formulas in *Common Sense*.[9] Evangelical eschatology was then politicized in an even more intense manner in the 1790s, when increasingly shrill reactions to the French Revolution mushroomed into millenarian mass movements that prepared the ground for the Second Great Awakening.

However, the millenarian rhetoric of the Revolution illustrates how difficult it is to align the eschatological hopes of evangelical theologians with the dynamics of political modernization. Most eighteenth-century evangelicals believed that the global advent of God's grace would be announced by profound secular changes. From this perspective, the overthrow of an unjust political regime indicated the coming deliverance, especially if that overthrow was carried out, at least nominally, under Protestant auspices. Thus, it is no surprise that many evangelical ministers were ready to team up with the political forces in the land. Their motives for doing so, however, were markedly different from the motives of secular leaders such as John Adams and Thomas Jefferson. In fact, the actions of evangelical revolutionaries may not even have reflected patriotic convictions but rather the belief that the imminent Christian apocalypse would level all differences among nations, effectively transcending all human institutions.[10]

Orthodox ministers, too, supported the Revolution, for reasons that often deviated from the goals and philosophies of secular leaders—and certainly from the underlying dynamics of modernization that generated such goals and philosophies. After the Revolutionary War broke out, orthodox ministers tended to be in favor of independence for the simple reason that they had something to lose: their social status in their communities depended to a large degree on their congruence with public opinion. Apart from this thinking, military defeat foreboded the establishment of an Anglican state church. Thus, the clergy had concrete privileges and freedoms to defend. These vested rights, however, were not necessarily identical to the vested rights at stake in the political struggle.[11] Unlike the more radical forces among urban artisans, for instance, most revolutionary ministers had no interest in annulling the traditional politics of deference.[12] Charles Chauncy supported colonial resistance because he saw it as a means of creating political unity, although he worried about its tendencies toward social differentiation. Here, as elsewhere, Chauncy sensed that religious institutions were forced to formulate an answer to the rapid modernization of social theories and practices in Revolutionary America—not by dismissing them, but by entering into coalitions with forces that otherwise would seem uncontainable. Orthodox and evangelical ministers alike felt that they could defend their privileged rhetorical positions within a modernizing society if they managed to declare religious faith as the foundation and origin—indeed, as the condition of possibility—of any enlightened public sphere.

One of the most tempting points of correspondence between religious and secular ideologies in this regard was their shared filiopietistic view of the past (i.e., the canonization of American "forefathers").[13] By embedding the colonial call for independence within a homegrown history of liberty, the revolutionary elite reacted to a threatening loss of cultural identity. Already, John Adams's *Dissertation on the Canon and Feudal Law* (1765) balanced its bold modernism ("The true source of our sufferings has been our timidity. We have been afraid to think. ... Let us dare to read, think, speak, and write") with an appeal to the values and virtues of the colonial past. Thus, "Let us dare ..." was complemented by "Let us recollect ..."[14] However, Adams did not advocate a restorative or religious revolution. He praised the original Puritan settlers not because he thought them superior to present-day colonists— not because their legacy was being lost—but because to him they looked exactly like the colonial protesters of 1765. In this respect, *Dissertation on the Canon and Feudal Law* was the very opposite of a Puritan jeremiad: Adams did not compare the deficiencies of the present to the achievements of an exemplary past, but he anchored present achievements in an ongoing history of liberty. Current conditions and policies were legitimized, not rebuked.

When Adams looked back on seventeenth-century New England, he discerned an already enlightened culture. He lauded his ancestors' education, their learnedness, and their cultivation of rational debate, which created newspapers and filled libraries. Above all, he praised the first Puritan settlers for their critique of "the feudal and canon law" (i.e., the obscurantist intermingling of secular and clerical power). According to Adams, this stance showed that the present resistance had sprung from a time-honored American tradition:

> It was this great struggle [against the canon and feudal law] that peopled America. It was not religion alone, as is commonly supposed; but it was a love of universal liberty and a hatred, a dread, a horror, of the infernal confederacy before described [of clergy and aristocracy], that projected, conducted, and accomplished the settlement of America.[15]

These settlers were political ancestors. Adams described a Puritan enlightenment that had instilled the rebels, not with piety, but with "a hereditary ardor for liberty and thirst for knowledge." As for the Puritan doctrine of grace and other theological concerns, Adams was willing to excuse such core elements of the tradition he extolled as unavoidable by-products of an otherwise rational mindset. Evangelical "enthusiasm," too, was honored as a "noble infirmity" and hence degraded to the status of a mere epiphenomenon: a useful accessory that imparted the necessary élan to the forefathers' desire for freedom.[16] This outlook was exactly Thomas Paine's attitude toward evangelical rhetoric when he used it as an effective means of political agitation. It is not surprising, therefore, that the new political powers repeatedly relied on techniques of religious publicity that, a generation earlier, Jonathan Edwards had already thought fit for changing the course of secular history: during the American War of Independence, the Continental Congress proclaimed at least sixteen national days of prayer, fasting, and thanksgiving.[17]

The Whig recruitment of Puritan forefathers not only satisfied acute desires for cultural identity, but also facilitated an enlightened reinterpretation of American settlement history. Colonial protest against imperial taxation hinged on the assumption that the English trade monopoly ought to be mutually beneficial for mother country and colonies. A more radical understanding of this theory came to the fore in the late 1770s: if the system turned out to be unprofitable for either party, that party had the right to dismiss the existing economic contract. For the revolutionary reading of settlement history, this interpretation had two implications. First, the economic autonomy of the initial colonists needed stressing so that Americans could claim the status of free contractual partners. From the perspective of the colonial Whigs, the original Puritan settlers were not simply refugees or functionaries of an English institution but, first and foremost, landowners. Benjamin Franklin explained in "Rules by Which a Great Empire May be Reduced to a Small One" (1773): "These remote Provinces have ... been acquired, purchas'd, or conquer'd, at the *sole Expense* of the Settlers or their Ancestors, without the Aid of the Mother Country."[18] In a similar manner, Richard Bland transformed religious ancestors into liberal entrepreneurs. In "An Inquiry into the Rights of the British Colonies" (1766), he argued against English economic interferences: "[Y]ou have been guilty of a gross Anachronism in your Chronology, and a great Errour in your Account of the first Settlement of the Colonies in North America." Bland's rationale was based on the claim that

the Colonies in North America, except those planted within the present Century, were founded by Englishmen; who, becoming private Adventurers, established themselves, without any Expense to the Nation, in this uncultivated and almost uninhabited Country.[19]

Interpreting religious émigrés as private proprietors, Bland, Franklin, and others strongly emphasized the materialistic dimensions of the Puritan "errand into the wilderness"—an interpretation that had the advantage of being largely based on fact. But this interpretation did more than provide historical accuracy to cultural semantics: it modernized the culture's very grounding in tradition. This is the second point to be noted. Stereotypically, revolutionary tracts praised the unique industry of the first settlers who wore animal skins and slept under trees (as the story went) but then created a flourishing civilization in less than a generation.[20] Under these terms, loss of property was identical to loss of custom. "We cannot bear the reflection that this country should be yielded to them who never had any hand in subduing it," Silas Downer maintained under the pseudonym "A Son of Liberty" in *A Discourse at the Dedication of the Tree of Liberty* in 1768.[21] Eight years later, Adam Smith concurred when he noted in *The Wealth of Nations* (1776) about the achievements of North American settlers: "The colonies owe to the policy of Europe the education and great views of their active and enter-prizing founders; and some of the greatest and most important of them, so far as concerns their internal government, owe to it scarce any thing else."[22]

By contrast, the filiopietistic rhetoric of the revolutionary clergy pro-duced different topoi and aimed at different effects. A chief ambition of the ministers was to use popular references to Puritan values and virtues to claim religion's fundamental share in revolutionary ideology and, there-fore, in the institutional prospects of an independent America. The chief goal of the ministers was to remind the political leaders that they could not look forward into an enlightened future without looking back and, hence, above. Where John Adams or Thomas Jefferson trusted in the world-shap-ing power of unhindered public reflection (what Immanuel Kant called *Selbstdenken*),[23] most religious supporters of the Revolution insisted that the legitimating value of the Puritan forefathers could not be had without accepting their heavenly father as well. In his sermon "Two Discourses on Liberty" (1774), Nathaniel Niles offered a warning that was typical of the times, claiming that former British subjects could not authorize themselves but needed transcendental sanction:

A thousand things may intercept our petitions on their way to an earthly monarch; but a combination of all our enemies in earth and hell cannot prevent a pious wish in its flight to Heaven; and let us remember, that the effectual fervent prayers of the righteous avail much. ... And if salvation has not come from our gracious sovereign King George, we cannot expect it from the hills. We must look still higher. ... Let us learn to live in the plain manner of our fore-fathers. It is high time for us to reform. We have had a rich inheritance and wasted it in riotous living. Let us soon return to our father's house, lest we be reduced to the want, even of husks to eat.[24]

Regularly, religious discourse aimed at deradicalizing the social transformations that attended the Revolution while affirming its political goals. "[W]hile we are nobly opposing with our lives and estates the tyranny of the British Parliament," preached Samuel West in "On the Right to Rebel Against Governors" (1776), "let us not forget the duty which we owe to our lawful magistrates; let us never mistake licentiousness for liberty."[25] A decade earlier, Jonathan Mayhew tried to reverse the egalitarian tendencies of the colonial protest movement without suffocating its patriotic will to resist. After the Stamp Act had been repealed, Mayhew—like many other moderates—declared that the time of militancy was over. Mayhew's concern for social peace was based on the fear that Whig principles in the hands of the common people could cause irreversible upheavals. In "The Snare Broken" (1766), he wrote:

Even the poor, and labouring part of the community, whom I am very far from despising, have had so much to say about government and politics, in the late times of danger, tumult and confusion, that many of them seemed to forget, they had any thing to do. Methinks, it would now be expedient for them, and perhaps for most of us, to do something more, and talk something less; every one "studying to be quiet, and to do his own business"; letting things return peaceably into their old channels, and natural courses, after so long an interruption.[26]

My point is not that there was a unified religious establishment that confronted an equally unified political sphere. There were moderates and radicals in both groups—in fact, both groups were "groups" only insofar as they were professionally instituted as such. My point is that we can describe the various forms of rhetorical alliance between religious and enlightened discourses as sincere and strategic at the same time because religious institutionalization involves particularly strong demands on an individual's activities in other fields of social incorporation. On the one hand, such alliances *committed* the historical actors to a common ideological framework that gave metaphysical justification to the new republic. On the other hand, alliances between secular and religious elites were always *competitions* over what kind of metaphysics was required by an enlightened—and geopolitically ambitious—nation. Thus, these alliances anticipated and, therefore, fostered the differentiation of religion and politics as autonomous spheres of action (i.e., as functional systems in a modern and modernizing society).[27]

Stated more concretely, patriotic representatives of the religious sphere such as Charles Chauncy and Jonathan Mayhew were very much aware that the new policies—whether Whig, liberal, or democratic—could not easily be subsumed under Christian or even classically republican paradigms. Therefore, the ministers attempted to direct the Revolution's self-interpretation in exactly this direction by entering into flexible coalitions with divergent strands of revolutionary thought. For instance, Mayhew's Puritanism was compatible with radical populist ideologies in its antimaterialism, thereby allowing common opposition to more ambitious economic models. Against democratic views of social organization, however, Mayhew sided with conservative conceptions of upholding the traditional politics of deference and checking radically egalitarian practices. In this context, his liberalist ethos of labor deftly invoked a rhetorically uncontroversial but ideologically adaptable revolutionary doctrine, because industry was a basic element of the democratic worldview as well.

Thus, although religious positions within the revolutionary spectrum were ideologically flexible, they were united in their efforts to simultaneously mobilize and check secular energies for institutional reasons. Religion promised to provide traditional legitimacy to a society (or a set of societies) whose grounding in tradition had been disrupted. Religion admonished "the people" to refrain from an endless revolution that would bring anarchy, followed by popular tyrannies; however, religion also confronted the Whig elite with a classical mirror of princes, reminding the aspiring political classes that even elected rulers of an autonomously organized body politic were limited by the power of a universal lawgiver—and hence, to a certain extent, by the interpretive authority of the clergy.

The creativity of religious rhetoric in the 1760s and 1770s can thus be described as a sign of institutional and communicative distress. Most Christian churches and denominations found it comparatively easy to embrace the Revolution in ideological terms, but the language of modern politics made strong demands on their claims to revealed truth. Conversely, if the political sphere sought to draw legitimacy from Christian traditions and values, its principled opposition to revelation and the *ius divinum* was in constant need of explication and adjustment. In this manner, the interaction between religious faith and political power in the United States has always been both close and contentious. Among the revolutionaries, there were only a few explicit opponents of established Christianity, but in view of the political utility of religious semantics, the ministers recognized that they confronted a mighty, discursive rival ("politics") in the officials and bureaucrats of an independent America. When Christian interpretations endowed radical developments with traditional legitimacy, thereby helping to divest modernization of some of its more frightening aspects, modernity could establish itself in a particularly sustainable, seemingly consensual manner.

This situation may well be the general dilemma of religious institutions in any modern, self-authorizing polity: once religion bids farewell to the theory of *ius divinum*, it plays a reputable but doctrinally diminished role in rational debates. In the 1780s, advocates and opponents of the new Constitution—and in the 1790s, Jeffersonians and Federalists—invoked Protestant values for their causes, but there was no necessary affinity between religious and political positions in these debates. Apparently, if religion did not want to become the ideological shibboleth of enlightened politics, it had to assert itself in the discursive field of the Enlightenment itself. A theological way of doing so was exemplified by Jonathan Edwards, who, a generation before the American Revolution, tried to entangle enlightened philosophies in contradictions, all the while hoping to show that the Enlightenment, rightly understood, was a fundamentally Christian affair. Most revolutionary ministers followed a modified version of this strategy. Instead of colonizing modern concepts of reason through esoteric inversions as Edwards had done, they seriously involved themselves in enlightened political practice.[28] In so doing, they thought they could place religion at a point of public debate where all ideological controversies converged and from which the centrifugal forces of modern politics could be controlled.

But once set in motion, modernity would not be controlled. Already, Jonathan Edwards blamed the end of his ministry in Northampton on the emergence of an autonomous public sphere in his hometown (including opposing parties in the English Country and Court system). He never reflected on the fact that the villagers dismissed him in an almost unanimous vote. Political disunity in Northampton could not have been so thorough as to prevent the partisan ringleaders from seeing a common opponent in their absolutist minister.[29] Decades later, in Revolutionary America, representatives of the religious sphere usually avoided this kind of open confrontation. Hence, they could always be found on both sides of any given ideological controversy. Two divergent conclusions can be drawn from this paradox: First, in a modern society, the desire to establish religion as a unified center of secular politics is doomed to fail because modernity—understood as the multiplication of options (experiential, social, ideological, etc.) competing in a public sphere—no longer allows unquestioned interpretive authority.[30] Second, however, desire for a unified semantic center survives and even thrives under such conditions. After the Revolution, such desire remained politically relevant in the form of increasingly sectarian competition among absolutist (religious) claims, all bent on offering themselves as the true embodiment of national faith rather than merely local positions. If there is an American pattern of religious–political associations, it probably can be found in this paradox.

1780s

When George Whitefield visited Boston on October 12, 1740, the politeness of his critics astonished him. Whitefield observed that Bostonians made a conscious effort to argue with tact and consideration; hence, theological controversies were addressed in a restrained manner, if they were addressed at all. Not surprisingly, Whitefield suspected, behind such civil affability was a particularly perfidious variety of religious formalism. What he encountered in America's most urban place was not rejection but the danger of tolerance. Indeed, from an absolutist perspective, the difference between silent forbearance and pure indifference may not be that significant. Ultimately, the peaceful coexistence of opposing forms of faith indicates the loss of status suffered by religion in a secularized market society.[31]

What Whitefield distrusted as a creeping subversion of religious authority in the 1740s was pursued as an explicit and self-aware policy by James Madison in the 1780s. In fact, Madison's groundbreaking idea of an extended republic—perhaps, the most innovative and historically consequential axiom of American constitutionalism—may have emerged directly from the enlightened principle of religious tolerance. In No. 51 of *The Federalist Papers*, at least, Madison traced back his theory of productive social differentiation to the example of modern church policy. The conflicting truth-claims of different denominations, Madison explained, could be best protected in their differences by devaluating the discursive capital of religion in general: the more sects there are, the harder it is for any individual sect to assert itself at the center of the religious field. If you want to avoid a majority religion, you need to increase the number of competing denominations: a maxim that Madison offered as a model for the sociopolitical and, perhaps, even economic organization of an extended republic as well.[32]

Based on this thought—and inspired by Jefferson's "Virginia Bill for Establishing Religious Freedom" (1779)—the Constitution, in its first amendment, prohibited the establishment of an American state church.[33] The establishment clause did not separate religious and political practices in public life, but it made a legal—and categorical—distinction between governmental and clerical institutions. In doing so, the Constitution tacitly prescribed a particular kind of national church policy—namely, a multidenominational one, portrayed by Sacvan Bercovitch as "a spiritual version of free enterprise."[34] The Federalist position on this point was clearly indebted to John Locke's *Epistola de Tolerantia* (1685/1689), which defined churches as self-organized associations ("religious societies") whose members, however, remained citizens, no matter which private groups they joined.[35] In this view, no denomination could limit the civil rights of its adherents or institute unlawful statutes for itself. Locke's policy guaranteed freedom of conscience, but it submitted religious institutions to political control. In essence, churches were seen as nationally incorporated subsocieties; they enjoyed legal autonomy only within a clearly demarcated constitutional frame. Hence, in interdenominational transactions, they behaved like private persons in the market: none could legislate for the other, but all were equally protected by the state in their common competition.[36]

The true provocation of this multidenominational policy was that it defined the search for salvation or metaphysical knowledge as a purely private affair. Thus, religion's discursive capital was not only devalued through inflation, but also forced to constantly reassert its buying power in the sphere of rational public truth production. Many members of the revolutionary clergy recognized exactly this threat when they criticized the federal Constitution, not because they disagreed with the proposed system of government but because that system abstained from seeking and paying tribute to transcendental legitimacy.[37] The rhetoric of the Constitution was conspicuously technical and free from zeal. The pathos of enlightenment— which during the war had allied itself with religious visions of transcendence—seemed now absorbed within a purely proceduralist understanding of political reason. When numerous ministers complained that at least the preamble could have struck a devout note, the Federalist writer "Elihu" replied that, although the Constitution honored and protected the free exercise of religion, it put an end to any kind of ecclesiastical obscurantism:

> Mankind are no longer to be deluded with fable. Making the glory of God subservient to the temporal interest of men is a wornout trick, and a pretense to superior sanctity and special grace will not much longer promote weakness over the head of wisdom. ... The most shining part, the most brilliant circumstance in honor of the framers of the Constitution is their avoiding all appearance of craft, declining to dazzle even the superstitious by a hint about grace of ghostly knowledge. They come to us in the plain language of common sense and propose to our understanding a system of government as the invention of mere human wisdom; no deity comes down to dictate it, not even a God appears in a dream to propose any part of it.[38]

There was nothing atheistic about these pronouncements. Like Thomas Paine on similar occasions, Elihu (who seems to have been a deist) interpreted the metaphysical silence of the Constitution as an expression of supreme worship because the delegates in Philadelphia had translated the divine law of nature into human words. But why, the ministers kept asking, did the Constitution refuse to profess this commitment to divine law? Benjamin Franklin seemed to have a similar question in mind when, on June 28, 1787, he suggested to the Constitutional Convention that it commence all sessions with a prayer. Because the delegates were venturing on an enterprise without precedence, Franklin argued, they ought to acknowledge that their human reason sprang from divine origins. A majority of delegates declined Franklin's proposal; the drafters of the Constitution seemed determined to bypass religious legitimacy in establishing the new order of government.[39]

Why, then, did the established denominations continue to feel committed to revolutionary ideologies—and why did most republican leaders refrain from publicly supporting deism or other radical stances toward Christianity? I submit that the Constitution's *proceduralist* understanding of reason played a crucial role in these affairs.[40] The process of modernization reached self-awareness in the United States earlier than it did in Europe, and it did so at the level of national(izing) institutions. The differences between European and American modernity in this respect (as Michael Broers discusses, for instance, in chapter 3 of this volume) have much to do with the fact that American constitutionalism recognized, accepted, and even fostered the functional differentiation of discrete social systems as the condition of possibility of a paradoxically extended republic. Improbably but consequentially, the Constitution provided nothing less than the pragmatics of modernization; it did not install beliefs or principles but rules and procedures (i.e., systematic, reusable tools) to regulate the interaction of increasingly autonomous spheres of action, thus reintegrating functional differentiation into continental nation-building.

Strikingly, this reintegration happened not only at the explicit level of construction of government but also, in a more implicit manner, at all levels of social differentiation, including religious–political transactions. As I argued earlier in this chapter, the government's doctrinal neutrality in matters of faith contained an institutional imperative: all churches had to submit to constitutional rules and regulations. This imperative demanded more of the individual denominations than merely tolerance vis-à-vis their competitors. Organized religion was now confronted with a troublesome alternative: it could either let go of metaphysical truth-claims altogether or establish those claims in a public sphere that was at least nominally committed to open debate and the verifiability of claims. There was a proto-evolutionist logic behind this policy, because enlightened thinkers such as Jefferson believed that public rationality would regulate itself and steadily progress by selecting the best arguments through contest and testing.[41] Accordingly, religious communication was forced to assimilate into modern practices of rationality even as it was trying to check or subvert them. The Constitution's multidenominationalism, in effect, guaranteed that the conditions of religious truth production were determined by the institutions of a secular and increasingly bourgeois society.

Thus, despite its ban on a state church, the Constitution did prefer a specific form of religious practice: legal tolerance privileged exactly the kind of faith that George Whitefield encountered in Boston—a restrained, service-oriented, modern church that kept the religious peace and fulfilled a social and, hence, civic function. In this manner, the Constitution may not have granted rational validity to religion outside enlightened debates, but it did grant to religious institutions rational utility within a procedurally established state and society. Whereas the new constitutional system did not itself compete with established denominations, it expected them to build faith in the nation.

Over and over, therefore, the political literature of the late 1780s stressed the social advantage of churchgoing citizens. Many authors on this topic did not even try to conceal the instrumental character of their pro-church stances. Benjamin Rush, in "A Plan for the Establishment of Public Schools and the Diffusion of Knowledge in Pennsylvania" (1786), declared that religious faith might well be a private matter between the individual and his God, but the *practice* of faith had to be understood as a public affair if the nation was to profit from it. According to Rush, it would be desirable for all citizens to be members of a church, regardless of the denomination: "A Christian cannot fail of being useful to the republic, for his religion teacheth him that no man 'liveth to himself.'" Rush's multidenominational tolerance was not limited to Christian confessions:

> Such is my veneration for every religion that reveals the attributes of the Deity, or a future state of rewards and punishments, that I had rather see the opinions of Confucius or Mohammed inculcated upon our youth than see them grow up wholly devoid of a system of religious principles.[42]

In the twentieth century, President Dwight D. Eisenhower reportedly summarized this idea with these words: "Our government makes no sense unless it is founded in a deeply felt religious faith—and I don't care what it is."[43] It would be a mistake to impute bad faith into such statements: they put into practice a core belief of the American Enlightenment—namely, the belief in the possibility of artificially constructing social happiness and political reason where neither comes naturally. Relying on a pessimistic anthropology and a generally skeptical attitude toward questions of metaphysical truth, the Federalists, in particular, sought to produce new forms of faith that were politically useful and could, nevertheless, be practiced in a sincere manner by those who believed in them. Benjamin Franklin recognized that no nation could be built on the intellectual basis of a deistic philosophy; yet he remained committed to an enlightened ethos of rational construction: "I began to suspect that [the] Doctrine [of deism] tho' it might be true, was not very useful," Franklin wrote in *The Autobiography*. Despite his realization that deism was morally deficient, Franklin refused to reconvert to any of the more socially "useful" forms of Protestant Christianity. Instead, he designed a new theology that he thought would do justice to both his critical and his normative interests:

> I form'd written Resolutions, (which still remain in my Journal Book) to practice them ever while I lived. Revelation had indeed no weight with

me as such; but I entertain'd an Opinion, that tho' certain Actions might not be bad *because* they were forbidden by it, or good *because* it commanded them; yet probably those Actions might be forbidden *because* they were bad for us, or commanded *because* they were beneficial to us, in their own Natures, all the Circumstances of things considered.[44]

Later, Franklin offered a multidenominational catalogue of principles said to contain "the Essentials of every known Religion," while being "free of everything that might shock the Professors of any Religion."[45] Ultimately, this basic version of faith was closer to enlightened conceptions of metaphysics than to traditional Christianity. On the whole, what Franklin presented was a natural religion with the additional assumption that God created humans not only as rational but also as moral beings.[46] This enlightened theology aimed not at establishing an unrivaled dogmatic truth but at organizing a peacefully inhabitable social environment in the face of religious diversity (doctrinal as well as geographic diversity). That Franklin did not want to have this project confused with premodern forms of worship was evident in the name he proposed for his new sect, which was to be organized as a private association: "the Society of the *Free* and *Easy*."[47] Such flippancy should not be written off as simply an act of substituting the old clergy with the new bourgeois priests of worldly reason. What the American Enlightenment attempted was nothing less than to create a self-perpetuating and self-referential (i.e., procedurally reproduced) republic that could not be wrecked by even the most irrational or immoral of rulers. What it actually achieved was something different but no less unlikely.

National multidenominationalism was implemented not without resistance on the part of the clergy and the individual states. Charles Chauncy fought in Boston for the continuation of a church tax. Connecticut, Massachusetts, and New Hampshire refused for a long time to abandon the old policy of the "two swords" (i.e., the close ideological cooperation of otherwise separated state and church institutions).[48] Many other states installed religious tests for civil servants (as a result, Jewish Americans in particular were banned from political office).[49] And political leaders displayed an increasingly antideistic attitude when more and more ministers voiced concern about the course of the French Revolution. Thus, although American society experienced dramatic secularization after independence—church membership reached a historic low between 1770 and 1790—this development was not accompanied by a corresponding loss of social authority among the clergy.[50] In fact, the ministers shrewdly took up the Federalist belief in religion's social utility and reinterpreted it once more as showing that the legal realities of the new nation were founded on Christian principles. Nicholas Collins, pastor of the Old Swede's Church in Philadelphia, wrote in 1787:

> A sermon every Sunday is a powerful antidote against selfish and malicious passions,—it would often dispose people for good government better than the wisest laws, and by promoting all the civil virtues, enable them to pay taxes, and to fulfill all the duties of a good citizen.[51]

In the young republic, this idea was conventional, but Collins gave a new spin to it. According to his interpretation, the social utility of religion showed that the constitutional nation-state was not a machine that would go "of itself" (i.e., regardless of the moral or intellectual condition of the electorate or the elected officials).[52] Collins explained:

> In the republican edifice, the people are not inanimate materials, but *living stones*. They must not only be sound and proper, but also willing to lie, to stand, *to join* as the architect wishes, nay, to go into their proper places; because in a free country there is no machinery strong enough to hoist massy stones and heavy timbers against their will.[53]

With such and similar pronouncements, representatives of the religious sphere functionalized the Federalist offer of national incorporation for their own purposes. Although religion was no longer able to operate at the discursive center of political debates, American constitutionalism could not, in turn, hope to transform religion into a mere instrument of social organization. As Tocqueville would later observe, there was something exceptionally American about this double development. Among other things, the American constitutional system was more reluctant than later republics, especially the French, to counter religious truth-claims with a normatively established institutional metaphysics of its own. "Civil" religion in the United States has always been a predominantly public—rather than an administrative—affair. Despite its ritualistic aspects, American civil religion has been characterized by an institutional informality and flexibility that so far has prevented it from becoming an ersatz denomination or a legally canonized instrument of political power.[54]

My point concerns once more the force of a proceduralist understanding of political reason in the American Enlightenment. With this view, it may no longer be important to decide whether the drafters of the Constitution envisioned the United States as a Christian or a secular nation. Whatever their personal beliefs, it seems unlikely that they intended the constitutional system to operate by authorial intent. What the Constitution did was to install a complex system of nationalizing institutions that allowed the generation and survival of self-regulating and self-perpetuating procedures (rather than contents), at the levels of both government and society. Neither government nor public institutions always worked in quite the manner expected or stipulated by the founders; the Constitution was no preprogrammed mechanism. But exactly this lack of programming may account for the Constitution's remarkable longevity. Successive governments and publics proved astonishingly competitive and cooperable in creating a livable environment for such unlikely phenomena as an American (national-continental) society and American history. I hold that these successive governments and publics were successful in doing so precisely because their original construction had not been programmatic but had already taken account of the evolutionary logic of competition and cooperability, thereby generating a system that both is able to adapt and requires constant adaptation from its elements—a system persistently producing its own oppositions and counterpublics.

The special conditions of public debate in a procedural republic prevent religion from becoming a mere function of constitutional rule. Constitutional multidenominationalism prefers and privileges particular forms of progovernmental faith, but it also prompts new religious movements to assert and reassert influence within the public sphere. This inevitable contest among changing denominations and forms of faith results in continued adaptive pressures. Isolated niches are difficult to maintain under such conditions, whereas creative reentries of religious practices and doctrines into social and political fields are frequent. In a sociogeographically differentiated nation without a formally decreed faith of its own, religion (both traditional and civil) is thus always contained and energized at the same time.[55] It is not only forced to rejuvenate itself perennially, but also given the means and conditions to do so. Even when it establishes itself in opposition to national governance, it usually stabilizes the system, paradoxically fostering commitment through competition and unity through diversification. In this sense, the surprisingly pluralistic and dynamic history of U.S. religion is always interwoven with the more general history of modern politics becoming aware of itself.[56]

Notes

1. See, for instance, the debate between John Adams and Thomas Paine in 1776, discussed in Frank Kelleter, "1776: John Adams Disclaims Authorship of *Common Sense*

but Helps Declare Independence," in *A New Literary History of America*, ed. Greil Marcus and Werner Sollors (Cambridge, MA: Harvard University Press, 2009), 98–103.

2. This rudimentary definition of *modernity* does not claim to compete with established sociological theories of modernization. For a good overview, see Wolfgang Knöbl, *Spielräume der Modernisierung: Das Ende der Eindeutigkeit* (Weilerswist, Germany: Velbrück, 2001). An analytical program based on my proposition would have to start by clarifying this program's relationship to advanced theories of social action (especially those of Erving Goffman and Pierre Bourdieu) and social systems (especially those of Talcott Parsons and Niklas Luhmann).

3. Such questions are asked and answered, for instance, in partisan quotation anthologies that show the founders to be "really" devout Christians or modern agnostics. See James H. Hutson, ed., *The Founders on Religion: A Book of Quotations* (Princeton, NJ: Princeton University Press, 2005); Stephen Abbott Northrop, ed., *A Cloud of Witnesses: The Greatest Men in the World for Christ and the Book* (Boerne, TX: Mantle Ministries, 1988). In general, concerning current issues, American scholars of the Revolution still tend to search the historical personnel for ideological allies or adversaries.

4. My theoretical frame overlaps with the descriptive tools in André Krischer's article in this volume, especially the notion of functional differentiation, which elegantly bypasses the problems of earlier models of secularization. My interest, however, is not in American religious history as a case study in the wider context of Luhmann's systems theory but in the modernizing agency of American revolutionary rhetoric.

5. The historiography of the American Revolution has a strong tendency to perceive individuals as unified representatives of social forces. This practice culminates in yes/no problems concerning, say, Thomas Jefferson's belief in God or the original intent of constitutional authors on a given social issue. When one scholar calls attention to the secularizing policies of this or that founder, another scholar will inevitably come along and show that the founder in question read the Bible. In this situation, we need a frame theory that acknowledges that a person can hold different beliefs and act differently in different contexts. When the correlation of (a) contexts and (b) beliefs and actions becomes consistent, I hold that we can speak of a social sphere; when these spheres become self-aware and institutionalized as autonomous (self-reproducing) contexts of action, we can investigate them as social systems.

6. Edmund Burke, *Selected Writings and Speeches*, ed. Peter J. Stanlis (Gloucester, MA: Peter Smith, 1968), 160. The quoted text is about the northern colonies. I refrain at this point from discussing Burke's assessment of southern religion; for this discussion, see Frank Kelleter, *Amerikanische Aufklärung: Sprachen der Rationalität im Zeitalter der Revolution* (Paderborn, Germany: Schöningh, 2002), 673–74.

7. See similar assessments in Bernard Bailyn, "Religion and Revolution: Three Biographical Studies," *Perspectives in American History* 4 (1970): 85–169; Jon Butler, *Awash in a Sea of Faith: Christianizing the American People* (Cambridge, MA: Harvard University Press, 1992), 194–224; Melvin B. Endy Jr., "Just War, Holy War, and Millennialism in Revolutionary America," *William and Mary Quarterly* 42, no. 1 (1985): 3–35; Thomas Cuming Hall, *The Religious Background of American Culture* (Boston: Little, Brown and Company, 1930).

8. For more about Adams and Chauncy, see John Corrigan, *The Hidden Balance: Religion and the Social Theories of Charles Chauncy and Jonathan Mayhew* (Cambridge, U.K.: Cambridge University Press, 1987), 7. On Chauncy's role in the Revolution, see Kelleter, *Amerikanische Aufklärung*, 333–50; Charles H. Lippy, *Seasonable*

Revolutionary: The Mind of Charles Chauncy (Chicago: Nelson-Hall, 1981), 89–105. On clerical support for the Revolution, see Charles W. Akers, *The Divine Politician: Samuel Cooper and the American Revolution in Boston* (Boston: Northeastern University Press, 1982); Catherine L. Albanese, *Sons of the Fathers: The Civil Religion of the American Revolution* (Philadelphia: Temple University Press, 1976); Alice M. Baldwin, *The New England Clergy and the American Revolution* (Durham, NC: Duke University Press, 1928); John F. Berens, *Providence and Patriotism in Early America, 1640–1815* (Charlottesville: University Press of Virginia, 1978); Patricia U. Bonomi, *Under the Cope of Heaven: Religion, Society, and Politics in Colonial America* (New York: Oxford University Press, 1986), 209–16; William Breitenbach, "Unregenerate Doings: Selflessness and Selfishness in New Divinity Theology," *American Quarterly* 34, no. 5 (1982): 479–502; William Breitenbach, "The Consistent Calvinism of the New Divinity Movement," *William and Mary Quarterly* 41, no. 2 (1984): 241–64; Cedric B. Cowing, *The Great Awakening and the American Revolution: Colonial Thought in the Eighteenth Century* (Chicago: Rand McNally, 1971), 178–225; Nathan O. Hatch, *The Sacred Cause of Liberty: Republican Thought and the Millennium in Revolutionary New England* (New Haven, CT: Yale University Press, 1977), 21–54; Alan Heimert, *Religion and the American Mind: From the Great Awakening to the Revolution* (Cambridge, MA: Harvard University Press, 1966); James Turner Johnson, ed., *The Bible in American Law, Politics, and Political Rhetoric* (Philadelphia: Fortress, 1985); Perry Miller, "From the Covenant to the Revival," in *The Shaping of American Religion*, ed. James Ward Smith and A. Leland Jamison (Princeton, NJ: Princeton University Press: 1961), 322–68; Edmund S. Morgan, "The Puritan Ethic and the American Revolution," *William and Mary Quarterly* 24, no. 1 (1967): 3–43; Mark A. Noll, *Christians in the American Revolution* (Grand Rapids, MI: Christian University Press, 1977); Mark A. Noll, "The Image of the United States as a Biblical Nation, 1776–1865," in *The Bible in America: Essays in Cultural History*, ed. Nathan O. Hatch and Mark A. Noll (New York: Oxford University Press, 1982), 39–58; Mark Valeri, "The New Divinity and the American Revolution," *William and Mary Quarterly* 46, no. 4 (1989): 741–69; Michael Walzer, "Puritanism as a Revolutionary Ideology," *History and Theory* 3, no. 1 (1963): 55–90; Donald Weber, *Rhetoric and History in Revolutionary England* (New York: Oxford University Press, 1988).

9. Ruth H. Bloch, *Visionary Republic: Millennial Themes in American Thought, 1756–1800* (New York: Cambridge University Press, 1985). On Paine's use of evangelical rhetoric, see Kelleter, *Amerikanische Aufklärung*, 452.

10. The prerevolutionary case of Jonathan Edwards is instructive here. As I have tried to show elsewhere (Kelleter, *Amerikanische Aufklärung*, 351–77, 452–53), there is nothing inherently revolutionary in Edwards's eschatology. I disagree on this point with, for example, C. C. Goen, "Jonathan Edwards: A New Departure in Eschatology," *Church History* 28, no. 1 (1959): 25–40; Heimert, *Religion and the American Mind*; Ernest Lee Tuveson, *Redeemer Nation: The Idea of America's Millennial Role* (Chicago: University of Chicago Press, 1968), 55–57. There seems to be no compelling correspondence between a "postmillennialist" eschatology on the one hand and a utopian political theory on the other; see Bloch, *Visionary Republic*, 18; James West Davidson, *The Logic of Millennial Thought: Eighteenth-Century New England* (New Haven, CT: Yale University Press, 1977). In fact, the very distinction between post- and premillennial theology does not seem to have played as decisive a role in the minds of the contemporaries as has been claimed by later observers. Equally questionable is the as-

sumption that Edwards believed in America's special covenant with God; see David C. Brand, *Profile of the Last Puritan: Jonathan Edwards, Self-Love, and the Dawn of the Beatific* (Atlanta: Scholars Press, 1991), 89–109; Harry S. Stout, *The New England Soul: Preaching and Religious Culture in Colonial New England* (New York: Oxford University Press, 1986). Even Edwards's *Some Thoughts Concerning the Present Revival of Religion in New England* (Boston: S. Kneeland and T. Green, 1742), which contains his most detailed and hopeful discussion of America in terms of sacred history, refrains from describing Americans as a chosen people. America—or rather, New England and, particularly, Northampton—is assigned a millenarian avant-garde role by Edwards for circumstantial rather than patriotic reasons; see C. C. Goen, ed., *The Works of Jonathan Edwards*, vol. 4 (New Haven, CT: Yale University Press, 1972), 353–55. Beyond that, "the coming of him who is the desire of all nations" puts an end to any special covenant; see John F. Wilson, ed., *The Works of Jonathan Edwards*, vol. 9 (New Haven, CT: Yale University Press, 1989), 247. The eschatological function of Jesus Christ, as Edwards described it, transcended exclusive revelations to a particular people, which is why Edwards was generally distrustful of covenant theology.

11. See the colonial debate about an Anglican episcopacy in North America (1767–1770). Parallel to the protests of the assemblies against an extension of imperial taxing authority, colonial ministers and theologians warned against the alleged plan of installing an American bishop. Under the direction of Charles Chauncy, who wrote three monumental books on the subject (*Appeal to the Public Answered*, *A Reply to Dr. Chandler*, and *A Compleat View of Episcopacy*), the New England clergy developed a militant and uncompromising line of resistance against any such scheme. John Adams—whose "Dissertation on the Canon and Feudal Law" also saw a connection between ecclesiastical and political corruption—later described the anti-episcopal movement as a decisive turning point in American revolutionary politics (Bonomi, *Under the Cope of Heaven*, 200; Lippy, *Seasonable Revolutionary*, 84). Rarely had the interests of secular and spiritual elites been so congruent. Adams's "Dissertation" is included in John Adams, *The Political Writings: Representative Selections*, ed. George A. Peek Jr. (New York: Liberal Arts Press, 1954). For Chauncy's position, see Charles Chauncy, *The Appeal to the Public Answered* (Boston: Kneeland & Adams for Leverett, 1768); Charles Chauncy, *A Reply to Dr. Chandler's "Appeal Defended"* (Boston: Kneeland for Leverett, 1770); Charles Chauncy, *A Compleat View of Episcopacy* (Boston: Kneeland for Leverett, 1771). On Chauncy and the question of an Anglican bishop in the colonies, see Edward M. Griffin, *Old Brick: Charles Chauncy of Boston, 1705–1787* (Minneapolis: University of Minnesota Press, 1980), 126–43; Lippy, *Seasonal Revolutionary*, 67–87. On evangelical attitudes, see Frank Lambert, *"Pedlar in Divinity": George Whitefield and the Transatlantic Revivals, 1737–1770* (Princeton, NJ: Princeton University Press, 1994), 214–25. For the controversy in general, see Bernard Bailyn, *The Ideological Origins of the American Revolution* (Cambridge, MA: Belknap Press, 1992), 96–8, 254–9; Bonomi, *Under the Cope of Heaven*, 199–209; Carl Bridenbaugh, *Mitre and Sceptre: Transatlantic Faiths, Ideas, Personalities, and Politics, 1689–1775* (New York: Oxford University Press, 1962); Arthur Lyon Cross, *The Anglican Episcopate and the American Colonies* (New York: Longmans & Green, 1902); Joseph J. Ellis, "Anglicans in Connecticut, 1725–1750: The Conversion of the Missionaries," *New England Quarterly* 44, no. 1 (1971): 66–81; Frederick V. Mills, "Anglican Expansion in Colonial America, 1761–1776," *Historical Magazine of the Protestant Episcopal Church* 39 (1970): 315–24; Bruce E. Steiner, "New England Anglicanism: A Genteel

Faith?" *William and Mary Quarterly* 27, no. 1 (1970): 122–35; Valeri, "The New Divinity and the American Revolution," 755.

12.   On the colonial *politics of deference* and its erosion in the course of the eighteenth century, see Carl Bridenbaugh, *Cities in Revolt: Urban Life in America, 1743–1776* (New York: G. P. Putnam's Sons, 1955); Richard L. Bushman, *From Puritan to Yankee: Character and the Social Order in Connecticut, 1690–1765* (Cambridge, MA: Harvard University Press, 1967); Thomas M. Doerflinger, *A Vigorous Spirit of Enterprise: Merchants and Economic Development in Revolutionary Philadelphia* (Chapel Hill: University of North Carolina Press, 1986); Richard S. Dunn, *Puritans and Yankees: The Winthrop Dynasty of New England, 1630–1717* (Princeton, NJ: Princeton University Press, 1962); James A. Henretta, "Economic Development and Social Structure in Colonial Boston," *William and Mary Quarterly* 22, no. 1 (1965): 75–92; Richard Hofstadter, *America at 1750: A Social Portrait* (New York: Vintage, 1973), 131–79; Stephen Innes, *Labor in a New Land: Economy and Society in Seventeenth-Century Springfield* (Princeton, NJ: Princeton University Press, 1983); Stephen Innes, *Creating the Commonwealth: The Economic Culture of Puritan New England* (New York: Norton, 1995); Jackson Turner Main, *The Social Structure of Revolutionary America* (Princeton, NJ: Princeton University Press, 1965); Darrett B. Rutman, *Winthrop's Boston: Portrait of a Puritan Town, 1630–1649* (Chapel Hill: University of North Carolina Press, 1965).

13.   Nina Baym, "Early Histories of American Literature: A Chapter in the Institution of New England," *American Literary History* 1, no. 3 (1989): 459–88; Joseph A. Conforti, *Jonathan Edwards, Religious Tradition, and American Culture* (Chapel Hill: University of North Carolina Press, 1995), 163–8; Philip Gould, *Covenant and Republic: Historical Romance and the Politics of Puritanism* (New York: Cambridge University Press, 1996); Udo J. Hebel, "Forefathers' Day Orations, 1769–1865: An Introduction and Checklist," *Proceedings of the American Antiquarian Society* 110, no. 2 (2003): 377–416; Udo J. Hebel, "The Rise and Fall of New England Forefathers' Day as a Site of National American Memory," in *Sites of Memory in American Literatures and Cultures*, ed. Udo J. Hebel (Heidelberg, Germany: Universitätsverlag Winter, 2003), 141–92.

14.   Adams, *Political Writings*, 18–19.

15.   Ibid., 7.

16.   Ibid., 8, 11. For a long time, Adams was seen as a secularized Calvinist; compare Bernard Bailyn, "Political Experience and Enlightenment Ideas in Eighteenth-Century America," *American Historical Review* 67, no. 2 (1962): 339–51; Paul K. Conkin, *Puritans and Pragmatists: Eight Eminent American Thinkers* (New York: Dodd, Mead and Company, 1968), 109–48; John P. Diggins, *The Lost Soul of American Politics: Virtue, Self-Interest, and the Foundations of American Liberalism* (New York: Basic Books, 1984), 55; Edmund S. Morgan, "John Adams and the Puritan Tradition," no. 4, *New England Quarterly* 34 (1961): 518–29; Barry Alan Shain, *The Myth of American Individualism: The Protestant Origins of American Political Thought* (Princeton, NJ: Princeton University Press, 1994), 27; Peter Shaw, *The Character of John Adams* (Chapel Hill: University of North Carolina Press, 1976). Adams's roots in enlightenment philosophies, especially deism, are stressed in Bernard Cohen, *Science and the Founding Fathers: Science in the Political Thought of Jefferson, Franklin, Adams, and Madison* (New York: Norton, 1995), 196–236; John P. Diggins, "John Adams and the French Critics of the Constitution," in *To Form a More Perfect Union: The Critical Ideas of the Constitution,*

ed. Herman Belz, Ronald Hoffman, and Peter J. Albert (Charlottesville: University Press of Virginia, 1992), 107–33; John P. Diggins, "1787–1790: John Adams Defends the New Constitution," in *A New Literary History of America*, ed. Greil Marcus and Werner Sollors (Cambridge, MA: Harvard University Press, 2009), 113–17; Zoltan Haraszti, *John Adams and the Prophets of Progress* (Cambridge, MA: Harvard University Press, 1952); John R. Howe, *The Changing Political Thought of John Adams* (Princeton, NJ: Princeton University Press, 1966); Correa Moylan Walsh, *The Political Science of John Adams: A Study in the Theory of the Mixed Government and the Bicameral System* (New York: G. P. Putman's Sons, 1915); and, particularly, C. Bradley Thompson, "Young John Adams and the New Philosophic Rationalism," *William and Mary Quarterly* 55 no. 2 (1998): 259–80, and C. Bradley Thompson, *John Adams and the Spirit of Liberty* (Lawrence: University Press of Kansas, 1998). A synthesis is attempted in Joseph J. Ellis, *Passionate Sage: The Character and Legacy of John Adams* (New York: Norton, 1993).

17.   On Edwards and techniques of religious publicity, see Kelleter, *Amerikanische Aufklärung*, 366–77.

18.   Benjamin Franklin, *Writings*, ed. J. A. Leo Lemay (New York: Library of America, 1987), 690.

19.   Richard Bland, "An Inquiry into the Rights of the British Colonies," in *American Political Writing during the Founding Era, 1760–1805*, ed. Charles S. Hyneman and Donald S. Lutz, vol. 1 (Indianapolis: Liberty Fund, 1983), 67–87, 75, 76.

20.   Here, as elsewhere, the American revolutionaries had only to Americanize British Whig topoi. Edmund Burke, in his "Speech on Moving His Resolutions for Conciliation with the Colonies" (1775), reminded the members of Parliament of their own Anglo-Saxon forefathers: "By adverting to the dignity of this high calling our ancestors have turned a savage wilderness into a glorious empire, and have made the most extensive and the only honorable conquests, not by destroying, but by promoting the wealth, the number, the happiness of the human race" (Burke, *Selected Writings and Speeches*, 185).

21.   Silas Downer, "A Discourse at the Dedication of the Tree of Liberty," in *American Political Writing during the Founding Era, 1760–1805*, ed. Charles S. Hyneman and Donald S. Lutz, vol. 1 (Indianapolis: Liberty Fund, 1983), 97–108, 108.

22.   Adam Smith, *An Inquiry into the Nature and Causes of the Wealth of Nations*, ed. Roy H. Campbell, Andrew S. Skinner, and William B. Todd, vol. 2 (Oxford, U.K.: Oxford University Press, 1976), 590.

23.   Compare Kant on the interdependence of reason and publicity: "Daher gibt es nur wenige, denen es gelungen ist, durch eigene Bearbeitung ihres Geistes sich aus der Unmündigkeit heraus zu wickeln, und dennoch einen sicheren Gang zu tun. Dass aber ein Publikum sich selbst aufkläre, ist eher möglich; ja es ist, wenn man ihm nur Freiheit lässt, beinahe unausbleiblich." See Immanuel Kant, *Werkausgabe*, ed. Wilhelm Weischedel, vol. 11 (Frankfurt: Suhrkamp, 1968), 54.

24.   Nathaniel Niles, "Two Discourses on Liberty," in *American Political Writing during the Founding Era, 1760–1805*, ed. Charles S. Hyneman and Donald S. Lutz, vol. 1 (Indianapolis: Liberty Fund, 1983), 257–76, 273.

25.   Samuel West, "On the Right to Rebel Against Governors," in *American Political Writing during the Founding Era, 1760–1805*, ed. Charles S. Hyneman and Donald S. Lutz, vol. 1 (Indianapolis: Liberty Fund, 1983), 410–48, 442.

26.   Jonathan Mayhew, "The Snare Broken," in *Political Sermons of the American Founding Era, 1730–1805*, ed. Ellis Sandoz (Indianapolis: Liberty Fund, 1991), 231–64, 262.

27. For the notion of functional systemic differentiation, see Niklas Luhmann, *Die Gesellschaft der Gesellschaft*, vols. 1 and 2 (Frankfurt: Suhrkamp, 1997).

28. For Edwards's esoteric inversions, see Kelleter, *Amerikanische Aufklärung*, 214–41.

29. Ibid., 355–66.

30. For secularization as a process of increasing options, see Charles Taylor, *A Secular Age* (Cambridge, MA: Harvard University Press, 2007).

31. George Whitefield, *Journals (1737–1741)*, ed. William V. Davis (Gainesville, FL: Scholar's Facsimiles & Reprints, 1969).

32. See James Madison, "Federalist No. 51," in *The Federalist Papers*, ed. Isaac Kramnick (Harmondsworth, U.K.: Penguin, 1987), 321: "In a free government the security for civil rights must be the same as that for the religious rights. It consists in the one case in the multiplicity of interests, and in the other in the multiplicity of sects. The degree of security in both cases will depend on the number of interests and sects; and this may be presumed to depend on the extent of country and number of people comprehended under the same government."

33. On Jefferson's "Bill," see Thomas E. Buckley, *Church and State in Revolutionary Virginia, 1776–1787* (Charlottesville: University Press of Virginia, 1977); Butler, *Awash in a Sea of Faith*, 262–68. On the First Amendment, see Thomas J. Curry, *The First Freedoms: Church and State in America to the Passage of the First Amendment* (New York: Oxford University Press, 1986); Leonard W. Levy, *The Establishment Clause: Religion and the First Amendment* (New York: Macmillan, 1986); Leonard W. Levy, Kenneth L. Karst, and Dennis J. Mahoney, eds., *The First Amendment: Selections from the Encyclopedia of the American Constitution* (New York: Macmillan, 1990); John F. Wilson and Donald Drakeman, eds., *Church and State in American History: The Burden of Religious Pluralism* (Boston: Beacon, 1987).

34. Sacvan Bercovitch, *The Rites of Assent: Transformations in the Symbolic Construction of America* (New York: Routledge, 1993), 53.

35. John Locke, *Epistola de Tolerantia: A Letter on Toleration*, ed. Raymond Klibansky and trans. J. W. Gough (Oxford, U.K.: Clarendon Press, 1968).

36. For a discussion of U.S. Supreme Court decisions on attendant questions of religious freedom and religious diversity, see Martha C. Nussbaum, *Liberty of Conscience: In Defense of America's Tradition of Religious Equality* (New York: Basic Books, 2008).

37. On the question of the Constitution's secularism, see Mitchell Meltzer, *Secular Revelations: The United States Constitution and Classic American Literature* (Cambridge, MA: Harvard University Press, 2005); Mitchell Meltzer, "1787: James Madison Keeps a Secret Transcript of the Constitutional Convention," in *A New Literary History of America*, ed. Greil Marcus and Werner Sollors (Cambridge, MA: Harvard University Press, 2009), 108–12; Noll, "Image of the United States"; M. Susan Power, *Before the Convention: Religion and the Founders* (Lanham, MD: University Press of America, 1984).

38. Quoted in Colleen Sheehan and Gary L. McDowell, eds., *Friends of the Constitution: Writings of "Other" Federalists, 1787–1788* (Indianapolis: Liberty Fund, 1998), 478.

39. Not surprisingly, Franklin's motion has been the object of an intense debate concerning the religious intent of the founders. Here, I am not interested in the partisan politics of this debate but merely in the way the Constitution institutionalizes

(and hence acknowledges and stabilizes) the functional differentiation of religion and politics.

40. For a detailed discussion of the emergence of proceduralist reason in the American enlightenment, see Kelleter, *Amerikanische Aufklärung*, 474–99.

41. In the 1790s and early 1800s, Jefferson had to learn that the public sphere worked very differently; see Kelleter, *Amerikanische Aufklärung*, 592–611.

42. Benjamin Rush, "A Plan for the Establishment of Public Schools and the Diffusion of Knowledge in Pennsylvania; to Which Are Added, Thoughts upon the Mode of Education, Proper in a Republic," in *American Political Writing during the Founding Era, 1760–1805*, ed. Charles S. Hyneman and Donald S. Lutz, vol. 1 (Indianapolis: Liberty Fund, 1983), 675–92, 681, 682.

43. Quoted in Robert Bellah, "Civil Religion in America," *Daedalus* 96 (1967): 1–21, 3.

44. Benjamin Franklin, *The Autobiography*, ed. J. A. Leo Lemay and Paul M. Zall (New York: Norton, 1986), 46.

45. Ibid., 78.

46. Franklin's universal theology comprised only six maxims: "That there is one God who made all things. That he governs the World by his Providence. That he ought to be worshipped by Adoration, Prayer and Thanksgiving. But that the most acceptable Service of God is doing Good to Man. That the Soul is immortal. And that God will certainly reward Virtue and punish Vice either here or herafter" (Franklin, *Autobiography*, 78). For a more detailed discussion, see Frank Kelleter, "Benjamin Franklin and the Enlightenment," in *The Cambridge Companion to Benjamin Franklin*, ed. Carla Mulford (Cambridge, U.K.: Cambridge University Press, 2008), 77–90.

47. Franklin, *Autobiography*, 163.

48. On the theory of the "two swords," see Jean-Pierre Martin, "The Two Swords: The Original Contribution of New England," in *The Transit of Civilization from Europe to America: Essays in Honor of Hans Galinsky*, ed. Winfried Herget and Karl Ortseifen (Tübingen, Germany: Narr, 1986), 53–7.

49. Butler, *Awash in a Sea of Faith*, 259; Edwin Scott Gaustad, *Faith of Our Fathers: Religion and the New Nation* (San Francisco: Harper & Row, 1987); Edwin Scott Gaustad, "Religious Tests, Constitutions, and 'Christian Nation,'" in *Religion in a Revolutionary Age*, ed. Ronald Hoffman and Peter J. Albert (Charlottesville: University Press of Virginia, 1994), 218–35.

50. Mark A. Noll, *A History of Christianity in the United States and Canada* (London: Society for Promoting Christian Knowledge, 1992), 163.

51. Quoted in Sheehan and McDowell, eds., *Friends of the Constitution*, 419.

52. The comparison of the American Constitution with "a machine that would go of itself" was first used by James Russell Lowell in 1888, but already in the 1780s, Federalist literature made excessive use of machine metaphors; see Michael G. Kammen, *A Machine That Would Go of Itself: The Constitution in American Culture* (New York: Knopf, 1986), 17. A similar image can be found in Kant's "Idee zu einer allgemeinen Geschichte in weltbürgerlicher Absicht" (1784), where Kant writes about the desirability of a self-organizing and self-perpetuating social structure ("die so wie ein *Automat* sich selbst erhalten kann"). See Kant, *Werkausgabe*, vol. 11, 43.

53. Quoted in Sheehan and McDowell, eds., *Friends of the Constitution*, 425.

54. On American civil religion, see Albanese, *Sons of the Fathers*; Bellah, "Civil Religion in America"; Robert Bellah, "The Revolution and the Civil Religion," in *Reli-*

gion and the American Revolution, ed. Jerald C. Brauer (Philadelphia: Fortress, 1976), 55–73; Jerald C. Brauer, ed., *Religion and the American Revolution* (Philadelphia: Fortress, 1976); Paul Goetsch, "In the Bully Pulpit: Presidential Rhetoric between Sermonizing and Agenda-Setting," in *Negotiations of America's National Identity*, ed. Roland Hagenbüchle and Josef Raab, vol. 1 (Tübingen, Germany: Stauffenburg, 2000), 330–46; Winfried Herget, "The Centrality of the Word," in *Negotiations of America's National Identity*, ed. Roland Hagenbüchle and Josef Raab, vol. 1 (Tübingen, Germany: Stauffenburg, 2000), 49–67; Frank Kelleter, *Louis Farrakhan's Nation of Islam, the Million Man March, and American Civil Religion* (Heidelberg, Germany: Universitätsverlag Winter, 2000); Heinz Kleger and Alois Müller, eds., *Religion des Bürgers: Zivilreligion in Amerika und Europa* (Munich: C. Kaiser, 1986); Sidney E. Mead, "The 'Nation with the Soul of a Church.'" *Church History* 36, no. 3 (1967): 262–83; Russel E. Richey and Donald G. Jones, eds., *American Civil Religion* (New York: Harper & Row, 1974).

55. James Gilbert's essay in this volume (chapter 7) traces a similar logic of religious life in the United States.

56. Such systemic self-awareness does not depend on the personal self-awareness of involved minds and bodies. The American system is designed to operate even if its actors lack understanding of its rationale or history. For *The Federalist Papers*, this was the very point of transferring "reason" from the realm of capacities to the realm of procedures. The risk of functional ignorance on the part of involved individuals, even governors (or historians?), is supposed as a rule.

Chapter 3

The Lingering Death of the Most Christian King: Pious Monarchs, Secular States, and Divided Societies in Europe, 1814–1851

Michael Broers

The Enlightenment, the French Revolution, and Catholic Europe

When one stands back from the maelstrom of the French Revolution and its Napoleonic sequel, both of which buffeted Europe in every aspect of its life and culture for more than a generation between 1789 and 1815, one cannot help but be struck by the place of the Catholic religion in the myriad conflicts and fundamental, often traumatic changes that marked these years.

The religious profile of Catholic Europe in 1789, on the eve of the French Revolution, was singular. Most Catholic states were exactly that: confessional polities; their rulers were Catholic kings, defenders of the faith, and public life was still restricted to members of the faith. Toleration, where it existed, meant toleration of Protestants and Jews, and no more; those of no faith at all simply did not exist, in law, which may have been just as well. In France, guided by Louis XVI's last Keeper of the Seals—the minister responsible for justice—toleration of Protestants had made headway, but they still remained beyond the pale of public life.[1] In the states of the Italian and Iberian peninsulas, such measures were simply beyond discussion.[2] In the Holy Roman Empire, at least officially, the faith of the sovereign still determined that of his subjects; this tradition may have become a legal formality in the Prussia of Frederick II, but it became more of a reality in the Catholic states, such as Bavaria. Where toleration of non-Catholic minorities existed, as in the electorate of the prince-bishop of Mainz, it was very much based on the model of France, where Jews and Protestants of various denominations went about their business in peace, but remained excluded from government service, law, and most of the other liberal professions.[3]

None of these practices set badly with the rural masses of Europe, or even with the majority of its urban bourgeois and artisan classes. Most Catholics were at least conventionally pious, and many of them were genuinely devout. Pilgrimages were still popular; miracles were still widely and deeply believed in; the Mass was celebrated frequently and was very well attended.[4] The Church had the adherence of both the state and the people in states that were designated officially as Catholic, right up to the outbreak of the French Revolution and beyond.

Nevertheless, the currents of enlightened skepticism had left none of the educated classes untouched, from the corridors of power to the reading rooms of provincial learned societies. The official boards of government censors in most countries were still dominated by the clergy, and in their eyes, the Enlightenment infected the music of Wolfgang Mozart, as well as the overtly anticlerical writings of the *philosophes*. The debate is still very much alive as to how far down the social scale the spirit of skepticism penetrated,[5] but two things can be said with some certainly: First, the Enlightenment remained an urban phenomenon; it did not reach the rural masses to any appreciable degree—a case of what did not happen in history proving as important as what did. Second, what did happen was a pervasive shift in the religious sensibilities of a significant—if not massive—segment of the European elites. Within France, the reforms of Vergennes were a clear sign of this shift, as was the careful, deliberate infiltration of the Board of Censors by the protégés of Voltaire, the overtly agnostic, skeptic arbiter of the unofficial literary world of French letters. This penetration of the Board of Censors allowed the officially forbidden books of enlightened thinkers to circulate freely within France.[6] Perhaps still more significant, if less tangible, was a diffuse tendency among the educated French classes, as well as those elsewhere, to live in a world where a tacit but very real division was made between religion and the practicalities of life, be they business dealings or the great affairs of state. As David Bell has put it, with acumen and eloquence, the triumph of the "creeping secularisation" of civilization was under way,[7] but only in certain urban, well-read quarters. Louis XVI stood out in his court as a genuinely devout soul; those close to him—his queen, his brothers, his ministers—did not share his view of the world, even if they went to Mass with him.[8] Indeed, one of the most interesting aspects of the influence of the Enlightenment is the effect it had within the Church itself, where the same currents of alienation existed between popular, traditional piety and an official outlook that increasingly suspected the more archaic manifestations of public piety and sought to curb or extirpate them. Most senior clerics of the last decades of the eighteenth century, in most Catholic states, supported the civil authorities over the curbing and even the outright prohibition of processions, pilgrimages, missions, and other forms of piety that produced disorder.[9] This whole process of the moderation of religion reached its apex in the support given by so many clergy, all over Europe, in the suppression of the Jesuits during the 1760s and early 1770s. The eventual dissolution of the order, by Rome in 1773, was seen at the time, and since, as the culmination of an intellectual movement within the Church, as well as a triumph driven in part from outside it, by enlightened currents.[10]

Hence, the religious profile of Catholic Europe on the eve of the Revolution was worrying and odd. The profile reveals an intelligentsia—and a wider spectrum of the educated, urban classes influenced by its writings—becoming increasingly alienated from the masses and states that outwardly conformed to the official faith, largely because it did not impinge on the workings of the states. In the circumstances of internal, civil peace that prevailed until 1789, such phenomena were simply currents of cultural and intellectual evolution. However, 1789 changed all that, and when Napoleon Bonaparte's conquests burst the bounds of France, these changes swept all over Europe. As will be seen in what follows in this chapter, these cultural divisions found their way into the core of the revolutionaries' reform programs. The revolutionaries attempted to reform the Church, to bring it under civil power, and to regulate its spiritual life. This effort caused conflict not only with papal officialdom, but also with the mass of society that had stood outside Bell's creeping secularization, to say nothing of the aggressive secularism espoused by many men brought to power by the Revolution.

Napoleon embodied much of this secularism. He was permeated by the secular and thus was almost emblematic of most educated Europeans of his generation. When he sought to reconcile Church and state, he did so very much on the terms of the Revolution, and his settlement did not last long or truly appease the masses, certainly not those outside of France. However, this secular view of the world was now backed and propagated by the most powerful army and state apparatus, governing the widest territorial hegemony that Europe had ever known up to that time. Under the regimes of the French Revolution and Napoleon, secularism no longer crept; it marched, it strutted, and it stamped loudly. The result was a cleavage in Catholic Europe that could amount to civil war in many places, as communities divided over support for the new regime or opposition to it. Outwardly, at least, and for as long as Napoleon continued to dominate most of Catholic Europe, the state triumphed, and the "enlightened" Church that had suppressed the Jesuits and embraced the Napoleonic Concordat of 1801 held the reins of power before and after the fall of Napoleon, in 1814.

This state of affairs lasted and yet did not last, a topic that forms the subject of this chapter. The religious reforms of the French revolutionaries and Napoleon left their mark on Europe, and the influence of the creeping secularization of the previous century remained very real. Nevertheless, the overt opposition that the revolutionaries and Napoleon had provoked from the Church and the people alike had also changed the spiritual and cultural landscape. Many skeptics of the Ancien Régime were now reborn as devout Catholics, and thus piety reentered the corridors of power in the decades after 1814. With this rebirth, the masses, both rural and urban, expected the Catholic religion—its archaic aspects most of all—would again take its place in the affections of those in power. Moreover, the strained relationship—and often utter hostility—between the Revolutionary-Napoleonic state and the Church had forged a new alliance between the formerly moderate and modernizing clergy and a recalcitrant laity: persecution and tension had led many clerics to seek rapprochement with a laity they had previously regarded with condescension bordering on contempt.[11] The first decades of the restoration period, thus, were confused and confusing to contemporaries. A powerful model of the state had been forged by secularists, in a decidedly secular mold, that restored rulers found more than attractive and useful. However, these same rulers were often among the reborn faithful themselves, whereas their loyalist supporters had clung to the Church as a symbol of resistance for almost a generation by 1814. The uneasy, often unclear relationship between these divergent forces forms the objective theme of this chapter, whereas its subjective thesis is that of the ultimate failure of the religious revival to reconquer the corridors of power and reverse the grip of creeping secularization on the new states of post-Napoleonic Europe, despite many conscious efforts to achieve exactly this.

The Climate of the Times

Napoleon's hegemony was swept away by a whirlwind as ferocious and sudden as the one he had originally ridden to the pinnacle of his power, but that hegemony had left a complex, pervasive, and—to the devout—pernicious legacy. For many to whom power had now fallen, it had to be expunged; for some, it had to be preserved as the only viable political system to emerge from decades of crisis; for more still, it had become part of their mental furniture, however unwelcome. Napoleon may have had to release Pius VII from his captivity in 1813, but the shackles he had placed on the Roman Church were not so easily broken.

Napoleon's reforms, far more than those of the revolutionaries of the 1790s, had shattered the foundations of the Ancien Régime, because Napoleon had formulated the challenge of reform in the manner of enlightened absolutism. However, he had been able to pursue absolutism's traditional enemies—the Church, the aristocracy, privilege in all its myriad manifestations—as a foreign conqueror, even in France, and do so without scruple for any sense of *vivre ensemble*, to say nothing of tradition or the voluntary constraints that bind familiars. In this clear-eyed spirit that mixed a need for efficiency driven by rapacity with a belief in enlightened symmetry in the public sphere, Napoleon undid the old order at the most fundamental levels of the state. Beyond Germany, his territorial and dynastic settlements may have been swept away as quickly as they had been created, but his methods of administration and the institutional framework through which they worked survived within most of the borders created or restored at Vienna. The public sphere of Western and Central Europe was henceforth cast in the image Napoleon and his collaborators had fashioned in the decade before 1814. In the departments of the Grand Empire, the new state was swallowed undiluted; in the *Mittelstaaten*, it was buffered by the German princes, but nonetheless adopted in its essentials; in Prussia and the restored realms of the Two Sicilies and the Netherlands, it took root through the grudging flattery of imitation. Even in Spain, that most ferocious bastion of resistance, the Napoleonic system would gradually seep into the body politic by the 1830s. By 1848, the Civil Code—the most thoroughly secular document produced in the Revolutionary era—was the bedrock of all the major states of western, continental Europe. That state was wholly and aggressively secular to a degree inconceivable even to Josephist absolutism.

Nevertheless, Napoleon had notably failed to secularize the European private sphere. By 1809, the much-vaunted Concordat of 1801 had been torn up by the Pope faster than Napoleon could himself manage; the Papal states were French departments, and Pius and his cardinals were all exiled and imprisoned. This outcome had been the culmination of a long, embittering process and, in retrospect, is not really surprising. Napoleon had dressed up the Concordat as a return to the Gallican powers of the old monarchy, but, in reality, the Concordat marked a return to the essence of the Civil Constitution of the Clergy of 1790: bishops were no longer elected by the laity, but rather were appointed by Napoleon on the approval of the Pope, and this was the aspect of the Concordat that did most to appease Catholics and appear to reverse the Revolution. However, the number of dioceses remained reduced to one per department, the number of Holy Days remained only six, and missions remained banned—as were most confraternities and the processions and private chapels they had fostered. There was no talk of restoring the regular clergy, save for a few teaching and nursing orders, nor was any confiscated Church property to be given back. The state, through the Ministry of Religions (*Cultes*) effectively ran the Church, as was envisaged in 1790. Above all, Napoleon reasserted emphatically freedom of conscience and equality of all.

The Roman Church had never been entirely happy with the terms of the original Concordat. Within those parts of Europe that had suffered most under the Revolution, it was, at best, seen as better than nothing. Pius had hesitantly accepted Napoleon's refusal to restore the regular clergy and his defense of freedom of worship exactly because, within the boundaries of Revolutionary France—which embraced Belgium, the left bank of the Rhine, and Piedmont by 1801—it was a restoration of sorts, however imperfect. When Napoleon imposed it on his new conquests, post-1805, and fostered broadly equivalent versions of it in his satellite kingdoms, Rome saw things differently. By 1808, as Napoleon imposed the French Concordat on the newly created Tuscan departments, Pius issued a circular to his bishops telling Napoleon that he was the friend of all faiths save the one in which he was baptized. Less than a year later, Rome itself was "the second city of the Empire" and Pius was no longer even its bishop. This was only the *cause célèbre* of a proto-*Kulturkampf* that had engulfed millions of Europeans of all classes, from great noble families who had newly discovered their piety following the loss of their political independence to the new hegemony. Simultaneously, isolated peasant communities now felt the full force of the new regime, as they lost their local saints, their shrines, and even their priests to the Concordat, along with their sons to Napoleonic conscription. This struggle was very different from the carefully choreographed sparring matches of Ancien Régime regalism.

In 1814, the Church and the faithful saw themselves as having engaged in, and emerged scathed but safe from, a battle for the soul of Europe. If Napoleon had not intended to destroy the body of the Church, it was widely felt that he was hell-bent on snatching its soul, just as he had its leader. This prevailing sense of deliverance—and the sense of chastening with which the restored regimes were imbued in 1814—enabled Rome to negotiate new and very favorable Concordats with most of the courts of Europe, including the Calvinist Netherlands. The political climate of the times allowed the Jesuits to return and prosper and permitted the missions—banned under the Napoleonic Concordat—to stream back into the European countryside. New monasteries and convents were built to replace those confiscated and converted to civic purposes or sold off by the revolutionaries and Napoleon. Even in the impoverished restored state of the Kingdom of Piedmont-Sardinia, a new diocese was created at Embrun and a new cathedral was built in Alessandria to replace the one blown up by the French—not in the course of war but because the Gothic structure was judged redundant. The architecture of much of Western Europe, both urban and rural, stands as witness to the determination of those in power to revive the faith and heal as many of the physical wounds of Napoleonic secularism as they could.

There were other wounds, however, all the deeper for being wounds of the mind and the spirit. Peter Fritzsche has argued brilliantly that the trauma of emigration induced the birth of the fundamentally new, wholly modern phenomenon of nostalgia; it produced a literature of loss, not only through the experience of exile, but also in the shock of returning to a changed world from that exile. Fritzsche emphasizes the autobiographical form of most of this literature, and so centers his thoughts on how these narratives "presupposed the internalization of historical time," while also forcing their authors to give these personal experiences a sense of historical context, "so that as more and more Europeans ... felt part of history, they insisted on their personal views and accounted their own damages."[12] This insight is penetrating and fecund, but it must be set within the context of the intense religious revival of the early Restoration. The sense of loss, dislocation, and alienation is palpable among the returned *émigrés*, yet so is the need among them to reach out beyond the isolated individuals they knew they risked remaining. The individual was the cornerstone of the Revolutionary-Napoleonic state; the damage done to the Church and to spiritual life began, at least, within the context of a wider assault on the matrix of corporate privileges that stood between the state and the citizen. The reconstruction of the Church, in physical and institutional terms, was in part—and soon in conflicting part—an attempt to rebuild networks and bonds between people. It might be useful to interpret this religious revival in terms of the emotional history of post-Napoleonic Europe as much as in political, cultural, or intellectual terms. Religious revival reflected a deeply felt need to fill the void of isolation in both the public and the private spheres and to reorient dislocated sensibilities.

Yet the religious revival also points to something else. In his seminal, if oddly neglected, masterpiece, *Studi sull'Età della Restaurazione*, written in the wake of World War II, the Italian historian of Restoration France, Adolfo Omodeo, discerned a "widely diffused sentiment of disgust and aversion among this new generation for their predecessors who had not kept faith with their own ideals."[13] For liberals, this meant the descent of 1789 into the Terror; for reactionaries, this meant the collapse of the Ancien Régime under the weight of its own cynicism. A spiritual restoration need not—and perhaps should not—equate to the reestablishment of the political and institutional norms of the old order, and even less to the retention of so much of the Napoleonic system. There was an instinct to look inward among the intellectuals of the period, to take fearful, insecure refuge in the personal, to become introspective and self-absorbed, and yet there was an equally perceived sense of urgency to rebuild bonds with others, to counter what one disillusioned Italian Jacobin had denounced as Napoleonic "government by geometry" with a religion of love and a paternalistic state that cared for its people above its ambitions.

The incongruities and ironies of Restoration Europe became increasingly clear to contemporaries. The physical could speak loudest. The new churches and religious houses, the restored roadside shrines, were on Napoleonic highways. Those highways were now often patrolled by clones of the Napoleonic Gendarmerie, a potent innovation that brought the rule of the state into the most remote peripheries of Europe; the men on horseback and their carbines could now represent the throne and thereby lessen its dependence on the parish clergy. The Concordats, however amenable to Rome in their intentions, were made with states now imbued with the secular, Napoleonic ethos. Monarchs and ministers, as well as the clergy, might fret about the purely civil marriages contracted prior to 1814, but in most states, the *état civil* remained. In the foreign country that was the pre-Napoleonic Ancien Régime, the rivalries between Church and state had often complicated and obscured the alliance of the throne and the altar. Henceforth, the throne had chosen to tie itself to a very secularized state apparatus; the altar had come to doubt ethos or the state itself. In many cases, the restored monarchs came to see that the only way to assuage these new tensions was through their own personal conduct and initiatives, yet even they would find themselves increasingly doing so on the fringes of their own bureaucracies and not through them. There were those on Left and Right—usually on their extremes, it must be said—who doubted that the circle could be squared.

The crossroads analogy is one of the most overworked in historiographies of all ages, but it certainly applies to the feelings and thoughts of the people of Western Europe in the decades after 1814. They felt pulled to look back, to look forward, and even more to look up, as it were: back to the old order, forward to the new regime forged under Napoleon, and up to a religious revival that could promise something quite different from a return to an old order that had failed its faithful by allowing the Godless world of the French Revolution and its bastard son to triumph so conclusively for so long. They knew that they lived in a heterogeneous world.

Choices: The Difference between Authority and Power

The rupture in the bodies politic of Western and Central Europe caused by the revolutionary and Napoleonic conquests created a void that was filled with nostalgia for the old order that frequently distorted its image for counter-revolutionaries left behind, just as exile could shape minds that famously both forgot and learned nothing. The clash of political and cultural aspirations nourished by embattled counter-revolutionaries and returned courts often proved even more problematic than the suspicions restored rulers harbored toward the servants and partisans of the former Napoleonic regimes. In many states, the practical aspirations of the restored rulers—or, in the case of the princes of the Confederation of the Rhine, the preserved rulers—fitted more readily with the centralized, highly professional, and thoroughly secular administrations they found in place. What the House of Orange; the French, Spanish, and Neapolitan Bourbons; and even the Pope found on their returns were structures that gave them power, more power than they could have dared hope for on their departures, and it was the kind of power—won from traditional nuisances—that they had always craved.

However, these reformed state structures were exactly what the counter-revolution "at home" had fought against so tenaciously, whether in the Tyrol, the Navarre, or the Vendée, as peasant communities battled the encroachments of the new regime. Equally, the retention of the essence of the new regime spelled the continued exclusion of the traditional aristocratic powerbrokers of the Ancien Régime from the corridors of power. In the absence of these rulers, a very ahistorical aura had grown around them. They came to symbolize the most archaic and corporatist aspects of the old order; they became the living embodiments of that world Alexandre Dumas expressed so well as "a time of less liberty and more freedom." This statement was more than gravely inaccurate nostalgia; it became concrete political aspiration in 1814, and it was swiftly dashed almost everywhere. The hopes were most coherently expressed by François-René de Chateaubriand when he famously beseeched the returning Louis XVIII not to listen to the Napoleonic *apparatchiks* and urged him to dismantle the state apparatus he found and to restore local government to the nobles.[14] Baron Karl vom Stein's stillborn plans for a "Third Germany" were quite similar. Ironically, the only effective way to protest for the ancient liberties was through constitutional states, France chief among them. In the wake of the Hundred Days, the *petite noblesse* fought back on the hustings as the Vendéans in the *bocage* never could, producing the Chambre Introuvable and forcing Louis XVIII to choose his path. That he did so is less predictable or ironic than the fact that he had to do so by further restricting an already narrow franchise, to exclude the poorer, more reactionary provincial nobility who had defied Jacobins and Bonapartes in succession. In other states, where parliamentary politics did not exist, a major reason for denying constitutions was to exclude the provincial nobility from power: The Sicilian Constitution of 1812 had shown how effective parliamentary politics could be to perpetuate baronial power; any form of elective or even nominated representation in Piedmont-Sardinia would have led to the attempted cessation of Liguria under its patrician families. The Spanish provincial *juntas*, who had done so much to sustain the resistance to Napoleon, found in Ferdinand VII the heir of Philip V, and so went the way of the more obvious, newer threat of the liberal *cortes*. Stein's plans to revive the *kreise* were strangled at birth by Karl August von Hardenberg and the princes of the former confederation. Monarchs returned to the realization that Napoleon, however detested, had understood their traditional aspirations better than they had themselves.

However, by embracing the structures of the new regime, the restored rulers risked losing the traditional sources of authority, founded on a respect for privilege and traditional hierarchies, that had given Ancien Régime sovereignty its aura, while often drawing its teeth. Authority seldom went hand in hand with effective state power in Ancien Régime Europe, as the difficulties encountered by Joseph II and his imitators in the future *Mittelstaaten* showed all too clearly. What the ferocity of counter-revolution had shown, however, was the depth of loyalty that deposed or embattled rulers could call on if they showed themselves to be defenders of traditional liberties and archaic, as opposed to Tridentine, piety. Perhaps the most striking illustration of this loyalty is the conduct of the Neapolitan Bourbons during the first French invasion of 1798–1799, when they appealed to the unruly communities of the Apennine periphery and to the bandits and their noble protectors, over whom the monarchy had struggled to impose its grip throughout the eighteenth century. Indeed, the Neapolitan example is all the more striking because it was such a volte-face when set in the context of the determined, if impotent, reform policies that the monarchy had sought to pursue in the decades before the French Revolution. Many of its more committed reforming ministers passed into Napoleonic service, and most of them were retained in 1815, when the Bourbons returned from exile in Sicily. However, in 1821, in 1848, and finally in 1860, the Bourbons would again turn to these traditional sources of support, appealing to them in traditional terms, and their pleas would be answered. Naples was but a harbinger of what would happen in Spain.

Traditional loyalty had two main wellsprings, one political and one cultural. The first, political authority, rested not on centralized power, but rather on bonds of reciprocal respect for the status quo; it turned on acceptance of the ancient liberties by the monarch, matched by residual loyalty to the crown—if not quite to the state—by provinces, corporations, and social castes. This source of authority was the patrimonial state in its last days. It was not of much use in normal times, and in the largely peaceful mid-eighteenth century, Philip V of Spain and his Neapolitan cousins set about earning the opprobrium of many of their subjects. The Habsburgs found it of little use in times of war, because eighteenth-century warfare demanded expensive, professional armies. The French Revolution and the Napoleonic onslaught changed all this. In 1814, contemporaries could not tell to what extent that onslaught was over. Louis XVIII made his choice when he jettisoned the Chambre Introuvable by 1816—a very courageous decision in the context of the Hundred Days. Things were not as clear to most of his contemporaries, however, both rulers and subjects alike.

The second source of traditional authority was more amorphous but all the more important. It hinged on a shared culture between rulers and ruled. As the gap widened between elite and popular culture in the course of the eighteenth century, and as elite culture became increasingly secular, the common bond of religion became increasingly important, in equal measure as it came under strain. When the French revolutionaries asserted the sovereignty of the nation in 1789, they changed the nature of kingship, so much so that no one thought it important to discuss whether France should be a republic. Louis XVI was such an irrelevance that he would have to overthrow himself, by his own actions. That he chose to do so reveals that Louis understood all too well what was at stake: not only the loss of power, but also the loss of the sacredness of kingship, the true basis of his authority. The future course of the Revolution within France and the resistance Napoleon met in his conquest of Western Europe proved the French revolutionaries' concept of political culture to be a minority view, but it was coupled to the creation of a powerful state.

Few returned rulers attempted as truly an *intégriste*, uncompromising restoration as the Savoyards, between 1814 and 1821. The Civil Code was torn up, the French administrative system was dismantled, and as much as possible, the services of the administrators and magistrates of the French occupation—which covered a period of more than fifteen years—were dispensed with. Thus, the Savoyard monarchy and its domains were something of a template in the post-1814 world, and their experience will be referred to at several points for this reason. The dynasty weathered a rather mild, elitist attempt at revolution in 1821, but the shock was enough to force the abdication of Victor Emmanuel I, to be succeeded by his brother, Charles Felix. Charles Felix received quite a bit of advice before he returned to Turin to take the vacant throne, but two petitions spell out very starkly the choice between the power supplied by the new regime and the authority conferred by respect for tradition. Few sectors of the Piedmontese elites had been shaken more by the policy of thoroughgoing reaction—*la Palmaverde*—than the magistracy, most of whom had been reared under the Civil Code. On May 28, 1821, every senior magistrate of the highest court in the realm, the Senate of Turin, addressed a petition to Charles Felix not only asking for restraint toward the rebels, but also warning that "A wise, strong, and prudent prince ... should not assume the exercise of supreme power if he proclaims his aversion to all innovation, or to resist it rigorously."[15]

In utter contrast, the Cardinal Bishop of Novara—a center of the military revolt—advised him thus: "I would be neglecting my duty if I did not draw to His Majesty's attention ... that the clergy, magistrates, and people of this city and province (as opposed to the garrison) are opposed and alien to any and all innovations."[16] The bishop was less at pains to protect his flock (there was no need) than to advise the new king of the climate of opinion—or at least of the climate of opinion the Church preferred. Charles Felix chose to rely on religion during his ten-year rule, but a closer examination of the nature of that choice—and of similar choices made elsewhere—shows that to submit to the altar did not really equate with a return to the Ancien Régime, as it might first appear. The Ancien Régime itself had become highly secularized before its collapse. There was no clear, integral road back.

The Construction of the Juste Milieu and the Eclipse of Kingship

The fragility—indeed, the incongruity—of the counter-revolutionary coalition was quickly exposed after the fall of Napoleon, at the very moment that its components most needed to unite against the deeply entrenched men and institutions of the new regime. The best, clearest, and most genuine source of unity in these circumstances was, without doubt, religion. Christian faith and devotion, both Catholic and Protestant, proved a real bond among all opponents of the new regime and could even attract those who were not counter-revolutionaries. Yet, even here, this shared sense of culture and purpose had to accommodate itself to the secular character of the new state the restored rulers had emphatically embraced.

There is a fine but vital distinction to be made in the relationship of religion to royalty in the post-Napoleonic world. A monarch's appeal to religion as a form of social, political, and cultural cement could take two forms. In the first form, it might, but seldom did, mark a deliberate reversion to Ancien Régime divine right absolutism: Ferdinand VII of Spain stood on these claims, supported by the political discourse developed by the *serviles* in the *cortes*, and Charles X of France deliberately evoked it in his neo-Gothic coronation ceremony of 1824. Absolutism was seldom invoked in practical politics, however. Until the electoral catastrophe of

1827, Charles X continued to work through the parliamentary regime created by the Charter of 1814. Throughout the years of restored Bourbon rule, but especially under Louis XVIII, French prefects showed a real dislike for the return of the missions, fearful of their explicitly ultra, divisive political pronouncements, but equally repelled by the fervent, emotionally intense character of their activities.[17] Just before his death in 1831, Ferdinand VII brushed aside the Salic law—and his reactionary brother, Don Carlos—by making his infant daughter, Isabella, the queen and her mother, Maria Cristina, the long-term regent. The motive for this flouting of traditional absolutism—and the final blow it dealt to any pretense to the survival of divine right—was his perceived need to restore many of the Napoleonic administrative reforms and, as happened in 1833, to convert Spain into a constitutional monarchy. The result was the First Carlist War, which ended only in 1839. When faced with the choice of abandoning the power given them by the new state for a return to traditional deference, most rulers looked forward rather than back.

The second form was quite different, because it was based less on revival of the monarch as the anointed of God than on an appeal by the monarch to a set of values and practices shared with his subjects. There is something of this form in Frederick William III's Church of the Prussian Union, founded in 1817, which Christopher Clark has compared to the Church of the Napoleonic Concordat as embodying "novel ways of thinking about the role of religion in the legitimation of state power."[18] On the one hand, the post-Napoleonic Prussian state could think of no other way to administer the established Church than to resort to that very French revolutionary technique—perfected under Napoleon—of turning it into a department of state under its own cabinet minister. On the other hand, when faced with a Catholic population vastly increased by the acquisition of the Rhine province, the king felt the need to rally all his Protestant subjects not around his person, but around a new, united Protestant Church. In post-1821 Piedmont, the appeal to religion took a slightly different turn, but it was also born less of suspicion of "Jacobinism" than of a newly discovered enemy within. The revolt of 1821 had been relatively insignificant in Piedmont compared with the events in Naples, Spain, and Portugal, but it had shaken Charles Felix's faith in the very pillars of the Ancien Régime state, the old aristocracy with its grip on the magistracy, the army, and the diplomatic corps. Indeed, Charles Felix turned on the army, the symbol of the Piedmontese nation surpassed only by the king. His suspicion of the old establishment led him to reverse centuries of Piedmontese diplomatic policy, thus putting the country under the virtual protection of Austria—the old enemy but, in his eyes, a fellow Catholic power. At home, he largely turned his back on the traditional elites, instead recruiting his ministers from the newly acquired Genoese patriciate and spending most of his time among them, away from Turin. In the Prussian and Piedmontese contexts, the appeal to Christianity meant something very different from a restoration, however illiberal. The king was most Christian, more intensely and sincerely so than in the past, but he was more clearly a lost child of the post-Napoleonic wreckage than a ruler confident in his divine right. It was a case of looking up rather than looking back or forward.

This sense of identification with their subjects' spiritual cravings made clear political sense in the context of the times, at least up to a point. Reactionary ideologues such as Louis Bonald were doing as much to reposition the sources of legitimacy and social stability as any liberal or radical, and rulers such as Charles Felix responded. Bonald, in particular, looked in new directions—upward, but also inward—for the wellsprings of stability and legitimacy. The family was the cornerstone of society for Bonald, not the state, and he regarded the sanctity of family property as essential to its survival. Beyond the family stood the social group, and together they were buffers against despotism and state interventionism. They shaped an organic society, which was not sustained by traditional royal absolutism any more than it was sustained by the individualism of the revolutionary Enlightenment.[19] The state was shaped not by its ruler, but by the families—as quite distinct from individuals—that constituted it.

Such responses may have been tacit admissions of the triumph of the creeping secularization of mores that David Bell has discerned in eighteenth-century French society, which is not at all the rabid anticlericalism referred to previously.[20] As Gérard Gengembre has pointed out, the counter-revolution developed a reply to the Revolution and, by so doing, created modernity, thus becoming part of it. The counter-revolution did not try to fight the Revolution through the "enlightened theology" of the previous century, itself a source of spiritual poverty. Rather, thinkers such as Bonald looked to Christianity to sanction a new *tabula rasa*, thus redirecting the fate of society away from man and toward God. In so doing, this strand of counter-revolution all but left Divine Right behind.[21]

In a very different sense, there was very little looking back in corridors of power, even among the most avowedly reactionary regimes. The grip of laissez-faire economics—perhaps even more than that of the Napoleonic Code and system of civil administration—made genuine returns to paternalism impossible, if not quite unthinkable, for most rulers. Charles X might touch for the king's evil, but he did not restore price fixing for the people of Paris in the lean, dangerous years after 1827. Instead, he allowed the myth of a Jesuit plot against the city to take root among the Parisian masses by 1830.[22] By 1833, the Spanish monarchy had granted a liberal constitution, had committed itself to ruthless administrative centralization, and had accepted military and financial aid from the liberal powers, Britain and France, to go to war against Carlism. Carlism was the greatest single expression of the diverse, often incongruous threads of the counter-revolutionary coalition. Don Carlos was a traditional absolutist—a Bourbon centralizer—but he was imbued with traditional piety; his victory would not have sat easily with the particularism of his guerrilla fighters in the Basque provinces or the Catalan hinterland. Looking back could only pose a threat to the new regime if it ignored the contradictions victory would bring, so it set religion firmly to the forefront in the meantime. Nevertheless, Carlism stood out in the 1830s as a force to be reckoned with. Its ultimate demise in 1839 was by negotiation and not the result of a crushing victory by the new regime, even with generous foreign help. Looking back—the power of local loyalties and lost privileges sustained by popular piety and the hope of a renewed royal paternalism—remained the aspiration of many ordinary people.

With this wider context in mind, we can return to the Savoyards for an almost unique example of a concerted attempt to return to Ancien Régime paternalism and its ramifications. Charles Felix's predecessor, Victor Emmanuel I, did more than purge his administration of as many servants of the French as he could. Between 1815 and 1821, he confronted the new regime on two fronts that most rulers by then considered lost—and probably worth losing: (a) internal free trade in grain and (b) family morality, to wit, the errant husband, liberated in so many ways by the Civil Code. In October 1816—during a year of famine throughout Western Europe—long columns of peasants from the Duchy of Parma-Piacenza appeared on the borders of the Savoyard king and eventually flooded into the port of Genoa. Ragged and hungry, the peasants were fed and reclothed but were finally dissuaded from their reported intention of taking ship for America. They had come this way, they said, because the news had spread that the king would not let them starve, that Victor Emmanuel cared for his people. Piedmontese and Genoese officials also reported that their own government in Parma and their own priests had encouraged them in these hopes.[23] In 1814, the Duchy of Parma-Piacenza had been given to Maria Luigia of Austria, Napoleon's second wife, who ran it as the last Napoleonic satellite kingdom and for whom economic nonintervention was a cardinal maxim. In contrast, Victor Emmanuel, against the firm advice of almost all his ministers, had reinstituted the royal grain store—the *Annona*—which had, indeed, done much to ruin royal finances and distort commerce, but which had also won the restored regime great popular support in the famine years that followed 1814. The *Annona* was reestablished in Genoa late in 1816, largely because official pressure was put on the private sector to provision it.[24] The governor of Chambéry applauded the decision to institute public works in the Duchy of Savoy in the same year, and the creation of the *Annona*, which would "prevent a large number of people hard pressed by hunger from starvation and threatening public order." Both actions accorded, for him, "natural justice."[25] The *Annona* had been a mainstay of Ancien Régime policy, but it did not survive long after 1814. Nevertheless, it is at least arguable that the efforts made—and seen to be made by Victor Emmanuel in this regard—did much to sustain the popularity of the regime with the masses in desperate times.

More intriguing still is Victor Emmanuel's recourse to a proactive *police des familles* in the same years, because it does not seem to have originated as government policy, but rather was driven by petitions to the "Most Christian King" from distraught wives and children. Whereas even the Church dithered in the face of these demands to arrest errant husbands and force them to provide for their families, the king acted decisively. In the years 1816–1820, fifty-six cases of what might collectively be termed *home wrecking* reached the king, all by private petitions and all involving bourgeois, provincial families. Many cases dealt with the husband in the most severe terms: several men finished in Fenestrelle, the state prison notoriously used for dangerous political prisoners, and they languished there because the king allowed their wives to decide whether to release them.[26] In this respect, at least, the king showed himself a paladin. He challenged the very core of the Civil Code, thus overthrowing the hierarchy it established within the family and the entire concept of the family as the untouchable nucleus of liberal society, to say nothing of his direct assault on the machismo of Revolutionary-Napoleonic culture.[27]

Toward a New Order: Romantic Nationalism

Many forces combined in the early nineteenth century to thwart the Restoration—just as many from within the ranks of supporters as within the ranks of liberal and radical opponents. However, as the pace of change and the degree of dislocation in society grew, even some of the most determined enemies of the Vienna settlement found themselves drawn to admit the one sentiment that held together all the diverse strands of reaction: the belief that the new regime—however useful to those in charge, however replete with power—was a cold-hearted being, as sterile and incapable of inspiring stability as it was able to implement policy.

The personal odyssey of Hugues Felicité Robert de Lamennais, from Catholic reactionary to Christian socialist, was a profound journey that took place within the compass of the political world created by the French Revolution but did not break out of its parameters. The counter-revolution fought to place God at the head of the nation. Joseph de Maistre, Bonald, Cesare d'Azeglio, and others saw the need for a more organic, neocorporatist society to fill the void left by revolutionary individualism: a society based on the family and on association was God's will, and the king was there to facilitate this social order and to protect it. What this vision had in common with that of the Revolution was its increasing view of the monarch as a tool—almost a deputy—rather than as the fount of all tangible power, or even of traditional authority. The monarch was there to serve the social order—families and groups of families—ordained by God. To the Revolution, the state—with or without a king—was similarly, if not identically, there to serve the individuals who comprised the citizenry. To both the state and the citizenry, absolutism had become a thing of the past.

Within the revolutionary framework, the terms for the survival of monarchical power had been spelled out in 1789. West of the Elbe, adherence to these terms would increasingly—if more gradually than is often allowed—dictate the survival of dynasties. The counter-revolution was also dictating new terms, however. In this vision, there was room for the throne, but less and less room for absolutism. For Bonald, real power came from God, and so the throne was inevitably subject to the altar, along with everyone else. The truly popular path was, perhaps, paternalist interventionism coupled with adherence to traditional corporatism shorn of noble privilege. This path became the core of Carlism, for example, and of the early years of the Savoyard restoration, when the dynasty survived—loved even by the reformers, if not esteemed—against all the rational odds. Such an approach to the governance of civil society commanded much affection, even hope, among the masses, but it could not survive the changing times or hope to oust the Napoleonic state.

It was Giuseppe Mazzini who broke the circle when he spoke of the French Revolution as "the exhaustion of the principle," as the last act of the Enlightenment. Jules Michelet and Alphonse de Lamartine were quick to follow. Their solution was as devastatingly simple as it was ethereal, the flowery language in which it was expounded notwithstanding. For the new generation of Romantic nationalists, God breathed life into the people, and the people—through democracy—breathed life into the state. The state, in turn, could hope to survive only in the context of the nation, the nation being the natural home of the people, a wider reflection of—not a replacement for—the family. This vision offered God without the Church and its privileges; it offered association without the antiquated strictures of corporatism; it put a living organism back in charge of the nation—no longer a king or the law, but the people.

Romantic nationalism caught the imagination of the educated classes from the 1830s onward, marrying as it did the institutions of the new regime and the yearnings for association of the earlier generation of counter-revolutionaries. If nothing else, an exploration of the relation of religion to power in *Vormärz* Western Europe reveals the pertinence of Romanticism as a political concept, however debatable its relevance to literature or the arts. Nonetheless, this conceptual breakthrough did not inspire the masses. Until well after 1848, the real competitors for popular support were truly populist. Old-style Jacobin radicalism spread from the cities to many parts of the countryside in France and western Germany; counter-revolution of the atavistic, Vendean kind was all that could rouse most rural areas throughout the period. The *realpolitik* of post-Napoleonic Europe is that of the triumph of state bureaucracies over the political extremes, of the precarious victory of the *juste milieu*, to the point that they exhausted their own vision, but not their power.

Notes

1. Munro Price, *Preserving the Monarchy: The Comte de Vergennes* (Cambridge, U.K.: Cambridge University Press, 1995).
2. Franco Venturi, *Settecento Riformatore: Da Muratori a Beccaria* (Turin: Einaudi, 1969). For an overview, see Owen Chadwick, *The Popes and the European Revolution* (Oxford, U.K.: Oxford University Press, 1981).
3. On Mainz, see T. C. W. Blanning, *Reform and Revolution in Mainz, 1743–1803* (Cambridge, U.K.: Cambridge University Press, 1974). On similar conditions in Aachen, Cologne, and Cleves, see Jeffrey M. Diefendorf, *Businessmen and Politics in the Rhineland, 1789–1834* (Princeton, NJ: Princeton University Press, 1980), 23–82.

4. See Chadwick, *Popes and the European Revolution*. For a recent overview, see Nigel Aston, *Christianity and Revolutionary Europe, 1750–1830* (Cambridge, U.K.: Cambridge University Press, 2002).

5. See especially Haydon T. Mason, ed., *The Darnton Debate: Books and Revolution in the Eighteenth Century* (New York: Norton, 1995).

6. On the penetration of the censors by Voltaire, see Robert Darnton, *The Literary Underground of the Old Regime* (Cambridge, MA: Harvard University Press, 1982). On the power of Voltaire's system, see Darrin M. McMahon, *Enemies of the Enlightenment: The French Counter-Enlightenment and the Making of Modernity* (Oxford, U.K.: Oxford University Press, 2001).

7. David Bell, "Culture and Religion," in *Old Regime France*, ed. William Doyle (Oxford, U.K.: Oxford University Press, 2002), 78–104. For the classic study, see Robert R. Palmer, *Catholics and Unbelievers in Eighteenth Century France* (Princeton, NJ: Princeton University Press, 1939).

8. See John Hardman, *French Politics, 1774–1789: From the Accession of Louis XVI to the Fall of the Bastille* (London: Longman, 1995), for a study that puts religious and cultural sensibilities at the center of politics.

9. Venturi, *Settecento Riformatore*; Chadwick, *Popes and the European Revolution*; Nigel Aston, *The End of an Elite: The French Bishops and the Coming of the Revolution, 1786–1790* (Oxford, U.K.: Oxford University Press, 1992); Monique Cottret, *Jansénismes et Lumières pour un autre XVIIIᵉ Siècle* (Paris: Bibliothèque Albin Michel, 1998); John McManners, *Church and Society in Eighteenth Century France*, vol. 1 (Oxford, U.K.: Clarendon Press, 1998); Antonio Mestre Sanchis, "Religión y Cultura en el Siglo XVIII," in *Historia de la Iglesia en España*, ed. Ricardo Garcia Villoslada, vol. 4 (Madrid: La Editorial Católica, 1974), 586–743.

10. Venturi, *Settecento Riformatore*; Dale Van Kley, *The Jansenists and the Expulsion of the Jesuits from France, 1757–1765* (New Haven, CT: Yale University Press, 1975); Graça da Silva Dias and José Sebastião da Silva Dias, *Os Primórdios da Maçonaria em Portugal*, 2 vols. (Lisbon: Instituto Nacional de Investigação Cientifica, 1980); Enrique de la Lama Cereceda, *J. A. Llorente, un Ideal de Burguesia: Su Vida y Su Obra hasta el Exilio en Francia, 1756–1813* (Pamplona, Spain: Ediciones Universidad de Navarra, 1991), 47–214.

11. Michael Broers, *Politics and Religion in Napoleonic Italy: The War against God, 1801–1814* (Basingstoke, U.K.: Routledge, 2002); James M. Brophy, *Popular Culture and the Public Sphere in the Rhineland, 1800–1850* (Cambridge, U.K.: Cambridge University Press, 2007), 253–299; Jonathan Sperber, *Popular Catholicism in Nineteenth-Century Germany* (Princeton, NJ: Princeton University Press, 1984); Judith Devlin, *The Superstitious Mind: French Peasants and the Supernatural in the Nineteenth Century* (New Haven, CT: Yale University Press, 1987); Gabrielle Turi, *Viva Maria! La Reazione alle Riforme Leopoldine* (Florence: Olschki, 1969).

12. Peter Fritzsche, "Specters of History: On Nostalgia, Exile and Memory," *American Historical Review* 106, no. 5 (2001): 1587–618, 1589.

13. Adolfo Omodeo, *Studi sull'Età della Restaurazione* (Turin: Einaudi, 1974), 48.

14. François-René de Chateaubriand, "Réflexions Politiques sur Quelques Écrits du Jour et sur les Intérêts de Tous les Français," in *Chateaubriand: Grands Écrits Politiques*, ed. Jean-Paul Clément, vol. 1 (Paris: Imprimerie Nationale, 1993), 151–276.

15. Archivio di Stato di Torino, Segretaria di Stato, Esteri: "Lettere e Suppliche dei Regi Sudditit alla LL MM, 1814–1821," Dossier: "Lettere Ricevute dal Re durante il

Suo Soggiornare in Modena dal Aprile al Ottobre 15, 1821," Senate of Turin to Charles Felix, May 28, 1821.

16. Archivio di Stato di Torino, Segretaria di Stato, Cardinal Bishop of Novara to Charles Felix, April 9, 1821.

17. Omodeo, *Studi sull'Età della Restaurazione*, 310–38.

18. Christopher Clark, "The Napoleonic Moment in Prussian Church Policy," in *Napoleon's Legacy: Problems of Government in Restoration Europe*, ed. David Laven and Lucy Riall (Oxford, U.K.: Berg, 2000), 217–35, 219.

19. Louis Gabriel Ambroise de Bonald, *Démonstration Philosophique du Principe Constitutif de la Société* (Paris: Clere, 1830), 449ff.

20. David A. Bell, "Culture and Religion," 78–104.

21. Gérard Gengembre, *La Contre-Révolution ou l'Histoire Désespérante* (Paris: Imago, 1989), 115–16.

22. Geoffrey Cubitt, *The Jesuit Myth: Conspiracy Theory and Politics in Nineteenth-Century France* (Oxford, U.K.: Oxford University Press, 1993).

23. For this correspondence, see Archivio di Stato di Torino, Segretaria di Stato, Affari Interni, Governatori e Comandanti, Mazzo 10 (1816). The archives show that they were not alone; similar incidents are reported throughout the period from 1816 to 1820 along the borders with France and the Swiss cantons.

24. Archivio di Stato di Torino, Segretaria di Stato, Affari Interni, Governatori e Comandanti, Mazzo 10 (1816), commandant of Genoa to foreign minister, December 2, 1816.

25. Archivio di Stato di Torino, Segretaria di Stato, Affari Interni, Governatori e Comandanti, Mazzo 11 (1817), governor of Chambéry to foreign minister, December 21, 1816.

26. Michael Broers, "Sexual Politics and Political Ideology under the Savoyard Monarchy, 1814–1821," *English Historical Review* 114, no. 457 (1999): 607–35.

27. Lynn Hunt, *The Family Romance of the French Revolution* (Berkeley: University of California Press, 1992).

Part II

Punishment

Chapter 4

Multiple Sanctions: Crime, Punishment, and Ideology in Early America

Daniel A. Cohen

Many New Englanders of the eighteenth and early nineteenth centuries considered themselves at once dutiful heirs of the Puritans, good children of the Enlightenment, and after 1776, patriotic devotees of the Revolution. Drawing together three distinct case studies, this chapter explores some of the ways in which such early Americans interwove those ideologi-

I would like to thank the City of Krefeld for sponsoring the Ninth Krefeld Historical Symposium—and Jürgen Martschukat and Volker Depkat for inviting me to participate. I am also grateful to Elizabeth Bussiere and the late Morris L. Cohen for reading early drafts of this chapter; Evi Girling and Anthony Santoro for their formal comments at Krefeld; all the other symposium participants for their observations and suggestions; the American Antiquarian Society and the National Endowment for the Humanities for generously supporting my scholarship with a long-term fellowship; the Johns Hopkins University Press and the Omohundro Institute of Early American History and Culture for permission to publish material (in the first and second parts of this chapter, respectively) that originally appeared in *American Quarterly* and *William and Mary Quarterly*; and Jared Bendis and the Freedman Center for Digital Scholarship at Case Western Reserve University for digitization assistance.

cal commitments in addressing issues of crime and punishment. The first part traces changing justifications of the death penalty in New England execution sermons of the 1670s through the 1820s, showing how Protestant ministers increasingly supplemented (or even, occasionally, replaced) scriptural or theological arguments with secular and patriotic ones. The second part analyzes explanations of interracial sexual violence in execution sermons of the 1760s through the 1810s, finding that clergymen often blended evangelical and Enlightenment concepts and values in rebutting protoracist understandings of such crimes. The third part moves beyond the pulpit and the gallows into the contentious and heterogeneous public sphere of Jacksonian America by examining a Protestant mob's interrelated sectarian and patriotic motives for burning an Ursuline convent outside Boston in 1834. Although the three case studies differ in several ways, they all reveal a common intellectual pattern: whether justifying capital punishment, explaining interracial criminality, or rationalizing extralegal violence, New Englanders of the eighteenth and early nineteenth centuries tended to intermingle both religious and secular arguments in grappling with controversial legal or social issues. In contrast to Europe's more polarized ideologues, who often pitted traditional religion against secular revolution or enlightened reform, many early Americans evidently felt most comfortable—and garnered most public support—when they could plausibly appropriate the multiple sanctions of Protestant belief, Enlightenment ideology, and Revolutionary patriotism.[1]

Religious and Secular Justifications of Capital Punishment

When criminals were hanged in early New England, Puritan ministers often addressed the cases in sermons that were subsequently published by local printers and booksellers. Over a period of a century and a half, from the mid-1670s through the mid-1820s, the range of concerns addressed in such works remained remarkably stable. Ministers berated condemned criminals for their misconduct, explained how they had arrived at so terrible a fate, warned others against similar wickedness, and sought to turn the awful spectacle at the gallows into an occasion for saving souls. One additional purpose of most of those sermons—and a primary aim of many—was to justify the execution itself. Indeed, Puritan clergymen apparently viewed themselves and were viewed by others as quasi-official apologists for the courts. Yet while ministers consistently defended the death penalty, their justifications varied considerably over the decades. By examining their arguments in conjunction with actual changes in the capital code, one can trace the changing rationale for criminal executions in colonial and early national New England.[2]

Puritan Justifications: God's Gallows

New England's earliest execution sermons relied heavily on biblical authority in justifying the death penalty. As in every other type of Puritan sermon, the minister would invariably begin with a particular passage of scripture (the *text*), draw a proposition or argument from that text (the *doctrine*), and then apply that doctrine to the particular events, circumstances, or issues of the day (the *application*). In some early execution sermons, the text, doctrine, and application all sought to justify the punishment about to be inflicted. For example, Increase Mather's *Sermon Occasioned by the Execution of a Man* (1686) vindicated the punishment of James Morgan for stabbing a companion to death with an iron spit. The sermon's text was taken from the book of Numbers: "And if he smite him with an instrument of iron (so that he die) he is a murderer, the murderer shall surely be put to death." The doctrine that Mather reasonably drew from the verse was, "Murder is a Sin so great and hainous as that whoever shall be found Guilty of it, must be put to Death by the hand of Publick Justice." And Mather's first application of his doctrine was to argue that it "justifieth the Authority here, in respect of the Sentence of death which has been passed on the Murderer, who is this day to be executed."[3]

Only when the justice of the capital sentence had been firmly established on the authority of scripture did ministers such as Increase Mather feel justified in moving on to other issues. That viewpoint should not be surprising; among conscientious Puritans, there could hardly be a more effective bulwark of judicial severity than that provided by Holy Writ. By defining capital crimes largely in theological terms, as offenses against the law of scripture and its heavenly Author, New England's early ministers shifted the burden of ultimate responsibility for capital sentences onto a magistrate far less vulnerable to popular challenge than any temporal authority. The moral sanction—and moral certainty—that they claimed was not merely Godlike but literally divine. Thus, in the very first execution sermon published in New England, *The Cry of Sodom Enquired Into* (1674), Samuel Danforth insisted that a teenager convicted of buggering a mare was not finally condemned by mortal jurors or judges but by God himself. The young offender

had become a "Monument" to the deity's "fierce Wrath and Indignation";
his judicial death would be a "Dreadful Example of Divine Vengeance."
Had the earthly court failed to execute such a judgment, it would have
drawn down "the wrath of God" upon the community as a whole.[4]

The clergy's reliance on divine decree as a warrant for judicial severity was more than mere rhetoric. That approach was actually consistent
with contemporary Puritan legal doctrine. In their attempts to reform the
penal code in seventeenth-century England, Puritans had sought to reduce
the number of property crimes already punishable by death, since biblical codes did not provide capital punishment for such crimes. Conversely,
they tried to introduce the death penalty for a number of offenses—such as
adultery, blasphemy, and sodomy—severely condemned by scripture but
not then capital under British law. These aims of Puritan legal reformers,
largely frustrated in England, were achieved in the earliest criminal codes
of Massachusetts. On the one hand, such crimes against property as larceny,
burglary, and robbery, which were punishable by death in England, were not
initially capital offenses in the Puritan colony. On the other hand, such biblically condemned sins as adultery, blasphemy, sodomy, and bestiality were
made capital in the Bay Colony.

Statutes imposing the death penalty were characterized by a closer fidelity to biblical law than was almost any other category of legislation in
seventeenth-century Massachusetts. Puritan lawmakers lifted some capital
provisions almost verbatim from relevant biblical texts and appended scriptural citations to the statutes. Not even Puritan legislators, however, viewed
scriptural precedents as binding in all cases. Rather, they were seen as justifications for capital statutes that were deemed otherwise socially expedient.
In other words, legal theorists of the time saw biblical precedent as a necessary but not always sufficient condition for the death penalty. Puritan doctrine also allowed for a significant measure of judicial discretion in dealing
with specific capital cases. Given that pragmatic outlook, Puritan ministers
occasionally went beyond the letter of scripture to justify particular executions by invoking the aggravated circumstances of individual cases. Still,
during the seventeenth century, biblical sanction remained paramount.[5]

Provincial Justifications: Sacred and Secular

The justifications of capital punishment offered by New England clergymen
during the first two-thirds of the eighteenth century continued to rest largely

on scripture. A few ministers drew their doctrines from biblical passages that directly condemned capital crimes; many others cited such texts in the course of their analysis.[6] Clergymen also continued to justify executions as the community's obligation to an avenging God; like their seventeenth-century predecessors, they insisted that criminal executions were necessary to "purify the land" and hence avoid divine judgments against society as a whole.[7] But despite the persistence of such pious arguments, some eighteenth-century ministers evidently sought to distinguish—and establish a rough equilibrium—between religious and secular justifications of capital punishment. The resulting hybrid pattern, suggestive of the early Enlightenment's love of "balance ... in all things," appears in three execution sermons produced over a period of forty years by Boston ministers of theologically liberal leanings: Benjamin Colman's *The Hainous Nature of the Sin of Murder* (1713), Samuel Checkley's *Murder a Great and Crying Sin* (1733), and Charles Chauncy's *The Horrid Nature and Enormous Guilt of Murder* (1754).[8]

These similar titles were matched by similar arguments in defense of capital punishment for murder. Each author explicitly justified the penalty on both religious and secular grounds. In defending the capital punishment of a murderer in 1713, Benjamin Colman declared of the authorities: "It is their *Obedience* to the Divine Law, and their *Fidelity* and *Tenderness* to Humane Society, that constrain them to the Condemnation and Execution."[9] Likewise, in 1733 Samuel Checkley insisted that both the "Law of God" and the "Safety of Mankind" called for "Vengeance on Murderers."[10] Two decades later, in 1754, Charles Chauncy condemned homicide in similar terms. "It is at once a Sin against *God* and *Man*," Chauncy explained. "It virtually *usurps God's sovereign Authority* ... and it does the *highest Injustice* to Man."[11] Each author thus stressed the hybrid nature of the offense of murder—and of the rationale for its punishment. The two types of justification were easily distinguishable in the sermons and seemed to be granted equal validity.

The specific religious arguments offered by the three ministers were virtually identical. All cited scriptural texts condemning murder, decried it as a violation of God's sovereignty (as well as a desecration of his image as embodied in human beings), and followed their seventeenth-century predecessors in suggesting that God required the community to punish murderers to cleanse the land. Their secular justifications were also remarkably similar. Each minister found a natural warrant for the capital punishment of killers in the fact that extreme penalties were imposed for murder by virtually all human societies, Christian and pagan. But beyond the presumptive authority of universal practice, with its implication of natural law, the secular argument most stressed by the clergymen was that of deterrence or, more broadly, society's right of self-defense.[12]

Much as the arguments of Increase Mather and Samuel Danforth during the 1670s and 1680s reflected contemporary Puritan legal doctrine, so too did the approach embraced by Colman, Checkley, and Chauncy at least loosely correspond to subsequent penal developments in the province. As noted earlier, the first criminal codes introduced in Massachusetts diverged from British practice by failing to provide capital punishment for property offenses and by imposing the death penalty for several biblically condemned moral and religious offenses that were not capital under English law. That break with British standards was gradually mended over the course of the seventeenth century as a number of property crimes were made capital, particularly for repeated offenses. The process of legal convergence was accelerated by successive reorganizations of the government of Massachusetts during the 1680s and 1690s.[13]

During the decades straddling the turn of the eighteenth century, the cohesiveness and influence of Puritan leaders waned, even as increasingly assertive English authorities intervened more frequently in the colony's civic affairs. As a result of both imperial coercion and local emulation of metropolitan models, the legal system of an increasingly mature and complex provincial society underwent a broad process of anglicization. On the one hand, colonial administrators struck some religious and moral offenses from the capital code. On the other hand, provincial legislators gradually stiffened punishments for crimes against property. Although burglary and robbery were capital only on a third conviction under the revised code of 1692, robbery became subject to the death penalty on a second conviction in 1711, and the most egregious type of burglary became capital even on a first offense in 1715. Murder, the crime addressed by Colman, Checkley, and Chauncy, may not have been directly touched by the legal changes just described. But the clergy's emphasis on the protection of public order and safety as legitimate grounds for capital punishment, independent of scriptural authority, was certainly consistent with the increasingly secular, property-oriented character of the capital code.[14]

Revolutionary Justifications: For the Public Good

Clergymen continued to offer hybrid justifications of capital punishment—such as those formulated by Colman, Checkley, and Chauncy—during the second half of the eighteenth century. However, several execution sermons of the Revolutionary decades shifted away from traditional religious justifications, with some ministers even questioning the applicability of scriptural laws to their own society. Biblical citations and invocations of divine wrath continued to appear, but the balance of discussion and the burden of justification had apparently swung toward the secular arguments. That change was undoubtedly related to broad shifts in public attitude and discourse generated by the political upheaval of those years. In an era of republican revolution against long-established royal authority, invocations of ancient scripture and divine sovereignty probably had less rhetorical resonance than assertions of pressing social need and the common good. On a theological level, the new pattern reflected the gradual erosion—even among New England's orthodox clergy—of Calvinism's theocentric approach to human obligation. The ministers were probably also influenced by the new social and penal theories of Enlightenment thinkers and republican ideologues, though there is scant evidence of direct borrowing in the sermons themselves.[15]

In addition to those broad changes in the intellectual climate, more immediate considerations were also involved. The earliest of the innovative sermons addressed hangings not for murder, an offense for which scripture repeatedly assigned the capital penalty, but for burglary and rape, crimes for which there was no explicit biblical provision of death. Some executions of burglars during that period generated significant popular opposition, and clergymen apparently felt constrained to update their rhetoric to combat it.[16] In part, then, the new secular arguments were ad hoc adjustments to controversial cases that violated the Puritan tradition of basing capital punishment on scriptural authority. But there was more to it than that: the increasingly secular orientation occasionally even infiltrated sermons addressing executions for murder.[17]

The new skepticism toward purely theological rationalizations of capital punishment was forcefully expressed in Peres Fobes's *The Paradise of God Opened to a Penitent Thief* (1785), an execution sermon delivered in the face of widespread public opposition to the hanging of a man for burglary in Taunton, Massachusetts. By the minister's own account, "a considerable number, chiefly of the populace, manifested their doubts and dissatisfaction concerning the lawfulness of the intended execution," with some even claiming that "it would be a murderous bloody deed." Fobes's observation that opponents of the penalty attacked the "judges and jury, the sheriff and state's-attorney, the prosecutor *and the preacher*" suggests both his own and the public's perception of the minister as a quasi-official apologist for the legal authorities. In fact, Fobes embraced just such a role in delivering a sermon that defended the execution and in appending to its published version an essay "On the Nature and Enormity of Burglary." His essay set out to defend the capital punishment of burglars on both religious and secular grounds but, in the end, discredited scripture as a foundation for contemporary penal codes.[18]

Fobes began his essay by laying out a number of strained scriptural arguments in defense of capital punishment for burglars. But then, midway through his discussion, the minister reversed himself and embarked on a completely different line of argument. He began by contrasting the wealth and luxury of his own time with the austere simplicity of material life during the time of the biblical Hebrews and during the early days of Anglo-American settlement. His point was that his own "advanced age" of prosperity required sanctions against theft more stringent than those of the earlier periods. It was therefore entirely appropriate—and perfectly just— that Massachusetts legislators had not made burglary a capital offense on first conviction until 1715, more than eighty years after the Puritans' initial arrival.[19]

Lest readers miss the broader implications of his argument, Fobes made them all but explicit by rhetorically demanding whether it was "possible to suppose, that a body of judicial laws, though made in heaven, for a people who existed some thousand years ago, and so different from us in their manners, connexions, pursuits, situation, soil, climate, and an endless variety of other circumstances, can, or ever ought, in equity, and in particular, to bind us, or any other nation on earth, at this day?" Montesquieu himself could hardly have stated the issue, or implied the answer, more clearly. Modern circumstances, in all their complexity, required modern legal codes, regardless of divine sanction; no longer did God or tradition provide the last word. Finally, to complete his case, the minister illustrated some of the absurd penal consequences of rigid adherence to scriptural precedent, citing such biblically capital crimes as "the loss of virginity before marriage, the striking of parents, and sabbath breaking." Fobes thus ridiculed the very enterprise of scriptural justification that had occupied the first half of his essay—and that had engaged the authors of New England execution sermons for more than a century.[20]

It should be emphasized that the changes reflected in Fobes's sermon were more than rhetorical. Rather, the new approach corresponded with a concurrent transformation in the actual enforcement of the criminal law. In a study of penal developments in late provincial and early national Massachusetts, William E. Nelson found a radical shift in law enforcement during the decades following the American Revolution, away from its traditional role as a regulator of religion and morality toward its modern emphasis on the protection of property. "The aims of the criminal law had now consciously become the preservation of order in society," David H. Flaherty has likewise concluded of postrevolutionary America, "without reference to the saving of souls or the building of God's kingdom on earth." Although Nelson implied that the change in approach occurred rather suddenly during the decades immediately following the Revolution, Flaherty and others have suggested that it happened more gradually, as a result of longer-term shifts in attitude. Although the timing of a transformation in legal theory and practice cannot be established on the basis of changes in ministerial doctrine, the pattern of development in sermons depicted here—featuring the transitional, hybrid justifications of the first half of the eighteenth century—is certainly more consistent with the gradualist view. New England's ministers were apparently moving in the same direction and at approximately the same pace as actual enforcers of the criminal law.[21]

Republican Justifications: Patriotism at the Gallows

Several execution sermons issued in the early republic introduced a new secular rationale for capital punishment. The defense was a formalistic one, based on the presumed fairness of the laws and legal procedures under which the criminal was condemned. It was often implied rather than explicitly stated, and it was generally offered as a supplement to rather than a substitute for more traditional justifications. The new procedural defense was apparently nurtured by Americans' patriotic pride in their government institutions and perhaps also by a weakening of the ministers' own faith in their other lines of defense. In at least two cases, it was also fostered by doubts concerning the condemned criminal's guilt. The legal-procedural defense seems to have been most popular during the ten years straddling 1800, when it appeared in at least four execution sermons.[22]

The Reverend Samuel Blatchford offered a particularly overt appeal to the pride of Americans in their new legal system in an address appended to Timothy Langdon's published *A Sermon Preached at Danbury* (1798) on the execution in Connecticut of "Anthony, a Free Negro" for rape. Although he was himself a recent immigrant to the United States, Blatchford's address featured a patriotic disquisition on the American form of government that particularly emphasized the fairness of its criminal procedures. "In most countries the life of a subject is at the will of his Lord; but here nothing is attempted against the life of a citizen, without an open and fair trial," Blatchford explained. "Evidences are required to make out the charge, and the utmost deliberation is used by those impartial judges of the fact, called jurors, before they deliver their verdict." The humanity of American law was still further demonstrated by its treatment of prisoners sentenced to death: executions were "deferred for a considerable time" to allow the condemned ample opportunity for prayer and repentance. "You who are come hither to-day to see this sad spectacle," the minister suggested, "will go away perhaps satisfied with the justice of your country."[23]

Moses C. Welch's *The Gospel to Be Preached to All Men* (1805), a sermon addressing a capital case in which the degree of the condemned man's guilt was in some doubt, offers another example of the legal-procedural defense. Samuel Freeman had been convicted for the murder of his common-law wife in Ashford, Connecticut. Although acknowledging that he had brutalized the woman, Freeman denied having intentionally killed her. "I know not, certainly, that you are guilty of the crime for which you are to die," Welch conceded to the prisoner. "The truth is known to God and your own soul." Yet that did not prevent the minister from implicitly justifying the fatal sentence:

> Having been accused of the crime of shedding human blood, the Grand-Jury of the county, after a due investigation of the case, have indicted you for Murder. You have been brought to the bar of the Honorable Superior Court, and assisted in your defence by able and learned counsel. But the evidence was so clear against you as to induce twelve sober, judicious, disinterested jurors, on their oath, to pronounce you guilty. The sentence of death, according to the law of the land, has been passed upon you.[24]

In the increasingly law-oriented and lawyer-dominated civic culture of America's early republic (a far cry from that of Puritan Massachusetts, whose authorities had once sought to ban the practice of law and later prohibited lawyers from holding public office), the mere recitation of well-ordered judicial procedures was apparently gaining, even for ministers, the sort of incantatory moral force traditionally reserved for invocations of sacred scripture.

That new emphasis on courtroom procedures was paralleled by a shift in crime genres. During the first decade of the nineteenth century, trial reports—pamphlet-size synopses or book-length transcripts of judicial proceedings—emerged in New England as popular literary alternatives to execution sermons. Such trial reports can be seen, in part, as a repackaging of the procedural justification of capital punishment in its own distinctly legalistic format. As a result, when gallows sermons began to slip out of literary vogue during the ensuing decades, defenders of judicial authority already had another popular genre to carry their message to a sometimes skeptical public. That trial reports occasionally treated cases in which defendants were acquitted, however, signaled the arrival of a more contingent (and, arguably, more democratic) approach to moral certainty. The truth was no longer baldly asserted by a single authoritative spokesman, whether minister or magistrate, but was mediated and accredited through the autonomous judgment of the community itself—as represented by jurors and, by extension, readers. If guilt no longer seemed as self-evident as it had often been portrayed in early execution sermons, New England readers might still pride themselves on a system of justice well equipped to sort through the uncertainty and ferret it out. And just as trial reports replaced execution sermons, so did the courtroom increasingly replace the gallows as the chief public site for communicating the moral truths and social lessons of crime and punishment. Indeed, during the 1830s and 1840s, states throughout New England and the Mid-Atlantic region sought to remove criminal executions from public view by concealing them behind prison walls.[25]

At first glance, this schematic account appears to confirm a straightforward secularization model: (a) sermons of the late seventeenth century defended capital punishment largely on scriptural or theological grounds; (b) several ministers of the early to mid-eighteenth century embraced a transitional approach, striking a balance between religious and secular justifications; (c) during the 1760s and thereafter, New England clergymen increasingly turned to secular arguments of various types; and, finally, (d) by the early nineteenth century, lawyers and judges had largely replaced ministers as the community's authoritative spokesmen on issues of crime and punishment—and trial reports (conveyed to readers both in newspapers and in separate publications) had replaced execution sermons as the region's most popular crime genre. Yet such a neat conceptualization, though accurate as far as it goes, is misleading on at least three grounds.

First, the secularizing trend tends to be somewhat exaggerated by my method of analysis, which highlights those sermons (and particular passages within those sermons) that presented new terminology and ideas. In fact, scriptural and theological justifications of capital punishment continued to appear—albeit often alongside more secular arguments—in many gallows sermons of the early republic. In a recent study, Scott D. Seay even argues that New Divinity theologians led a significant retreat from Lockean (i.e., Enlightenment) understandings of civil government and a corresponding revival of "tradition Puritan political ideas" in execution sermons of the late eighteenth century.[26]

Second, the linear secularization model tends to elide the degree to which the alternating—and later synergistic—influence of religious and secular ideologies had *together* served to narrow the application of the death penalty by the early nineteenth century. Initially, Puritan ideology had discouraged that penalty for various property crimes punishable by death in early modern England but had sanctioned capital punishment for various religious and moral offenses strongly condemned by scripture. Subsequently, Anglicization—a particular type of secularization—had eliminated most of the Puritans' biblical additions to the capital code but had also sanctioned the reintroduction of capital punishment for property crimes. (In fact, between the 1730s and 1790s, a substantial proportion of executions in New England were for serious property offenses, such as burglary and robbery.) By the late eighteenth century, however, executions of property criminals had become increasingly controversial in the region precisely because they were sanctioned neither by traditional religious authority nor by newer Enlightenment ideas, such as the principle of proportionality in punishment. As a result, after 1800, most executions in New England were for the crime of murder—an offense for which the ultimate sanction was justified both by scripture and, at least arguably, by notions of proportionality. In other words, Yankees of the early republic tacitly struck a compromise on the death penalty—"yes" for homicide but generally "no" for property crimes such as robbery or burglary—that reflected the ongoing influence of both Christian and Enlightenment ideologies.[27]

Third, the secularization pattern is to some degree an illusion created by the timing of the demise of the execution sermon as a literary form. Not long after that genre had petered out during the mid-1820s, the debate over capital punishment actually reverted to the older religious approach. When a new wave of agitation for abolition of the death penalty swept the country during the 1830s and 1840s, clergymen from orthodox Protestant denominations led the defense of the gallows. Although they used a variety of arguments, such ministers spearheaded a significant revival of traditional scriptural justifications of capital punishment. Perhaps drawn in by those arguments, even opponents of the death penalty often made biblical claims. The reversion to scriptural authority was probably fostered by the revivalism of the Second Great Awakening and reflected the increasing bibliolatry of nineteenth-century Calvinist orthodoxy. Whatever the explanation, once the chronological scope of analysis is extended into the 1830s and 1840s, any simple secularization model becomes untenable.[28]

Evangelical and Liberal Constructions of Interracial Rape

Eighteenth-century New England clergymen tended to draw on both religious and secular ideologies not only in *justifying* capital punishment but also in *explaining* the origins of violent criminality. Whereas earlier Puritan ministers tended to explain the actions of murderers and other capital criminals in essentially theological terms (e.g., as the products of natural depravity), those of the mid-eighteenth century and thereafter often combined such spiritual understandings with secular insights derived from Enlightenment ideology. My own research confirms that pattern even with respect to the subcategory of capital cases involving alleged crimes of sexual violence by African American men against Caucasian women. Although several modern scholars have traced the popularization of the racist myth of African American men as "black beasts" (prone to raping or murdering white women) to a group of eighteenth-century New England execution sermons and criminal narratives, my own reading of these same sources has led me to a very different conclusion.[29]

Contrary to conventional scholarly wisdom, the ministers who produced execution sermons on such interracial cases rarely emphasized—and often ignored or even repudiated—the sorts of protoracist images or stereotypes sometimes attributed to them. Instead, ministers tended to promote two nonracist explanations of violent crimes allegedly committed by African Americans, in each case as an integral aspect of a much broader understanding of human character and behavior. First, the dominant *evangelical* construction postulated natural depravity as the source of sexual violence (irrespective of the offender's race) and prescribed spiritual transcendence, or Christian redemption, as the solution. That evangelical construction, firmly grounded in the fundamental theological convictions of New England Protestants, pervaded the region's execution sermons, regardless of the capital crime involved.[30] Second, the *liberal* construction likewise denied essentialist racial explanations of crime; arraigned various forms of social injustice as contributory causes of sexual violence, as well as other forms of criminality; and advocated social reform as part of the solution. That approach's designation as *liberal* does not denote any specific political or theological positions but rather a self-conscious, Enlightenment-inspired rejection of "bigotry" or "narrow prejudice" (racial or otherwise) and openness to "new ideas or proposals" for reform.[31] Though the evangelical and liberal constructions of violent crime were different in both diagnosis and prescription, authors of execution sermons and other popular crime genres sometimes combined or intertwined elements of both in their writings— once again illustrating the American preference for blending religious and secular ideologies, rather than pitting one against the other.

An early example of such interweaving of evangelical and liberal arguments was evoked by the case of a sixteen-year-old household slave named Bristol, born in Africa and brought to New England at about the age of eight, who was convicted in 1763 of murdering his master's unmarried sister in Taunton, Massachusetts. Sylvanus Conant of Middleborough addressed the case in a sermon titled *The Blood of Abel, and the Blood of Jesus Considered and Improved* (1764). Appended to the published version was a short account of the crime and its principals, written by Bristol's defense counsel (and Conant's friend), Robert Treat Paine. According to the pamphlet, Bristol had been "treated with all the Tenderness and Instruction that could be desired" and had lived for years in the same household with the victim—"a young Lady of a chearful Disposition" and "an even generous Temper." "He always appeared happy in his Situation," Paine insisted, "and shewed an uncommon Readiness to do his Business, and Faithfulness to perform what he undertook, without the least Appearance of Sullenness or Malice." Despite the reported absence of any immediate provocation, Bristol allegedly struck the woman with an iron implement as she stooped over a hearth, knocked her into the fire, dragged her to the cellar, and finally struck her with an ax. After his arrest, Bristol "appeared very penitent," "expressed his Sorrow for the Crime," and "declared constantly … that he never had any Anger against the deceased, nor any of the Family." Supposedly, his only explanation for the homicide was that "he was prompted to it by a Negro Boy of his Acquaintance, who threatned to kill him if he did not do it."[32]

Sylvanus Conant's sermon on Bristol's case was a typical gallows discourse in the evangelical tradition. He warned his audience against the perils of sin and exhorted both Bristol and the broader community to seek redemption through the saving "blood of Jesus." As in many other eighteenth-century execution sermons, the minister asserted an essential kinship between the condemned criminal and the broader community, insisting that all human beings had "the same vicious Seeds of Enmity, Prejudice, Wrath, Malice, Envy, Hatred, and the like in ... [their] Hearts, that were the guilty Cause of the Murder we now lament." Conant also emphasized that neither the crime nor the criminal should be distinguished from others on the basis of race; although the minister nominally addressed that message to Bristol himself, he clearly intended it for a wider audience as well:

> You are not to imagine, that you are treated with any greater Severity meerly because you are a black Boy, and bro't from your native Country among us, for you are not: If any of us had done such a horrid Thing as you have, we should be treated as you are: Your being of a different Colour from us, makes no Odds in this Matter. You have not only an immortal Soul as we have, but you are of the same Kind of Flesh and Blood that we are; for GOD *hath made of one Blood, all Nations of Men, for to dwell on all the Face of the Earth.*

Not content to rest his assertion of human sameness on scriptural authority alone, the minister also supported his claim with a quotation from a British commentary on Johann Gottlieb Heineccius's popular eighteenth-century German exposition of universal law: "Men by Nature are equal, being composed of the same essential Parts: Whence, every one ought to treat every other as equally a Man with himself." Conant thus sought to bolster traditional Puritan notions of spiritual equality with a newer form of secular egalitarianism, rooted in Enlightenment thought, that explicitly condemned prejudice based on complexion or nationality as illiberal. Although Conant did not say so directly, he probably intended these passages to challenge others in the community who viewed Bristol's case in essentially racial terms.[33]

Indeed, although Conant's published sermon deployed both evangelical and liberal assertions of human equality in an effort to preempt any racial construction of Bristol's case, one rambling and somewhat ambiguous passage in Robert Treat Paine's appendix suggested far more ambivalent racial attitudes. Paine began by attributing Bristol's crime to "the Weakness of human Nature" and "the horrid Effects of our ungovern'd Passions" in the absence of "virtuous Principles." But he then immediately moved his analysis from the implied universality of corrupt human nature to certain distinctive traits imputed to African Americans. Bristol's crime, he insisted, "naturally calls upon those who have the Care of Negroes to be very vigilant in removing the Prejudices of their barbarous Disposition by Instruction, and to instill into their Minds such Christian Principles as may influence their Actions when absent from the Eye of their Masters." And in apparent reference to Bristol's claim that he had acted on the orders of another "Negro Boy," Paine further urged white masters to supervise the "companying together" of African Americans, describing their potentially violent "Conspirings" as "that grand Source of all the Evils that have arisen so frequently from this Nation."[34]

Conant's sermon and Paine's ambivalent appendix together suggested both the limits and the possibilities for racial explanations of crime in a setting where traditional Christian and insurgent Enlightenment ideologies shared moral and intellectual authority. Although both ideological systems asserted the essential universality of human nature, each allowed openings for invidious distinctions between groups based on their varying access to proper education or training. For an enlightened Christian, one variant of the universal need to counteract "ungovern'd Passions" with "virtuous Principles" was the more particular need to counteract "the Prejudices" of an alien group's "barbarous Disposition" with "Christian Principles." In the absence of proper instruction, members of such a group might be particularly prone to various forms of criminality, particularly if they were allowed to consort and conspire with one another without proper supervision. In short, both the tribalism (or chauvinism) of reformed Christianity and the environmentalism of Enlightenment psychology allowed *some* room for racial or quasi-racist constructions of criminality. However, as suggested by the publication on Bristol's case, such racial ideas tended to be counteracted, or at least qualified and contained, by an overarching belief in the essential kinship and uniformity of humankind.[35]

Most ministers discussing cases of alleged interracial rape in late eighteenth-century New England showed considerably less interest in racial issues than did Sylvanus Conant and Robert Treat Paine. As suggested by its title, Thaddeus MacCarty's *The Power and Grace of Christ Display'd to a Dying Malefactor* (1768), addressing the execution of "Arthur, a Negro" for rape, was a standard evangelical gallows sermon. The minister from Worcester, Massachusetts, took a passage from the Gospel according to Luke on the dying Savior's conversion of the thief on the cross as his scriptural text, and his exposition emphasized the universal human need for salvation through Christ. MacCarty assured Arthur that, if he could obtain God's favor before his execution, he would be assured of a safe "passage to the glorious presence of Christ in paradise." And he urged his wider audience to feel pity and compassion for the condemned rapist—one of their "fellow-creatures" whose "soul" was as "precious" as their own. The sermon contained no discussion whatsoever of racial issues or of the racial backgrounds of the defendant and the victim.[36]

Timothy Langdon's *A Sermon Preached at Danbury* (1798) on the execution of "Anthony, a Free Negro" for rape was more overtly political than MacCarty's but showed no greater interest in the race of the condemned criminal. As with many earlier evangelical sermons, Langdon's oration focused primarily on God's vengeance against the wicked and the sinner's need for repentance. But Langdon also explicitly linked the spiritual concept of sin to the forces of social revolution in contemporary Europe. Citing hostile accounts of the French Revolution, the minister insisted that the biblical crimes of Cain and Judas were only pallid foreshadowings of the horrors that would result wherever anti-Christian revolutionaries gained the upper hand. "It [sin/revolution] is the grand principle of disorganization," Langdon explained. "As it operates in Europe, at the present day, it threatens the ruin of religion, government and morals." Yet Langdon never asserted any special connection between African Americans in general—or African American criminals in particular—and the forces of social revolution, either in Europe or anywhere else. From Langdon's perspective, American rapists such as Anthony and European revolutionaries certainly had something fundamental in common: they were dangerous and egregious sinners. But the minister never suggested that their kinship, or their sinfulness, had anything to do with their race.[37]

Not only did eighteenth-century execution sermons on cases of alleged interracial rape generally fail to discuss, let alone to emphasize, racial issues, they did not always even *identify* the racial backgrounds of condemned criminals. Execution sermons on such cases (not otherwise discussed here) by James Dana (1790) and Noah Worcester (1796) *nowhere* indicated that their subjects were African Americans, either in the texts or on the title pages; without independent knowledge of the cases, readers of those sermons would have had no way of determining the men's racial backgrounds. The published sermons of Thaddeus MacCarty and Timothy Langdon did identify the condemned in their subtitles as "Arthur, a Negro" and "Anthony, a Free Negro," respectively. That such brief designations were intended as derogatory epithets, however, is by no means clear; rather, they likely served primarily as substitutes for conventional surnames or as devices to explain the absence of such surnames. That onomastic rationale may also help account for the complete absence of racial identifiers on Dana's and Worcester's title pages. Because their criminal subjects (Joseph Mountain and Thomas Powers, respectively) had conventional surnames, racial designations were not needed for reasons of clarity and hence were omitted.[38]

Yet postrevolutionary New England was by no means a color-blind society—slavery actually lingered on in Connecticut and Rhode Island well into the nineteenth century—and the authors of all these sermons were no doubt quite aware of the racial backgrounds of the criminals whose cases they addressed.[39] Their decisions not to discuss, or even mention, the issue of race in their discourses were probably grounded both in immediate rhetorical strategies and in broader ideological convictions. The clergymen who delivered execution sermons in New England almost invariably sought to emphasize the underlying spiritual kinship between condemned criminals and other members of the community—and hence play down any essential moral or social differences between them—as a way of hammering home their central evangelical message that all people stood in as much need of repentance and reform as the malefactor at the gallows.[40] Any emphasis on the racial backgrounds or imputed racial traits of African American criminals would have tended to undermine that message by accentuating superficial differences between the black convict and the minister's wider audience (which, in New England, was always predominantly white). More broadly, evangelical Christians of the early modern period—believing in the biblical Creation story—took the common descent and essential kinship of all human beings, regardless of race or nationality, as a fundamental article of faith. Finally, in the wake of the Enlightenment, most humane and well-read New England clergymen of the late eighteenth century would have dismissed essentialist racial distinctions as not only unscriptural but also illiberal.

Not until the publication in 1817 of William Andrews's *A Sermon Delivered at Danbury* on the execution of Amos Adams in Connecticut did a New England minister offer substantial racial commentary on African Americans in the context of a capital rape case. Most of the address was devoted to the usual evangelical verities. Andrews insisted that variations in people's moral conduct were "not to be ascribed to any innate difference of moral character." To the contrary, the Bible taught that "all sinners, in a natural state, possess the *same* moral character." Nor could a convicted rapist like Amos Adams be denied the promise of Christian redemption as a result of his racial background. "Believe in Christ, Amos; and you shall this day experience the full benefit of his atoning blood," the minister exhorted. "You shall pass from nature to grace, from earth to heaven, from the gallows to glory."[41]

In a long paragraph toward the end of the sermon, however, Andrews directly addressed social distinctions based on race. Acknowledging that "a few" of the "people of color" in Connecticut were "virtuous members of society," the minister insisted that many others were "engaged in every evil work," particularly "crimes and misdemeanors." He claimed that "one-third or more" of all offenders from the county sentenced to state prison during the previous twenty-six years had been "colored people." During that same period, two of the three criminals convicted of capital offenses had also been "negroes." But Andrews immediately suggested that these statistics implicated the white population as much as the black:

> Is no part of their sin chargeable upon us? What but the most cruel avarice brought them here? And what but this has kept so many of them to this day in ignorance and degradation? In this land of boasted light, how many thousands are there, as ignorant as the brutes that perish! They have been taught nothing but to labor and to sin. To them, our countrymen have generally appeared in the character of tyrants and executioners.[42]

Andrews seemed to believe that many African Americans were ignorant, degraded, and even criminal; yet he attributed these tendencies not to any intrinsic difference between the black and white (or African and European) branches of humanity, but rather to the tyrannical oppression and exploitation of the former by the latter. The minister's proposed solution to the imputed problem of black criminality further suggested a social or environmental (rather than essentialist) view of racial difference, one animated by an underlying confidence in the potential for social amelioration and reconciliation:

> Our interest and our duty point to the same course. They [African Americans] must be enlightened. They must be instructed in the principles of the christian religion. They must be raised to the rank of rational beings, and be made to feel as much as possible, the force of moral obligation. The shameful fact must be confessed that our countrymen are largely their debtors. The mention of their claims, so long neglected, ought to

affect every heart and crimson every face. Be it ours to recognize, and discharge our obligations. There is not any benevolent society to which I could more heartily lend my feeble support, than to an association for the purpose of reforming the morals and improving the condition of our blacks.[43]

Andrews's sermon thus contained all the essential elements of what was to become the standard white liberal response to racial injustice over the next two centuries: expressions of guilt, obligation, and condescension; calls to activism; and faith in the possibility of reconciling the interests of oppressor and oppressed through benevolent outreach, moral uplift, and social reform. Compared to the more strictly evangelical constructions offered by earlier ministers, Andrews's secular analysis of the (alleged) problem of black criminality allowed greater conceptual space both for invidious constructions of racial difference and for liberal explanations and solutions. In other words, the gradual weakening of older theological understandings of human character and criminal behavior could alternately lead the thinking of white New Englanders in liberal or protoracist directions—or in both directions simultaneously. Indeed, by 1817, one can begin to trace the emergence of a modern American discourse on race, crime, and sexual violence. To the extent that the once-dominant evangelical construction of crime was deemphasized, explicitly racial considerations and related sociological issues came to the fore, with liberal constructions of black criminality contending in a curiously symbiotic ideological struggle with protoracist images, epithets, and arguments.[44]

Protestant and Patriotic Justifications of Mob Violence

Even after the demise of the execution sermon genre during the 1820s, nineteenth-century New Englanders continued to blend religious and secular ideas when grappling with issues of crime and punishment. In an increasingly heterogeneous society, however, no single figure—whether minister, prosecutor, judge, or journalist—could hope to speak with unchallenged authority. Indeed, even the line between crime and punishment was sometimes blurred and contested; in an era notorious for its riots, American mobs of the 1830s and thereafter often took the law into their own hands, inflicting rough justice on a variety of unpopular groups, including racial, ethnic, and religious minorities. Whether they defended or condemned such mob violence, those who sought to influence American public opinion generally did so by appealing to a combination of religious and secular values. This third case study—of an episode of anti-Catholic mob violence and the prolonged controversy that followed—moves beyond sermon doctrines, showing how religious and secular ideologies remained stubbornly intertwined in the disorderly, sectarian, and intensely partisan public sphere of antebellum America.[45]

Throughout the first several decades of the nineteenth century, as the pace of European immigration gradually increased, Roman Catholics established dozens of academies for girls across the United States. Although the schools were often operated by nuns and attached to convents, many of their students came from wealthy Protestant families. During the early 1830s, an Ursuline community operated one such institution on a picturesque hilltop estate called Mount Benedict in Charlestown, Massachusetts, near Boston. Surrounding the Ursuline establishment, however, were several brickyards operated by rough Scots-Irishmen from New Hampshire—men with deeply embedded ethnocultural traditions of hostility toward Catholicism. In August 1834, a Protestant mob, led by some of those brickmakers (acting in collaboration with Boston and Charlestown firemen), ransacked and burned the Ursuline convent. Although ostensibly trying to rescue a nun who was supposedly being held against her will, the rioters had destroyed what they perceived to be an anti-American institution; the attorney general of Massachusetts, however, indicted more than a dozen of the rioters on charges of burglary and arson.[46]

In the aftermath of the Charlestown riot, supporters of the Ursulines tended to blame two figures for inciting the mob: One was Lyman Beecher, a prominent Presbyterian clergyman, who had reportedly delivered three anti-Catholic sermons in Boston on the day before the riot. The second alleged instigator was Rebecca Reed, the impoverished daughter of a local farmer who, though born and raised a Protestant, had converted to Catholicism and entered the Charlestown convent in 1831. Reed soon became unhappy at Mount Benedict, left the institution, and began telling tales of various abuses there. Several months after the riot, Reed published an exposé titled *Six Months in a Convent* that quickly became antebellum America's first great anti-Catholic bestseller, reportedly selling more than 50,000 copies in less than a year. The Ursuline superior responded with a bitter refutation of Reed's charges, issued amid a spate of polemical publications on both sides of the conflict. Far more than a passing trauma, the Charlestown convent riot was a formative generational event that would intermittently inflame Bay State politics and popular culture over the next twenty years, culminating in the stunning takeover of the government of Massachusetts by the nativist Know-Nothing Party during the mid-1850s.[47]

As suggested by the effort to blame Lyman Beecher, many contemporary observers saw the burning of the Charlestown convent as an act of religious bigotry, inspired by evangelical Protestant extremists. Thus, in a series of caricatures published several months after the riot, the popular Boston graphic artist David Claypoole Johnston launched a powerful satirical assault on the Protestant fanaticism that had allegedly motivated the anticonvent mob. Three of the images are representative of the entire set:

- "Fanatical Inspiration" (figure 4.1) shows a Protestant preacher (probably Lyman Beecher) spouting "Bigotry, Prejudice, calumny, Black lies, Self interest, Envy, self conceit, and Bible perversions," while the devil, or a satanic imp, fans the flames of anti-Catholic bigotry.
- "Defenders of the True Faith" (figure 4.2) depicts a pig-faced leader addressing an equally animalistic mob. The leader tells his followers, "Remember that the greatest blessing secured to us by the constitution is Religious liberty, which means ... that if you dont approve of the religion of your neighbour, you are at liberty to burn his house down...."
- "Anti-Catholic Doings" (figure 4.3) shows the swinish rioters, armed with clubs and torches, brutalizing the Ursulines and their students, dragging the corpse of a deceased nun out of a coffin, and setting the convent on fire.

Fig. 4.1. "Fanatical Inspiration"

Fig. 4.2. "Defenders of the True Faith"

Fig. 4.3. "Anti-Catholic Doings"

Johnston's association of the rioters and their apologists with Protestant fanaticism tended to be confirmed, albeit inadvertently, by the sponsors of Rebecca Reed, who audaciously compared *Six Months in a Convent* to the "little treatise" of Martin Luther that had launched the Protestant Reformation three centuries earlier.[48]

Yet some of the rioters also appear to have understood the burning of the Charlestown convent as an act of patriotism, comparable to the acts of mob violence that had marked the American Revolutionary crisis. As in those earlier attacks against British officials and their property (or against other embodiments of threatening imperial policies), concerned citizens mobilized to assail an alien institution that was perceived to be both anti-democratic and anti-American. Thus, the particular Boston volunteer fire company that was most damningly implicated in the riot was a straight-laced contingent of young patriots who, in 1832, had renamed their unit after Thomas Melvill, one of the last surviving participants in the Boston Tea Party. The filiopietistic group had established a veritable shrine to Melvill in their stationhouse, hung a painting of the Tea Party on their wall, and nearly adopted Revolutionary-style cocked hats as part of their official uniform. There is also reason to believe that the convent rioters had originally planned to stage their assault on August 14, the well-known and once widely commemorated anniversary of Boston's Stamp Act riots of 1765—another famous mob action of the Revolutionary crisis. During one of the subsequent trials of the alleged convent rioters, supporters of the accused vandals circulated handbills addressed to the "Sons of Free-dom," invoking the Revolutionary era slogan of "Liberty or Death!" And after the trials were over, at about the time that the Ursulines were forced to retreat to Canada, somebody planted an American flag on the ruins of Mount Benedict—as if marking the country's repossession of a conquered enemy stronghold. Finally, bits and pieces of evidence suggested that Yan-kee Protestants had also absorbed the Old World's revolutionary brand of anti-Catholic propaganda; thus, a Charlestown brickmaker touted Napoleon's destruction of European convents, and an anticonvent handbill issued shortly before the riot claimed, "When Bonaparte opened the nun-nerys of Europe, he found crowds of Infant sculls!!!!!"[49]

Those who condemned the Charlestown mob also appealed to patriotic and Revolutionary values—a winning stance, one might have thought, given the Constitution's and the Founding Fathers' tacit commitments to denomi-national pluralism and sectarian tolerance. Unfortunately for the Ursulines, however, many Americans who condemned the riot also shared the mob's suspicion of Roman Catholicism as potentially antithetical to American religious and political freedom. Nevertheless, for twenty years after the burning of the Charlestown convent, Protestant supporters of the Ursulines repeatedly tried, albeit without success, to obtain financial compensation from the Massachusetts legislature for the fire's victims. In 1845, in the midst of those efforts, a popular Boston novelist and story-paper editor named Justin Jones published a fictionalized account of the convent riot titled *The Nun of St. Ursula*. Though Jones's novelette formally endorses convent compensation, it expresses as well the sort of visceral Yankee hostility toward Catholicism that prevented the measure from ever being enacted into law. In light of the world's current "clash of civilizations," *The Nun of St. Ursula* also provides a startling reminder of the mutability of religious animosities. To judge by Jones's potboiler, mid-nineteenth-century American Protestants saw less to fear in armed Muslims than in Ursuline nuns.[50]

Here is a brief summary of Jones's fanciful and convoluted plot: One day, Harvard student Fred Gray runs into his old childhood chum, Jack Melville, on the streets of Cambridge. Melville tells a fantastic tale. After having been shipwrecked, rescued by Turkish sailors, and adopted by a Turkish admiral, Jack had converted to Islam in order to marry Zillah, the Turkish admiral's adopted Greek daughter. Zillah, however, had subsequently been kidnapped by pirates and (unknown to Jack) had only recently been deposited in the Charlestown convent. Meanwhile, Fred Gray has fallen in love with Cecile Melville, Jack's younger sister. Unfortunately, Cecile has been sent by her widowed mother to the Ursuline school in Charlestown, where a lecherous Canadian monk, Padre Francis, has persuaded her to become a novice. When Cecile has second thoughts, Padre Francis and the Ursulines decide to drug Cecile and initiate her into the order anyway. In the story's climax, Fred, Jack, and his crew of Turkish sailors rescue both Cecile and Zillah from the burning convent. The denouement features a final rush of happy developments. Fred Gray marries Cecile Melville. Jack and Zillah, Fred and Cecile, and the Widow Melville all sail to Constantinople. After two years abroad, Fred and Cecile return to Cambridge with old Mrs. Melville, but as the story ends, they are looking forward to a visit from their "eastern relatives."[51]

In *The Nun of St. Ursula*, Justin Jones reworks the real story of the Charlestown convent riot in an effort to appeal to the prejudices of Yankee Protestant readers. Thus, he concocts several characters that conform to the crudest of anti-Catholic stereotypes, such as Padre Francis, the lecherous Canadian monk. He also replaces the controversial anti-Catholic agitator,

Rebecca Reed, with an ideal Protestant "damsel in distress," Cecile Melville. But what are we to make of Jones's elaborate Turkish subplot? Of course, on one level, it simply provides *The Nun of St. Ursula* with several standard requisites of a successful adventure story of the mid-1840s: shipwrecks, naval battles, exotic settings, a cross-cultural romance, and several surprising plot twists. But on another level, it also serves to advance Jones's anti-Catholic agenda, albeit in a somewhat indirect way. In effect, Jones splits the bulk of his novel's foreigners into two main categories: "good" Turkish Muslims and "bad" Roman Catholics. Jack Melville's life is saved by Turkish sailors, he is adopted by a Turkish admiral, he falls in love with a Muslim girl, and he converts to Islam after observing its admirable "moral precepts" and the "good faith" of its believers. Even the elderly Mrs. Melville is reconciled to her son's conversion once Jack explains that the Muslim prays to "the *same* God" as the Christian and that the typical Turk is not only a person "of honesty," "morality," and "piety" but also "of benevolence and kindness." Near the end of the novel, Fred and Cecile's Protestant friends celebrate their nuptials in an elaborate multicultural extravaganza of oriental cuisine, decor, apparel, music, and dance. In light of such conspicuous broadmindedness, the reader is invited to conclude that Yankee hostility toward Roman Catholicism must be based not on mere provincialism or bigotry but rather on well-grounded fears of "papal power" and popish vice.[52]

Jones's struggle to reconcile his own distaste for Roman Catholicism with his broader cosmopolitan self-image is reflected in a number of editorial comments near the beginning and end of the novel. At the outset, Jones emphatically describes the convent ruins "as a monument of intolerance" and as a "disgrace" to "the good old Commonwealth of Massachusetts!" He juxtaposes the shameful ruins on Mount Benedict to the nearby Bunker Hill Monument, commemorative of Revolutionary valor and American liberty. And he suggests that it would be both "expedient and just" for the state legislature to pay compensation to the riot's victims. He also endorses the presence of the Catholic Sisters of Charity in Massachusetts, because, unlike the Ursulines, the Sisters of Charity are not cloistered. But after all those concessions, Jones still warns against any plan to reestablish an Ursuline convent in New England; such an *enclosed* institution, he insists, would be "repugnant to the feelings of the great mass" of Yankees. "Go on and multiply your churches," he invites Roman Catholics in conclusion, "but have no secret auxiliaries—and both Protestants and Catholics may yet worship the same God in the same community without jealous rivalry—without wrangling—without rioting!"[53]

The ambivalent positions staked out by Justin Jones in *The Nun of St. Ursula* reflected the viewpoints of many moderate antebellum Protestants. On the one hand, such Americans were deeply hostile toward Roman Catholic beliefs, rituals, and institutions. On the other hand, they liked to view themselves as liberal, tolerant, and cosmopolitan—that is, as good children of the Enlightenment—and they were genuinely shocked by the disorderly violence of the convent riot. Such attitudes were particularly characteristic of the Bay State's urban Whigs, the party that dominated Massachusetts politics for most of the twenty years following the convent riot. Thus, it is not surprising to learn that Justin Jones edited a Whig newspaper in Boston during the early 1850s and even served as a Whig representative to the state legislature. But by then, the somewhat *soft*—or accommodationist—anti-Catholic stance staked out by urban Whigs such as Jones was about to be overwhelmed by a much *harder* form of popular anti-Catholicism.[54]

In April 1853, the Massachusetts House of Representatives finally passed a bill to provide state compensation for the victims of the Charlestown riot; that fleeting victory, however, provoked a fierce backlash that led to the measure's narrow defeat on reconsideration. Significantly, those votes divided the legislative contingents of each of the state's three major political parties (Whigs, Democrats, and Free Soilers) almost precisely in half, evidently demonstrating to many Bay State Protestant voters that *none* of the existing parties could be counted on to stand up against the growing political influence of Roman Catholics. Within a matter of months, irate Protestants had begun to organize themselves into secret nativist lodges as an alternative to politics as usual. During the fall of 1854, as statewide elections approached, two of Boston's popular literary weeklies (or story papers) suddenly began filling their pages with viciously anti-Catholic and anticonvent tales, including several fictionalized retellings of the Charlestown convent riot. That November, the insurgent Know-Nothing Party pulled off one of the most shocking upsets in the history of American politics. In a massive electoral landslide, the Know Nothings won every single statewide office, every congressional race, all forty state senate seats, and all but a handful of the 379 seats in the state's House of Representatives. Twenty years after the burning of the Ursuline convent, tens of thousands of Massachusetts voters—acting both as Protestants and as patriots—had tacitly vindicated the Charlestown rioters and handed the nativist movement its greatest political victory.[55]

Conclusion

This essay's three disparate case studies all strike variations on the same broad theme. In grappling with potentially controversial issues of law, crime, violence, and punishment (whether legal or extralegal), early Americans tended to invoke both religious and secular arguments in support of their policies, actions, or beliefs. As early as the first half of the eighteenth century, New England clergymen constructed hybrid defenses of capital punishment that carefully balanced scriptural and social justifications; later, secular arguments occasionally even displaced the religious ones. During the second half of the eighteenth century, ministers formulated dual evangelical and Enlightenment-liberal constructions of interracial sexual violence that effectively countered protoracist understandings of black criminality. And during the first half of the nineteenth century, Yankee rioters and their sympathizers offered both sectarian and patriotic justifications for a controversial act of extralegal mob violence. Though religious conservatives occasionally assailed Enlightenment or Revolutionary ideas and social radicals sometimes repudiated traditional Christianity, shrewd New Englanders of the eighteenth and early nineteenth centuries understood that they were most likely to persuade their fellow citizens when they deployed the multiple sanctions of Christian, Enlightenment, and Revolutionary belief.[56]

Notes

1. That American and French revolutionaries held contrasting attitudes toward traditional religion was noted by Alexis de Tocqueville, as discussed by Frank Kelleter in chapter 2 of this volume.

2. The first part of this chapter is largely drawn from Daniel A. Cohen, "In Defense of the Gallows: Justifications of Capital Punishment in New England Execution Sermons, 1674–1825," *American Quarterly* 40, no. 2 (1988): 147–64; that article appears in a slightly different form in Daniel A. Cohen, *Pillars of Salt, Monuments of Grace: New England Crime Literature and the Origins of American Popular Culture, 1674–1860* (New York: Oxford University Press, 1993), 101–14. For more on early New England execution sermons, see Cohen, *Pillars of Salt, Monuments of Grace*, 3–13, 41–58, 83–100; Scott D. Seay, *Hanging between Heaven and Earth: Capital Crime, Execution Preaching, and Theology in Early New England* (DeKalb: Northern Illinois University Press, 2009); Karen Halttunen, *Murder Most Foul: The Killer and the American Gothic Imagination* (Cambridge, MA: Harvard University Press, 1998), 11–32; Louis P. Masur, *Rites of Execution: Capital Punishment and the Transformation of American Culture, 1776–1865* (New York: Oxford University Press, 1989), 25–49; Ronald A. Bosco,

"Lectures at the Pillory: The Early American Execution Sermon," *American Quarterly* 30, no. 2 (1978): 156–76; Walter Lazenby, "Exhortation as Exorcism: Cotton Mather's Sermons to Murderers," *Quarterly Journal of Speech* 57, no. 1 (1971): 50–56; Wayne C. Minnick, "The New England Execution Sermon, 1639–1800," *Speech Monographs* 35, no. 1 (1968): 77–89.

3. Increase Mather, *A Sermon Occasioned by the Execution of a Man* (Boston: J. Brunning, 1686), 1, 4, 14. For biographical treatments of Increase Mather, see John Langdon Sibley, ed., *Biographical Sketches of Graduates of Harvard University in Cambridge, Massachusetts, 1642–1658*, vol. 1 (Cambridge, MA: Charles William Sever, 1873), 410–70; Robert Middlekauff, *The Mathers: Three Generations of Puritan Intellectuals, 1596–1728* (New York: Oxford University Press, 1971), 77–187.

4. S[amuel] D[anforth], *The Cry of Sodom Enquired Into* (Cambridge, MA: M. Johnson, 1674), 8. For a biographical sketch of Danforth, see Sibley, *Biographical Sketches*, vol. 1, 88–92.

5. George Lee Haskins, *Law and Authority in Early Massachusetts* (New York: Macmillan, 1960), 145–54; Edwin Powers, *Crime and Punishment in Early Massachusetts 1620–1692* (Boston: Beacon Press, 1966), 252–72; Barbara Shapiro, "Law Reform in Seventeenth Century England," *American Journal of Legal History* 19, no. 4 (1975): 290, 296–97, 311; Kathryn Preyer, "Penal Measures in the American Colonies: An Overview," *American Journal of Legal History* 26, no. 4 (1982): 332–33; Daniel A. Cohen, "In Defense of the Gallows," 149–50.

6. For sermon texts condemning capital crimes, see Eliphalet Adams, *A Sermon* (New London, CT: T. Green, 1738), 1; Charles Chauncy, *The Horrid Nature and Enormous Guilt of Murder* (Boston: T. Fleet, 1754), 5; Timothy Pitkin, *A Sermon Preached at Litchfield* (Hartford, CT: Green and Watson, 1768), 3.

7. Benjamin Colman, *The Hainous Nature of the Sin of Murder* (Boston: John Allen, 1713) [published in volume with Cotton Mather, *The Sad Effects of Sin*], 14; Samuel Checkley, *Murder a Great and Crying Sin* (Boston: T. Fleet, 1733), 14–15; Chauncy, *Horrid Nature*, 21.

8. On the early Enlightenment's love of balance, see David Lundberg and Henry F. May, "The Enlightened Reader in America," *American Quarterly* 28, no. 2 (1976): 265; Henry F. May, *The Enlightenment in America* (New York: Oxford University Press, 1976), 1–101. For biographical treatments of Colman, Checkley, and Chauncy, see Clifford K. Shipton, ed., *Biographical Sketches of Those Who Attended Harvard College in the Classes 1701–1712*, vol. 5 (Boston: Massachusetts Historical Society, 1937), 120–37; Clifford K. Shipton, ed., *Biographical Sketches of Those Who Attended Harvard College in the Classes 1713–1721*, vol. 6 (Boston: Massachusetts Historical Society, 1942), 74–78, 439–67; Charles Burke Giles, "Benjamin Colman: A Study of the Movement toward Reasonable Religion in the 17th Century" (PhD diss., University of California, Los Angeles, 1963); Edward M. Griffin, *Old Brick: Charles Chauncy of Boston, 1705–1787* (Minneapolis: University of Minnesota Press, 1980); Charles H. Lippy, *Seasonable Revolutionary: The Mind of Charles Chauncy* (Chicago: Nelson-Hall, 1981). Similar arguments also appear in Nathaniel Clap, *Sinners Directed to Hear and Fear* (Boston: J. Allen for N. Boone, 1715), 39–40.

9. Colman, *Hainous Nature*, 14.

10. Checkley, *Murder*, 14–16.

11. Chauncy, *Horrid Nature*, 17.

12. Colman, *Hainous Nature*, 6–14; Checkley, *Murder*, 3, 8, 14–16, 23; Chauncy, *Horrid Nature*, 5, 10, 12, 14–17, 21. Similar secular arguments had appeared earlier in Mather, *Sermon Occasioned*, 9–11.

13. Powers, *Crime and Punishment*, 269–72, 303–8; Preyer, "Penal Measures," 333–34, 342, 348; David Thomas Konig, *Law and Society in Puritan Massachusetts: Essex County, 1629–1692* (Chapel Hill: University of North Carolina Press, 1979), 158–88, passim.

14. For a groundbreaking scholarly account of anglicization, see John M. Murrin, "Anglicizing an American Colony" (PhD diss., Yale University, New Haven, CT, 1966); on the anglicization of the Massachusetts legal system, in particular, see John M. Murrin, "The Legal Transformation: The Bench and Bar of Eighteenth-Century Massachusetts," in *Colonial America: Essays in Politics and Social Development*, ed. Stanley N. Katz and John M. Murrin (New York: Knopf, 1983), 540–72. On changes in the criminal code, see *The Charters and General Laws of the Colony and Province of Massachusetts Bay* (Boston: T. B. Wait, 1814), 239, 392–93, 406–7; Powers, *Crime and Punishment*, 303–8; Preyer, "Penal Measures," 342.

15. Despite shifts in public discourse on such issues as crime and punishment, the Revolution itself was by no means an entirely secular movement—a point amply confirmed by Frank Kelleter's essay in this volume (chapter 2). On the gradual demise of Calvinist theocentrism in eighteenth-century New England, see Joseph Haroutunian, *Piety versus Moralism: The Passing of the New England Theology* (New York: Henry Holt, 1932), 30–42, 86–87, 145.

16. On the lack of biblical sanction for the death penalty in cases of burglary and rape, see Powers, *Crime and Punishment*, 264, 269. For evidence of opposition to the execution of Massachusetts burglars, see later discussion in this chapter and "Theft and Murder! A Poem" (Boston: Isaiah Thomas, 1773); see also Stuart Banner, *The Death Penalty: An American History* (Cambridge, MA: Harvard University Press, 2002), 88–100, passim.

17. For examples of the new secular orientation not discussed here, see Noah Hobart, *Excessive Wickedness, the Way to an Untimely Death* (New Haven, CT: T. and S. Green, 1768), 6, 12–14, 19 (execution for burglary); Stephen West, *A Sermon, preached in Lenox in the County of Berkshire, Massachusetts, December 6, 1787: at the Execution of John Bly and Charles Rose* (Pittsfield, MA: E. Russell, 1787), 4–8 (burglary); James Diman, *A Sermon: Preached at Salem, January 16, 1772* (Salem, MA: S. and E. Hall, 1772), 7 (rape); James Dana, *The Intent of Capital Punishment* (New Haven, CT: T. and S. Green, 1790), 5–13 (rape); Aaron Bancroft, *The Importance of a Religious Education* (Worcester, MA: I. Thomas, 1793), 22–23 (murder).

18. Peres Fobes, *The Paradise of God Opened to a Penitent Thief* (Providence, RI: Bennett Wheeler, 1785); "Appendix," 1–12 (quoted at 1, emphasis added). For a biographical sketch of Fobes, see Clifford K. Shipton, ed., *Biographical Sketches of Those Who Attended Harvard College in the Classes 1761–1763*, vol. 15 (Boston: Massachusetts Historical Society, 1970), 229–35.

19. Fobes, *Paradise*, "Appendix," 2–8.

20. Ibid., 11–12.

21. William E. Nelson, "Emerging Notions of Modern Criminal Law in the Revolutionary Era: An Historical Perspective," *New York University Law Review* 42 (1967): 450–82; William E. Nelson, *Americanization of the Common Law* (Cambridge, MA: Harvard University Press, 1975), 117–21; David H. Flaherty, "Law and the Enforce-

ment of Morals in Early America," *Perspectives in American History* 5 (1971): 245–48, quoted at 248; Michael Stephen Hindus, *Prison and Plantation: Crime, Justice, and Authority in Massachusetts and South Carolina, 1767–1878* (Chapel Hill: University of North Carolina Press, 1980), 67–69; Richard Gaskins, "Changes in the Criminal Law in Eighteenth-Century Connecticut," *American Journal of Legal History* 25, no. 4 (1981): 309–11, passim.

22. On one minister's weakening faith in the scriptural defense, see the earlier discussion of Fobes's sermon; on another's loss of faith in the effectiveness of capital punishment as a deterrent, see Thomas Baldwin, *The Danger of Living without the Fear of God* (Boston: James Loring, 1819), 17. For doubts concerning a condemned man's guilt, see the discussion of Moses C. Welch's sermon later in this chapter; for the legal-procedural defense in a sermon on another such case—that of Jason Fairbanks—see Thomas Thacher, *The Danger of Despising the Divine Counsel* (Dedham, MA: H. Mann, 1802), 17–24, particularly 20 and 24. Elements of the new defense had appeared earlier, in embryonic form, in Thaddeus MacCarty, *The Guilt of Innocent Blood Put Away* (Worcester, MA: Isaiah Thomas, 1778), 16, and Fobes, *Paradise*, 8. For another example of the legal-procedural defense, see Enoch Huntington, *A Sermon, Preached at Middletown, June 28, 1797* (Middletown, CT: M. H. Woodward, 1797), 15–17.

23. S[amuel] Blatchford, "Address," in *A Sermon Preached at Danbury*, by Timothy Langdon (Danbury, CT: Douglas & Nichols, 1798), 20–22. For a biographical sketch of Blatchford, see Samuel Orcutt, *A History of the Old Town of Stratford and the City of Bridgeport Connecticut*, vol. 1 (New Haven, CT: Fairfield County Historical Society, 1886), 630–31.

24. Moses C. Welch, *The Gospel to Be Preached to All Men* (Windham, CT: J. Byrne, 1805), 16. For a biographical sketch of Welch, see Frank Bowditch Dexter, *Biographical Sketches of the Graduates of Yale College with Annals of the College History*, vol. 3 (New York: Henry Holt, 1903), 459–63. These New England execution sermons expressed none of the hostility toward modern legal procedures attributed to English preachers by André Krischer in chapter 5 of this volume. On the increasingly law-oriented culture of America's early republic, see Alexis de Tocqueville, *Democracy in America*, ed. Richard D. Heffner (New York: Mentor, 1956), 123–28; Perry Miller, *The Life of the Mind in America* (New York: Harcourt, Brace & World, 1965), 96–265; Maxwell Bloomfield, *American Lawyers in a Changing Society, 1776–1876* (Cambridge, MA: Harvard University Press, 1976), 57–58; Gerard W. Gawalt, *The Promise of Power: The Emergence of the Legal Profession in Massachusetts, 1760–1840* (Westport, CT: Greenwood Press, 1979), 5, 117–18, passim; Robert A. Ferguson, *Law and Letters in American Culture* (Cambridge, MA: Harvard University Press, 1984), 11–15, 20. On Puritan hostility toward lawyers and on the rapid entry of lawyers into positions of political leadership on the eve of the Revolutionary period (a pattern that persisted throughout the Revolution and into the era of the early republic), see Murrin, "Legal Transformation," 541–42, 556, 568; also, on increasing litigiousness in the early republic, see William E. Nelson, *Dispute and Conflict Resolution in Plymouth County, Massachusetts, 1725–1825* (Chapel Hill: University of North Carolina Press, 1981), 76–152.

25. Cohen, *Pillars of Salt, Monuments of Grace*, 26–31, 112. On the shift away from public executions during the 1830s and thereafter, see Masur, *Rites of Execution*, 93–116, but on the persistently public or performative aspects of prison executions, see

Jürgen Martschukat, "Nineteenth-Century Executions as Performances of Law, Death, and Civilization," in *The Cultural Lives of Capital Punishment: Comparative Perspectives*, ed. Austin Sarat and Christian Boulanger (Stanford, CA: Stanford University Press, 2005), 49–68 (I am grateful to Evi Girling for bringing this book to my attention); Banner, *Death Penalty*, 154–68; Michael Madow, "Forbidden Spectacle: Executions, the Public, and the Press in Nineteenth-Century New York," *Buffalo Law Review* 43 (1995): 461–562.

26. See Seay, *Hanging between Heaven and Earth*, 127–36.

27. For a comprehensive listing of legal executions in New England, see Daniel Allen Hearn, *Legal Executions in New England: A Comprehensive Reference, 1623–1960* (Jefferson, NC: McFarland, 1999); see also Alan Rogers, *Murder and the Death Penalty in Massachusetts* (Amherst: University of Massachusetts Press, 2008), 43. Between 1780 and 1789, nineteen executions took place for the crimes of robbery and burglary in New England, compared to eleven for murder. Between 1790 and 1799, there were thirteen executions for murder (including four instances linked to mutiny or piracy), six for burglary, and three for rape. Between 1800 and 1809, there were eleven executions for murder, one for rape, and none for robbery or burglary. And between 1810 and 1839, there were thirty-seven executions in New England for murder (albeit sometimes linked to piracy or mutiny), ten for piracy (without murder), five for rape, four for robbery, three for arson, and none for burglary. For details on these executions, see Hearn, *Legal Executions*, 162–225. Opposition to the death penalty for property criminals was not restricted to New England; see Banner, *Death Penalty*, 88–143, passim.

28. On the movement to abolish the death penalty, which was promoted not only by Enlightenment ideas but also by the values of Romanticism and sentimentalism, see David Brion Davis, "The Movement to Abolish Capital Punishment in America, 1787–1861," *American Historical Review* 63, no. 1 (1957): 29–46; Philip English Mackey, *Voices against Death: American Opposition to Capital Punishment, 1787–1975* (New York: Burt Franklin, 1976), xviii–xxix, 1–119; Philip English Mackey, *Hanging in the Balance: The Anti-Capital Punishment Movement in New York State, 1776–1861* (New York: Garland, 1982), 112–319; Masur, *Rites of Execution*, 3–24, 93–163; Banner, *Death Penalty*, 88–143; Paul Christian Jones, "The Politics of Poetry: The *Democratic Review* and the Gallows Verse of William Wordsworth and John Greenleaf Whittier," *American Periodicals* 17, no. 1 (2007): 1–25; Paul Christian Jones, *Against the Gallows: Antebellum Writers and the Movement to Abolish Capital Punishment* (Iowa City: University of Iowa Press, 2011). On opposition to that movement by orthodox clergymen, see Mackey, *Voices against Death*, xxiii–xxiv; Mackey, *Hanging in the Balance*, 95n16, 125, 136, 145, 154–63, 214–17, 280, 318, passim; Masur, *Rites of Execution*, 141–59, passim. Conversely, the movement itself was led, in part, by ministers of the unorthodox Universalist, Unitarian, and Quaker denominations; see Mackey, *Voices against Death*, xxiii; Mackey, *Hanging in the Balance*, 214–16, 318. On the "bibliolatry" of nineteenth-century New England Calvinism, see Haroutunian, *Piety versus Moralism*, 186–87. The reemergence of orthodox American clergymen as leading public defenders of the death penalty during the 1830s and 1840s may be analogous to the "appropriation of capital punishment by religion" in mid- to late-eighteenth-century England, as described by André Krischer in chapter 5.

29. Richard Slotkin, "Narratives of Negro Crime in New England, 1675–1800," *American Quarterly* 25, no. 1 (1973): 3–31; Daniel E. Williams, "The Gratification of That Corrupt and Lawless Passion: Character Types and Themes in Early New England

Rape Narratives," in *A Mixed Race: Ethnicity in Early America*, ed. Frank Shuffelton (New York: Oxford University Press, 1993), 194–221; Daniel E. Williams, *Pillars of Salt: An Anthology of Early American Criminal Narratives* (Madison, WI: Madison House, 1993), 51–58, passim; Seay, *Hanging between Heaven and Earth*, 65–70. For important social-historical discussions of interracial rape in early America, see Sharon Block, *Rape and Sexual Power in Early America* (Chapel Hill: University of North Carolina Press, 2006), 163–209, passim; Cornelia Hughes Dayton, *Women before the Bar: Gender, Law, and Society in Connecticut, 1639–1789* (Chapel Hill: University of North Carolina Press, 1995), 231–84. On interracial sexuality and rape in the South, see Diane Miller Sommerville, *Rape and Race in the Nineteenth-Century South* (Chapel Hill: University of North Carolina Press, 2004); Martha Hodes, *White Women, Black Men: Illicit Sex in the Nineteenth-Century South* (New Haven, CT: Yale University Press, 1997); Paul Finkelman, "Crimes of Love, Misdemeanors of Passion: The Regulation of Race and Sex in the Colonial South," in *The Devil's Lane: Sex and Race in the Early South*, ed. Catherine Clinton and Michele Gillespie (New York: Oxford University Press, 1997), 124–35; Diane Sommerville, "The Rape Myth in the Old South Reconsidered," *Journal of Southern History* 61, no. 3 (1995): 481–518. The second part of this chapter is abstracted from a more comprehensive study, based on a larger and more varied group of popular crime publications; see Daniel A. Cohen, "Social Injustice, Sexual Violence, Spiritual Transcendence: Constructions of Interracial Rape in Early American Crime Literature, 1767–1817," *William and Mary Quarterly* 56, no. 3 (1999): 481–526.

30. On evangelical themes in execution sermons and in the closely related genre of criminal conversion narratives, see Cohen, *Pillars of Salt, Monuments of Grace*, 41–80, passim; Seay, *Hanging between Heaven and Earth*, 47–105; Daniel E. Williams, "'Behold a Tragic Scene Strangely Changed into a Theater of Mercy': The Structure and Significance of Criminal Conversion Narratives in Early New England," *American Quarterly* 38, no. 5 (1986), 827–47.

31. John Simpson and Edmund S. Weiner, eds., *The Oxford English Dictionary*, vol. 8 (Oxford, U.K.: Oxford University Press, 1989), quoted at 882. The *Oxford English Dictionary* locates usages of *liberal* with that meaning as early as 1781. Such usages of the term *liberal*, or its opposite *illiberal*, appear in several early American crime publications—but also correspond to modern conceptions of racial liberalism. An early example of that usage (not discussed elsewhere in this essay) appeared in Henry Channing's sermon on the execution in 1786 of Hannah Ocuish, a twelve-year-old "mulatto" servant, for the murder of a six-year-old girl in Connecticut. The minister criticized masters for failing to educate their servants and condemned the attribution of Ocuish's crime to her "*complexion*" as "*illiberal*." Henry Channing, *God Admonishing His People of Their Duty, as Parents and Masters* (New London, CT: T. Green, 1786), quoted at 23.

32. See Sylvanus Conant, *The Blood of Abel, and the Blood of Jesus Considered and Improved, in a Sermon* (Boston: Edes and Gill, 1764), 32–34. The victim was twenty-six or twenty-seven years old at the time of her death. On Robert Treat Paine's authorship of the appended account and other material on the case, see Stephen T. Riley and Edward W. Hanson, eds., *The Papers of Robert Treat Paine*, vol. 2 (Boston: Massachusetts Historical Society, 1992), 248–49, 255–57, 277–78, 281–86. For another scholarly treatment of the case, see Rogers, *Murder and the Death Penalty*, 26–28. For court files on the case, see Suffolk Files 145054, 113–14 (microfilm), Massachusetts State Archives, Boston. Newspaper accounts of Bristol's crime, trial, and conviction

were rather brief and did not emphasize his race except to identify him as a "Negroe Fellow" or "Negro Boy." See *Massachusetts Gazette and Boston News-Letter*, June 9, 1763; October 20, 1763; December 9, 1763.

33. See Conant, *Blood of Abel*, 5–31, quoted at 20–21, 27. The British commentary quoted was identified by Conant as "[George] Turnbull's *Notes on Heinec's Universal Law*." On Heinec, or Johann Gottlieb Heineccius, the "renowned" eighteenth-century jurist who wrote the German treatise, see David M. Walker, *The Oxford Companion to Law* (Oxford, U.K.: Oxford University Press, 1980), 559. On "religious equalitarianism," see Winthrop D. Jordan, *White over Black: American Attitudes toward the Negro, 1550–1812* (Baltimore: Penguin, 1969), 194–215. On the "secular equalitarianism" that condemned racial prejudice as "illiberal" and that became increasingly popular in Anglo-America after about 1760, see Jordan, *White over Black*, 276–96, passim, but especially at 276–77. Although such assertions of human equality in connection with the status of a slave may seem grossly hypocritical to present-day readers, abstract assertions of *spiritual* or *natural* equality routinely coexisted (with only occasional evidence of uneasiness) in prerevolutionary America with a wide range of hierarchical social relationships based on age, rank, family, gender, race, nationality, and religion.

34. Conant, *Blood of Abel*, 35.

35. Ibid., 35; but cf. Timothy H. Breen, "Making History: The Force of Public Opinion and the Last Years of Slavery in Massachusetts," in *Through a Glass Darkly: Reflections on Personal Identity in Early America*, ed. Ronald Hoffman, Mechal Sobel, and Fredrika J. Teute (Chapel Hill: University of North Carolina Press, 1997), 74–77.

36. Thaddeus MacCarty, *The Power and Grace of Christ Display'd to a Dying Malefactor* (Boston: Kneeland and Adams, 1768), 5, 21, 25. The scriptural passage from Luke on Christ's conversion of the thief on the cross was the text most frequently selected for New England execution sermons (irrespective of the race of the malefactor); see, for example, Ephraim Clark, *Sovereign Grace Displayed in the Conversion and Salvation of a Penitent Sinner* (Boston: John Boyle, 1773); Andrew Eliot, *Christ's Promise to the Penitent Thief* (Boston: John Boyle, 1773); Fobes, *Paradise*; Timothy Hilliard, *Paradise Promised by a Dying Saviour to the Penitent Thief on the Cross* (Boston: E. Russell, 1785), all addressing the cases of white criminals. Given white domination of New England both socially and demographically, readers would almost certainly have assumed that a rape victim not otherwise identified by race was white; however, the absence of explicit racial labels describing the victim, in this and other sermons, suggests that the authors did not want to emphasize that fact to readers or to use the victim's race to inflame white outrage toward the alleged rapist.

37. Langdon, *Sermon Preached at Danbury*, quoted at 10. Cf. Slotkin, "Narratives of Negro Crime," 24–25. For court records on the case of Anthony, see Connecticut Superior Court Records, Fairfield County, vol. 1 (1798–1808), August 1798 term, unpaginated; see also, Anthony's petition for a more lenient punishment, in Connecticut Archives, Crimes and Misdemeanors, 2nd ser., vol. 4, doc. 109 (microfilm), both in State Archives, Connecticut State Library, Hartford. According to the court records, Anthony's alleged victim, Mary Knap, was "under the age of Nineteen Years"; assuming that she was the "Mary Knap" born in Stamford, Connecticut, town records appear to suggest that she was approximately seventeen years old at the time of the alleged crime; see Stamford Vital Records, vol. 2, 104, Genealogical Index, State Archives, Connecticut State Library, Hartford.

38. Dana, *Intent of Capital Punishment*; Noah Worcester, *A Sermon Delivered at Haverhill, New Hampshire* (Haverhill, NH: N. Coverly, 1796). It should be noted that some other eighteenth-century crime publications did include both conventional surnames and racial identifiers, further suggesting that Dana and Worcester may have intentionally sought to obscure the racial backgrounds of their subjects for ideological reasons. Cf. Williams, *Pillars of Salt: An Anthology*, 55.

39. On the gradual abolition of slavery in Connecticut and Rhode Island, see John Wood Sweet, *Bodies Politic: Negotiating Race in the American North, 1730–1830* (Philadelphia: University of Pennsylvania Press, 2003), 240–63, passim; Joanne Pope Melish, *Disowning Slavery: Gradual Emancipation and "Race" in New England, 1780–1860* (Ithaca, NY: Cornell University Press, 1998), 50–118, passim; Bernard C. Steiner, *History of Slavery in Connecticut* (Baltimore: Johns Hopkins Press, 1893), 30–35; William D. Johnston, *Slavery in Rhode Island, 1755–1776* (Providence: Rhode Island Historical Society, 1894), 22–25, 56. Although the Connecticut state legislature passed a gradual emancipation law in 1784, it was not until 1848 that slavery was absolutely forbidden; Rhode Island also passed a gradual emancipation act in 1784.

40. Cohen, *Pillars of Salt, Monuments of Grace*, 83–84, 247; Halttunen, *Murder Most Foul*, 7–32, passim.

41. William Andrews, *A Sermon Delivered at Danbury* (New Haven, CT: T. G. Woodward, 1817), quoted at 4–5, 18.

42. Ibid., 14–15.

43. Ibid.

44. An early hint of this symbiosis is evident earlier in Sylvanus Conant's sermon on the case of Bristol, as issued with Robert Treat Paine's appendix. My formulation here is *not* intended to imply a moral equivalence between the liberal and protoracist (or racist) positions.

45. For several key studies of mob violence in Jacksonian America, see David Grimsted, *American Mobbing, 1828–1861: Toward Civil War* (New York: Oxford University Press, 1998); Paul A. Gilje, *Rioting in America* (Bloomington: Indiana University Press, 1996), 60–86; Michael Feldberg, *The Turbulent Era: Riot and Disorder in Jacksonian America* (New York: Oxford University Press, 1980); Leonard L. Richards, *"Gentlemen of Property and Standing": Anti-Abolition Mobs in Jacksonian America* (New York: Oxford University Press, 1970).

46. For accounts of the Charlestown convent, its destruction, and the controversy that followed, see Nancy Lusignan Schultz, *Fire and Roses: The Burning of the Charlestown Convent, 1834* (New York: Free Press, 2000); Daniel A. Cohen, "Passing the Torch: Boston Firemen, 'Tea Party' Patriots, and the Burning of the Charlestown Convent," *Journal of the Early Republic* 24, no. 4 (2004): 527–86; Daniel A. Cohen, "Alvah Kelley's Cow: Household Feuds, Proprietary Rights, and the Charlestown Convent Riot," *New England Quarterly* 74, no. 4 (2001): 531–79; Daniel A. Cohen, "The Respectability of Rebecca Reed: Genteel Womanhood and Sectarian Conflict in Antebellum America," *Journal of the Early Republic* 16, no. 3 (1996): 419–61; Daniel A. Cohen, "Miss Reed and the Superiors: The Contradictions of Convent Life in Antebellum America," *Journal of Social History* 30, no. 1 (1996): 149–84; Jeanne Hamilton, "The Nunnery as Menace: The Burning of the Charlestown Convent, 1834," *U.S. Catholic Historian* 14, no. 1 (1996): 35–65; Wilfred Joseph Bisson, *Countdown to Violence* (New York: Garland, 1989); James Gillespie Blaine II, "The Birth of a Neighborhood: Nineteenth-Century Charlestown, Massachusetts" (PhD diss., University of

Michigan, Ann Arbor, 1978), 55–128; Robert H. Lord, John E. Sexton, and Edward T. Harrington, *History of the Archdiocese of Boston*, vol. 2 (New York: Sheed & Ward, 1944), 205–39; Ray Allen Billington, *The Protestant Crusade, 1800–1860* (New York: Macmillan, 1938). Only one of the accused participants—a teenager—was convicted for his role in the riot, and he was soon pardoned.

47. Rebecca Theresa Reed, *Six Months in a Convent* (Boston: Russell, Odiorne & Metcalf, 1835). On Reed, see works cited in the previous note, especially Cohen, "Respectability of Rebecca Reed"; Cohen, "Miss Reed and the Superiors." On Beecher's alleged role, see Schultz, *Fire and Roses*, 165-66; Billington, *Protestant Crusade*, 72–73. Though originally ordained as a Presbyterian, Beecher at times affiliated with the Congregational denomination.

48. David Claypoole Johnston, *Scraps ... for the Year 1835* (Boston: D. C. Johnston, 1834); Georgianne McVay, "Yankee Fanatics Unmasked: Cartoons on the Burning of the Charlestown Convent," *Records of the American Catholic Historical Society of Philadelphia* 83 (1972): 159–68; Reed, *Six Months in a Convent*, 3–6. Johnston's depiction of some of the rioters as pig-like may be an allusion to the vulgar designation of Charlestown residents of the period (especially youth) as "Charlestown Pigs."

49. Cohen, "Passing the Torch," 528–34, 548–53, 579–80 (brief quotations at 579); Cohen, "Alvah Kelley's Cow," 558; Lord, Sexton, and Harrington, *History of the Archdiocese*, vol. 2, 214 (quotation on Bonaparte). Little in the Charlestown rioters is suggestive of the sort of radical alienation, anti-institutionalism, and antiauthoritarianism characteristic of American religious terrorists of the late twentieth century, as described by Michael Hochgeschwender in chapter 12 of this volume.

50. Harry Hazel [pseud. for Justin Jones], *The Nun of St. Ursula, or, the Burning of the Convent: A Romance of Mount Benedict* (Boston: F. Gleason, 1845). On the Constitution's and the Founding Fathers' commitments to denominational pluralism, see Frank Kelleter's discussion in chapter 2 of this volume.

51. Hazel, *The Nun of St. Ursula*.

52. Ibid., 10, 28–29, 54, passim.

53. Ibid., 16, 63.

54. On the Whig Party's dominance in Massachusetts from the mid-1830s through the late 1840s, see William F. Hartford, *Money, Morals, and Politics: Massachusetts in the Age of the Boston Associates* (Boston: Northeastern University Press, 2001); Ronald P. Formisano, *The Transformation of Political Culture: Massachusetts Parties, 1790s–1840s* (New York: Oxford University Press, 1983), 245–320. On Jones, see Timothy D. Murray, "Jones's Publishing House," in *American Literary Publishing Houses, 1638–1899*, ed. Peter Dzwonkoski (Detroit, MI: Gale Research, 1986), 231; Victor A. Berch, "Retrospective Notes," *Dime-Novel Round-Up* 57 (1988): 93–94; Ronald J. Zboray and Mary Saracino Zboray, "The Mysteries of New England: Eugene Sue's American 'Imitators,' 1844," *Nineteenth-Century Contexts* 22, no. 3 (2000): 457–92; Paul Erickson, "New Books, New Men: City-Mysteries Fiction, Authorship, and the Literary Market," *Early American Studies* 1, no. 1 (2003): 279, 295–96. My notions of *soft* and *hard* anti-Catholicism are loosely based on Alexander Saxton's concepts of *soft* and *hard* racism. See Alexander Saxton, *Rise and Fall of the White Republic: Class Politics and Mass Culture in Nineteenth-Century America* (London: Verso, 1990), 148–150, 259–60, 281–83.

55. On the convent compensation struggle, see Lord, Sexton, and Harrington, *History of the Archdiocese*, vol. 2, 232–33, 237–38. Throughout the Massachusetts leg-

islative session of 1853, Free Soilers and most Democrats were joined in a coalition against the Whigs, but party discipline was not maintained on the issue of convent compensation. For examples of anticonvent tales originally published in Boston story-papers during the fall of 1854 (and repeatedly reprinted as novelettes), see Charles W. Frothingham, *The Convent's Doom: A Tale of Charlestown in 1834* (Boston: Graves & Weston, 1854); Frothingham, *Six Hours in a Convent: The Stolen Nuns! A Tale of Charlestown in 1834* (Boston: Graves & Weston, 1855). On the Know-Nothing victory in Massachusetts, see John B. Mulkern, *The Know-Nothing Party in Massachusetts: The Rise and Fall of a People's Movement* (Boston: Northeastern University Press, 1992), 61–86; Tyler Anbinder, *Nativism and Slavery: The Northern Know Nothings and the Politics of the 1850s* (New York: Oxford University Press, 1992), 87–94; Mark Voss-Hubbard, *Beyond Party: Cultures of Antipartisanship in Northern Politics before the Civil War* (Baltimore: Johns Hopkins University Press, 2002), 105–37.

56. Southerners may have been less inclined than New Englanders to blend these different ideologies, especially by the antebellum period. On Southern exceptionalism with respect to the death penalty, in particular, see Judith Randle, "The Cultural Lives of Capital Punishment in the United States," in *The Cultural Lives of Capital Punishment: Comparative Perspectives*, ed. Austin Sarat and Christian Boulanger (Stanford, CA: Stanford University Press, 2005), 97–106; Banner, *Death Penalty*, 137–43. For an interpretation that posits a massive backlash against revolutionary ideology in the early republic, see Larry Tise, *The American Counterrevolution: A Retreat from Liberty, 1783–1800* (Mechanicsburg, PA: Stackpole, 1998); also see Larry Tise, *Proslavery: A History of the Defense of Slavery in America, 1701–1840* (Athens: University of Georgia Press, 1990).

Chapter 5

The Religious Discourse on Criminal Law in England, 1600–1800: From a Theology of Trial to a Theology of Punishment

André Krischer

In his *Memoirs*, Samuel Romilly recalled his anger over the publication of Martin Madan's pamphlet *Thoughts on Executive Justice* in 1784.[1] Romilly (1757–1818), the leading figure of the capital punishment reform movement in England around 1800, characterized the publication as "a small tract, in which … he [Madan] absurdly insisted on the expediency of rigidly enforcing, in every instance, our penal code, sanguinary and barbarous as it is."[2] Madan's tract had fatal consequences. In 1783, one year before it was published, fifty-one delinquents were executed in London. In 1785, a year after its publication, the execution rate nearly doubled to ninety-seven.[3] Romilly believed that Madan was also responsible for reviving the spectacle that appeared so detestable in the eyes of the reformers: "It was recently after the publication of this book that was exhibited a spectacle unseen in London for a long course of years before, the execution of nearly 20 criminals at a time."[4] Like other advocates of penal reform, beginning in the 1770s Romilly published his criticism of the prevailing opinion of capital punishment anonymously. Furthermore, his *Observations on a Late Publication, Intituled, Thoughts on*

Executive Justice "had so little success with the public, that it sold not more than a hundred copies."[5]

By contrast, Martin Madan's appeal for the intensification of capital punishment, both in quality and quantity, echoed the religious discourse of the previous fifty years. As Randall McGowen has shown, in such discourse criminal justice was typically compared to the torments of hell, and the gallows was interpreted as an instrument of fear, teaching publicly and unmistakably the dreadful lesson that crime does not pay.[6] The scaffold served as a visual representation of God's justice, which, according to the preachers, was essentially a merciless retribution for sinful crime. This discourse was most prominently presented in assize sermons, spiritual instructions inaugurating the biannual sessions of the provincial law circuits.[7] Almost all of these sermons were later printed in London and received extensive publicity in the metropolis.

Historians often see the discourse of the assize sermons as evidence for the pervasiveness of religion in eighteenth-century criminal justice. As McGowen writes, "divine justice was the normative model for human justice."[8] At first glance, this conclusion seems plausible, but there are reasons to look again at the relationship between law and religion. My belief is that the sermons did not constitute a prescription for criminal justice or a "demonstration of the cooperation between church and state"[9] but were instead a reaction to the process of secularization. Printed assize sermons can be found dating from the end of the sixteenth century. However, seventeenth-century preachers communicated an entirely different message. They usually reminded the judges, magistrates, and local elites that they should demonstrate Christian compassion and benevolence when exercising their duties in the grand and petty juries.

To understand this paradoxical paradigm shift from an approval of mercy to a call for terror, I suggest modifying our understanding of secularization such that it is not primarily defined in terms of the loss of faith and piety, the individualization of lifestyle, or the decrease in the number of clergymen in administration. Secularization is also a side effect of the emergence of autonomous social systems.[10] In early modern Europe, autonomous social systems did not exist. Politics in the late medieval and early modern centuries were interpenetrated by religion; science by criteria of social morality, honor, and credibility; and, of course, law by religion.[11] The boundaries of premodern social systems were still open, and thus legal communication was also religious communication, a fact that yielded significant overlap between what would later become two distinctive codes. Religion claimed omnicompetence in all realms of social interaction, evaluating them as true or untrue, lawful or unlawful, moral or immoral.

During the eighteenth century, however, English criminal law went through significant processes of reform, chiefly concerning the law of evidence and the admission of defense counsel. These reforms dramatically accelerated the development of a legal system that operated with its own logic and codes. Whereas system differentiation in the period between the premodern and the modern world was a process of modernization for law, politics, science, and other spheres of society, it was a process of loss for religion, which forfeited its former position as normative regulator for society as a whole. The evolution of religion as a social system corresponded to its social decentralization. The eighteenth-century sermons and their bizarre theology of punishment reflect the process of the exclusion of religion from law and the emergence of distinctive codes in both systems. To reevaluate the paradoxes of the Enlightenment and the changing relationship between religion and law around 1800, I will first outline the religious discourses on criminal justice in the seventeenth century. The second section will depict changes in legal discourse after 1700. Finally, in the third section I will concentrate on the religious appropriation of the meaning of public execution in the late eighteenth century.

A Theology of the Trial: The Discourses of Seventeenth-Century Assize Sermons and the Early Modern Criminal Trial

More than 200 assize sermons were published between 1600 and 1700, and they focused on a variety of themes. The alleged corruptibility of the judges and magistrates was a popular theme, as was anti-Catholicism. But the main theme of the sermons was criminal law. In contrast to their eighteenth-century counterparts, churchmen were not concerned most about punishment or the lessons of justice. Rather, they presented a complex theology of the trial: a religious justification for, explanation of, and prescription for the actions and proceedings of the court. In this context, the sermon's theology of the trial showed five characteristic dimensions: (a) the appointment of magistrates and judges as God's representatives, (b) the interpretation of the trial as a quest for universal truth, (c) restrictions against the defense counsel, (d) the connection between judgment and mercy, and (e) the interpretation of the scaffold as a forum of truth.

The Appointment of Magistrates and Judges
as God's Representatives

The authority of magistrates and judges was conferred on them by God. This dictum from Romans 13 served as the leitmotif in the churchmen's analysis of legal power. "The Magistrate is ... Gods own image," concluded Henry Glover in 1663, as did many other preachers.[12] Because of the divine installation of secular authority, the divines perceived a natural "Alliance betwixt the Bench and the Pulpit."[13] This alliance primarily meant that the preachers regarded themselves as being in the position of instructors to the lawyers. The divines acted as interpreters of God's will, helping the judges administer the God-given common law.[14] Because all authority and law derived from God, the magistrate depended on preachers to distinguish between good and evil. They interpreted God's will and taught the lawyers what was right and wrong.

The Interpretation of the Trial as a Quest for Universal Truth

Preachers usually cited Psalm 111:10 ("The fear of the Lord *is* the beginning of wisdom") to outline the principles of the criminal trial: it was a search for truth in the presence of the divine.[15] It was as if the Last Judgment were nothing but a "Grand Assize," and an ordinary assize was an anticipation of the Last Judgment. Preachers declared that God was always "present in a Court of Judicature"; he participated not only by observing "all things that are there transacted, but by approving and ratifying every right sentence pronounc'd by the Judge."[16] Antony Fawkner preached in 1627 that God was "Witnesse, Iury, and Iudge"[17] not only at the Last Judgment, but in every English court as well. This transcendentally guided trial accumulated evidence and gathered matters of fact by hearing witnesses who were directly linked to God by their oath. Oaths were the core of the early modern trial and were regarded as generators of truth. Except for the audience and the defendant, all participants were put under oath: the judges and justices of the peace; the clerks, bailiffs, constables, and sheriffs; the witnesses; and, of course, the jurymen who "haue their name ... from their Oath; and therefore as often as they are called by that name, so often are they put in minde of that bond betweene God, and their own souls."[18]

In the traditional trial, an oath was not only a medium of communication that created the fiction that the speaker told the truth but a legal instrument itself.[19] St. Paul asserts this view in Hebrews 6:16: "an oath for confirmation is ... an end of all strife."[20] The importance of oaths corresponded with the early modern legal doctrines concerning the conscience.[21] The conscience was regarded as a book in which all actions and thoughts were documented and that was to be opened on Judgment Day. Because the transcript of the conscience provided a complete documentation of life, it was considered to be the best form of evidence. An oath immediately affected the conscience, obliging it vehemently. In 1623, Immanuel Bourne preached that a "mans conscience is as a thousand witnesses to acquite or condemne before God or men, and the voice of conscience is far more sure than the report of many others."[22] When someone participated in a trial, this "outward Tryall" was always accompanied by a "Tryall of Conscience" that was infallible, because the conscience was also an "eye-witness" that could not be deceived.[23]

Because of the advantages of oaths and the conducting of the criminal trial as an examination of conscience, preachers regarded a separate law of evidence to be unnecessary. All the laws required to evaluate evidence were perfectly contained in the Bible, especially in the Ten Commandments. Exodus 20:16, for example, applied to the examination of witnesses: "Thou shalt not beare false witness against thy Neighbour."[24] John Squire preached in 1616 that the whole trial could be structured by means of this simple commandment. It also applied to the plaintiff, whom the preachers usually suspected of being overwhelmed by his vengefulness: "if hee prosecute it for hatred, like Doeg, or for couetousness, like Jezebell, then dare I boldly say to such a man, Thou dost beare false-witness against thy neighbour."[25]

The early modern sermon described the pre-1700 trials quite precisely and ascribed a meaning to the proceedings that corresponded to the legal discourse.[26] In his famous account of the English criminal trial in the Tudor era, Thomas Smith (1513–1577) defined the essentials of the proceeding as an "inquisition of the twelue men within themselves, and their own conscience."[27] With the verdict, the jurors "discharged their Conscience"; they were sworn to tell the truth "according to the evidence, and their conscience."[28] Sworn witnesses were originally called only to give supplementary evidence. The "solemn use of Oaths" and the calling on the witness of God, who, "rather than Man, appears to decide the Cause,"[29] show that the penetration of religion into the early modern trial indeed constituted the forensic reality in the seventeenth century. A visible analogy existed between concrete practice in the law courts and the divines' theology of the trial.

Restrictions against the Defense Counsel

In 1683, Thomas Willis preached at the Kingston assizes that "truth is the Soul of Justice ... the very Basis of all ... Proceedings ..., without which Courts of Judicature are but Shops of Cruelty."[30] The divines could even describe how truth was revealed in the courtroom, for example, when the defendant "trembled at the bar ... looking pale, while the Judge is pronouncing the Sentence of Death upon him."[31] Legal practitioners also stressed that "the very Speech, Gesture and Countenance, and Manner of Defence of those who are Guilty, when they speak for themselves, may often help to disclose the truth."[32] Such a "record of gestures" that served as a lie detector could only be generated when the defendant spoke for himself and not when advocates acted on his behalf. This necessary record of gestures was not, however, the only reason that divines were skeptical of criminal defense. Barristers "wonderfully amplified small matters with great words."[33] Worst of all was that an advocate acted as an "Iustifier of the wicked."[34] In other words, he "knowingly promotes and willingly joins with a Person in an unjust Cause."[35] In a Christian society, any advocate had to act under the Ninth Commandment ("You shall not bear false witness against your neighbour").[36] "Two things are requiste" for a defense that was not "repugnant to the ordinance and glory of God. ... First, That they speake the Truth, Substantially: that they speake it Syncerely."[37]

The Connection between Judgment and Mercy

The most conspicuous difference between the early modern and the eighteenth-century sermons was in their evaluation of mercy as an essential virtue of authority.[38] For Madan, any form of clemency was the beginning of the nation's ruin and a perversion of God's command. But when Samuel Burton based his 1619 Warwick sermon on Romans 13:4 ("for he [the magistrate] beareth not the sword in vain"—a dictum that became topical in the later theology of punishment), he formulated a completely different ideal of the Christian regime. Burton argued that magistrates ought to take a lesson from the old church and its "*consuetudinem intercedendi pro reis....* But if the manner of ancient Bishops was to intreat and begge for pardon, it is not meet for us to call for vengeance and blood out of the Pulpit. It is better to answer God for mercy, than for iustice; and safer for a Magistrate to saue the liues of many malefactors, than to cast away one innocent."[39] In

1623, Thomas Scott preached that judges "sometimes in strict obseruance of iustice doe the greatest iniustice."[40] Mercy and justice, Scott argued, were "no such opposites as is thought, for they kisse and embrace each other; yea, that is no true mercy which is vnjust, nor that good iustice which is cruell."[41] Humfrey Babington called mercy and judgment "the harmony of the Universe, ... an admirable pair of Sister virtues." The judges ought to consider Luke 6:36: "Be ye merciful as your heavenly Father also is mercifull."[42] In strikingly unvarnished language, preachers explained what would happen if the judges did not follow their advice: "Today you take away life, tomorrow you may lose your owne.... If your peruert iustice while the staffe is in your hand, expect a deserued misery.... God will punish you, lege talionis, by a iust law."[43]

The Interpretation of the Scaffold as a Forum of Truth

Whereas Madan's judges could not be merciless enough, the very salvation of the seventeenth-century judge depended on his mercy. Mercy was an integral part of the theology of the trial, in which religion was directly interwoven into criminal law. However, this practice did not necessarily mean total reprieve and salvation from the gallows. Mercy and capital punishment definitely went hand in hand. "The Sword of Justice is to be bathed in the Oyle of Mercy, that it may at once wound and heal,"[44] but it was still a sword. Mercy could be granted even in executions; as Babington put it, "mercy would mitigate the rigor of some severe, yet necessary Laws."[45] Mercy entailed care for the salvation of the condemned. Good spiritual guidance in the days between judgment and execution should be able to prevent desperation. A consolatory expectation of life after execution, however, came with strings attached. "Mercy designs not the punishment, but the reformation of Offenders,"[46] but this reformation required the offender's remorse for his crimes. The most important sign of remorse, though not sufficient in itself, was the confession. A sinner ought to confess "of thy sinnes before God, and renewing of thy repentance, more seriously asking pardon and forgiuenesse, and in all humility desiring reconciliation in Christ."[47] The place for this confession by the condemned was the scaffold, in accordance with the Protestant act of penance, which had to be public (unlike the Catholic auricular confession).[48] Significantly, this "penitential confession"[49] was not only the churchmen's concern, offering "absolution at the hand of God"[50] after candid signs of remorse "in the eye with tears and tongue with confession."[51] It was just as crucial for the law as it was for the trial.

Early modern panegyrists of common law were proud of the evident differences between the English trial and the continental inquisitorial system, under which proceedings were often based on confessions extorted from prisoners under torture.[52] However, the traditional English trial was also not able to achieve legitimacy for death sentences through legal procedure alone. The system was in need of the public execution as a touchstone for the truthfulness and legitimacy of capital judgment. The truth of the judgment was avowed by the ritualistic speeches at the execution. At stake was not only moral certainty in terms of the modern law of evidence,[53] but the *transcendental certainty* that could be established by the convict's affirmation in his "last dying speech."[54] The ordinaries and chaplains of the prisons worked on the condemned before their execution, day and night if necessary, trying to achieve the delinquents' "happy conuersion, contrition and Christian preparation."[55] Criminal justice created legitimate sentences of death by referring to "pastoral power" (Michel Foucault) and spiritual therapy.[56] In many cases, the seventeenth-century judges acted as preachers themselves. After pronouncing judgment in cases in which the condemned dissented from the ruling, they usually delivered harangues. In such cases, the judges tried to convert the condemned by preaching: "Do not think of any Time here, make your Peace with God, which must be done by Confession, and by the Discovery of those that are Guilty of the same Crime with you. God have mercy upon you; and if you do so, he will have mercy upon you."[57]

Because of this reciprocity of criminal law and religion, the necessity of confessing the crime as a sin and the sin as a crime on the scaffold, the "theo-legal" social logic of the early modern criminal trial could turn against itself. As long as oaths were the promoters of truth, protestations of innocence on the scaffold were as good as the most sacred oaths of purgation.[58] He who solemnly declared his guiltlessness minutes before he was to appear before God must have had a pure conscience, which was, according to the theology of the trial, better than a "thousand witnesses to acquite or condemne before God or men."[59] The English audience, like audiences at continental public executions, was usually disturbed by a vow of innocence and openly questioned the legitimacy of the judgment in those cases. Because dissenting "dying speeches" could effectively undermine the ruling of criminal justice, there was almost no alternative to this cooperation between law and religion. In many cases, the prison's ordinary truly brainwashed the convict to bring him to confession. The divines' postulate that there existed an "Alliance betwixt the Bench and the Pulpit" was accurate, but this alliance began to dissolve after 1700.[60] Religion was placed at a disadvantage by this process of differentiation and lamented its loss of importance in the assize sermons of the eighteenth century.

The Decentralization of Religious Discourses in Eighteenth-Century Law

With the expulsion of the Stuart monarchy in 1688, the old, lawyer-free criminal trial disappeared. The Treason Trials Act of 1696, which fundamentally changed the shape of the criminal trial,[61] allowed prisoners in treason trials to be represented by defense counsel in most sequences of the trial.[62] By the 1730s, the advantages of the Treason Trials Act had been incorporated into ordinary criminal proceedings. The criminal law of the eighteenth century made its first clear break with the traditional parallels between the religious and legal establishment of truth when it introduced professional counsels for both the prosecution and the defense.[63] The consequence was the evolution of a distinctive and elaborate system of forensic communication. This change was accompanied by a law of evidence that had not existed in the old trial, at least not as a distinct set of rules.[64] The consequences of this legal evolution included not only previously unknown safeguards for defendants, but also the formation of a specific *legal* truth. Even if the legal practitioners of the eighteenth century still believed in the solemn obligations of an oath for the trial, they knew that several paradoxes would arise if the court relied solely on it. What if people "to whom the divine doctrines of the Gospel were unknown"[65] or who did not profess to the Christian religion at all had to appear on trial as witnesses? At the beginning of the seventeenth century, Edward Coke designated all "infidels" as enemies of the law.[66] Their testimony was nothing but the voice of the devil, and therefore, they could not serve as witnesses, let alone be placed under oath. However, around 1660, Matthew Hale thought more pragmatically and suggested that the reliability of the testimony of a Jew or a Turk "must be left to the jury."[67] This solution became the predominant practice in the subsequent period. Trials still used oaths, but the legal system increasingly diverged from a strictly religious interpretation of the oath.

In the courtrooms of the eighteenth century, oaths became profane mediums of communication, lending credibility to the statements of those who completed the usual external rituals compulsory for an oath. When in 1739 an Indian who professed the Gentoo religion appeared before English commissioners in a civil proceeding in Calcutta, the judges decided that he should be sworn in "according to the ceremonies of his own religion."[68] Confronted with an increase in such alternative forms of swearing, the judges decided that oaths ought to be administered by the people "according to their own opinions and as it most affects their consciences."[69] Thus, the colonial expansion of the British Empire was accompanied by a de-Christianization of the legal proceeding. This pragmatic tolerance not only of indigenous religions but also of British libertines, nonjurors, and Quakers in legal proceedings had been discussed intensively since the 1740s. It became clear that whether an oath truly affected the conscience of a witness or a juror was not a question of legal proceedings.[70] Indispensable were only those ceremonies that showed the people in the courtroom that someone had been put under oath.

What we see in this example is a characteristic feature of modern law, in which it defines for itself what ought and ought not be considered law within legal procedure. In Luhmann's words, the legal system programmed its own codes.[71] This development in the law of evidence was watched closely by the theologians, who feared losing another battle in the process of modernization. In their interpretation, trials were perverted by "subtlety of Penetration ... Rhetorick of Language ... Misrepresentation of Facts"[72]—a complaint that referred directly to the courtroom activities of lawyers. In 1759, William Sellon worriedly voiced the concern of most of his fellow churchmen: "What authority and confirmation would be in an Oath, which is indispensably requisite as *an end of all strife* ... did not the Supreme Being charge the mind, and men reverence that sacred name, by which they swear ... what could ever replace oaths as guarantees of truth in criminal trials?"[73] Jeremy Bentham later answered this question, mentioning a practice that had already been in use for some time: cross-examinations. Cross-examinations became the functional equivalent of oaths and replaced the latter "as the fundamental safeguard for the receipt of oral evidence."[74] They occurred first in state trials, which constituted the most elaborate legal procedures before 1700, and then beginning in the 1730s in common trials for felonies as well. In this context, the clear analogy between forensic practice and the divines' legal theology began to disappear, and the traditional theology of the trial changed into a theology of punishment.

A Call for Terror: The Religious Appropriation of the Meaning of the Public Execution

Even if deterrence had been an important motive behind the practice of public executions since the late Middle Ages,[75] it was not the primary purpose of capital punishment until the 1750s. When the theo-legal interpretation of common law prevailed, capital punishment was seen instead as a ritual of retaliation, a symbolic reversion of the perversion caused by the crime, a restoration of the universal order.[76] The fact that public executions fulfilled a didactic function was always secondary. The constitutive elements of premodern English capital punishment—physical violence and publicity—had different origins. Violence was a component of the execution as a ritual of retaliation, and public performance was a part of Protestant penitential practice *and* the necessary result of the old criminal trial, confirmed by the confession of the condemned.

The public execution lost its traditional procedural function at the beginning of the eighteenth century. Further research on the question is needed, but it seems likely that the elimination of such features in the authority's staging of the execution was related to the fact that in the new system, legitimation was already procured by the criminal procedure.[77] The introduction of the defense counsel and the construction of forensic truth by the reformed law of evidence not only benefited the accused, but also strengthened the legal procedure itself by enforcing legal autonomy and diminishing religion's claim to being the sole arbiter of truth. With the emergence of the reformed, adversarial criminal trial, additional forms of legitimation that had traditionally been provided by public confessions became less important or at least legally superfluous.

This transformation cleared the way for a fundamental change in the public execution. Before 1700, capital punishments had been carefully orchestrated to present the capital convicts as sincere penitents. After 1700, different forms of dying became typical. The condemned died in accordance with gender- or class-related modes of dying,[78] while the spectators would "make a day of it."[79] With the authority's withdrawal from the official interpretation of the execution, the spectacle was appropriated from below. The scenes at scaffolds cannot, in fact, be described in terms of a "plebeian carnival,"[80] but neither can they be considered as moral instructions for the public, bloody examples of delinquents that deterred "others, from treading in their steps."[81] Contemporaries were fully aware of this dilemma with regard to public executions. Bernard Mandeville and

Henry Fielding commented insistently on the failure of public executions to educate the society, and William Hogarth congenially visualized this spectacle, which did everything but prevent crime.[82] William Blackstone asked whether it was "found upon farther experience, that capital punishments are more effectual" at deterring men from offences than other forms of punishment and warned that the death penalty ought to be only "ultima ratio" because "life is the immediate gift of God to man."[83]

The penal reformers' critique targeted not only the practice of public executions of the later eighteenth century, but also, more importantly, those who defended this practice. Headed by John Wesley's evangelical Methodists, preachers had started a campaign against what they called false lenity and the abuses of mercy in criminal justice. The call for terror began to appear in sermons in the 1740s and slowly but steadily grew to be the core of the texts. The typical argument was that until Judgment Day it was "necessary to have recourse to human Judicatures, where the Punishment is visible and exemplary.... No Terrors will be of so much Efficacy, as those, which concern Sensation."[84] The Churchmen relied on the rigors of criminal law even as an illustration of the destiny of sinful human beings as such.[85] They tried to persuade their listeners that the "natural condition of guilt turns anybody into a prisoner," and "in consequence of such a character ... death eternal must be every man's punishment."[86] People should watch the prisoners at the bar carefully as well as "the judge pronouncing their doom, the officers of justice dragging them forth, a public spectacle of infamy and terror, and the agonies of a violent death seizing upon their devoted bodies," because such "painful and bitter sensations" were "by no means peculiar to condemned criminals" but gave a foretaste of "God's tribunal of eternal justice trying the sins of men."[87]

The doctrine of the inevitable eternal death for even the most marginally sinful offense ("one single lie, one passionate look, one proud thought, or covetous desire, or evil purpose") was obviously a reaction to the Enlightenment debate about the eternity of hell's torments.[88] Even unorthodox Anglican bishops like John Tillotson had questioned the doctrine of everlasting hellfire for every sin and sinner.[89] Wesley, however, preached that after the Last Judgment, souls either "shine forth as the sun" or "shall go away into eternal punishment."[90] He radicalized the conception of mercy, understanding it in the strict Protestant sense of grace as the ultimate precondition of eternal life. At the Last Judgment, mercy was not to temper God's justice toward malefactors, but applied only to those who had sincerely tried not to commit any sin throughout their entire lives and had sinned notwithstanding: "there is not a man on earth that liveth and sinneth not," but anybody who had committed a crime, however slight, was lost and would be "punished with everlasting destruction." [91] Because legal proceedings—which were perverted by the unholy rhetorical subtleties of barristers, who could achieve acquittals for even the worst criminals—could no longer teach this essential lesson about the "the grand Assize," the divines started to concentrate on capital punishment.[92] At this point, the courts of law did not overflow with religious language, and the radicalized assize sermons of the later century were not a "demonstration of the cooperation between church and state."[93] Instead, the unremitting cries for terror and bloody examples from the pulpit were a kind of appropriation of capital punishment by religion—just as the condemned had appropriated the meaning of the execution by "dying bravely" and "like a man."[94] Tragically, the theology of punishment proved to be extremely effective in preventing the reform of penal law in Britain, eventually becoming the new ideology of public execution.

Against this backdrop, Madan published his *Thoughts on Executive Justice*. Romilly commented that it was "a strong and vehement censure upon the judges and the ministers for their mode of administering the law, and for the frequency of the pardons which they granted."[95] Madan accused the judges of having set themselves "above the law ... wanting to govern without them."[96] He depicted specific examples of false "scruple of conscience in the Judges" that led to the reprieve of criminals.[97] Such a judicial scruple or the suspicion of having condemned an innocent endangered the theology of punishment's claim that the "certainty of punishment" for even the slightest offenders corresponded with God's merciless legal practice.[98] To maintain the terror of punishment, Madan's extreme penal theology clearly justified the execution of an innocent who was actually innocent only in legal terms. According to certain theologians, an innocent man's crimes were always sin enough to have him brought to the scaffold and from there to eternal death in hell. The same message was preached in the last two decades of the century from pulpits all over England and in the American colonies.[99] The preacher's most convincing argument was that mercy ridiculed the authority of the law, and "justice is laughed at."[100] The popular fear of the supposed social erosion caused by "lower ranks of life"[101] and their "natural" disposition to commit crimes meant that Madan and the preachers had public opinion on their side. Obviously the "crowd" could not be bridled by preaching, but only by carrying "terror to the hearts" and "making examples of the guilty."[102]

Madan's pamphlet enjoyed considerable success. "Some of the judges, and the government, for a time, adopted his reasoning," remarked Romilly. Yet this time lasted longer than Romilly had imagined it would. As late as 1810, he had to argue against Edward Law, Lord Chief Justice Ellenborough, in Parliament, who claimed that "terror alone could prevent the commission of … crime."[103] Even if Romilly (born in 1757) had not committed suicide in 1818, he would not have lived to see any reform of England's capital punishment practices. Executions continued to be carried out in public until 1868, and the faith in the deterrent character of bloody examples was imperturbable. My focus here is not the reform process[104] but rather the following contention: it was not the law's permeation by religious discourse that led to the perpetuation of public executions, but rather the differentiation of law and religion. In this process, religious doctrines about criminal law became ideological. The example of English penal law—particularly in regard to capital punishment and corresponding religious discourse in the seventeenth and eighteenth centuries—demonstrates that it is inaccurate to conceptualize secularization as religion's loss of importance. In the process of system differentiation, religion had appropriated fields of meaning—in this case the meaning of public execution—that the legal system had not yet programmed with its own codes.

Conclusion

This chapter deals with the relation between religion and criminal law in seventeenth- and eighteenth-century England. It focuses on the question of why Anglican theologians and preachers in the Age of Enlightenment were so preoccupied with the necessity of the merciless execution of capital judgment. Historians have usually taken this view as evidence of religion's infiltration of criminal law, but this interpretation is fragmentary at best. My suggestion is to view this problem in the more complex light of its long historical development. In fact, legal semantics in eighteenth-century England were less and less leavened by religious references. Particularly in regard to the law of evidence, religious rhetoric was largely excluded. Here, and also with respect to other aspects of the criminal procedure, law and religion were differentiated from each other.

What the differentiation of law and religion meant for religion becomes evident in the analysis of the assize sermons, which offer us the most important sources for theologians' interpretation of criminal law between 1600 and 1800. Thus, in the center of the chapter is a study of the change of theo-legal discourses. Prior to 1700, when the criminal procedure was still performed traditionally as a trial of conscience based on oaths, religion was indeed a crucial factor in law, as reflected by the theology of the trial presented by preachers in their assize sermons. After 1700, however, when trial procedure was reformed significantly, religion lost its pervasive status in criminal law and procedure. Theologians and their sermons increasingly focused on the execution, which they tried to interpret as a visualization of hell's torments on earth. Any form of mercy and milder, more modern punishments interfered with this interpretation. Thus, the theology of punishment should actually be understood as a rearguard action (or reaction) of religion in the context of modernization. Nevertheless, it did play an important role in reformulating the function of the scaffold. Traditionally, the scaffold was a forum of truth where the convicts either confirmed the legitimacy of the judgment with their confessions or subverted it with protestations of innocence. However, in the context of a reformed legal procedure that did not depend on the public execution as a touchstone for the "truth" of the death sentence, theologians offered a justification of the scaffold as a forum for social instruction and a symbol of the alliance between God and the authorities in the fight against crime. Because of this new ideology, religion proved to be a serious obstacle for the abolition of capital punishment at the turn of the nineteenth century.

Notes

1. Samuel Romilly, *Memoirs of the Life of Sir Samuel Romilly, Written by Himselfe*, vols. 1 and 2 (London: John Murray, 1841); Martin Madan, *Thoughts on Executive Justice with Respect to Our Criminal Laws, Particularly on the Circuits* (London: Printed for J. Dodsley, 1784).

2. Romilly, *Memoirs*, vol. 1, 65.

3. Ibid.

4. Ibid.; Peter King, *Crime and Law in England, 1750–1840: Remaking Justice from the Margins* (New York: Cambridge University Press, 2006).

5. Romilly, *Memoirs*, vol. 1, 66; Samuel Romilly, *Observations on a Late Publication, Intituled, Thoughts on Executive Justice* (London: T. Cadell, 1786).

6. Randall McGowen, "The Changing Face of God's Justice: The Debate over Divine and Human Punishment in Eighteenth-Century England," *Criminal Justice History 9* (1988): 63–98.

7. James S. Cockburn, *A History of English Assizes 1558–1714* (Cambridge, U.K.: Cambridge University Press, 1972), 65ff.

8. Randall McGowen, "'He Beareth Not the Sword in Vain': Religion and the Criminal Law in Eighteenth-Century England," *Eighteenth-Century Studies* 21, no. 2 (1987–1988): 192–211, 193.

9. McGowen, "He Beareth Not the Sword," 194.

10. For an excellent introduction to this topic, see Michael King and Chris Thornhill, eds., *Niklas Luhmann's Theory of Politics and Law* (New York: Palgrave Macmillan, 2003).

11. Steven Shapin, *A Social History of Truth: Civility and Science in Seventeenth-Century England* (Chicago: University of Chicago Press, 1994).

12. Henry Glover, *Ekdikesis or a Discourse of Vengeance* (London: printed for Henry Brome, 1664), 10.

13. John Martin, *Lex Pacifica: or Gods Own Law of Determining Controversies Explain'd and Asserted* (London: J. G. for Richard Royston, 1664), 1.

14. Thomas Hurste, *The Descent of Authoritie* (London: Clarke, 1637).

15. John Bury, *The Schole of Godly Feare* (London: Fetherstone, 1615).

16. Thomas Willis, *God's Court Wherein the Dignity and Duty of Judges and Magistrates Is Shew'd* (London: printed by B. W. for Ralph Smith, 1683), 15, 25.

17. Antony Fawkner, *The Widowes Petition* (Oxford, England: Lichfield, 1635), 13.

18. Ibid., 24.

19. Thomas Andrew Green, *Verdict According to Conscience: Perspectives on the English Criminal Trial Jury 1200–1800* (Chicago: University of Chicago Press, 1985).

20. John Tillotson introduced a sermon with this maxim. See John Tillotson, *The Lawfulness, and Obligation of Oaths* (London: Aylmer, 1681).

21. Harald E. Braun and Edward Vallance, eds., *Contexts of Conscience in Early Modern Europe, 1500–1700* (Basingstoke, U.K.: Palgrave Macmillan, 2004).

22. Immanuel Bourne, *The Anatomie of Conscience* (London: Butter, 1623), 11.

23. Ibid., 11.

24. John Squire, *A Sermon Preached at the New Churchyard on White-Sunday, 1619* (London: Pyper, 1621), 2.

25. Ibid, 21.

26. John H. Langbein, *The Origins of the Adversary Criminal Trial* (Oxford, U.K.: Oxford University Press, 2003).

27. Thomas Smith, *The Common-wealth of England* (London: Will. Stansby for J. Smethwicke, 1635), 163.

28. Smith, *Common-wealth of England*, 147.

29. Thomas Comber, *The Nature and Usefulness of Solemn Judicial Swearing* (London: Lambert, 1682), 31.

30. Willis, *God's Court*, 15.

31. Ibid.

32. William Hawkins, *Treatise of the Pleas of the Crown*, vol. 2 (London: E. and R. Nutt, and R. Gosling, 1721), 400.

33. James Johnson, *The Judge's Authority* (Cambridge, England: Simpson, 1670), 21–22.

34. Thomas Scott, *Vox Dei* (London: I. L. for Richard Rounthwait, 1623), 22.

35. Laurence Echard, *The Hainousness of Injustice Done under the Pretence of Equity* (London: M. Wotton, 1698), 15–16.

36. Squire, *A Sermon*, 16.

37. Fawkner, *Widowes Petition*, 21.

38. Willis, *God's Court*, 7; see Krista J. Kesselring, *Mercy and Authority in the Tudor State* (Cambridge, U.K.: Cambridge University Press, 2003).

39. Samuel Burton, *A Sermon Preached at the Generall Assises in Warwicke* (London: Stansby, 1620).

40. Scott, *Vox Dei*, 14.

41. Ibid., 24.

42. Humfrey Babington, *Mercy and Judgment* (Cambridge, England: Dickinson, 1678), 7.

43. Antony Fawkner, *Nicodemus for Christ* (London: Felix Kyngston, 1630), 20.

44. Willis, *God's Court*, 10–11.

45. Babington, *Mercy and Judgment*, 15.

46. Ibid.

47. Bourne, *Anatomie of Conscience*, 30.

48. Thomas Ailesbury, *A Treatise of the Confession of Sinne* (London: Crook, 1657), 7.

49. Ibid., 10.

50. Ibid., 32.

51. *Sin Dismantled* (London: J. Best for William Crook, 1664), 13–14.

52. See John Fortescue, *A Learned Commendation of the Politique Lawes of England* (London: Tottell, 1573). For a more complex picture, see John H. Langbein, *Torture and the Law of Proof: Europe and England in the Ancien Régime* (Chicago: University of Chicago Press, 1977). For the inquisitorial trial, see Jürgen Martschukat, *Inszeniertes Töten: Eine Geschichte der Todesstrafe vom 17. bis zum 19. Jahrhundert* (Cologne, Germany: Böhlau Verlag, 2000), 33.

53. Barbara J. Shapiro, "To a Moral Certainty: Theories of Knowledge and Anglo-American Juries, 1600–1850," *Hastings Law Journal* 38 (1986): 153–93.

54. See, for this genre, James Anthony Sharpe, "'Last Dying Speeches': Religion, Ideology, and Public Execution in Seventeenth-Century England," *Past and Present* 107 (1985), 144–67.

55. Henry Goodcole, *A True Declaration of the Happy Conuersion, Contrition, and Christian Preparation of Francis Robinson, Gentleman* (London: Edw: All-de dwelling neere Christ-church, 1618).

56. Peter Lake and Michael C. Questier, "Prisons, Priests, and People," in *England's Long Reformation 1500–1800*, ed. Nicholas Tyacke (London: University College London Press, 1998), 195–234.

57. Thomas B. Howell, ed., *A Complete Collection of State Trials*, vol. 13 (London: T. C. Hansard, 1816), 429.

58. For this interpretation see Andrea McKenzie, *Tyburn's Martyrs: Execution in England 1675–1775* (London: Hambledon Continuum, 2007).

59. Bourne, *Anatomie of Conscience*, 11.

60. Martin, *Lex Pacifica*, 1.

61. James R. Phifer, "Law, Politics, and Violence: The Treason Trials Act of 1696," *Albion* 12, no. 3 (1980): 235–56.

62. The privilege of a full defense was not granted until 1836.

63. Langbein, *Origins of the Adversary Criminal Trial*, 106ff.

64. Ibid., 178ff.

65. Thomas Peake, *A Compendium of the Law of Evidence* (Walpole, NH: Thomas & Thomas, 1804), 98.

66. Daniel J. Hulsebosch, "The Ancient Constitution and the Expanding Empire: Sir Edward Coke's British Jurisprudence," *Law and History Review* 21, no. 3 (2003): 439–82.

67. David Saunders, "The Judicial Persona in Historical Context: The Case of Matthew Hale," in *The Philosopher in Early Modern Europe: The Nature of a Contested Identity*, ed. Conal Condren, Stephen Gaukroger, and Ian Hunter (Cambridge, U.K.: Cambridge University Press, 2006), 140–59.

68. Peake, *Compendium*, 95.

69. Ibid.

70. William Blackstone, *Commentaries on the Laws of England*, vol. 3 (London: Butterworth, 1772), 449.

71. Niklas Luhmann, *Das Recht der Gesellschaft* (Frankfurt: Suhrkamp, 1997), 165–213.

72. William Dodwell, *The Nature Extent and Support of Human Laws Considered* (Oxford, U.K.: printed for James Fletcher, 1750), 30.

73. William Sellon, *A Sermon Preached at the Assizes Held at Guildford* (London: J. Hughes, 1759), 13.

74. John H. Langbein, "Historical Foundations of the Law of Evidence: A View from the Ryder Sources," *Columbia Law Review* 96 (1996): 1168–202, 1194.

75. Kesselring, *Mercy and Authority*, 145.

76. Katherine Royer, "The Body in Parts: Reading the Execution Ritual in Late Medieval England," *Historical Reflections/Réflexions Historiques* 29, no. 2 (2003): 319–39.

77. See Niklas Luhmann, *Legitimation durch Verfahren* (Berlin: Luchterhand, 1969).

78. Andrea McKenzie, "Martyrs in Low Life? Dying 'Game' in Augustan England," *Journal of British Studies* 42, no. 2 (2003): 167–205.

79. V. A. C. Gatrell, *The Hanging Tree: Execution and the English People 1770–1868* (Oxford, U.K.: Oxford University Press, 1986), 109.

80. Thomas Walter Laqueur, "Crowds, Carnival, and the State in English Executions, 1604–1868," in *The First Modern Society: Essays in English History in Honour of Lawrence Stone*, ed. A. L. Beier, David Cannadine, and James M. Rosenheim (Cambridge, U.K.: Cambridge University Press, 1989), 305–55.

81. Henry Venn, *Man a Condemned Prisoner, and Christ the Strong Hold to Same Him* (London: Printed for E. and C. Dilly, G. Keith, W. Harris, and J. Gurney, 1769), 9.

82. Randall McGowen, "'Making Examples' and the Crisis of Punishment in Mid-Eighteenth-Century England," in *The British and Their Laws in the Eighteenth Century*, ed. David Lemmings (Woodbridge, U.K.: Boydell Press, 2005), 182–205.

83. Blackstone, *Commentaries*, vol. 4, 10–1.

84. Reeve Ballard, *The Necessity of Magistracy from the Vices of Mankind* (London: printed for H. Pemberton, 1745), 6–7.

85. McGowen, *Changing Face of God's Justice*, 71.

86. Venn, *Man a Condemned Prisoner*, 5.

87. Ibid., 20; for similar statements in other sermons, see McGowen, *Changing Face of God's Justice*, 73.

88. McGowen, *Changing Face of God's Justice*, 74.

89. John Tillotson, *Of the Eternity of Hell-Torments: A Sermon Preach'd before the Queen at White-Hall, March the 7th, 1689/90* (London: H. Hills, 1708).

90. John Wesley, *The Great Assize* (London: T. Trye, 1758), 12.

91. Ibid., 14.

92. Ibid.

93. Randall McGowen, "He Beareth Not the Sword," 193–94.

94. McKenzie, *Tyburn's Martyrs*, 195.

95. Romilly, *Memoirs*, vol. 1, 65.

96. Madan, *Thoughts on Executive Justice*, 46.

97. Ibid.

98. Ibid., 64.

99. Daniel A. Cohen, "In Defense of the Gallows: Justifications of Capital Punishment in New England Execution Sermons, 1674–1825," *American Quarterly* 40, no. 2 (1988): 147–64.

100. Madan, *Thoughts on Executive Justice*, 102.

101. William Pugh, *A Sermon Preached at the Assizes Held at Buckingham* (London: Printed for J. Townsend, 1765), 20.

102. Madan, *Thoughts on Executive Justice*, 11, 64.

103. Quoted from Randall McGowen, "A Powerful Sympathy: Terror, the Prison, and Humanitarian Reform in Early Nineteenth-Century Britain," *Journal of British Studies* 25, no. 3 (1986): 312–34, 316.

104. See Randall McGowen, "Civilizing Punishment: The End of the Public Execution in England," *Journal of British Studies* 33, no. 3 (1994): 257–82.

Chapter 6

Between Moral Certainty and Morally Certain: The Religious Debate over the Death Penalty in the United States

Anthony Santoro

The 2005 Virginia gubernatorial race featured, for the first time in the modern era, a major-party candidate who openly opposed the death penalty.[1] The conventional wisdom held that this position was a political kiss of death in a state where the majority of voters strongly support the death penalty. Virginia, after all, is second only to Texas in the number of executions carried out in the modern era, since capital punishment resumed in the United States following the U.S. Supreme Court's decision in *Gregg v. Georgia*.[2] Republican candidate Jerry Kilgore, a strong supporter of the death penalty, repeatedly attacked his opponent, Democrat Timothy Kaine, for Kaine's opposition to capital punishment. Kilgore stressed his belief that the death penalty is just and necessary to protect citizens and help prevent crime. Kaine just as frequently stressed that his Catholic faith taught him that the death penalty is morally wrong, but that he would carry out his duties if elected governor. The open disagreement over both the propriety of capital punishment and the religious issues surrounding it provided voters a chance to evaluate their beliefs in light of their own religions traditions, and brought this debate to the fore.[3]

The continued salience of religious viewpoints in the contemporary debate over capital punishment is indisputable, as is the effect of that debate.[4] In the case of the Virginia gubernatorial race, a majority of respondents polled stated that although they disagreed with Kaine's stance, they accepted that his religious belief was sincere and thus took him at his word when he pledged to carry out his duties as governor. Kaine's articulation of his religious beliefs thus mitigated what could have potentially been a serious political liability.[5] In December 2004, a Zogby International Poll found that, for the first time, a minority of Catholic respondents (48 percent) supported capital punishment. Prior polling found that Catholics tended to support capital punishment in roughly the same proportion as Americans in general, averaging about 70 percent over the past several decades. Respondents credited church teachings as the primary reason for the drop in support.[6] Nor is religion meaningful only in the abstract; recent studies have shown that religion may be as important as race and gender in predisposing capital jurors to vote a certain way in a death penalty case.[7] Some people also believe that the geographic disparity in the use of capital punishment—which is predominantly a southern institution[8]—may be partially explained by the dominant religion in the region.[9]

Certainly, major theological differences exist between abolitionist and retentionist churches, as the official statements explaining their position make clear. Those differences break down principally to two related questions:

- How is the Bible to be read and understood?
- What is the relationship between the teachings of Jesus of Nazareth and those contained in the Old Testament?

In other words, should the believer read the Bible literally to look for the letter of the law, as the Southern Baptist Convention's statement indicates,[10] or should the believer try to seek out the spirit of the law as, for example, the United Church of Christ suggests?[11] Does the message of love, mercy, and forgiveness preached by Jesus counter Old Testament teachings, or does nothing in the New Testament contradict what is contained within the Old?[12] These theological differences are well beyond the scope of this essay, but it is important to recognize them before turning to the issues at the core of the contemporary debate: the understood structure of the political state, its duties, and the means by which those duties may legitimately be discharged.

In describing her position on capital punishment, political philosopher Jean Bethke Elshtain remarked that the death penalty tempts us to view the state as an idol, giving it ultimate power over life and death.[13] At the same time, however, she admits that taking seriously the inherent dignity and worth of every individual conflicts with this opposition, particularly in cases where the "moral certainty of the guilt of a person for a particularly horrific crime" is not in question.[14] This tension—between (a) the ideals of retribution, atonement, and vengeance and the mechanisms that we invest with the authority to seek such in our names and (b) questions of the inherent value and dignity of the individual[15]—remains the center of the religious debate about capital punishment in the United States. The debate is far ranging and expansive, but it is dominated by two sincerely held needs: the need to be morally certain and the need for moral certainty. The first of these needs is a question with regard to the state, the second with regard to individual defendants, and each has a strong procedural component. As to the first, the need to be morally certain is the need to answer the question of whether the state has the right to punish crimes by taking a person's life, whether under any circumstances or under narrow, specific circumstances. This need is affected and complicated by questions of whether the death penalty can be executed perfectly, whether it need be, and whether either of these questions materially changes our assessment of whether we can be morally certain that the state possesses the right to take life as punishment. The question of moral certainty, on the other hand, is a question of whether we can be certain that the specific defendant being sentenced to death is truly guilty of the crime for which he or she is being sentenced. Tracing these two lines of argument through the debate does more than clarify the reasons that the respective religious bodies support or oppose capital punishment in the contemporary political state and the grounds on which they do so. Following these rhetorical skeins enables the observer to see the respective bodies' understandings of the nature of crime and punishment generally.

Although this essay confines itself to the contemporary debate over the death penalty, it is worth pausing over the basic question suggested by the title, that being the question of morality and the idea of the moral. Briefly defining both *religion* and *punishment* will help clarify this question. As David Garland explains, *punishment* is "the legal process whereby violators of the criminal law are condemned and sanctioned in accordance with specific legal categories and procedures."[16] Condemnation, assignation of an offense to a category of crime and an appropriate range of sanctions, and the ritual imposition of the punishment—all are a part of the social institution of punishment. As will be shown, the churches' statements are in essential agreement that punishment is simultaneously an expression and a communication of our collective morality, which is to say an expression and a communication of our understandings of morality in the modern moment, in response to the particular conditions of "living-in-the-world."[17]

Religion too is concerned with the particular conditions of living-in-the-world. As Bruce Lincoln clarifies, religion is minimally characterized by a transcendent discourse that informs practices designed to bring about either a proper human world or proper human subjects. This, in turn, gives rise to a community that identifies itself with regard to those discourses and practices, as well as to an institution capable of and charged with regulating those discourses and practices and modifying them, where necessary, while preserving their transcendent validity.[18] The basic question of human living, then, can be variously phrased as "What am I to do?" and "Who are we to be?" That is to say, religion as a source of morality—of discourses and actions capable of guiding and helping to create the proper world or proper subjects—is a question of the identification of our rights and duties, relative to the divine, to the human social order, and to one another, pursuant to trying to answer and live up to the questions of what we are to do and to be.[19]

Here then, religion and punishment exist synergistically. Religion provides one basis for punishment, not in the sense that punishment is or should be designed to carry out religious dicta, but in the sense that, as is reflected in the churches' articulations of their position on capital punishment, punishment is an expression of and communicates our common, shared morality. Insofar as the churches and their adherents are concerned, the basic moral question of who we are to be and what we are to do provides a basis for justifying as well as limiting punishment. In the discourses and debates over the death penalty, the need to be morally certain that the state has the right to punish with death, then, and the need to achieve moral certainty regarding an individual's guilt are overlapping, simultaneous procedural and ethical needs. If punishment is in part an expression of our collective morality, then the procedural problems attendant in perfectly expressing that morality—such as racially, geographically, or economically biased application; poor quality of counsel; evidentiary concerns; or procedural barriers to postconviction relief—are cause for concern. At the same time, understanding punishment as this expression demands continual reexamination of that morality. This reexamination is at the heart of the most basic element of the religious debate over capital punishment: whether human life is best honored and protected by taking the life of those who kill. The need for moral certainty and the need to be morally certain are expressions of this ethical tension as it arises via living-in-the-world.

Morally Certain

In the churches' official statements and the debates, the need for moral certainty is a need to be sure, beyond a reasonable doubt, that the accused are truly guilty of the crimes for which they can be sentenced to death and are truly deserving of that punishment. This aspect focuses on the system of death in the United States and whether it is sufficiently free of errors in its application that the requisite level of certainty can be attained.

The need to be morally certain, in contrast, speaks to the question of perceptions of the state, its rights and responsibilities, its limitations, and its purviews. Does the state have the right to take the lives of its citizens as punishment for certain crimes, or does it not? Within this debate over the rights and responsibilities of the state are two other debates that simultaneously question and define the perceived role of the state from the perspective of the religious body or individual in question. The first is the question of the relationship between limitations placed on the individual and those placed on government. The second is the question of the construction of government itself and where it stands relative to the individual citizen believer.

Because it is from within those two broad debates that all the issues that surround the death penalty are evaluated, it is helpful to begin exploring these issues by first detailing the three broad camps within which most of the various religious bodies fall. The first and largest group consists of those churches and religious organizations that believe that the state does not possess the right to punish with death. The churches in this group cite the failings within the system—primarily racial, geographic, economic, and social inequalities in application and the chance of executing an innocent—and use that awareness of those failings to argue against the right of the state to execute in the contemporary moment. This view accords with the teachings of their faiths, which are various articulations of the idea that all life is sacred and that it is God's right alone to take life.

A second group, which includes the Southern Baptist Convention and the National Association of Evangelicals, believes not only that the death penalty is permissible but also that the state should use it. The third group acknowledges that the state has the right to take life but argues that right should be used only in cases of last resort. According to these churches, were the situation such that no other way to protect human life or to protect society existed other than to execute, then, and only then, would the death penalty be permissible. These bodies, which include the Catholic Church and the Evangelical Lutheran Church in America (ELCA), argue that the contemporary situation is such that this is not the case, however. And since the state has less than lethal options at its disposal to protect itself and its citizens, there is no circumstance under which the imposition of the death penalty is justifiable.

Parsing the churches' official statements regarding capital punishment demonstrates how questions of moral certainty and the need to be morally certain are weighted and considered as well as the movement from one problem to the other. There are, of course, several issues on which there is broad agreement. The sanctity of human life is unquestioned, as is the notion that the system, as it currently stands, is insufficiently capable of ensuring that no mistakes are made—that no executions of innocents or other miscarriages of justice can occur. And there is essential agreement that racial, social, and economic factors play too great a role in deciding who lives and who dies. There is broad agreement that reforms are necessary, whether to bring the system closer to infallibility or as necessary resolutions of specific problems en route to eventual abolition. Finally, there is no question that one of the primary responsibilities of the state is to protect the lives of its citizens. However, the conclusions to which these principles lead are in dispute.

All these concerns speak to specific cases and to the application of capital punishment in general, but they do not address the question of whether one can be morally certain that the state possesses the right to execute in response to certain crimes. The essential question here—and the primary point of departure between the abolitionist and retentionist churches—can be phrased simply: What is capital punishment? It is not necessary here to delve into theories of punishment or penology; for our purposes, it is sufficient to consider two major differences in the way the churches approach this problem. The first is the question of whether punishment is an intrinsic good or an intrinsic evil. This question has a continuum of opinions, divided between two poles that treat punishment as necessary and intrinsically good and as inherently evil and always in need of justification. In its statements on the death penalty, the National Association of Evangelicals argues that crime cannot be considered violative absent reciprocally harsh punishment. Punishment is thus a necessary good. From that viewpoint, to cavil about the incidence of heinous crimes—or any infractions—makes no sense when the proposed remedy falls short of reciprocity. Capital punishment is not only justified from this point of view but also demanded: to punish a murderer with less than death is to communicate to criminals and the public alike that the inherent value of human life is diminished.[20] Retribution is the dominant rationale for supporting punishment in these arguments, and it is both necessary and proper to explicitly seek retribution.

The opposite claim—that "punishment, since it involves the deliberate infliction of evil on another, is always in need of justification"[21]—is advanced in various forms by the abolitionist churches. Although not denying the state the right to imprison or otherwise sequester individuals who are dangerous to others or to society itself, they demand that "punishment … be determined with a view to the reformation of the criminal and his reintegration into society (which may not be possible in certain cases)."[22] Retribution is generally rejected as a valid rationale for punishment, particularly when that punishment involves taking life.[23] Indeed, the abolitionist churches, in rejecting the validity of retribution as a penal aim, denounce it as incompatible with justice[24] and lament that the Supreme Court has legitimated retribution as a valid penal aim.[25]

If the question of retribution is rephrased as a question of the legitimacy of vengeance, the disagreement stands in starker relief and highlights the different conceptions of capital punishment per se. Retentionist denominations, such as the Lutheran Church–Missouri Synod (LCMS), hold that the death penalty is not revenge, whereas the Southern Baptist Convention notes that although God denies humans the right to take personal vengeance, he nevertheless gave the magistrate—the state—the power to take life in response to crime.[26] The Assemblies of God avers that both the Old and New Testaments deny the legitimacy of personal vengeance.[27] Conversely, the Christian Church (Disciples of Christ) maintains that "Holy Scriptures clearly mandate that we are not to … render evil for evil, and that we are not to seek retribution with vengeance for the evil done to us."[28] Finally, the ELCA states, "People often respond to violent crime as though it were exclusively a matter of the criminal's individual failure. The death penalty exacts and symbolizes the ultimate personal retribution."[29]

This statement brings to the fore another area in which the churches disagree: what do crime and punishment communicate about responsibility and by whom it is borne. Retentionist denominations treat the matter of responsibility as beginning and ending with the offender. At the same time, they argue for a division between the citizen and the government in questions pertaining to life, paralleling the division between "God's kingdom of grace and His rule in power."[30] Supreme Court Justice Antonin Scalia makes this point as well, stating that the death penalty "is undoubtedly wrong unless one accords to the state a scope of moral action that goes beyond what is permitted to the individual."[31] Under this theory, the idea that government morality and individual morality are one and the same is a fallacy, a viewpoint that is echoed in the statements of the retentionist denominations. The difference in moralities reflects the different roles and responsibilities of individuals and states. On the one hand, individuals are forbidden to kill, except in narrowly prescribed circumstances, such as self-defense or just war.[32] Governments, on the other hand, "[do] not bear the sword in vain;"[33] charged as they are with protecting their citizens, governments may legitimately take the lives of those who have committed murder. In this way, the sacredness of human life is upheld and the state communicates to its citizens and any would-be murderers both the value with which life is held and the penalty to be levied for violating the image of God, the imago dei.[34]

The state, regardless of its composition, is seen as necessarily distant from citizens and believers. For individuals, killing is a choice; for the state, it is an obligation to punish murder by taking the lives of those who kill. The element of choice is implied even when it is not directly stated, as in the LCMS statement: the more frequent imposition of the death penalty on the poor and on minorities, the statement holds, is the result of a greater number of "crimes against person," including murder, arising from those within "subcultures of violence" within the inner cities.[35] Leaving aside the factual infelicity—capital crimes committed in inner cities are punished with the death penalty far less frequently than those committed in the suburbs and exurbs[36]—the description of subcultures of violence implies an element of willful belonging, an element that aggravates rather than mitigates the abstract murder in question.

The abolitionist denominations express a different conception of the distance between believer–citizens and their government. These bodies posit minimal distance between believer–citizens and the state, particularly where life is concerned, and between the lawful and the unlawful. They likewise grant that the state has powers and rights that individuals do not have; none of them, for instance, argues against incarceration on the grounds that it represents a power greater than that enjoyed by the individual. At the same time, however, the abolitionist denominations all draw up short on the question of life. In matters of life and death, the state's rights and responsibilities are equivalent to the individual's, and here is where the perceived distance between the individual and the state closes. Capital punishment necessarily forecloses any possibility of rehabilitation, reconciliation, and redemption[37] and devalues the "God-given dignity of every human life, even those who do great harm."[38] This devaluation has several consequences. First, as some of the churches argue, it is a further devaluing of the victim, whose memory is joined even more fully with death.[39] Second, it communicates contradictory lessons: that we can protect life by taking life and that we can teach that killing is wrong by killing. For these arguments to be posed as contradictory, the distance between the individual and the state, in the capacity to act, must be dismissed.[40] Even the two bodies that grant that the state possesses the right to punish with death—the Catholic Church and the ELCA—limit that right to cases of absolute necessity, when no other options are available. The distance is thus simultaneously granted in the abstract and denied in the current social and political situation. Because "modern society has the means of protecting itself, without definitively denying criminals the chance to reform,"[41] the state is limited to "incapacitat[ing] offenders in a manner that limits violence, and hold[s] open the possibility of conversion and restoration."[42]

Although the state has the power to act in ways that the individual cannot, it lacks the authority to do so when it need not do so; it need do so only in cases that are most analogous to individual self-defense. Importantly, the abolitionist churches do not distance the criminal from the law abiding as the retentionists do. They do not question the matter of choice and the personal responsibility that follows from actions voluntarily undertaken; on this point the two sides agree. They differ, however, as to how these actions are to be understood in their broader societal meaning. Whereas the retentionists begin and end with the crime itself, the abolitionists seek to place it into a broader picture, which leads to different understandings of moral certainty.

Two Understandings of Moral Certainty

In their considerations of whether we can be morally certain that the state has the right to execute convicted criminals, the abolitionist churches bemoan two consequences attendant with the devaluation of life that they see in the death penalty: (a) further devaluing the murder victim by linking him or her to yet another death and (b) communicating contradictory lessons about the utility of killing to demonstrate our abhorrence of killing. To these consequences a third should be added, one that follows from and conflicts with the commitment to seek the redemption of the offender. This result is the distortive effect that this devaluation has on our approach to crime more generally. Despite being morally certain that the state has no right to take life as punishment, the abolitionist bodies approach the issues surrounding moral certainty more thoroughly than do the retentionists.[43] As the history of the death penalty shows, "its application has been discriminating with respect to the disadvantaged, the indigent, and the socially impoverished."[44] The American Baptist Churches notes that the majority of people on death row are "poor, powerless, and educationally deprived," and roughly half of those on death row belong to a minority group.[45] The United Church of Christ goes further, stating that the death penalty has been demonstrably discriminatorily applied to "Blacks, Hispanics, [and] Native Americans."[46] This concern persists: The Presbyterian Church (USA) opens its 2000 statement calling for a moratorium with a lengthy argument that the death penalty remains racist in its application, focusing on the Supreme Court's 1987 decision in *McCleskey v. Kemp*, in which the Court "refused to act on data demonstrating the continuing reality of racial bias."[47]

Along with observations that the death penalty continues to be administered in a racially biased way are various twists on the cliché that "capital punishment means that those without the capital get the punishment."[48] The American Baptist Churches and the Fellowship of Reconciliation both note the preponderance of indigent among those ultimately receiving the death penalty, and the National Council of the Churches of Christ in the USA made the economic injustices inherent in the application of the death penalty a plank in its original declaration of opposition to capital punishment.[49] Accompanying the arguments of racial and economic bias are observations that the execution of an innocent remains an ever-present threat; the Presbyterian Church (USA) cites a study suggesting that as many as 8 percent of death row inmates are innocent of the crimes for which they were convicted.[50] When former Illinois governor George Ryan emptied his state's death row, the primary reason he gave was the disproportionate number of innocents found there. At the time that Ryan declared first a moratorium and then a blanket commutation, Illinois had executed twelve people since 1976, whereas thirteen had been exonerated in that same span.[51]

Retentionists express the same worry that an innocent person may be executed,[52] but their response to this possibility points to a different understanding of moral certainty than that held by the abolitionist churches. The solution to the possibility of an innocent person's being executed is to call for death sentences to be handed down "only when the pursuit of truth and justice result in clear and overwhelming evidence of guilt."[53] By focusing their attention on whether one can possess moral certainty that the defendant sitting in the courtroom is guilty of the crime for which he or she has been charged, retentionists render questions of unfairness of application less relevant from their perspective and demonstrate a more narrow understanding of moral certainty. If the guilt of the defendant can be ascertained with moral certainty, and if it is morally certain that the state may legitimately impose a death sentence, then any inherent bias in the system—racial, socioeconomic, or otherwise—is irrelevant. Moral certainty, for retentionist churches, extends only to specific cases, to specific defendants.

Abolitionists, in contrast, tend to approach the question of moral certainty from a broader understanding of its demands; abolitionists demand to know whether *this* defendant—however certain his or her guilt—is particularly noteworthy among a class of like defendants. Although abolitionist churches are morally certain that the state does not possess the authority to execute, they nevertheless invest far more energy in dealing with the question of moral certainty than do retentionists and to a different end, to compounding the argument against the state's right to take life. Not only does the state not have the right, they argue, but even were that not the case, it could never be done in such a way as to remain a just application of power. When the ELCA states that it "increasingly question[s] whether the death penalty has been and can be administered justly,"[54] it gives every indication that it believes that the death penalty cannot be administered in a just manner, for the reasons previously discussed. Justice is better served, the ELCA argues—indeed, can only be considered justice—when it is directed toward rehabilitative and restorative ends. And when the ELCA's statement against vengeance is reconsidered, the reason is immediately apparent: "People often respond to violent crime *as though it were exclusively a matter of the criminal's individual failure*."[55] Seeing only individual failure, the ELCA feels, is misleading and harmful, because it ignores the failures of the greater community and its corporate responsibility.

The idea of corporate responsibility for crime is driven in part by the nature of the response: "The use of the death penalty in a representative democracy places citizens in the role of the executioner."[56] The "fallacy" that Justice Scalia spoke of is clearly displayed here. Individual and government morality are not distinguished one from the other, nor is there any posited distance between the state and the citizen; for all intents and purposes, the citizen and the state are interchangeable. This concept is, of course, the meaning of the phrasing within the legal system, the reason that criminal cases are brought by the people of the jurisdiction against the defendant. The very phrasing that communicates that the state is also a victim of the transgression makes all citizens culpable in the punishment administered. The abolitionist denominations accept the consequence of this responsibility and fit it into their theological framework, expressing their understanding of the culpability borne by the society at large. This awareness is what the Presbyterian Church (USA) means when it states that Christians cannot isolate themselves from the "corporate responsibility" that they bear both for victims and for executions.[57] Expressions of this sense of corporate responsibility can take the form of more personalized expressions of regret for shortcomings, as in the Mennonite Church and General Conference's statements acknowledging that they have fallen short in their Christian duties in "preventing crime and restoring from its effects."[58] It can also find expression in arguments that the death penalty, because it "ignores corporate and community guilt"[59] and "exacts and symbolizes the ultimate in personal retribution,"[60] is an illegitimate and unfair response to social problems that we have failed adequately to address or to work to solve.

Conclusion

Punishment levied in response to violent crime is always characterized by a strong exilic element, in which the offender is removed from society forcibly and either is detained in a temporary or permanent state of exile, via incarceration, or is exiled from society permanently via execution. Neither retentionist nor abolitionist churches dispute the right of society to exile dangerous individuals. They continue to debate, however, about whether that right to exile extends even unto taking life. This dispute is not merely about whether the state has the right to kill its own citizens, though that question has been directly answered by a majority of faith groups, most often in the negative. The debate ultimately is about the interpellation of the criminal as *the other*, and when and how that happens.

On the one hand, in statements issued by retentionist denominations, the criminal becomes *the other*,[61] someone recognizably different from the remainder of the populace, when he or she chooses to commit the crime whose punishment can be or is a death sentence. At that point, the killer has chosen to undertake an action that can, and should, lead to exile from (and for the protection of) society via his or her death at the hands of the state, which is seen as distant from and bound to operate under different moral rules than individuals. For abolitionists, on the other hand, when it comes to the question of taking life, the distance between the citizen and the state is far less, and with diminishing distance comes an equivalence of moral responsibility. If individuals are prohibited from killing, except in cases of absolute necessity, so too is the state, which means, in the current historical moment, that because modern society can protect itself without taking life, it is bound to engage less violent means of protection in place of more violent or lethal means.

That said, however, for abolitionists too the criminal is an *other*, though the commission of the crime is more the signal of that otherness than the signal event. The inclusive and embracing rhetoric and vision of justice tempered by mercy—justice turned toward rehabilitation and reconciliation, so that, when possible, the errant can be returned to society—reveal an understanding of that criminal as also alien, as "not like us." This otherness can be for any number of reasons. Although the workings of the criminal justice system contain documented and demonstrable biases that disproportionately affect racial minorities, the poor, and the uneducated, the holistic vision of society projected by abolitionist churches in their denunciations of the death penalty stands in contrast to the visions of the *other*, against which that vision is posited. In addressing the questions of whether one can be morally certain that the state has the right to kill and whether one can possess moral certainty that a particular defendant is sufficiently guilty to be executed, both sides trade in concepts of exile, though for different reasons and to different ends.

Finally, the resolution of these questions produces different communicative effects. Retentionists intend for the death penalty to stand as a sign of what society absolutely cannot and will not tolerate, even if it means destroying humans made in the image of God to achieve that end.[62] Abolitionists reject the notion of protecting society "by making killers of all of us because one of us kills."[63] Nor are abolitionist groups entirely comfortable with the implications of giving the state the power over life. Recalling Elshtain's observation that the death penalty tempts us to see the state as an idol, Church Women United's statement on the death penalty decries the "false confidence" placed in capital punishment as a solution to violent crime,[64] which "is, in part, a reminder of the human failure to ensure justice for all members of society."[65] Lastly, whereas retentionists argue that individuals can forfeit their right to live by their actions,[66] thus declaring in favor of a derivative view of rights, in which even the right to life can be said to derive from the state,[67] abolitionists, by denying the state the legitimate authority to take life as a punishment, can plausibly claim to hold and communicate a natural rights view of life. In all, the difference in views regarding the nature and construction of the state in the current political moment and our role in relation to it underlies the divergence of opinion over the death penalty in the churches.

Notes

1. This essay confines itself to the debate among Christian churches and groups. Official statements from Buddhist, Islamic, and Jewish bodies, as well as the Christian churches discussed here, can be found at "Religion and the Death Penalty," Death Penalty Information Center, Washington, DC, http://deathpenaltyinfo.org/religion-and-death-penalty, and "Religious Groups' Official Positions on Capital Punishment," Pew Forum on Religion and Public Life, Washington, DC, http://www.pewforum.org/Death-Penalty/Religious-Groups--Official-Positions-on-Capital-Punishment.aspx.

2. *Gregg v. Georgia*, 428 U.S. 153 (1976).

3. For a succinct depiction of the debate over the death penalty during the 2005 campaign, see Pamela Podger and Michael Sluss, "Death Penalty Debate Makes Religion an Issue," *Roanoke Times*, October 16, 2005, http://www.roanoke.com/news/roanoke.wb/3649.

4. See, for example, John Witte Jr., *God's Joust, God's Justice: Law and Religion in the Western Tradition* (Grand Rapids, MI: William B. Eerdmans, 2006); Erik C. Owens, John D. Carlson, and Eric P. Elshtain, eds., *Religion and the Death Penalty: A Call for Reckoning* (Grand Rapids, MI: William B. Eerdmans, 2004).

5. Robert Barnes, "Kilgore Ads Seek to Divide Democrats," *Washington Post*, October 13, 2005.

6. United States Conference of Catholic Bishops, "Catholic Campaign to End the Use of the Death Penalty," Publication 5-715, USCCB Publishing, Washington, DC, 2005. For more information about the Zogby International Poll for the USCCB, see John Zogby's statement to the USCCB at http://nccbuscc.org/sdwp/national/deathpenalty/zogby.shtml.

7. Chester L. Britt, "Race, Religion, and Support for the Death Penalty: A Research Note," *Justice Quarterly* 15, no. 1 (March 1998): 175–91; Theodore Eisenberg, Stephen P. Garvey, and Martin T. Wells, "Forecasting Life and Death: Juror Race, Religion, and Attitude toward the Death Penalty," *Journal of Legal Studies* 30, no. 2 (2001): 277–311.

8. "Number of Executions by State and Region since 1976," Death Penalty Information Center, Washington, DC, http://deathpenaltyinfo.org/number-executions -state-and-region-1976#region.

9. See the comments of Dr. Barrett Duke, vice president for public policy and research for the Southern Baptist Convention's Ethics and Religious Liberty Commission, at the Pew Forum on Religion and Public Life, in "Religious Reflections on the Death Penalty," Washington, DC, June 5, 2001, http://pewforum.org/events/?EventID=10. In the ten states with the highest execution totals—Texas, Virginia, Oklahoma, Missouri, Florida, North Carolina, Georgia, South Carolina, Alabama, and Louisiana—the Southern Baptist Convention, an evangelical denomination, is the largest reporting religious body in the state. By contrast, in the Northeast and the Upper Midwest, where the majority of states have abolished the death penalty, the Catholic Church and the Evangelical Lutheran Church in America, two abolitionist denominations, are the dominant church bodies. See Dale E. Jones, Sherri Doty, Clifford Grammich, James E. Horsch, Richard Houseal, John P. Marcum, Kenneth M. Sanchagrin, and Richard H. Taylor, *Religious Congregations and Membership in the United States, 2000* (Nashville, TN: Glenmary Research Center, 2002).

10. Southern Baptist Convention, "Resolution on Capital Punishment," Southern Baptist Convention, Orlando, FL, June 2000, http://www.sbc.net/resolutions /amResolution.asp?ID=299.

11. United Church of Christ, "Resolution of the 12th General Synod of the United Church of Christ" (1979), in *The Death Penalty: The Religious Community Calls for Abolition*, ed. Pat Clark (Philadelphia: American Friends Service Committee, 1998), 24–25.

12. Though the Assemblies of God takes no formal position on capital punishment, the denomination's position paper deals with these two issues succinctly and clearly. See Assemblies of God, "Capital Punishment," Assemblies of God, Springfield, MO, http://www.ag.org/top/Beliefs/contempissues_08_capital_punish.cfm.

13. Jean Bethke Elshtain, *Who Are We? Critical Reflections and Hopeful Possibilities* (Grand Rapids, MI: William B. Eerdmans, 2000).

14. Jean Bethke Elshtain, "Foreword," in *Religion and the Death Penalty: A Call for Reckoning*, ed. Erik C. Owens, John D. Carlson, and Eric P. Elshtain (Grand Rapids, MI: William B. Eerdmans, 2004), xii.

15. Thorsten Sellin, *The Death Penalty: A Report for the Model Penal Code Project of the American Law Institute* (Philadelphia: American Law Institute, 1959).

16. David Garland, *Punishment and Modern Society: A Study in Social Theory* (Chicago: University of Chicago Press, 1990), 17.

17. Talal Asad, *Formations of the Secular: Christianity, Islam, and Modernity* (Stanford, CA: Stanford University Press, 2003), 14.

18. Bruce Lincoln, *Holy Terrors: Thinking about Religion after September 11* (Chicago: University of Chicago Press, 2006), 5–8.

19. G. Scott Davis, "Ethics," in *The Blackwell Companion to the Study of Religion*, ed. Robert A. Segal (Oxford, U.K.: Blackwell, 2006), 239–54.

20. National Association of Evangelicals, "Capital Punishment 1972," National Association of Evangelicals, Washington, DC, http://nae.net/index.cfm?FUSEACTION= editor.page&pageID=187; National Association of Evangelicals, "Capital Punishment 1973," National Association of Evangelicals, Washington, DC, http://www.nae.net/ government-relations/policy-resolutions/95-capital-punishment-1973.

21. USCCB, "Statement on Capital Punishment," USCCB, Washington, DC, 2001, 3.

22. Ibid., 4.

23. United Methodist Church, "Capital Punishment" (1980), in *The Death Penalty: The Religious Community Calls for Abolition*, ed. Pat Clark (Philadelphia: American Friends Service Committee, 1998), 25.

24. Mennonite Central Committee, "Death Penalty" (December 4, 1982), in *The Death Penalty: The Religious Community Calls for Abolition*, ed. Pat Clark (Philadelphia: American Friends Service Committee, 1998), 19.

25. American Friends Service Committee, "Statement on the Death Penalty," American Friends Service Committee, Philadelphia, undated, 7; United Methodist Church, "Capital Punishment," 25.

26. LCMS, *Report on Capital Punishment* (St. Louis, MO: Concordia Publishing House, 1980), 4; Southern Baptist Convention, "Resolution on Capital Punishment."

27. Assemblies of God, "Capital Punishment."

28. Christian Church (Disciples of Christ), "Resolution Concerning Opposition to the Use of the Death Penalty" (1980), in *The Death Penalty: The Religious Community Calls for Abolition*, ed. Pat Clark (Philadelphia: American Friends Service Committee, 1998), 10.

29. ELCA, "Social Statement on the Death Penalty," ELCA, Chicago, 3, http://www.elca.org/What-We-Believe/Social-Issues/Social-Statements/Death-Penalty.aspx.

30. LCMS, *Report on Capital Punishment*, 5.

31. Antonin Scalia, "God's Justice and Ours: The Morality of Judicial Participation in the Death Penalty," in *Religion and the Death Penalty: A Call for Reckoning*, ed. Erik C. Owens, John D. Carlson, and Eric P. Elshtain (Grand Rapids, MI: William B. Eerdmans, 2004), 234.

32. Indeed, the rhetorical similarities between legitimizations of killing in self-defense and in a just war extend beyond the merely analogous.

33. Romans 13:4. All biblical citations are taken from the New Revised Standard Version.

34. Genesis 1:27; Southern Baptist Convention, "Resolution on Capital Punishment"; LCMS, *Report on Capital Punishment*, 10.

35. LCMS, *Report on Capital Punishment*, 9.

36. On the geographic and racial disparities involved, see, for example, Andrew Ditchfield, "Challenging the Intrastate Disparities in the Application of Capital Punishment Statutes," *Georgetown Law Review* 95, no. 3 (2005): 801–30; Michael Kroll, "Chattahoochee Judicial District: Buckle of the Death Belt—The Death Penalty in Microcosm," Death Penalty Information Center, Washington, DC, http://deathpenaltyinfo.org/chattahoochee-judicial-district-buckle-death-belt-death-penalty-microcosm; and Michael J. Songer and Isaac Unah, "The Effect of Race, Gender, and Location on Prosecutorial Decisions to Seek the Death Penalty in South Carolina," *South Carolina Law Review* 58, no. 1 (2006): 161–209.

37. See Bruderhof Communities, "Statement on the Death Penalty," in *The Death Penalty: The Religious Community Calls for Abolition*, ed. Pat Clark (Philadelphia: American Friends Service Committee, 1998), 9; Presbyterian Church (USA), "Capital Punishment, 106th General Assembly, 1966," in *Public Policy Statements of the Presbyterian Church (U.S.A.): Capital Punishment* (Louisville, KY: General Assembly Council, 2000), 9; USCCB, "Statement on Capital Punishment," 4.

38. USCCB, "Catholic Campaign."

39. See United Methodist Church, "Capital Punishment," 25; Church Women United, "Capital Punishment" (1981), in *The Death Penalty: The Religious Community Calls for Abolition*, ed. Pat Clark (Philadelphia: American Friends Service Committee, 1998), 11.

40. USCCB, "Catholic Campaign," USCCB, "A Good Friday Appeal to End the Death Penalty," Publication 5-327 (Washington, DC: USCCB, 1999).

41. Pope John Paul II made this statement in an address in St. Louis, Missouri, on January 27, 1999; see USCCB, "Good Friday."

42. ELCA, "Social Statement," 13.

43. Among the retentionist denominations, the LCMS statement includes the greatest consideration of issues of moral certainty. See LCMS, *Report on Capital Punishment*, 9–10.

44. USCCB, "Statement on Capital Punishment: Committee on Social Development and World Peace" (March 1, 1976), in *The Death Penalty: The Religious Community Calls for Abolition*, ed. Pat Clark (Philadelphia: American Friends Service Committee, 1998), 26.

45. American Baptist Churches, "Resolution," in *The Death Penalty: The Religious Community Calls for Abolition*, ed. Pat Clark (Philadelphia: American Friends Service Committee, 1998), 6. See also Fellowship of Reconciliation, "An Appeal to End All Executions," in *The Death Penalty: The Religious Community Calls for Abolition*, ed. Pat Clark (Philadelphia: American Friends Service Committee, 1998), 15.

46. United Church of Christ, "Resolution," 25.

47. Presbyterian Church (USA), "Moratorium on Capital Punishment, PCUSA 212th General Assembly, 2000," in *Public Policy Statements of the Presbyterian Church (U.S.A.): Capital Punishment* (Louisville, KY: General Assembly Council, 2000), 1–3; *McCleskey v. Kemp* 481 U.S. 279 (1987).

48. Helen Prejean, "Would Jesus Pull the Switch?" *Salt of the Earth*, March–April 1997, 13.

49. American Baptist Churches, "Resolution," 6; Fellowship of Reconciliation, "Appeal," 14; National Council of the Churches of Christ in the USA, "Resolution Opposing Capital Punishment and Racism in Sentencing" (May 26, 1988), in *The Death Penalty: The Religious Community Calls for Abolition*, ed. Pat Clark (Philadelphia: American Friends Service Committee, 1998), 21.

50. Presbyterian Church (USA), "Moratorium," 2.

51. George Ryan, "Reflections on the Death Penalty and the Moratorium," in *Religion and the Death Penalty: A Call for Reckoning*, ed. Erik C. Owens, John D. Carlson, and Eric P. Elshtain (Grand Rapids, MI: William B. Eerdmans, 2004), 221–30.

52. See, for example, Duke's comments at the Pew Forum in "Religious Reflections."

53. Southern Baptist Convention, "Resolution on Capital Punishment."

54. ELCA, "Social Statement," 13.

55. Ibid. (emphasis added). The ELCA cites Matthew 5:38-39 and John 8:3–11 as illustrative of restorative justice.

56. Presbyterian Church (USA), "Moratorium," 2.

57. Presbyterian Church (USA), "Resolution on a Continuing Witness to Abolish the Death Penalty, 1977," in *Public Policy Statements of the Presbyterian Church (U.S.A.): Capital Punishment* (Louisville, KY: General Assembly Council, 2000), 6. This idea was reaffirmed in the Presbyterian Church (USA)'s 1985 "Opposition to Capital Punishment," and its 2000 "Resolution," in *Public Policy Statements of the Presbyterian Church (U.S.A.): Capital Punishment* (Louisville, KY: General Assembly Council, 2000), 4 and 2, respectively.

58. Mennonite Church, "Statement on Capital Punishment" (August 1965), in *The Death Penalty: The Religious Community Calls for Abolition*, ed. Pat Clark (Philadelphia: American Friends Service Committee, 1998), 20; General Conference Mennonite Church, "Capital Punishment" (July 16, 1965), in *The Death Penalty: The Religious Community Calls for Abolition*, ed. Pat Clark (Philadelphia: American Friends Service Committee, 1998), 17.

59. Reformed Church in America, "Resolution on Capital Punishment" (1965), in *The Death Penalty: The Religious Community Calls for Abolition*, ed. Pat Clark (Philadelphia: American Friends Service Committee, 1998), 23.

60. ELCA, "Social Statement," 13.

61. *The other* is a constant motif in literature pertaining to the death penalty. For two examples considering the societal ramifications of the creation of the other and of the imposition of otherness on the families of offenders, see Austin Sarat, *When the State Kills* (Princeton, NJ: Princeton University Press, 2002); Susan F. Sharp, *Hidden Victims* (New Brunswick, NJ: Rutgers University Press, 2005).

62. Southern Baptist Convention, "Resolution on Capital Punishment." See also Duke's comments at the Pew Forum in "Religious Reflections" and LCMS, *Report on Capital Punishment*.

63. Reverend Joseph Lowery at the Pew Forum in "Religious Reflections."

64. Church Women United, "Capital Punishment," 11.

65. ELCA, "Social Statement," 13.

66. Duke at the Pew Forum in "Religious Reflections."

67. On derivative rights, see Ronald Dworkin, *Life's Dominion: An Argument about Abortion and Euthanasia* (London: HarperCollins, 1993).

Part III

Science

Chapter 7

Fraternal Twins: American Science and American Religion

James Gilbert

I do not believe in decisive ruptures, in an unequivocal 'epistemological break', as it is called today. Breaks are always, and fatally, reinscribed in an old cloth that must continually, interminably be undone. This interminability is not an accident or contingency; it is essential, systematic, and theoretical. And this in no way minimizes the necessity and relative importance of certain breaks, of the appearance and definition of new structures....

—Jacques Derrida[1]

American religions, particularly Protestant denominations and their derivative sects, have had an intimate, long-standing, and sometimes troubled relationship with science. This situation is nothing new, as the troubled European acceptance of astronomy and geology, particularly up to the nineteenth century, also reveals. The difference is that this anxious dialogue persists in American culture in a more intense form, with profound effects on both sides of the conversation. It may even be argued that religious hesitations about some key scientific concepts are responsible for American antiscience attitudes and high levels of scientific illiteracy. Certainly other societies have serious reservations about science—Europe is a case in point—but ambiguity about science there does not stem largely from religious belief.[2]

This chapter explores some of the contours of the historic interactions of religion and science in the United States. Its particular focus is on the ideological and structural organization of American religions and their relationships and interactions with the scientific establishment. It seeks to identify elements of American civilization that account for the peculiar modern dynamism of (largely) Protestant faiths and their place and function within traditions of localism, individualism, and democracy and their response to and empowerment by those traditions.[3]

Religion

The explanation for this continued intense interaction lies in the history of American religious and scientific institutions and, especially, in the complex circumstances that have made religious belief a growing rather than diminishing element of culture in the United States. For example, general estimates place church membership only at around 10 percent of the American population in 1800. By 1890, church membership had risen to around 45 percent. By 1980, the figure stood at about 62 percent.[4] In many respects, this special condition of growth depends on the unique dispensation and dispersion of European (and to a lesser extent African, Asian, and Latin American) religious beliefs into American culture and the persistent immigration of new peoples and faiths. But even by the time of the American Revolution, the religious landscape was already taking on a familiar shape with its characteristic variegations, local loyalties, and regional concentrations. As Wilbur Zelinsky writes in his *Cultural Geography of the United States*, by 1776, there already were at least five large, major Protestant denominations and a considerable number of smaller ones, including Methodists, German Lutherans, the Dutch Reformed, Catholics, Moravians, and Mennonites. In the 230 years since then, American religions have proliferated and expanded with new denominations and wholly new religions of U.S. origin, and today some 250 distinct religious bodies can be identified.[5]

In establishing the institutional framework for the practice of American religion, there is no better beginning than the American Revolution and the constitutional limits on and guarantees of religion and free speech. The

European Enlightenment, in its political translation onto American soil, deeply infused and colored the thoughts and designs of those who drew up the Constitution of the United States. But the American Enlightenment did not occur in a cultural vacuum, nor was it simply a system of generalized reason. Its Lockean affinities, with an appeal to a Christian conception of God, are apparent and have led to a great deal of speculation about whether the founders were Christians or Deists.[6] Important traditions from the earliest settlements and political designs made their way into the Constitution with the better-known influence of contemporary European thought. Most notably expressed in the famous First Amendment to the Constitution, the Enlightenment placed the fundamental rights of liberty with the individual—in other words, removing from government the power to abrogate ultimate political rights and looking to reason rather than divinity for ultimate sanction. This was particularly the case in America's rejection of any formal links between the state and religious organizations. Although this separation might have been murky in its implications at first, because some states had all but established religious institutions, the goal was clear enough. In its American version, the Enlightenment ideal was to prevent the government from favoring or underwriting one particular sect. In other words, the design was a marketplace of contending groups, unencumbered by unfair advantage. To level the competition and promote denominational growth, the federal and state governments exempted religious and non-profit civic organizations from taxation. This historic disestablishment (and simultaneous encouragement of religion—subsidy, if you will) had two distinct and contradictory purposes, depending on circumstances and perspective. One focused on protecting civil society from the imposition of a state church. The other was to protect religious institutions from state interference while encouraging their economic viability. But because the amendment was largely concerned with fundamental institutions of state and silent on goals for society and social legislation, there remained a huge area of potential controversy over possibilities that religious groups might secure moral sanctions derived from religious belief through legislation.[7] Interpreters from Alexis de Tocqueville onward have underscored this separation of church and state and the open arena for competition as a key factor in understanding America's particularly vibrant religious culture.[8]

The settlement of constitutional rights proved to have long-term disquieting effects because it encouraged two profoundly different tendencies. One was to place religion squarely in the marketplace, with groups vying with one another for members, economic resources, and influence. Quite literally, denominations needed to appeal to members for finances or, on occasion, to engage in money-making business endeavors. In the latter half of the twentieth century, this need led to the wholesale adoption of market research, advertising, and other practices borrowed from business.[9] At the same time, the very size, variety, and mobility of the American population, washed over by waves of immigrants carrying their own religious traditions, encouraged the proliferation of sects. What began in Europe with the splintering of the Catholic Church and the declension of Protestantism into various tendencies was continued and was greatly exaggerated in the United States, creating a landscape of ethnic churches tied in some manner to the old country, as well as a vast potential for new recruits to existing denominations. At the same time, the very ease with which splits and offshoots occurred created what might be likened to an evolutionary analogy, where new species emerged to respond to a new and rapidly changing environment. In this sense, American religious proliferation was a consequence of English and continental efforts to reform and purify the Christian church. The result in the United States has been the surprisingly large inventory of new religions, among which Mormons, Scientologists, Christian Scientists, Jehovah's Witnesses, Fundamentalists, Seventh Day Adventists, and Pentecostals are well-known examples.

Given relatively unpopulated land and the tendency of some communities to displace themselves from Europe or from the Eastern United States as whole bodies, religious communities were sometimes also geographic communities, with their own institutions, schools, and customs—sometimes even languages. Examples would be the Mennonite and Amish communities in Pennsylvania and southern Indiana.[10] Inevitably, the Babel of Protestant tongues in America encouraged waves of evangelism, beginning in the late eighteenth century and recurring at regular intervals, all of them aiming to unify a splintered Christianity.[11] However, this response to the disorder and variety of American religious sects may, in the end, have only contributed to the proliferation of new sects and freestanding, loosely affiliated congregations. In other words, there is a kind of dialectic among American sects that is based on coming together and splitting apart. So, if the Constitution separated church from state, it said nothing about church and society, a situation that American religions took as an opportunity to define themselves as central to their mission. Indeed, it was precisely here where religious groups struggled to take advantage of the opportunities enacted by the disestablishment amendment and to compete and reform to gain new adherents and as they faced new circumstances.

Another tradition affirmed by the Constitution and prolonged by custom is localism. The persistently local focus of power and the frequent and fervent hostility toward centralization, state authority, and anything identified with old world political systems have been characteristic of Protestant suspicion toward the Catholic Church and, on occasion, toward the English Episcopal Church. But there are far larger implications. This tradition of localism, which I shall call *congregational culture*, had profound effects and was based on the practice of self-governance by local churches and their power to replace ministers; they often modified theological tenets as well. Congregational culture extended beyond the narthex, reaching out to embrace political and social institutions and ideals. If "all politics is local politics" remains, even today, the reigning cliché of American elections, it is equally significant that other institutions, such as the public schools, share with politics and the church deep roots in the immediate community. Certainly, there are contradictory tendencies that pull in the opposite direction toward centralization, but politics, religion, and education in America have historically functioned close to the community and to the individual, despite the powerful centripetal forces of nationalism, corporate capitalism, and the statist impulse of federalism.

Traditions of the congregational culture have had a parallel and powerful intellectual and moral component. It is not just political and religious energy and control that emanate from the local community, but also ideas, which frequently receive their validation from the same community. It is a long-held and much-revered notion that the "common man," whose opinions are expressed within the local community, is fully capable of understanding and deciding questions of truth without having to appeal to higher human authority or, sometimes, to the Highest Authority.

Although this sanctified individualism has energized the autodidactic tendency of American attitudes generally, it has also affected Americans' understanding of science and technology. If the United States is a nation of tinkerers (or, at least, so the mythology goes), invention itself seems the outcome of individual and local effort, rarely associated with institutions— even if this comforting narrative is a deeply dysfunctional and inaccurate description of the way prevailing technological and scientific enterprises are organized. Because experimentalism is so highly prized, grand theory is much less so. Laypersons often view the complexities of science—particularly when science and technology issues enter the political discussion or dispute religious precepts—as a challenge to the local community; the very difficulty and esoteric complexities of science have become a metaphor for statism, foreignness, and corporate science and have created a situation in which the term *scientific theory* can be defined as a questionable assertion.

None of these characteristics would matter if the local community were weak, isolated, and disorganized. But access to power is always an invitation to exercise it, and local institutions such as school boards and city councils, local administrations, and elected officials, have shown no reluctance to exercise this power. Armed with the democratic notion that the community can decide not just whom to elect (and how to worship and which ministers to employ) but also what ideas to teach in the public schools, local common sense sometimes trumps scientific expertise from outside the community.

It is precisely around this point that the perennial conflicts over Darwinism and various other scientific hypotheses have been carried on. Because of this belief in the ascendancy of local and individual reason and the capacity of the community to determine truth, popular literature rejecting Darwinian ideas has exercised a powerful sway in some American bywaters. The reasoning has not changed much since William Jennings Bryan's two-part rejection of Darwinism in the 1920s. First, he declared that German militarism in World War I had emerged from enacting the idea of the survival of the fittest (a concept he wrongly credited to Charles Darwin). But he also argued, in a metaphoric and simplistic reading of the second law of thermodynamics, that Darwinism was scientifically implausible. This common-sense argument provided a rationale for local school boards and, occasionally, state boards of education—none or few of whose members were practicing scientists or engineers—to reject perhaps the most powerful explanatory tool in biology on "scientific" grounds as well as moral principles. The same reasoning persists today among televangelists, who seem perfectly comfortable giving lectures to their virtual audiences on the scientific validity of any number of varieties of creation science.[12]

In some respects, this powerful denial and negation of mainstream science does not impinge quite as much as it could because of the deep separation between scientific theory and technology in American thought and practice. If religious organizations have been antagonistic to some of the general theories of modern science, such as the Big Bang, relativity, or global warming, they have been very comfortable about embracing technology, particularly when it relates to spreading the Word. No Luddites, they! This paradox is not a new phenomenon in American culture. If we define technology in two respects—as human engineering and the practical application of invention—we find religious organizations often at the forefront of both areas. From the late colonial period, traveling ministers roamed the bustling middle territories between the seacoast and the frontier, holding camp meetings and organizing crowds in community social and intellectual encounters that helped arouse local spirit and democratic community among dispersed settlers. Peripatetic ministers experimented with rudimentary concepts of crowd psychology by inventing tools and techniques for exciting belief. These techniques have persisted within American religious (and political) organizations. Theologically, these men wrenched open the steely grasp of Calvinism on American Protestantism, releasing every man and woman to be his or her own interpreter of scripture and responsible for his or her own salvation and fortune.

One result of this emphasis on individual and community salvation has been the remarkable fluidity of belief and divergent religious organizations, both in colonial America and then following the American Revolution. Perhaps no other people have invented more new denominations and sects and more contending religious organizations. These religious activities have taken three basic forms: (a) the invention of entirely new religions, (b) the proliferation of subclasses of denomination, and (c) the creation of mixed secular–religious organizations that would fall under the rubric of what Robert Bellah (and Jean-Jacques Rousseau) called "civil religion."[13] In the course of only a few hundred years, American culture has produced Mormonism, Christian Science, Scientology, Pentecostalism, Fundamentalism (not exactly a sect), and many others. Denominational profligacy and the evolution of competing groups within the same general rubric have brought, for example, the Southern Baptists, Primitive Baptists, liberal Baptists, Total Emersion Baptists, and Foot-Washing Baptists; indeed, there are more than twenty-five identifiable subgroups in the Baptist denomination alone. Religious and secular sects, stressing a utopian return to nature and "holism"; religiously inflected twelve-step cures for alcoholism and every imaginable compulsion and addiction; and scientific–religious organizations such as the American Scientific Affiliation add a powerful religious component to the organizational texture of American culture.[14] And beneath this religious landscape lies the sacralized patriotism of civil religion, with its hallowed mythologies of American exceptionalism and its panoply of sacred symbols and apostles.

Two points should be made about these phenomena. First, many of these groups, religious or semireligious, organized themselves in response to important social or deep-seated technological change. Thus, we see important religious developments partly as a response to changes in science and technology. For example, Mary Baker Eddy's Christian Science was deeply imbedded in a particular and popular American Victorian attitude toward medicine and society. Scientology, as its name suggests, proposed the use of modern sociology, personality tests, and social engineering concepts as the basis for a new religion. (I think, by the way, that the German and French refusal to designate this sect as a religion underscores my point about America's generous definition of religions). Fundamentalism, although it appeared to look backward and deny the modern world, in fact, had a streamlined, lean, and supple message that made communication through the mass media even more effective and compelling.

This readiness to embrace technology suggests a second, related point. American religious organizations, particularly Evangelical groups, have positioned themselves at the cutting edge of communication technology. Among the earliest groups to see the inherent possibilities in new communication techniques, they experimented early on with radio proselytizing and later developed the important innovations associated with televangelism (a technique that merged two forms of 1950s television presentation: the Billy Graham revivals and the broadcast homilies of Catholic Bishop Fulton J. Sheen). During the twentieth century, Evangelical groups produced hundreds of movies and documentaries and experimented with a huge variety of printing and mailing enterprises. This broadcasting and publishing modernism has, in turn, reinforced the mass culture structure of many of their theoretical beliefs, so that technology and theology have interacted to reinforce each other. Positioned, as they were, to recognize and then exploit technological shifts in mass culture delivery systems and intellectual and cultural fashions and enthusiasm, modern faiths have evolved rapidly and in step with these changes. Indeed, one of the contemporary controversies of American Christianity is whether churches have embraced too completely a marketing and advertising ethic.

There is further explanation for why American religious organizations have sustained their presence and dynamism in the midst of cultural change. Without a positive orientation and an optimistic and antitraditionalist perspective, religious groups might never have achieved their power to intervene in discussions of American politics, science, and the application of technologies. This forward position has emboldened religious individuals and organizations not just to adopt innovations in communication, but also to intervene powerfully in discussions about the applications of these technologies. Although some fundamentalist Protestants have waged (in alliance with the Catholic hierarchy) a still unsuccessful battle to amend or ban the technologies of birth control, their efforts to shift the argument to another technology—abortion—have come very close to success. They have been able, quite remarkably, to dominate the discussion about when life begins. They have effectively isolated science and scientists within a confusing technical and defensive vocabulary, and the very efforts of scientists to ensure the viability of a fetus have undercut their ability to define when life begins. The point is that religious organizations have positioned themselves credibly at the focal point of such discussions, drowning out secular arguments on both sides and forcing the discussion into a mode that challenges the relevance of opposing scientific ideas.

In part, this reflex opposition reflects the cultural process elsewhere called *covering*, which religious groups have borrowed from other areas of mass culture.[15] Given the amazing diversity and inventive energy of American cultural production, plus its lack of respect for preserving archaic and traditional forms, its best formula for commercial success often has been the incorporation and cover of the most innovative trends in popular culture, even in their rawest or most ethnic forms. This phenomenon has been most visible and marked in the endless borrowings from and adaptations of black culture. But what holds true in this case is similar elsewhere: cover culture is the American way of life and adaptability, its lifeblood. In similar fashion, churches and religious organizations have engaged in covering. They too adapt parallel versions of popular culture—the most notable perhaps being Christian rock 'n' roll, although many other important examples exist. Their aim is audience share: the creation of a friendly and receptive public or, rather, an opportunity to attract a larger secular mass audience. Making religion relevant to other aspects of American culture strengthens its pertinence to issues of science and technology.

Science

A crucial characteristic of the scientific–technological–religious interchange also stems from the basic way that American science has been organized historically. Although there were efforts during the nineteenth century to create an official scientific establishment in America—the Smithsonian Institution in Washington, D.C., made some gestures in this direction—by and large, scientific organizations have flourished privately, without much official sanction. This situation has changed considerably in recent decades, primarily because of the Cold War. The best example of this new situation is the National Science Foundation, which was established in 1950 by the federal government to direct and fund research. Although not ostensibly a credentialing body, its actual operation of funding projects exerts a powerful influence in determining the boundaries of legitimate science. It rejects fringe theories and projects. Its scientific board is, in most cases, self-governing, although on occasion politicians have attempted to influence its direction. This model is also typical of other government scientific research bodies, such as the National Institutes of Health, a much older research agency. Another organization, the National Academy of Sciences, is perhaps the closest to a state-sponsored national scientific bureau; however, its function is limited and its membership small, select, and often honorific.

The major scientific organization in the United States, the American Association for the Advancement of Science, is a private organization with a relatively open membership policy. It welcomed antievolutionist crusader William Jennings Bryan as a member of its astronomy section in 1925, for example. The organization also has been the site of struggles over fringe beliefs, such as creation science, cold fusion, and the like. Like all scientific organizations, one of its functions is border patrol—that is, attempting to maintain an open membership but with a limited definition of legitimate science.

Looking at the history of American higher education, one sees additional traces of a contest—or, at least, a lively dialogue—between centralizing, internationally oriented universities and a huge coterie of religiously founded private colleges. This divide reproduces to some degree the division between large, centralized science and localism. During the nineteenth century, with the initial expansion of American college and university education, a significant percentage of new colleges, and even some universities, were founded by religious organizations. Even in the twentieth century, church-accredited colleges and universities numbered more than 2,000.[16] Although these schools certainly taught the sciences as well as the humanities and religion, many were founded to train ministers and missionaries for a particular sect or faith. The large component of Catholic institutions of higher education generally followed the particular order that sponsored them. In general, most of these religious schools (outside the Catholic faith) gradually secularized until, in contemporary society, only relatively few strictly retain the old model. Thus, it is instructive to mention one institution that looks back to an earlier day to see how it manages the interface of fundamentalist religion and science. At Wheaton College in Illinois, the biology department's catalog preface quotes Colossians 1:16–17: "For by Him all things were created; things in heaven and on earth, visible and invisible, whether thrones or owners or rulers or authorities: all things were created by Him and for Him." And yet this preamble introduces a fairly typical selection of biology courses for a major—but with a difference. As a geologist from the college explains, "Thorough coursework in both geology and biblical studies in the general education curriculum generally moves the student from conflict to a complementary view of mainstream geology and history."[17] In other words, he implies that the notions of "intelligent design" and "theistic evolution" resolve the conflict between biblical and Darwinian accounts of origins.

Most major American universities, particularly during the important phase of institution building at the end of the nineteenth century, instituted thoroughly secularized curricula, and leaders in the sciences and the social sciences conscientiously organized curricula, departmental structure, and research enterprises on what they understood to be the prevailing German model. A large cohort of American students who matriculated at German universities, particularly in Heidelberg, brought back with them ideas of organization, initiative, and in particular a decidedly materialist and functionalist orientation to research.[18]

The eventual result was the organization of university science investigation and research by teams. Although this model also certainly prevails in corporate research, it is particularly the mark of contemporary academic science, with a mentor, perhaps several partners, and graduate students constituting the research group. Indeed, this is now so much the model that university bureaucratic language has evolved to describe the structure, with the lead researcher known as the *PI*, or *principal investigator*.

This organizational model might pass unremarked, except that it flies in the face of prevailing popular mythology about scientific discovery and the dynamics of scientific advancement. The narrative that Americans recount to themselves, despite considerable evidence of corporate and cooperative research, is the story of the heroic individual—the ingenious autodidact who creates a string of inventions, applies for patents for his discoveries at the U.S. Patent Office, and makes a fortune. These are the chronicles of Thomas Edison, Alexander Graham Bell, and Steve Jobs, as well as countless others. Their stories are nothing more than the typical American success story, as are those of rock stars, politicians, movie stars, executives, millionaires, and athletes. The American success story expresses a faith in individual initiative and, by implication, hostility to government bureaucracies and, with regard to science, to theoretical work. It is also a model narrative of the lives of the American saints, the evangelical ministers from the rural South or small towns or backwaters of New England, such as Joseph Smith, Dwight Moody, and Billy Graham, who defied established churches, centralized denominations, and credentialing organizations to create their own sets of beliefs and the powerful associations and megachurches to spread them. The biographies of these religious figures, along with those of inventor geniuses, constitute an important piece of the folklore of American culture. They embody the deepest affirmations of American mythologies: soaring inspirational stories of society driving the history of progress. Although their basic outlines contain some true elements, they are stories of very special individuals, and one must, in the end, conclude that neither the great inventor nor the brilliant harvester of souls is really just like everyone else.

What are the implications of this dual narrative of science and religion in American culture? We can begin our assessment with what is not unusual. American society, like those of other advanced nations, manages to maintain a fundamental separation between professional scientific organizations and laboratories and mainline religious organizations and schools of theology. They meet along jealously guarded frontiers. But these profound separations can sometimes be breached. As a result, American culture is awash with contending models of thought, in turn resulting in competing explanations and frequent challenges to the application of science and technological projects when they appear to encroach on strong religious explanations or moral regulations. This dual narrative is a sign of the continuing struggle between the disenchantment and the reenchantment of the world.[19]

This opposition has remained strong since World War II, in part because of the achievements and accumulating power of the scientific establishment, as well as the parallel rise of politically powerful evangelical forces and their dramatic entrance into politics. One result was the obvious doctoring of science by the George W. Bush administration to accommodate the hesitations of some of its key political-religious constituencies on issues of birth control technology, global warming, stem cell research, and so forth. At the same time, the forces of congregational democracy that operate at the local level continue to propose expelling the teaching of evolution from the public schools (although, generally, *not* from university biology departments) or pairing it with some version of creation science.

Perhaps even more important are proliferating shadow religious institutions: religious-scientific organizations comprising myriad religious versions of secular institutions. The almost limitless energy expended to copy and imitate reaches into all levels of American cultural life, keeping religious thinking at the forefront of politics, mass culture, and even science. This energy is readily apparent, for example, in the website Beliefnet.com, a meeting place for pop culture ecumenism that publishes articles, blogs, advertisements, editorials, and news stories aimed at helping the surfer find an appropriate faith using its "Belief-o-Matic" set of questions.[20] And one has only to look at the most widely purchased popular novels in the past 10 years, published under the general moniker "Left Behind Series" to measure this energy at work. The sixteen novels in the series by Tim LaHaye and Jerry Jenkins have sold an amazing 65 million copies, making them one of the greatest success stories in publishing history anywhere. Distributed by the Christian publishing company Tyndale House, these novels explore the days of the Final Judgment, the Tribulation, and other end-time predictions; however, they are set in the modern world, with timely allusions to current events. Using the tools of popular fiction, adventure stories, romance novels, mysteries, and science fiction, these eclectic books try to ground the biblical predictions of the end of the world in contemporary and modern scientific terms. Through the use of mass culture formats, they read the Bible as a blueprint for secular history, inventing a fictional narrative in which a religious explanation of human and natural events seems to make sense in scientific and secular terms. These novels are a far cry from the staid philosophizing of organizations such as the Institute on Religion in an Age of Science, with its membership of university professors and old-line religious affiliations devoted to finding some intellectual coherence between religion and science. And yet the two endeavors reflect something of the same compulsion of American culture to break down the separation of science and religion.

There are many other tangible results of this mix of science and religion in American life, one of them, remarkably, revealed in the beliefs of scientists about evolutionary theory. Performed in 2006, the latest Gallup Poll on the issue of evolution revealed that 55 percent of Americans asserted that humans were created by God in their present form. Another 27 percent subscribed to theistic evolution—in which God guides the process. Only 13 percent affirmed that humans evolved without divine intervention. In other words, 82 percent of Americans believed in some version of biblical or divine explanation. But an even more astonishing result came from a

1997 poll of scientists (broadly defined). As expected only, 5 percent subscribed to the biblical account of creation. Fifty-five percent affirmed some kind of naturalistic account. Still, an amazing 40 percent chose some version of theistic account, with God directing evolution. Perhaps, this finding is nothing more than evidence of Pascal's Wager.[21] However, it is revealing nonetheless that close to half of those polled believed in some form of divine explanation for human existence.

It might be argued that theistic evolution does not really matter, and that one can certainly engage in advanced science even while holding a vague belief that God is somehow hovering over the outcome or, at least, defining the principles of the universe. But the significance lies elsewhere, I think. It symbolizes the extraordinary cultural relevance of religion in all areas of American life. The result is a complex texture that seems to rest on the special elements of American culture, politics, government, and organizational life and, especially, on the particular spirit of congregational democracy and the way by which the continent was peopled, which gives American culture plausibility and power. In a market-driven universe, this gravitational attraction to religion is something that should not be underestimated.

Notes

1. Jacques Derrida, *Positions*, translated by Alan Bass (Chicago: University of Chicago, 1981), 24.

2. See table 7-9 in National Science Board, *Science and Engineering Indicators 2006*, vol. 1 (Arlington, VA: National Science Foundation, 2006), 7–38, http://www.nsf.gov/statistics/seind06/. The annual evaluation of science and technology in the United States, which is funded by the U.S. Congress, reveals some very interesting trends in American attitudes. For example, from 1977 to 2004, there was a marked decline in the prestige of scientist as a profession (falling from 66 percent to 52 percent), even though the level of prestige remains relatively high. The prestige of priest or minister as a profession fell by the same ratio in this time period, from 41 percent to 32 percent. Public attention to scientific news is also relatively low; it places near the bottom of items listed, next to religion.

3. An interesting book on American religion is by literary critic Harold Bloom, *The American Religion: The Emergence of the Post-Christian Nation* (New York: Simon & Schuster, 1992). Specifically on the interaction of religion and science, see James Gilbert, *Redeeming Culture: American Religion in an Age of Science* (Chicago: University of Chicago Press, 1997). See also Stephen J. Gould, *Rock of Ages: Science and Religion in the Fullness of Life* (New York: Ballantine, 1999). A large and important literature defines the perimeters of American religious behavior. See, for example, R. Laurence Moore, *Religious Outsiders and the Making of America* (New York: Oxford University Press, 1986); Ronald L. Numbers, *The Creation-*

ists (New York: Alfred A. Knopf, 1992); George M. Marsden, *Fundamentalism and American Culture: The Shaping of Twentieth Century Evangelicalism* (New York: Oxford University Press, 1980); Ronald L. Numbers, "Science and Religion," in *Historical Writing on American Science: Perspectives and Prospects*, ed. Sally Gregory Kohlstedt and Margaret W. Rossiter (Baltimore: Johns Hopkins University Press, 1986), 59–80.

4. Roger Finke and Rodney Stark, "Turning Pews into People: Estimating 19th Century Church Membership," *Journal for the Scientific Study of Religion* 25, no. 2 (1986): 186–87.

5. Wilbur Zelinsky, *The Cultural Geography of the United States* (Englewood Cliffs, NJ: Prentice-Hall, 1973), 13.

6. For a discussion of this important affinity, see Dipesh Chakrabarty, *Provincializing Europe: Postcolonial Thought and Historical Difference* (Princeton, NJ: Princeton University Press, 2000), 235–36.

7. Frank Lambert, *Religion in American Politics: A Short History* (Princeton, NJ: Princeton University Press, 2008), 14–40.

8. Nathan Hatch, *The Democratization of American Christianity* (New Haven, CT: Yale University Press, 1989).

9. On church finances, see, for example, James Hudnut-Beumler, *In Pursuit of the Almighty's Dollar: A History of Money and American Protestantism* (Chapel Hill: University of North Carolina Press, 2007). See also John Hardin, "Retailing Religion: Business Promotionalism in American Christian Churches in the Twentieth Century" (PhD diss., University of Maryland, College Park, 2011).

10. Other groups, such as the Moravians, were important as well as controversial. See Aaron Spencer Fogleman, *Jesus Is Female: Moravians and the Challenge of Radical Religion in Early America* (Philadelphia: University of Pennsylvania Press, 2007).

11. William McLoughlin, *Revivals, Awakenings, and Reform: An Essay on Religion and Social Change in America, 1607–1977* (Chicago: University of Chicago Press, 1978).

12. On the Scopes Trial, see Edward J. Larson, *Summer of the Gods: The Scopes Trial and America's Continuing Debate over Science and Religion* (New York: Basic Books, 1997). The same sort of hesitation, coupled with an intensive advertising campaign of energy-supplying companies, has generated widespread doubt about mainstream scientific acceptance of global warming and its causes.

13. Robert Bellah, "Civil Religion in America," *Daedalus* 96, no. 1 (1967): 1–21.

14. For information on the American Scientific Affiliation and its attitudes toward religion and science, see James Gilbert, *Redeeming Culture* (Chicago: University of Chicago Press: 1997), 147–69.

15. I do not wish to imply that American religions are distinct from mass culture. Indeed, they constitute an important element of it.

16. Constant H. Jacquet Jr., ed., *Yearbook of American and Canadian Churches, 1973* (Nashville, TN: Abingdon Press, 1973), 109–10.

17. Stephen O. Moshier, "History and Future of the Relationship between the Geosciences and Religion: Litigation, Education, Reconciliation?," *Geological Society of America Abstracts with Programs* 35 (2003): 610. Other colleges with similar programs include Calvin College in Grand Rapids, Michigan, and Bryan College (named after William Jennings Bryan) in Dayton, Tennessee, the scene of the Scopes Trial.

18. Dorothy Ross, *The Origins of American Social Science* (New York: Cambridge University Press, 1991).

19. One scientist suggested in 1977 that the differences between science and religion had been minimized among scientists because, he said, "We are not wise to have that body politic seeing science as antagonistic to spiritual commitment." In effect, he was arguing that these differences might have compromised public funding of science. Gregg Easterbrook, "Science and God: A Warming Trend?," *Science* 277, no. 5328 (1977): 890–93.

20. See http://www.beliefnet.com/About-Us/Our-Mission.aspx. One of the featured articles tries to reconcile evolution and creation: "Conversations with God," a blog by Neale Donald Walsch. The site also includes recipes, advice, movie guides, spiritual suggestions, horoscopes, and other entries.

21. French philosopher Blaise Pascal argued that it was impossible to prove the existence of God but, nonetheless, with nothing to lose, living as though God exists was a bet worth making.

Chapter 8

Science, Religion, and the Modern State: A View from the History of Science

Ronald E. Doel

Wine glasses clinked worldwide in 2009 as scientists toasted the 200th anniversary of Charles Darwin's birth. It was a landmark year for another reason: it marked the 150th anniversary of *On the Origin of Species*, the seminal work in which Darwin developed the theory of natural selection, a cornerstone of modern biology. In Western Europe—where 70 to 80 percent of the population accepted the idea that humans evolved from earlier life forms—Darwin's ideas were celebrated as a profound intellectual achievement.[1]

I am very grateful for critical comments on an earlier draft by Volker Depkat, Gary B. Ferngren, James B. Gilbert, Kristine C. Harper, Jürgen Martschukat, and numerous colleagues at the Krefeld Historical Symposium in 2008. I am no less grateful for support for this research from the Department of History at Florida State University, the BOREAS Programme of the European Science Foundation, and the National Science Foundation (Grant 0922651).

In the United States, however, public commemorations of Darwin's anniversary had an edgier tone. Despite America's status as a leading scientific and economic superpower, only four in ten Americans accepted that evolution had actually occurred. A quarter of the population firmly believed evolution to be false. A major court battle over the teaching of intelligent design (*Kitzmiller v. Dover Area School District*, dubbed *Scopes II*) had just ended in 2005, eighty years after the famous Scopes Trial had addressed the issue of teaching evolution in public schools. As *The Economist* noted, among industrial nations only Turkey—the largest democracy in the Muslim world, its secular government in power since only 1923—ranked lower than the United States in public acceptance of evolution, at 25 percent.[2]

Concerning evolution, the United States (compared to its industrial, democratic counterparts) is indeed exceptional. But focusing on flashpoint conflicts between science and religion may distract us from what is particularly interesting about their relationship. A quarter-century ago, historians of science became convinced that the presumed warfare between science and religion was a myth. They did so, however, only after examining a related topic, the relationship between ideology and science—spurred on in the West by national leaders interested in discovering links between science and democratization during the early decades of the Cold War.

This story is largely unfamiliar to historians of religion and culture. At the same time, historians of science are still laboring to grasp the extent to which the large narrative of the Enlightenment—the rise of rationality and its application to material culture through technology—is only one strand of conflicting metanarratives about meaning, spirituality, and values. A growing number of historians sense that much remains to be done to bridge what historian Peter Harrison has termed the dissociation of wisdom and science.[3] Our insights about these issues nevertheless remain limited because heated evolution–creationist battles have often distracted scholars from examining how larger religious and scientific matters have played out across the political and scientific spectrum in the United States and elsewhere during the twentieth century.

To appreciate the current state of affairs requires understanding how historians of science over the past century constructed—and then revised—an account of science's relation to religion. This chapter begins by revealing how historians in the early Cold War period came to see ideological influences of any kind as distortions of the production of knowledge, thereby limiting appreciation of the extent to which scientific practices are influenced by society and culture. It then addresses the challenges of writing narratives about the engagement of science and religion in the United States since the start of the twentieth century, with the hardening cultural divide between those who favor materialist explanations for natural phenomena and those who see the universe in spiritual terms. It ends by considering what we still do not know about the intersection between religion and science and how biographical narratives can profitably reveal these relationships.

Creating and Dispelling Myths about the War between Religion and Science

The idea that science and religion have been at war with each other emerged during the nineteenth century. It first arose between 1810 and 1840, when, as historian Ronald L. Numbers argued, "men of science pushed successively to replace the supernatural creation of the solar system with the nebular hypothesis, to expand the history of life on earth from 6,000 to millions of years, and to shrink Noah's flood to a regional event in the Near East," leaving some theologians convinced that "infidel science" was exposing Christians to attack.[4] But it took on its modern form, as a conflict between competing worldviews, in the final decades of that century. In 1896, Andrew Dickson White published *A History of the Warfare of Science with Theology in Christendom*. President of Cornell University from 1866 to 1885, White had insisted that "Christian theologians had a long history of opposing scientific progress in the interest of dogmatic theology." His self-proclaimed role was to let "the light of historical truth into that decaying mass of outworn thought which attaches the modern world to decaying mediaeval conceptions of Christianity, and which still lingers among us—a most serious barrier to religion and morals, and a menace to the whole normal evolution of society."[5]

White was not the first to make this argument in the United States; the chemist and historian John William Draper had made similar points in his 1874 *History of the Conflict between Religion and Science*.[6] But White's book, published during the second Industrial Revolution and amid the reforming impulses of the Progressive Era, gained a wide audience. White's polemic was motivated by several factors. He insisted on limiting religious influences in U.S. universities, where graduate programs were just taking root.[7] As U.S. ambassador to Russia when he completed his book, White also came to see the "barbarism of the Russian czars" as undermining scientific autonomy, which he defined as "the exceptional agency of great men striving against deeply pernicious character traits instilled by theological training."[8] White's assessment, as historian of religion Gary Ferngren accurately notes, soon became "the predominant view of the relationship between science and religion among scientists and laymen alike" into the twenty-first century, wedding "a triumphalist view of science with a patronizing view of religion."[9]

Historians and sociologists with an interest in science—very few of either existed until the 1930s—generally ignored these arguments. They were, by and large, interested in other issues. At Harvard University, George Sarton, the Belgian-born scholar now regarded as the father of the modern discipline of history of science, labored to complete a general introduction to the history of science from Homer to the twentieth century, finishing only through the fourteenth century before his death.[10] Sociologist Robert K. Merton, also at Harvard through 1938, sought to find the norms of science, later denoted by the acronym CUDOS: communalism, universalism, disinterestedness, and organized skepticism. But Merton was equally intrigued by the influence of religious and cultural values on science. The Merton Thesis, stemming from his 1935 dissertation research, held that modern science had been given a boost in seventeenth-century England by the reformed Protestant movement of Puritanism, whose emphasis on diligence, industry, and education—combined with increased trade and international commerce—had stimulated new interest in studying nature.[11]

One might have expected that the Merton Thesis would have encouraged further research into cultural influences on the production of knowledge. Scholars at the time recognized that Merton had written on science in Protestant England in part to refute a study by the Soviet historian Boris Hessen, presented at the Second International Congress of the History of Science in London in 1931, that partially attempted to explain Isaac Newton's achievements as an effort to solve technical problems facing the English bourgeoisie.[12] Although some dismissed Hessen's work as "vulgar Marxism," he was among the first to challenge the prevailing idea that science was the product of genius rather than a community activity shaped by local values.[13] That this did not happen owes in part to World War II and the influence of James B. Conant, president of Harvard University, wartime science administrator, and one of the nation's most influential educators.

A key challenge that Conant took up during the war was how to teach science in the postwar world. In 1943, Conant had set up the Harvard Committee on the Objectives of a General Education in a Free Society, which two years later produced *General Education in a Free Society*, one of the most influential texts in the history of U.S. higher education.[14] His particular concern was to foster the "necessary bonds and common ground" among citizens living now in a "technological age" that had "accelerated democracy's natural tendency to produce difference and division."[15] Conant saw history of science (in the high schools as well as at the university level) as particularly suited for this task: free inquiry in science would aid capitalism, the modern industrial state, and democratization. The issue became more urgent after the United States used atomic weapons against Japan in 1945. The atomic bomb, Conant declared, was the price paid for "health and comfort in this scientific age"; citizens needed to understand that technology was a tool that democratic states could safely use. Conant's "case studies" approach, developed at Harvard immediately after the war ended, sought to reveal the "tactics and strategy of science," progressing from technical details to the nature of science itself. As historian Michael A. Dennis has observed, "A society educated through the case studies Conant envisioned would possess an immunity to totalitarianism as well as a desire to support scientific research."[16]

In certain respects—certainly on an academic level—Conant's program was extraordinarily influential. It inspired the first professional generation of historians of science to examine the production of knowledge in the natural sciences, particularly during the Scientific Revolution, when the natural sciences had taken root. Occurring within the context of the Cold War, Conant's program also inspired certain practitioners to focus on the intersection of ideology and science, including the efforts of states to promote "ideologically correct" science. As historian Mark Walker has noted, this emphasis led to several seminal studies, including Charles C. Gillispie's examination of science during the French Revolution, David Joravsky's study of the rise of Lysenkoism in the Stalinist era, and numerous accounts of National Socialism's influence on German science. Few of these works explicitly addressed religion. But an undercurrent of this scholarship was that religious influence was a form of ideology: a distorting influence that was pernicious to the pursuit of objective knowledge about the natural world.[17]

Conant's determination to illuminate the boundaries between science and nonscience (in his view, between rational, reliable knowledge and superstition) and how these borders became established bore poignant fruit— particularly in the writings of one of his Harvard instructors, Thomas S.

Kuhn. Like many young scholars in his generation, Kuhn was particularly concerned with what later generations would call "internal" history of science: a history of ideas, with their external applications relegated to the distinct realms of history of technology and history of medicine. Like Conant, he was interested in the dynamic interplay between conceptual schemes and experiment.[18] In working through his ideas—from his 1956 *Copernican Revolution* to his 1962 *Structure of Scientific Revolutions*—Kuhn considered how knowledge was generated and affirmed within scientific communities.[19] *Structure* became not only his most celebrated work, but also one of the most important humanities texts in the twentieth century. It made clear that scientific ideas were not strictly cumulative but could face periods of upheaval and discontinuity during times when distinct paradigms—such as geocentricism and heliocentrism—shifted. Kuhn was not particularly interested in the role that religion played in developing ideas about the natural world. But *Structure* was a slow-acting time bomb, for in it Kuhn reaffirmed the idea that science was influenced by social and cultural factors and that the study of science needed to simultaneously examine larger sociopolitical issues.[20]

Some time passed before historians began to explore the ramifications of Kuhn's ideas for religion. Indeed, much writing about the history of modern science in the 1960s and early 1970s continued to reinforce the special character of science and its relationship to Western values. For instance, Herbert Butterfield's widely used *The Origins of Modern Science* (1957 revised edition) proclaimed that the Scientific Revolution had outshone "everything since the rise of Christianity and reduces the Renaissance and Reformation to the rank of mere episodes, mere internal displacements within the system of medieval Christendom."[21] Butterfield had built his reputation on his 1931 *The Whig Interpretation of History*, which had critiqued accounts that cast historical developments moving toward an inevitable and glorious present.[22] But Butterfield—a British citizen intimately aware that radar had won the battle of Britain during World War II and that the atomic bomb had ended it—had himself written a Whiggish history of science, one in which the triumph of good scientific ideas seemed inevitable.[23]

By the 1970s, however, a new generation of historians of science began to question these narratives—a development that would have profound consequences for understanding the role of cultural factors in the production of knowledge. One of the most influential of these new undertakings came from the early modern scholar Betty Jo Teeter Dobbs, who devoted much of her career to examining the life of Newton. Instead of focusing on Newton's achievements in terrestrial and celestial physics and optics—which left him seemingly an eighteenth-century "modern" who was intellectually orphaned in the early seventeenth century—Dobbs examined Newton's philosophical and religious commitments. In her influential works, including *The Foundation of Newton's Alchemy, or "The Hunting of the Green Lyon"* (1975) and *The Janus Faces of Genius: The Role of Alchemy in Newton's Thought* (1991), Dobbs portrayed a Newton far from a premature "modern" and instead firmly embedded in his time: her Newton was concerned with Biblical chronologies, with discovering uncorrupted original texts and recovering untainted early knowledge to discern divine activity in the world. He was deeply engaged with the religious views of his age.[24]

Not surprisingly, Dobbs's interpretation—as well as those that followed hers—was less than enthusiastically received by scientists (just as many scientists had been perturbed by Kuhn's unintended challenge to the objectivity of science and his claim that successful lines of research under old paradigms were sometimes abandoned in their successors).[25] Indeed, Dobbs found that a previous keeper of Newton's papers, the British Astronomer Royal David Brewster, had privately written in 1855 that "we cannot understand how a mind of such power, and so nobly occupied with the abstractions of geometry, and the study of the material world, could stoop to be even the copyist of the most contemptible alchemical poetry, and the annotator of a work, the obvious production of a fool and a knave."[26] This historical Newton deeply challenged Conant's confident expectation that the history of science would disclose the clear boundary between science and superstition.[27]

Nevertheless, Dobbs's studies—reinforcing other original interpretations that had begun to demonstrate the influence of social and cultural factors on the production of natural knowledge, such as those by Frances Yates, Alexandre Koyré, and Michael Polanyi—opened a floodgate of new scholarship.[28] In recent years, historians of science have begun exploring intimate and sometimes surprising relationships between religion and various branches of twentieth-century science. For instance, historians have realized that Soviet cosmologists in the 1960s were genuinely concerned that their Western counterparts seemed unduly enamored by Judeo–Christian idealizations about the beginning of the world when the Big Bang theory gained popularity over the competing steady-state model. Within the United States, historians of science came to recognize that Frederic E. Clements's theory of ecological succession—one of the most influential concepts in mid-twentieth-century ecology—contained in its concept of a climax community a distinct teleological element.[29]

Several insights from this new research are particularly profound. Perhaps the most important case may be in the consideration of the historical relationship of science and religion in Islam. Postwar historical accounts held that Islamic science reached an apex between the twelfth and fifteenth centuries, diminishing just as medieval European science began showing signs of life. The presumed cause of this decline was an imposition of Islamic religious rule following the sacking of Baghdad in 1258. But historian of science David C. Lindberg recently reached a very different conclusion. He finds no evidence of a decline, which was an assumption that earlier scholars could have refuted by using manuscript sources. Islamic scholars continued to make advances into the fifteenth century, even after the Christian reconquest of Spain was well under way. For Lindberg, the better question to ask was not when Islamic science declined or which culture had outperformed the other in the race for superiority in natural science, but rather, "How is it that an intellectual tradition began in such unpromising circumstances developed an astonishing scientific tradition that endured as long as it did?" Indeed, Lindberg has concluded that Islamic preeminence in the mathematical sciences "lasted well over half a millennium—a longer period than the interval between Copernicus and ourselves."[30] It is hardly the only misconception of this kind to have been recently overturned. Since the beginning of the twentieth century, generations of American schoolchildren were taught that Christopher Columbus's sailors were terrified about sailing off the edge of the flat earth—a false narrative designed to discredit the Catholic Church that fit well into White's antireligious framework.[31] We cannot feel confident that our narratives about the relationship of science and religion are reliable if, as Lindberg puts it, they served primarily as useful tools "in religious polemics over the relative merits of Islam and Christianity: which religious culture wins the natural sciences sweepstakes?"[32]

Clashing Worldviews and Polemical Accounts: Ethics, Morality, and Standing

What historians of science now insist is the most accurate interpretation of the engagement between science and religion—that there was and is no

war—has not escaped the ivory tower. Historian Ronald Numbers has succinctly framed the issue: "The secular public, if it thinks about such issues
at all, *knows* that organized religion has always opposed scientific progress
(witness the attacks on Galileo, Darwin, and Scopes). The religious public
knows that science has taken the leading role in corroding faith (through
naturalism and antibiblicalism)."[33]

Numbers has put his finger on something important here, for these two
competing master narratives have come to embody perceptions of interactions between science and religion in America. For modernists, conservative religious advocates opposed to evolution are battling against reason
and rational thinking—attacking Enlightenment values and a hard-won understanding of the natural world. But for literalist religious conservatives,
privileging the claims emerging from scientific inquiry limits insights into
ethics, morality, and transcendent truths, a process the historian Peter Harrison has termed "the disassociation of wisdom and knowledge."[34] That the
terms *science* and *religion* sometimes defy clear definition—the French
philosopher Auguste Comte promoted a "religion of humanity" whereas
the early nineteenth-century scriptural geologists demonstrated the planet's
considerable age—has mattered little for those seeking to use these master
narratives to win larger cultural and political debates.[35]

Although the historians John Brooke and Geoffrey Cantor have correctly noted that one can "construct a narrative very different in flavour
from those preoccupied with conflict"[36]—with the advantage of illuminating cultural, political, and social issues left unaddressed in more polemical
accounts—such accounts are rare. The more familiar narrative is certainly
reflected in Draper's 1874 *History of the Conflict between Religion and
Science*, in which Draper argued that the history of science was "a narrative of the conflict of two contending powers, the expansive force of the
human intellect on one side, and the compression arising from traditional
faith and human interests in the other."[37] This view—equating rejection
of evolution with a rejection of modernity itself, owing to fundamentalist
beliefs and anti-intellectualism—was reinforced just after the Scopes Trial
not only by the prominent essayist H. L. Mencken but also by the journalist and crusader Maynard Shipley, who declared in *The War on Modern
Science* (1927) that religious fundamentalists were "bitterly opposed ... to
the *method of science* in general."[38] At the time that Mencken and Shipley
were writing, the catch-all term *American fundamentalism* came into widespread use, and what defined it was the conflict over teaching evolution in
public schools.[39]

In the present, with some 15 percent of U.S. citizens telling pollsters that they interpret the Bible literally, including a literal six-day creation, conflict narratives have remained popular.[40] Journalist and cultural historian Susan Jacoby, noting that an additional 15 percent of Americans not identified as religious conservatives also reject evolution, has argued that what is truly exceptional about America is that its citizens are woefully ignorant about basic scientific concepts. Two-thirds of Americans surveyed at the beginning of the twenty-first century could not identify DNA as the basis for heredity, nine in ten had no grasp of radioactivity, and one in five thought the sun revolves around the earth. Like Mencken and Shipley eighty years earlier, Jacoby found the religion–evolution battle "a microcosm of all the cultural forces responsible for the prevalence of unreason in American society today."[41] To a large extent, Jacoby drew her inspiration from Richard Hofstadter's classic 1963 *Anti-intellectualism in American Life*,[42] which argued that anti-intellectualism was "the flip side of America's democratic impulses in religion and education."[43] Because fundamentalists sought a personal relationship with God, they were resistant to ecclesiastical structures and equally opposed to "the modernizing and secularizing trends long associated with intellectualism."[44] Hofstadter had identified a key fault line in the American political fabric, and subsequent studies would confirm that religious conservatives were indeed correct that scientists were more secular than the public at large: 38 percent of U.S. scientists in 2008 did not believe in God (with 41 percent of biologists self-identifying as atheists), while at its most elite levels, fully 72 percent of National Academy of Sciences members were atheists and 21 percent agnostic; only 7 percent admitted belief in a personal God.[45] But although Hofstadter's insightful study portrayed crucial aspects of American exceptionalism, his broadbrush characterization of fundamentalism provided little light on the diversity of views among conservative religious Americans.[46]

We may learn more by focusing less on battles over evolution and more on attitudes toward technology, where in America the first and second Industrial Revolutions caused remarkably little conflict for religious conservatives. As historian James B. Gilbert has argued, literalists in general have wholeheartedly supported the advance of technology, and—like the population at large—accepted that science and technology are intimately related.[47] Indeed, Americans of all stripes have long shown a deep, abiding faith in technology. Perry Miller, the mid-twentieth-century intellectual historian who introduced the term *technological sublime*, declared that New England Puritans gleefully "flung themselves in the technological torrent ... and cried to one another as they went headlong down the chute that here was their destiny."[48] The story is remarkably rich. One reason that many fundamentalists embraced technology was that it resonated with the common-sense realism at the heart of Baconianism, widely accepted by English and American Protestants.[49] Historian David Noble has also noted that technology—a measure of modern enlightenment—draws deeply on religious myths, and religious belief is manifest in the technological enterprise: "Perhaps nowhere is the intimate connection between religion and technology more manifest than in the United States," he wrote, "where an unrivaled popular enchantment with technological advance is matched by an equally earnest popular expectation of Jesus Christ's return."[50] Religious symbolism certainly permeated the public pronouncements of Wernher von Braun, director of the National Aeronautics and Space Administration's Marshall Space Flight Center and the preeminent rocket engineer of his generation.[51] Acceptance of technological advancements by religious conservatives may also explain why Americans are less concerned over genetically modified foods than their Western European counterparts and why, in contrast to Europe, ethical criteria do not figure in U.S. patent law.[52]

But if many Americans, from strict biblical literalists to secularists, have an abiding faith in technology (and technological fixes), it is equally the case that few seem willing to accept science as the final word on the boundary between spirituality and the rational world. Herein may lie yet another narrative that is less well explored. Although the late astrophysicist and science popularizer Carl Sagan declared in his successful 1980 *Cosmos* television series that scientific inquiry was a satisfying substitute for religious faith, relatively few U.S. citizens agreed.[53] More remained convinced that science was helpful, even exciting and wondrous, but hardly infallible. As the mathematician and philosopher Alfred North Whitehead put it in 1925, there were discarded scientific ideas as well as theological ones—and despite the modernist expectation that when science and religion clashed, "religion was always wrong, and ... science is always right," real-life cases turned out to be more complex.[54]

We can learn a great deal by studying such instances. One illuminating boundary clash of this sort involves contemporary studies seeking to determine the evolutionary basis for ethics, and whether religious belief itself is an outgrowth of biological evolution. Recent-generation historians of science, including Paul Lawrence Farber, have used historical studies to challenge contemporary researchers confident that norms of ethical behavior can be better explained by biology than by historical interpretations

of human societies at distinct periods. For instance, Farber has challenged
the evolutionary biologist Edward O. Wilson's claim, rooted in his theory
of sociobiology, that because certain adaptive social practices appear pref-
erentially selected over time, evolutionary biologists are better equipped
than historians and social scientists to analyze human history. For Farber,
prior claims by biologists about the average intelligence of distinct ethnic
groups and the desirability of applying eugenics to weed out criminality
ought to warn us that confident claims of knowledge sometimes reflect cultural biases—today as in the past.[55] This caution could also perhaps apply
to the work of secular scholars studying the evolution of the human brain.
Several such scholars have become increasingly convinced that a preference for religious feelings is driven by evolution—a line of reasoning, for
instance, used by biologist Richard Dawkins in his polemics against the
legitimacy and value of religion.[56] Some researchers have been surprised
to discover that, in the words of science writer Robin Marantz Henig, individuals expecting religion would be invoked to answer fewer questions
about the natural world in an age of science were wrong: "No matter how
much science can explain, it seems, the real gap that God fills is an empti-
ness that our big-brained mental architecture interprets as a yearning for
the supernatural."[57]

Put another way, it may be another instance where master narratives
of conflict fail to adequately illuminate larger societal tensions. The arguments of Dawkins aside, secular thinkers have pointed to the loss of
coherent larger stories in modern society to explain the human condition.
Philosopher of science Michael Ruse has argued that we cannot appreciate larger cultural conflicts over spirituality without realizing that religion
itself has struggled since the Enlightenment to provide a clear picture of
the future. Ruse found "surprising similarities between evolutionist and
creationist thinking" in their mutual hostility, as well as their evangelical
drive to gather new recruits. In his view, these two ideologies have, since
the Enlightenment, "offered rival religious responses to a crisis of faith—
rival stories of origins, rival judgments about the meaning of human life,
rival sets of moral dictates, and above all what theologians call rival es-
chatologies—pictures of the future and what lies ahead for humankind."[58]
Historian Peter Harrison similarly has argued that a key problem is that
"the science–religion relation is a creature of the categories 'science' and
'religion' that emerged during the course of the sixteenth and seventeenth
centuries," masking a boundary dispute between professions over cultural
power and prestige. By the nineteenth century, science was seen to exclude

aesthetic, ethical, and theological considerations, whereas wisdom came "to denote a holistic, non-technical, mode of knowing" that was "the antipathy of scientific knowledge." The disjuncture of wisdom and science, Harrison argued, and their disengagement from the inner moral compasses of individuals, is what has fundamentally shaped the contemporary engagement of science, theology, and religion.[59]

These insights by Ruse and Harrison may help place contemporary conflicts over religion, science, and evolution in America into more fruitful categories of analysis and shift the focus further from well-trod tales of conflict. This move may nevertheless prove difficult for contemporary issues now at center stage in the "science versus religion" divide. The Dover, Pennsylvania, trial over the teaching of intelligent design in 2005 — presided over by Judge John E. Jones III, who was appointed to the federal bench by the conservative U.S. president George W. Bush — concluded that intelligent design was a religious notion rather than a scientific theory. Judge Jones's verdict that intelligent design was a modified form of creationism and, thus, had no place in public school science classes reaffirmed federal policies in place for more than a quarter-century and was widely praised by many contemporary observers, not least because of the questionable ethics of then–Dover Area School District school board members.[60] The *Dover* decision came amid new challenges to evolution promoted by the Discovery Institute, a well-funded and politically sophisticated Seattle-based think tank. (Despite declaring religious neutrality, several Discovery Institute leaders have averred that modernity's commitment to rationality and science, while excellent in discerning regularities in nature, is "woefully deficient at discerning the hand of God against the backdrop of those regularities."[61]) The religious right is better organized politically than at any point in U.S. history; creation ministries have flourished; and the issue of evolution, in ways never experienced in Europe or Japan, is now interwoven into national partisan divisions, with the conservative wing of the Republican Party having included it in its political platform.[62] Significant as these developments are, however, they challenge the historian to conceive of interpretations that go beyond affirming master narratives of conflict that seem less satisfying when set in the nineteenth or early twentieth centuries.[63]

It is, of course, a challenge for many contemporary historians of modern science to remain emotionally disengaged from attacks, whether religiously or politically based, on the most well-established and supported scientific theories of their own age, including the theory of evolution. Similarly challenging is the hot-button issue of anthropogenic climate change, which suggests for those who accept the validity of the science certain urgent political actions, with a tragedy-of-the-commons outcome for those who ignore evidence of accelerating warming.[64] As with evolution, polls show a significant partisan and educational gap over public attitudes toward global warming, with conservatives growing more convinced over time that news of global warming "is generally exaggerated."[65] But a less often noticed criticism voiced by individuals who reject both evolution and anthropogenic climate change is that both scientific fields for them appear tainted by ideology and beholden to interested patrons offering grants: they see few differences between climate modelers, evolutionary biologists, or tobacco company researchers who found no evidence linking cigarettes to cancer.[66] In part, this view reflects a declining faith in experts in the United States, which—like trust in government—fell precipitously after the late 1950s (an 80 percent decline by 1976).[67] It is perhaps ironic that the largest legacy of James B. Conant's case studies program, via Thomas Kuhn's work, was increased public awareness that cultural factors could affect science.

Francis Fukuyama's post–Cold War optimism that Western liberal democracy was the pinnacle of humanity's sociocultural evolution—*The End of History*, as he termed it—now seems very misplaced.[68] A large divide clearly remains between those who hold spiritual views of the universe and those who favor materialist explanations. Complex issues involving science, ethics, religion, and meaning will certainly continue to roil industrial nation-states.[69]

Unanswered Questions and Fruitful Topics

All of this discussion reminds us how little we actually know about the relationship of science and religion in the modern state. Apart from the well-studied conflict between creationists and the scientific community in twentieth-century America, we understand relatively little about certain basic issues: for instance, how Catholics viewed potential careers in science or the extent of Jesuit influence on research in fields where its adherents specialized, such as seismology.[70] We also have surprisingly few insights into Jewish traditions and influences within American science, apart from studies documenting the depth of anti-Semitism within U.S. university departments and research facilities, particularly before the outbreak of World War II.[71] Overarching inquiries into the nature of Jewish scientists and the secularization of U.S. culture—such as David A. Hollinger's *Science, Jews, and Secular Culture*—are rare.[72] It is this dearth of scholarship that makes the insights of James Gilbert (chapter 7) and Monika Wohlrab-Sahr and Thomas Schmidt-Lux (chapter 9) in this volume particularly important.[73]

Our ignorance about these relationships at least partially reflects the inadvertent narrowing of inquiry inspired by Cold War assumptions about what mattered for science, democratization, and secular culture. For instance, when the Center for History of Physics of the American Institute of Physics established an oral history program in the history of physics in the 1960s, framework questions were drawn up to be asked of all interviewees in addition to those specific to each individual: What kinds of homes did you grow up in? Who were your parents, and what did they do? Which newspapers and magazines did you read? What hobbies did you pursue? This approach was wise, for these standard questions ultimately yielded an immense storehouse of information for demographic analysis. Yet the only explicit question asked about religion was, "Were your parents religious when you were growing up?" A final question—"As you look back over your life, were there any guiding principles, religious or philosophical, that you've felt have been very important to you?"—did inspire some scientists to reflect on their movement toward (or away from) faith during their lives. But implicit in the framework question set was an assumption that religious issues were more important to the family of origin than to the interviewee. This was a missed opportunity to learn more about religious views of American scientists.[74]

The mixed messages elicited by the final framework question also remind us that scientists' commitment to faith is often more variable over time than their commitment to the values of their professional community. Historian Gary Ferngren correctly argues that historians of science now "attempt to avoid presentist and essentialist approaches, which often have influenced our historical understanding of both religion and science."[75] But the essentialism that Ferngren has in mind, that "an idea or a discipline is basically the same in all ages," must also be applied to *individuals*.[76] This is famously the case for Darwin himself, whose religious faith, already weakening as he sailed on the *Beagle*, was deeply undermined by the deaths of his father in 1849 and his beloved daughter Annie in 1851, when Darwin was forty-two.[77]

A clearer understanding of the dynamic interactions between religion and science will emerge when we have more life stories of scientists that include this dimension. As historians Brooke and Cantor have rightly argued, "a biographical approach may show that ... piety and a commitment to the investigation of nature could co-exist in one and the same person. It may reveal anxiety, even torment, as new ideas were assimilated. It may reveal a whole range of strategies worked out by a particular individual to preserve a living faith and a scientific integrity. Or again, it may reveal impiety and hostility toward established religions."[78] This approach has already yielded illuminating portraits of religious naturalists struggling with the materialistic implications of Darwinism at the turn of the twentieth century.[79]

A hint of what may continue to emerge from such future work can be gleaned from the life story of the geochemist J. Laurence Kulp (1921–2006). A Princeton PhD, Kulp joined the Department of Geology at Columbia University in 1947 at a time when the earth sciences were rapidly expanding. Soon thereafter, Kulp spent time at the University of Chicago with the nuclear chemist Willard Libby, who had developed the technique of radioactive carbon dating and applied it to a wide range of problems in archeology (assigning dates to Egyptian mummies and to ancient fossils). By the early 1950s, Kulp began applying this technique in the physical environmental sciences, using radioactivity produced by U.S. atomic tests in the Pacific to study the motion of deep ocean currents, which were then little understood. Simultaneously, he became coleader of an initially secret project, which was code-named Project Sunshine and funded by the Atomic Energy Commission, to determine the extent to which humans around the world had been exposed to nuclear fallout. By the 1960s, Kulp had gained a solid reputation for evaluating the global spread of nuclear fallout, for studying the dynamic environment of the world oceans, and for training a new generation of U.S. geochemists to use these revolutionary techniques. Sensing commercial opportunities, Kulp left Columbia University to manage a company he had founded, Isotopes Inc., and later directed a controversial acid rain assessment for the Reagan administration.[80]

That was the Kulp known to earth scientists. But for individuals primarily concerned with the intersection of Christian faith and science in mid-twentieth-century America, Kulp was best known as a promising junior star of the American Scientific Affiliation (ASA), a big-umbrella organization of evangelical scientists who sought to undermine "unscientific defenses of the Bible" by correlating "the facts of science and the Holy Scriptures."[81] Before he reached Princeton, Kulp was a graduate of conservative Wheaton College in Illinois and was initially opposed to evolutionary theory. Kulp had hoped to inspire youth toward Christianity by reducing apparent contradictions between modern science and theology. In the late 1940s, Kulp introduced to ASA members the dating methods he learned from Libby, arguing that human origins had occurred at least hundreds of thousands of years in the past. Increasingly convinced that Christians needed to accommodate their readings of scripture according to modern science, Kulp blasted literal readings of Noah's account, arguing that the "science of geology precludes certain interpretations of Genesis, but does not make impossible acceptance of plenary inspiration of the scriptures."[82]

Kulp's declarations came at the same time as the publication of a singularly influential book by the theologian Bernard Ramm, *The Christian View of Science and Scripture* (1954), which sought to reconcile fundamentalist and modernist approaches through the concept of progressive creation. Although Ramm hoped that his theological formulation would undermine support for flood geology and young-Earth traditions within American fundamentalism, his arguments—joined by Kulp's insistence on the primacy of scientific evidence—in fact divided evangelicals in the United States and caused a rupture within the ASA. Outraged by Ramm, Kulp, and the willingness of ASA leaders to accept evolution—and also convinced that their views subverted the foundations of Christianity—then–ASA members John C. Whitcomb and Henry Morris (a hydrological engineer by training) in 1961 wrote *The Genesis Flood*, an instant hit among literalist Christians, with sales ultimately exceeding 200,000 copies. More than any other single factor, *The Genesis Flood* inspired the energetic creationist movement that emerged in the second half of the twentieth century. The willingness of Kulp and many other ASA members to accept evolution also inspired Morris to establish the Institute for Creation Research, which insisted on a literal and common-sense reading of scripture in interpreting the physical world.[83]

These two narratives appear to be distinct. But they are, in fact, intertwined: Kulp was a single individual, and tracing the unitary thread of his life reveals fascinating intersections between American science and religious faith. At Columbia University in the 1950s, Kulp saw himself promoting a more progressive theology among fellow fundamentalists, thereby creating a pathway for young, conservative Christians to enter science. But his more secular colleagues at Columbia regarded Kulp—and the army of clean-cut young evangelicals (most wearing white bobby socks) that he recruited to his geochemical laboratory—as "theochemists." Indeed, some of Kulp's colleagues believed that Kulp was hoping to discover evidence favoring Bishop James Ussher's 1654 calculation that the world had been created in 4004 B.C.[84] His former graduate student Wallace Broecker, who succeeded Kulp as director of Columbia's Geochemistry Laboratory and later won the U.S. National Medal of Science, later dismissed Kulp as "Elmer Gantry," the infamous narcissistic preacher from Sinclair Lewis's late 1920s novel.[85] But Broecker himself had been a conservative evangelical Christian as a teenager, had attended Wheaton College (where Kulp had recruited him to Columbia), and had remained an active member of the ASA well into the late 1950s. Although later in life Broecker drifted far from his conservative religious roots, others trained by Kulp, including Karl Turekian of Yale University, remained well connected to evangelical Christianity throughout their adult lives.[86]

Narratives of conflict and war fascinate us more than tales of cooperation. But the ASA story, as historian Mark Kalthoff reminds us, was in fact one in which "certain American egalitarian evangelicals who, with no intention of compromising their religious commitments, dared to join in and follow America's scientific elites. They took the dare believing that, since the Bible and the book of Nature shared a common Author, they were employing the one best tool for compelling all rational people to embrace their vision of the Christian faith."[87] We will learn much more about the relationship of science and religion within the modern state by looking beyond our horrified fascination with the creationist–evolution wars to probe what it was like to bridge the modern divide.

Notes

1. "Insight: Evolution," *Nature* 457, no. 7231 (2009): 808–48; "Belief in Evolution: Untouched by the Hand of God," *Economist,* February 5, 2009, http://www.economist.com/daily/chartgallery/displaystory.cfm?story_id=13062613.

2. Joe Palca, "Darwin, Britain's Hero, Is Still Controversial in U.S.," *Weekend Edition Sunday,* National Public Radio, February 8, 2009, http://www.npr.org/templates/story/story.php?storyId=100379229; "Belief in Evolution." See also Debora MacKenzie, "The Battle for Turkey's Soul," *New Scientist* 202, no. 2703 (2009): 20–21.

3. Peter Harrison, "Disjoining Wisdom and Knowledge: Science, Theology, and the Making of Western Modernity," in *Wisdom or Knowledge? Science, Theology, and Cultural Dynamics,* ed. Hubert Meisinger, Willem B. Drees, and Zbigniew Liana (London: T&T Clark, 2006), 51–73. Equally significant is John Brooke and Geoffrey Cantor, *Reconstructing Nature: The Engagement of Science and Religion* (New York: Oxford University Press, 1998).

4. Ronald L. Numbers, "Introduction," in *Galileo Goes to Jail and Other Myths about Science and Religion* (Cambridge, MA: Harvard University Press, 2009), 1.

5. Andrew Dickson White, *A History of the Warfare of Science with Theology in Christendom* (New York: D. Appleton, 1903): v–vi. On this issue, see Gary B. Fern-

gren, ed., *Science and Religion: A Historical Introduction* (Baltimore: Johns Hopkins University Press, 2002).

6. John William Draper, *History of the Conflict between Religion and Science* (New York: D. Appleton, 1897).

7. Robert E. Kohler, "The Ph.D. Machine: Building on the Collegiate Base," *Isis* 81, no. 4 (1990): 638–62; Laurence R. Veysey, *The Emergence of the American University* (Chicago: University of Chicago Press, 1965).

8. Michael D. Gordin and Karl Hall, "Introduction: Intelligentsia Science Inside and Outside Russia," *Osiris* 23 (2008): 1–19, 5.

9. Ferngren, *Science and Religion*, ix.

10. Arnold Thackray and Robert K. Merton, "On Discipline Building: The Paradoxes of George Sarton," *Isis* 63, no. 4 (1972): 473–95.

11. Robert K. Merton, "Science, Technology, and Society in Seventeenth Century England," *Osiris* [original series] 4, pt. 2 (1938): 360–632; H. Floris Cohen, *The Scientific Revolution: A Historiographical Study* (Chicago: University of Chicago Press, 1994), 314–15; Edward P. Davis and Michael P. Winship, "Early Modern Protestantism," in *Science and Religion: A Historical Introduction*, ed. Gary B. Ferngren (Baltimore: Johns Hopkins University Press, 2002), 117–29.

12. Steven Shapin, "Understanding the Merton Thesis," *Isis* 79, no. 4 (1988): 594–605.

13. Michael Aaron Dennis, "Historiography of Science: An American Perspective," in *Science in the Twentieth Century*, ed. John Krige and Dominique Pestre (London: Harwood Academic Press, 1997), 1–26, 5.

14. Harvard Committee on the Objectives of a General Education in a Free Society, *General Education in a Free Society* (Cambridge, MA: Harvard University Press, 1945).

15. Dennis, "Historiography of Science," 10.

16. Ibid., 13.

17. Mark Walker, "Introduction," in *Science and Ideology: A Comparative History*, ed. Mark Walker (New York: Routledge, 2003), 1–2, 7.

18. Dennis, "Historiography of Science," 14.

19. Thomas S. Kuhn, *Copernican Revolution: Planetary Astronomy in the Development of Western Thought* (Cambridge, MA: Harvard University Press, 1957); Thomas S. Kuhn, *The Structure of Scientific Revolutions* (Chicago: University of Chicago Press, 1962).

20. Kuhn later recoiled in horror from this interpretation. See Keay Davidson, "Why Science Writers Should Forget Carl Sagan and Read Thomas Kuhn: On the Troubled Conscience of a Journalist," in *The Historiography of Contemporary Science, Technology, and Medicine: Writing Recent Science*, ed. Ronald E. Doel and Thomas Söderqvist (London: Routledge, 2006), 15–30, 23; Peter J. Bowler and Iwan R. Morus, *Making Modern Science: A Historical Survey* (Chicago: University of Chicago Press, 2005), 8–9.

21. Herbert Butterfield, *The Origins of Modern Science* (New York: Free Press, 1957), 7.

22. Herbert Butterfield, *The Whig Interpretation of History* (London: G. Bell and Sons, 1931).

23. Steven Shapin, *The Scientific Revolution* (Chicago: University of Chicago Press, 1996), 1–2; B. J. T. Dobbs, "Newton as Final Cause and First Mover," *Isis* 85, no. 4 (1994): 633–43.

24. B. J. T. Dobbs, *The Foundations of Newton's Alchemy, or "The Hunting of the Green Lyon"* (New York: Cambridge University Press, 1975); B. J. T. Dobbs, *The Janus Face of Genius: The Role of Alchemy in Newton's Thought* (New York: Cambridge University Press, 1991); Margaret J. Osler, "The Canonical Imperative: Rethinking the Scientific Revolution," in *Rethinking the Scientific Revolution*, ed. Margaret J. Osler (New York: Cambridge University Press, 2000), 16. See also Brooke and Cantor, *Reconstructing Nature*, 1; Rebekah Higgitt, *Recreating Newton: Newtonian Biography and the Making of Nineteenth Century History of Science* (London: Pickering & Chatto, 2007).

25. Bowler and Morus, *Making Modern Science*, 10.

26. Quoted in Dobbs, "Newton as Final Cause and First Mover," 641.

27. Dennis, "Historiography of Science," 1.

28. Frances A. Yates, *Giordano Bruno and the Hermetic Tradition* (Chicago: University of Chicago Press, 1964); Alexandre Koyré, *From the Closed World to the Infinite Universe* (Baltimore: Johns Hopkins University Press, 1957); Michael Polanyi, *The Tacit Dimension* (New York: Anchor Books, 1967). See also Bowler and Morus, *Making Modern Science*, 7–8. Later studies have continued to reevaluate the interplay between natural philosophers and religious authority, including the still controversial argument by Pietro Redondi that Galileo Galilei's more troubling *theological* heresies were concealed by the Church's condemnation of his assertions regarding celestial bodies; see Pietro Rodondi, *Galileo: Heretic* (Princeton, NJ: Princeton University Press, 1989). For significant reassessments of recent historiography, see Martin J. S. Rudwick, "Senses of the Natural World and Senses of God: Another Look at the Historical Relationship of Science and Religion," in *The Sciences and Theology in the Twentieth Century*, ed. Arthur R. Peacocke (Notre Dame, IN: University of Notre Dame Press, 1981), 241–61; and especially Brooke and Cantor, *Reconstructing Nature*.

29. Loren R. Graham, *Science in Russia and the Soviet Union: A Short History* (New York: Cambridge University Press, 1993). On Clements, see Peter J. Bowler, *The Earth Encompassed: A History of the Environmental Sciences* (New York: W.W. Norton, 2000), 520; Robert E. Kohler, "Plants and Pigeonholes: Classification as a Practice in American Ecology," *Historical Studies in the Natural Sciences* 38, no. 1 (2008): 77–108; Michael G. Barbour, "Ecological Fragmentation in the Fifties," in *Uncommon Ground: Rethinking the Human Place in Nature*, ed. William Cronon (New York: Norton, 1996), 233–55 and 510–14.

30. David C. Lindberg, *The Beginnings of Western Science: The European Scientific Tradition in Philosophical, Religious, and Institutional Context, Prehistory to A.D. 1450* (Chicago: University of Chicago Press, 2007), 190–91. See also Edward Grant, *Science and Religion, 400 B.C. to A.D. 1550: From Aristotle to Copernicus* (Baltimore: Johns Hopkins University Press, 2006). Natural scientists have continued to argue that the perceived decline of Islamic science supports the lesson of limiting state political intrusion into science; see Steven Weinberg, "Without God," *New York Review of Books* 55, no. 14 (2008): 1.

31. Jeffrey Burton Russell, *Inventing the Flat Earth: Columbus and Modern Historians* (New York: Praeger, 1997).

32. Lindberg, *Beginnings of Western Science*, 190–91.

33. Numbers, *Galileo Goes to Jail*, 6 (emphasis in original).

34. Harrison, "Disjoining Wisdom and Knowledge," 64.

35. Brooke and Cantor, *Reconstructing Nature*, 8, 18; see also Martin J. S. Rudwick, *Bursting the Limits of Time: The Reconstruction of Geohistory in the Age of Revolution* (Chicago: University of Chicago Press, 2005).

36. Brooke and Cantor, *Reconstructing Nature*, 19.

37. Quoted in Numbers, *Galileo Goes to Jail*, 1.

38. Maynard Shipley, *The War on Modern Science: A Short History of the Fundamentalist Attacks on Evolution and Modernism* (New York: Alfred A. Knopf, 1927), xii (emphasis in original).

39. Susan Jacoby, *The Age of American Unreason* (New York: Vintage, 2009), 21.

40. Jon D. Miller, Eugenie C. Scott, and Shinji Okamoto, "Public Acceptance of Evolution," *Science* 313, no. 5788 (2006): 765–66.

41. Jacoby, *Age of American Unreason*, xvii, quoted 22.

42. Richard Hofstadter, *Anti-intellectualism in American Life* (New York: Alfred A. Knopf, 1963).

43. Jacoby, *Age of American Unreason*, xv.

44. Ibid. See also A. Hunter Dupree, *Science in the Federal Government: A History of Policies and Activities* (Baltimore: Johns Hopkins University Press, 1986).

45. Elaine Howard Ecklund and Christopher P. Scheitle, "Religion among Academic Scientists: Distinctions, Disciplines, and Demographics," *Social Problems* 54, no. 2 (2007): 289–307; Edward J. Larson and Larry Witham, "Leading Scientists Still Reject God," *Nature* 394, no. 6691 (1998): 313. Levels of religious faith vary between distinct scientific disciplines, and religious faith is strikingly low among evolutionary biologists.

46. Dismissive attitudes toward the presidential campaigns of William Jennings Bryan by Hofstadter and other progressive historians for his antievolutionary views may have limited appreciation of Bryan's progressive views in other realms, or so one recent historian has argued: "in the long shadow of the Scopes trial, other memories of Bryan gradually faded from public consciousness [even as other] Bryan biographers did point out that a rigorously Christian liberalism was not a contradiction in terms"; see Michael Kazin, *A Godly Hero: The Life of William Jennings Bryan* (New York: Alfred A. Knopf, 2006), 302.

47. James B. Gilbert, *Redeeming Culture: American Religion in an Age of Science* (Chicago: University of Chicago Press, 1997).

48. Perry Miller, "The Responsibility of a Mind in a Civilization of Machines," *American Scholar* 31 (Winter 1961–62): 51–69. Historians of technology agree with Miller's assessment; see Thomas P. Hughes, *American Genesis: A Century of Invention and Technological Enthusiasm, 1870–1970* (Chicago: University of Chicago Press, 2004).

49. Walter H. Conser Jr., "Baconianism," in *The History of Science and Religion in the Western Tradition: An Encyclopedia*, ed. Gary Ferngren, Edward J. Larson, Darrel W. Amundsen, and Anne-Marie E. Nakhla (New York: Garland, 2000), 169–71.

50. David Noble, *Religion of Technology: The Divinity of Man and the Spirit of Invention* (New York: Penguin, 1999), quoted 3, 5; see also 191, 195.

51. On von Braun, who developed the rockets that propelled Apollo astronauts to the moon, see Michael J. Neufeld, *Von Braun: Dreamer of Space, Engineer of War* (New York: Alfred A. Knopf, 2007).

52. Daniel J. Kevles, "Principles, Property Rights, and Profits: Historical Reflections on University/Industry Tensions," *Accountability in Research* 8, no. 4 (2001): 12–26; Dietram A. Scheufele, Elizabeth A. Corley, Tsung-jen Shih, Kajsa E. Dalrymple,

and Shirley S. Ho, "Religious Beliefs and Public Attitudes toward Nanotechnology in Europe and the United States," *Nature Nanotechnology* 4, no. 2 (2008): 91–94.

53. Keay Davidson, *Carl Sagan: A Life* (New York: John Wiley & Sons, 1999).

54. Quoted in Ferngren, *Science and Religion*, 163. Whitehead's vision served as a rival view of science from that espoused by most twentieth-century scientists; see Bowler and Morus, *Making Modern Science*, 5.

55. Paul Lawrence Farber, *The Temptations of Evolutionary Ethics* (Berkeley: University of California Press, 1994); Paul Lawrence Farber, *Finding Order in Nature: The Naturalist Tradition from Linneaus to E. O. Wilson* (Baltimore: Johns Hopkins University Press, 2000). See also Stephen Jay Gould, *The Mismeasure of Man* (New York: W.W. Norton, 1996).

56. A leading example of the work of Richard Dawkins (an evolutionary biologist at Oxford University) is *The God Delusion* (Boston: Houghlin Mifflin Harcourt, 2006).

57. Robin Marantz Henig, "Darwin's God," *New York Times Magazine*, March 4, 2007, http://www.nytimes.com/2007/03/04/magazine/04evolution.t.html.

58. Michael Ruse, *The Evolution–Creation Struggle* (Cambridge, MA: Harvard University Press, 2005), 3; Michael Ruse, "Is Evolution a Secular Religion?," *Science* 299, no. 5612 (2003): 1523–24.

59. Harrison, "Disjoining Wisdom and Knowledge," 65–67. As science became increasingly secularized, Nature also ceased to be God's Book, undermining arguments that those who studied nature were virtuous through this process. See Steven Shapin, *The Scientific Life: A Moral History of a Late Modern Vocation* (Chicago: University of Chicago Press, 2008), 23–28.

60. Barbara Forrest and Paul R. Gross, *Creationism's Trojan Horse: The Wedge of Intelligent Design* (New York: Oxford University Press, 2007).

61. Forrest and Gross, *Creationism's Trojan Horse*, 191–92.

62. Miller, Scott, and Okamoto, "Public Acceptance of Evolution," 766; Stephanie Simon, "Their Own Version of a Big Bang," *Los Angeles Times*, February 11, 2006.

63. One historian of science and medicine attempted to encourage such an inquiry by inviting an essay from a leader of the intelligent design movement to contribute to his historical encyclopedia on religion and science. See William A. Dembski, "The Designer Argument," in *The History of Science and Religion in the Western Tradition: An Encyclopedia*, ed. Gary B. Ferngren (New York: Garland, 2000), 335–44.

64. Although the level of current consensus favoring the theory of climate change is extraordinarily high, historians of science understand that a few scientific near certainties of earlier eras—classical physics and the rejection of continental drift—were later judged spectacularly wrong. On climate change science, see Naomi Oreskes, "The Scientific Consensus on Climate Change," *Science* 306, no. 5702 (2004): 1686; Naomi Oreskes and Erik Conway, *Merchants of Doubt: How a Handful of Scientists Obscured the Truth on Issues from Tobacco Smoke to Global Warming* (New York: Bloomsbury Press, 2010); Spencer R. Weart, *The Discovery of Global Warming: Revised and Expanded Edition* (Cambridge, MA: Harvard University Press, 2008), 197–204. On larger challenges of objectivity in history, see Peter Novick, *That Noble Dream: The "Objectivity Question" and the American Historical Profession* (Cambridge, U.K.: Cambridge University Press, 1988).

65. Quoted in a Gallup Poll report, Joseph Carroll, "Americans Assess What They Can Do to Reduce Global Warming," Gallup, Washington, DC, April 24, 2007, http://www.gallup.com/poll/27298/Americans-Assess-What-They-Can-Reduce-Global-Warming.aspx.

66. For helpful discussions, see Robert N. Proctor and Londa Schiebinger, eds., *Agnotology: The Making and Unmaking of Ignorance* (Stanford, CA: Stanford University Press, 2008); Roger A. Pielke Jr., *The Honest Broker: Making Sense of Science in Policy and Politics* (New York: Cambridge University Press, 2007).

67. Seymour Lipset and William Schneider, "The Decline of Confidence in American Institutions," *Political Science Quarterly* 98, no. 3 (1983): 379–402.

68. Francis Fukuyama, *The End of History and the Last Man* (New York: Free Press, 1992).

69. Robert Kagan's *The Return of History and the End of Dreams* (New York: Alfred A. Knopf, 2008) critiques Fukuyama's *End of History*.

70. Prominent exceptions include Daniel J. Kevles, *The Physicists: A History of a Scientific Community in America* (Cambridge, MA: Harvard University Press, 1995), which treats the experiences of Catholic and Jewish physicists inter alia, and Carl-Henry Geschwind, "Embracing Science and Research: Early Twentieth Century Jesuits and Seismology in the United States," *Isis* 89, no. 1 (1998): 27–49. For helpful recent assessments of this broad field, see John A. Heitmann, "Doing 'True Science': The Early History of the Institutum Divi Thomae, 1935–1951," *Catholic Historical Review* 88, no. 4 (2002): 702–22; Steven J. Harris, "Roman Catholicism since Trent," in *Science and Religion: A Historical Introduction*, ed. Gary B. Ferngren (Baltimore: Johns Hopkins University Press, 2002), 247–60.

71. Thomas Bender, *Intellect and Public Life: Essays on the Social History of Academic Intellectuals in the United States* (Baltimore: Johns Hopkins University Press, 1993); Laura Smith Porter, "From Intellectual Sanctuary to Social Responsibility: The Founding of the Institute for Advanced Study, 1930–1933" (PhD diss., Princeton University, Princeton, NJ, 1988).

72. David A. Hollinger, *Science, Jews, and Secular Culture: Studies in Mid-Twentieth Century American Intellectual History* (Princeton, NJ: Princeton University Press, 1998).

73. See, in addition, Gilbert, *Redeeming Culture*.

74. Ronald E. Doel, "Oral History of American Science: A Forty-Year Review," *History of Science* 41, no. 4 (2003): 349–78.

75. Ferngren, *Science and Religion*, xi.

76. Ibid.

77. Adrian Desmond and James Moore, *Darwin: The Life of a Tormented Evolutionist* (New York: W.W. Norton, 1994).

78. Brooke and Cantor, *Reconstructing Nature*, 32.

79. For instance, an entry into the life story of the naturalist and physician Philip Henry Gosse (1810–88) and other contemporaries may be gleaned from John Rendle-Short, *Green Eye of the Storm* (Carlyle, PA: Banner of Truth, 1998). Better known is the literary classic by Gosse's son, Edmund Gosse, *Father and Son: A Study of Temperaments* (New York: Scribner, 1907), which cast Philip Henry Gosse as a fanatically religious despot standing in opposition to an emerging modernist perspective—a polemical narrative in the model of Andrew Dickson White's *Warfare* treatise, which had appeared one decade before.

80. Ronald L. Numbers, *The Creationists* (New York: Alfred A. Knopf, 1992); J. Laurence Kulp oral history interview by Ronald E. Doel, April 12, 1996, Columbia University Oral History Research Office; Wallace S. Broecker, "Better Living through Geochemistry: Tracking Chemical Clues to Investigate the Earth," in *Lamont-Doherty*

Earth Observatory: Twelve Perspectives on the First Fifty Years, 1949–1999, ed. Laurence Lippsett (New York: Columbia University, 1999), 49–58.

81. Mark Alan Kalthoff, "The New Evangelical Engagement with Science: The American Scientific Affiliation, Origin to 1963" (PhD diss., Indiana University, Bloomington, 1998), 18.

82. Kalthoff, "New Evangelical Engagement with Science," 690–92; Numbers, *The Creationists*.

83. Bernard Ramm, *The Christian View of Science and Scripture* (Grand Rapids, MI: William B. Eerdmans, 1954); John C. Whitcomb Jr. and Henry M. Morris, *The Genesis Flood: The Biblical Record and Its Scientific Implications* (Phillipsburg, NJ: Presbyterian and Reformed Publishing, 1961); Gary J. Dorrien, *The Remaking of Evangelical Theology* (Louisville, KY: Westminster John Knox Press, 1998), 123; Kalthoff, "New Evangelical Engagement with Science," 690–92; Numbers, *The Creationists,* 187.

84. Tanya J. Levin and Ronald E. Doel, "The Lamont–Doherty Earth Observatory Oral History Project: A Preliminary Report," *Earth Sciences History* 19, no. 1 (2000): 26–32.

85. Sinclair Lewis, *Elmer Gantry* (New York: Harcourt, Brace, 1927); Mark Schorer, *Sinclair Lewis: An American Life* (New York: McGraw-Hill, 1961). Broecker's assessment appears in Wallace Broecker oral history interview by Ronald E. Doel, December 29, 1995, Oral History Research Office, Columbia University, New York, 22.

86. Kalthoff, "New Evangelical Engagement with Science," 532; see also Karl K. Turekian, "Threads: A Life in Geochemistry," *Annual Reviews of Earth and Planetary Sciences* 34, no. 1 (2006): 1–35.

87. Kalthoff, "New Evangelical Engagement with Science," 737.

Chapter 9

Science versus Religion: The Process of Secularization in the GDR as a Specific Response to the Challenges of Modernity

Monika Wohlrab-Sahr and Thomas Schmidt-Lux

The present debate about religion among historians and sociologists is one of competing exceptionalisms. Whereas, from the European perspective, the United States was for a long time considered an exceptional case of highly stable religiosity and of the absence of atheism, Europe is considered an exceptionally areligious part of the world.

Whatever one may think of this competitive exceptionalism, the developments that took place in the German Democratic Republic could certainly be added to the list. The decline in church membership and religious belief during the Socialist Unity Party of Germany (Sozialistische Einheitspartei Deutschlands, or SED) regime gave the East German population the lowest levels of religiosity and church affiliation in the world, creating an effect that would endure until the present day.

But exceptionalism is not very satisfying as an explanation[1] because it always refers to a normative master trend from which the exceptional case deviates. Sometimes it seems to tell us more about the pet ideas of social science research than about the reality that this research is trying to grasp. Until the 1980s, a seemingly universal secularization process was supposed to represent such a master trend, whereas nowadays seculariza- tion has been taken over by the idea of a worldwide revitalization of religi- osity—a "return of the sacred." But a sociologist may curiously ask, "Why is there no significant atheism in the United States?" as well as, "Why is there such a high and stable degree of atheism in East Germany?"

Such questions lead us to analyze the specific historical and social con- ditions in the respective countries, and they also reveal some general devel- opments in the unfolding process of modernity. We will undertake in this chapter an analysis of the secularization process in the GDR as the result of a specific political and ideological way of dealing with a general tension in modernity: the tension between science and religion.[2]

This analysis does not intend to add another single-factor explanation to the existing ones. Rather, it aims at highlighting an important aspect of the secularization process that has not been taken very seriously so far. The SED was obviously able not only to enforce church disaffiliation but also to create a predominantly secular habitus in its population.[3] Our hypoth- esis is that this habitus was made possible through (a) the sharp accentua- tion of an antagonistic, irreconcilable conflict between science and religion and (b) the acceptance of this conflict among large parts of the population. Thus, the socialist party could refer to a rich history of secularist ideas, al- lowing the antireligious politics of the SED to stand on the shoulders of the giants of secularist thinkers in Europe for whom the conflictive relation- ship between science and religion was a central idea. Whereas repression against church members in the GDR was clearly one of the political means of establishing secularism, the popularization of secularist ideas through mass institutions of adult education was another, no less important means.

As we will show with references to interviews with East German fami- lies and survey data, the framework of a science–religion conflict is still evident in the everyday thoughts of East Germans. Even newly emerging religious-like perspectives—such as the growing belief in an afterlife—are often constructed on the basis of "scientistic" ideas.

Despite the particularity of the GDR's development, we will argue that the conflictive framework does, nevertheless, refer to a general tension be- tween different societal spheres as part of modern development itself—a tension that does *not*, however, predefine the ways in which it is being handled in different contexts. We argue that one can differentiate multiple types of secularization according to the different ways in which this tension is being dealt with. Although the history of the Enlightenment established an important stock of ideas regarding this tension, the movement certainly did not define a single outcome.

On the theoretical level, this differentiation implies five different levels in the process of secularization that may serve as a guideline for comparative research:

1. The mode and degree of functional differentiation between religion and other societal spheres, such as science
2. The interpretative framing of secularization processes, which may not only include the irreconcilability of science and religion but also attempt to bridge the gap between the two spheres[4]
3. The role of conflicting interests and the engagement of religious and secular actors
4. The extent to which the interpretive framing of the secularization process could be spread among the population
5. The degree of religious decline or stability, fragmentation, or homogeneity and its relationship to the process of functional differentiation

When we talk about religion, we refer to it, first of all, as a social system[5] with a specific communication code—namely, the distinction (and relationship) between the immanent and the transcendent. This perspective blurs the seemingly clear distinction between functional and substantial definitions of religion: religion can always be analyzed regarding its function *and* its content or form. On the one side, religion fulfills certain functions for society as well as for individuals, especially the function of dealing with fundamental insecurity and contingency. On the other side, the system of religion deals with the fundamental problem of insecurity and uncertainty *in a specific way* that clearly differs from the methods of other societal spheres (such as the economy or politics) and, thereby, makes "religious" interpretations identifiable as such.[6] This approach can be seen in reference to problems of mortality and death, which all religions have dealt with and for which they have provided semantics, images, and interpretations. Thomas Luckmann has, therefore, relegated to specific religions the responsibility to cope with "big transcendences."[7]

Related to the concept of religion as a social system—which is not identical to specific religions such as Christianity, Islam, or Judaism—is a variety of belief systems (such as Catholic, Protestant, or Sunni Muslim beliefs); organizations (such as churches, sects, denominations, or orders); and communities (in which people interact face-to-face in common religious practices).

Related to these specific belief systems, as well as to the religious system, are the concrete beliefs and practices of individuals, which can be referred to as *religiosity*. Their beliefs may differ from the religious beliefs of certain communities or from the dogmas of religious organizations. However, these beliefs and practices must relate to the distinction or relationship between immanence and transcendence to be identified as religious perspectives by those who adopt them and by others.

According to this conceptualization of religion, not only does secularization imply that other societal spheres are being "purified" of religious modes of communication (level 1); it may also imply that religious communication, as such, is being questioned as a legitimate model of communication (level 2) by certain actors and through specific institutions (level 3). Secularization may also mean that the religious distinction or relationship between immanence and transcendence, including the specific forms that this relationship took, has lost its plausibility as a framework for interpreting life, mortality, and death for growing parts of the population (levels 4 and 5).

Modernity, Religion, and Secularization in the GDR

Almost twenty years after the German reunification, East Germany is still one of the most highly secularized regions in the world in terms of religious decline. Whereas in 1949—the year in which the GDR was established—more than 80 percent of East Germans were church members, in 1989 that proportion had declined to 29 percent and has continued to drop ever since.[8] This decline certainly has to be interpreted as a lasting consequence of the conflictive relationship between religion and politics during the GDR regime and of the repression that church members faced during that period. Even if churches were the only relevant institutional actor besides the state during the GDR regime, and even if they were at the core of the "peaceful revolution," this important political role obviously was not able to compensate for the losses in church membership, religious affiliation, and belief.

But another important and enduring aspect of the secularization process in the GDR has to be taken into account. The SED, as the leading party, not only put pressure on the East German population to resign their church activities and membership but also managed to effectively construct a dichotomy between religion and science in the public mind. Thus, an older antagonism, set up by positivist and evolutionist thinkers in the nineteenth century and given a specific profile by Austrian neopositivism and German monism in the early twentieth century, was revived and given a new form.[9]

Against the background of antireligious theories and their presumed influence on present sociological thinking, especially on secularization theories, American sociologists of religion have questioned the empirical validity of an assumed conflict between religion and science.[10] If we, nevertheless, take such a conflict as our starting point, we do not imply the assumption of any kind of "natural" contradiction or "fundamental" hierarchy between the two, as evolutionist thinkers such as Auguste Comte have suggested. Instead we look at the specific conditions under which such antagonism has been effectively constructed.[11] This perspective is in line with the proposal of several historians and sociologists that secularization not be analyzed as an unavoidable result of a historical master trend but rather as the specific outcome of concrete sociopolitical conflicts.[12]

Nevertheless, it would be negligent to completely ignore any tensions between science and religion in the course of modernity. European history—that is, not only the history of postcommunist societies—is full of examples of such tensions evolving from the internal development of the natural sciences as scientists started to liberate themselves from the religious definition of their fields, even in cases in which the scientists may have themselves been deeply religious. The case of Galileo Galilei is a prominent example of this tension. That the debate over the invitation to the pope to give Sapienza University of Rome's 2008 inaugural address was accompanied by references to this historic case indicates how deeply such developments and conflicts are engrained into the historic memory of the respective societies. Galileo played an important role in the GDR as well. The Berlin Ensemble, which used to be directed by Bertolt Brecht, played "The Life of Galileo" 242 times in only five years after its premiere on January 15, 1957.

In the cradle of Protestant fundamentalism in the United States stood the conflict between creationism and Darwinism, which is very much alive today, as creationist views are espoused by almost half of the American population.[13] But in spite of such tensions, it is obvious that science *and* religion were able to flourish in both Italy and the United States. In contrast, the case of the GDR is interesting because the SED regime was so successful in establishing an antagonism between science and religion at the expense of religion.

Science and Religion:
Its Conflictive Relationship in Early Sociology

For the early sociologists at the turn of the twentieth century, the relationship between religion and science was at the core of their analyses of the modernization process and of the destiny of religion in the course of this process. This focus was especially evident in evolutionist approaches such as Comte's,[14] which reserved religion for an early stage of human and societal development, assuming that it would be replaced by social science in the course of history. But in a more complex way, this view also is found in Max Weber's approach. Weber fundamentally differs from evolutionist thinkers inasmuch as he saw rationality originally arising from religion.[15] Nevertheless, he did not expect a peaceful coexistence between the different social spheres. Weber's concept of the autonomization of value spheres can be considered an early version of a theory of social differentiation,[16] of which Niklas Luhmann's theory of social systems is a late example. But unlike Luhmann and his concept of the coexistence of self-regulatory systems, Weber essentially presents a theory of *conflict* between the spheres that is caused by their immanent tendencies of rationalization:

> The tension between religion and intellectual knowledge definitely comes to the fore wherever rational, empirical knowledge has consistently worked through to the disenchantment of the world and its transformation into a causal mechanism. For then science encounters the claims of the ethical postulate that the world is a God-ordained, and hence somehow *meaningfully* and ethically oriented, cosmos. In principle, the empirical as well as the mathematically oriented view of the world develops refutation of every intellectual approach which in any way asks for a 'meaning' of inner-worldly occurrences.[17]

Weber concludes: "[C]ulture's every step forward seems condemned to lead to an ever more devastating senselessness."[18]

According to Weber, religion repels the attack of the self-relying intellect by claiming a type of knowledge that is essentially different from intellectual knowledge. Nevertheless, religion is always in danger of becoming inconsequential by intruding into the realm of science. This inconsequentiality occurs—in Weber's view—when religion abandons the incommunicability of the mystic experience by interpreting the world's meaning in rational terms. However, he integrates a kind of pessimistic evolutionism into his theory of rationalization, inasmuch as the process of rationalization—as he conceives it—actually had its origin in the religion and myth that it would eventually come to undermine.

Weber did not assume that science would some day take over the position of religion. Nevertheless, he predicted a developmental pattern in which religion would become the "arational" or irrational power in the world—and would be increasingly restricted to this perspective—but in which religion would also be in constant danger of undermining its own autonomous position with its need to argue within the framework of scientific rationality.

Unlike later theories of functional differentiation such as Luhmann's, Weber's notion of the autonomization of value spheres implies the idea that some of the other spheres—such as art or the erotic sphere—compete with religion in its own field by providing a means of inner-worldly salvation.

Although Weber was much more skeptical regarding the potential of science and rationality to offer a means of inner-worldly salvation, he also discussed one exception to this rule. He perceived the German plebeian intellectualism as "religious," particularly because it implied a socialist eschatological belief. Thus, it was radically antireligious with respect to the beliefs of the church. In this case, science was given the role of a "prophet of the revolution" that was believed to terminate the class society.[19] So next to the idea of the functional differentiation of value spheres in Weber's theory, we also find the notion of a competition *between* the spheres over their promises of inner-worldly salvation and over the idea that religion may be tempted to adapt to scientific rationality and thereby undermine its own specificity. Weber's theory deals with processes of not only differentiation but also *de-differentiation* between the spheres: science may be used like religion, and religion may argue with the means of science.

Constructing an Antagonism between Science and Religion: From Positivism to Socialism

In some of the recent theories of secularization that follow in Weber's footsteps, we can still find the notion of a teleological development undermining religion's position, with the changing role of science being crucial to this development.[20] This type of argument remains within the perspective of one master trend of modernization and secularization, without reflecting on the very different societal developments and their specific circumstances.

Other scholars have delivered historical evidence for the tension between religion and science, especially for the European context. Historians such as Hugh McLeod[21] and sociologists such as José Casanova have highlighted the secularizing influence of social movements that propagated Enlightenment ideas in Europe, which they considered as one important factor for the European secularization process.[22]

But, despite the critical attitude of several Enlightenment thinkers toward church and religion, the movement actually did not establish a strict antagonism between religion and science.[23] In addition to anticlerical and atheist positions, there were also many deist thinkers among the philosophers of the Enlightenment. Furthermore, Protestantism itself was an important element of the Enlightenment tradition. More influential in establishing such a dichotomy was positivism, with its double strategy of disenchanting the world and establishing science as a religion of its own—a universal scientific religion.[24] This concept comes close to Weber's idea about the different value spheres competing for inner-worldly salvation.

The antagonism between science and religion was enforced by the logical positivism of the Vienna Circle,[25] which developed the notion of *wissenschaftliche Weltauffassung*, or a scientific world concept, which explicitly contrasted religion. The Vienna Circle was in line with Comte's evolutionism inasmuch as it paralleled Christianity with the outdated worldview of the Middle Ages, which needed to be overcome by scientific progress. In the footsteps of this movement (with explicit reference to Comte), the Association of Monism was founded in Germany in the early twentieth century. The association actually created a monistic *Weltanschauung* (or ideology), which followed the idea that nature and science are guided by the same laws. The members explicitly claimed a fundamental hiatus between their scientific Weltanschauung and Christianity. Consequently, their ideology can be considered the "ideal-type of a scientistic ideology," aiming at the substitution of Christianity with a newly established Monist "church" that was supposed to govern society on the basis of scientific and ethical principles.[26]

On the other side of the spectrum, the rise of Protestant fundamentalism in the United States in the beginning of the twentieth century also emerged from a perceived tension between religion and the natural sciences, especially with reference to Darwin's theory. This tension—as we know from ongoing conflicts about the teaching of Darwinist theory in schools—has still not vanished today, even though the U.S. Supreme Court regularly limits creationists' influence on school curriculums.[27] Surveys indicate broad support for creationist beliefs in the population. According to a Gallup poll from 1999, 47 percent of Americans were in favor of this statement: "God created human beings pretty much in their present form at one time within the last 10,000 years."[28] But this poll also shows that in the United States, where the conflict between supporters of creationism and supporters of evolutionism started from religious groups rather than from scientists, this antagonism was not carried out at the expense of religious beliefs.

Probably because of this very circumstance, the predominant sociological approaches in the United States do not give much weight to the tension between religion and science as a factor in the secularization process. Rodney Stark and Roger Finke interpret the mere idea that a conflict may exist as a heritage of ideological secularization theories.[29] Referring to a 1969 survey among American academics, Stark and Finke show that natural scientists are much more likely to be religious than are psychologists and anthropologists.[30] On the basis of this evidence, they conclude that science–religion antagonism is a secular doctrine of social scientists themselves rather than an empirical finding.[31] More recent studies, however, show that scientists in the United States are much more likely not to believe in god than the general population. Even if they are skeptical regarding fundamental differences between natural and social scientists, Ecklund and Scheitle, in their survey of American academics at elite institutions, nevertheless show that certain groups of scientists—especially physicists, biologists, and political scientists—stand out as being more inclined to atheist or agnostic positions and as being less likely to practice a religion than other groups of scientists.[32]

Steve Bruce also questions the assumption of a clash, especially between natural science and religion, by showing that it is not natural scientists but anthropologists who constitute the most areligious group of academics.[33] He concludes that "the greatest damage to religion has been caused not by competing secular ideas but by the general relativism that supposes that all ideologies are equally true (and hence equally false)."[34]

These findings, however, are not as evident as presented. The respective surveys obviously do not deal with the relationship between science and religion as social systems; rather, they concern the relationship between scientists as individuals and religion. A scientist's personal relationship with religion, however, is an entirely different issue than the relationship between science and religion as social systems. As systems, science and religion may entirely follow their own logic and force actors that are included into the system because of their social roles (as scientists or ministers) to accept this logic. As individuals, however, scientists may very well be able to adhere to harmonistic views about the relationship between both spheres. How easy scientists find this task depends on the sociocultural framing rather than on the inner development of the spheres and the relationship between them. Structure, culture, and agency need to be analyzed separately to understand their relatedness and to understand the origins and mechanisms of societal conflicts.[35]

If we deal with the above-mentioned science–religion antagonism in the European positivist tradition, and with its influence in socialist and post-socialist societies, we see that it is this exact sociocultural framing that we try to grasp. In this respect, Germany is a good case. We are able to compare East Germany and West Germany with their different developments, as well as examine different time periods and see how lasting certain effects of the socialist regime have been. Not all of this analysis can be done in detail in this chapter, but we will draw an outline of this development, place it in its wider context, and collect some empirical evidence from recent research to sketch our theoretical perspective.

"Scientism" versus Religion: The East German Case

Most of the socialist regimes, especially (but not only) in countries with predominantly Protestant or Orthodox populations, were able to cause a rapid decline in church membership and Christian belief.[36] The governing party of the GDR—the SED—managed to turn the East German population into the people with the world's lowest rate of church membership and highest rate of professed atheists.[37]

Historians have shown that, in some parts of the later GDR, the population was already rather detached from the church after the National Socialist regime in Germany and even earlier.[38] Using church statistics in the Protestant part of Germany since 1850, Lucian Hölscher indicated that in terms of participation in church activities, the later East–West division in Germany had already begun in 1910.[39] The regions with low participation in church activities were industrial areas at that time, and secular movements were popular not only among the intellectual elite but also among the Social Democratic Party, which was preaching "a synthesis of Marxism and Darwinism."[40] These findings imply that East Germany was a historical setting where different kinds of secularizing effects coincided—with secular movements that were based on the antagonism between science and religion being one of them. These influences, as well as the secularizing effect of the Nazi regime, created the soil on which the SED could plant its secularist ideas.

But despite such broader historical trends, an enormous decline in church membership and religiosity did occur under the socialist regime.[41] Obviously, this decline resulted from several factors:[42]

- *State oppression.* The oppression of church members included severe social disadvantages.
- *Conflicts over ritual participation, membership, and loyalty.* This conflict was induced through the introduction of the *Jugendweihe*, a coming-of-age ritual meant as a substitute for the Protestant confirmation. The practice was shaped as a conflict between membership in the church and membership in the Socialist party, which had become a mass institution of the GDR.[43] It was framed as a general conflict of loyalty in which one had to avow his or her fidelity to one of the two sides. A lyric from a song that was sung at Jugendweihe expressed the conflict clearly: "Tell me where you stand!"
- *Socializing effects of nonmembership and areligiosity.* At a certain time, these effects had become the "normal" pattern in East German society. Hence, they constitute an influential factor of their own.
- *Cultural transformation.* Some social scientists have also pointed to the cultural transformation in the GDR, which has been described as the emergence of a "worker society," focusing on issues of immediate necessity and practicality. Obviously, these issues were not in accordance with religious practice and belief.[44]
- *Dominance of Protestantism.* With its high degree of "internal secularization," compared to that of Catholicism, Protestant dominance was a significant factor.
- *Scientific worldview.* This factor refers to the creation and spread of a scientistic ideology that is based on the competition between religion and science: the so-called scientific worldview.

Without neglecting the relevance of all the influences highlighted, we want to focus on the scientific worldview, which stressed the scientific character of Marxism–Leninism and the interpretation of science as the only path to a glorious future. From this point of view, science was meant to explain and predict *all* aspects of human life and nature. The German word *Weltanschauung* hints at the all-embracing notion of this worldview, opposing the idea of functional differentiation that would consider religion, science, and politics as autonomous spheres that may exist next to each other and refer to different functional problems in society.[45] According to this "imperialistic version," science was meant not only to explore appropriate means and measures to reach certain goals but also to define those very goals.[46]

The term *wissenschaftliche Weltanschauung* was an important ideological topic and could be found in almost any official GDR document. Sometimes, it was used as a synonym for Marxism–Leninism, and sometimes it was defined as a worldview that should enable people "to orient themselves in a fast-changing, antagonistic and conflict-burden world, to define our place, our goals, and the path that leads to these goals."[47]

Characteristic of the rationale of the scientific worldview was the explicit attempt to compete with a Christian worldview. Focusing solely on empirical and provable phenomena and promising to guide individual lives and make sense of life and death, the scientific worldview claimed to supersede all forms of religion.

The socialist and communist groups of the nineteenth and early twentieth century had already framed religion and science as antagonistic counterparts. This interpretation was immediately established as the official program and ideology of the new East German state: "Since time immemorial, religion has been the enemy of science."[48] According to this position, religion is opposed to any materialistic or objective reality and simply results from fear and helplessness. Whereas science aims at abolishing those drawbacks, religion is interested in keeping people in ignorance. Religion and science are perceived as two combating agents with deep-rooted divergent interests. During the nineteenth and early twentieth century, religion and science were seen as strictly contradicting spheres on a societal and individual level. Religious beliefs were perceived as "relics of an ancient consciousness" that would soon vanish.[49]

Compared to religion, this imperialistic interpretation considered science a superior way of thinking.[50] Science was perceived to have better means and to supersede religion in all spheres of life, even in moral and social questions. Thus, the scientific worldview of the East German regime was a new version of the old narrative about the superiority of science.

Obviously, similar ideologies existed in other former communist countries as well. The outcome, however, was different. Paul Froese, for example, speaks of "scientific atheism" becoming "a thing of the past" in Russia;[51] however, for East Germany, that statement holds true only for the official programs and not for personal convictions. Therefore, we have to look for the conditions under which the ideology of scientific atheism was spread to the broader population and for the ways in which it was appropriated on the individual and family levels. The assumption that worldviews that were adopted under dictatorial conditions would necessarily be dropped when those conditions were gone is obviously much too simple.

The Role of Secularist Institutions and Agents

The GDR created several institutions that were supposed to spread the scientific worldview on a very popular level. Institutions of adult education, such as Urania, were set up in many cities to deal with scientific and ideological matters. The establishment of popular observatories throughout the country and of astronomy as a general subject in school is also important in this respect. None of these institutions were *only* ideological; all of them actually spread scientific knowledge throughout the overall population. However, they popularized the worldview within the framework of creating a scientific Weltanschauung that was explicitly intended to substitute for religion and "superstition."[52] Therefore, these institutions must be considered instruments of a general process of disenchantment that did not just "occur" but was purposely initiated. Even if the practice was more or less ideological in different places and in different periods of the GDR regime, the moment of disenchantment remained essential.[53]

The attempt to not only spread knowledge but also change the worldviews of the population can be observed throughout the existence of this institution under the GDR. In a Urania protocol from 1954, this purpose was addressed in the following way:

> The spread of scientific knowledge must contribute to the formation of the scientific and materialist worldview of our population. Lectures have to point out that nature proceeds according to natural laws and dialectically, that there are no miracles, that the world can be comprehended and changed by us, and that we do not depend on "higher beings." ... Lectures in natural sciences therefore have to be consciously used as instruments to fight superstition, non-scientific ideas, and mysticism.[54]

As a certain counterpart to this development, the Leopoldina—a prestigious academy of the natural sciences that existed throughout the GDR

as an all-German institution and that managed to maintain some independence under the socialist regime—invited West German members, such
as Carl Friedrich von Weizsäcker, who gave lectures in the rooms of the
churches, explicitly as a Christian *and* a scientist. But, by its nature, this
academic institution could not exert the same influence as a mass institution like the Urania.

A comparative analysis of biology books in the GDR and West Germany from 1948 through 1989 also supports these findings for secondary
schools.[55] It shows that, with reference to the theory of evolution and the
question of how the world and human life came into being, West German
biology books tended to point out the difference between scientific, philosophical, and religious ways of addressing those questions but explicitly
underlined the legitimacy of the religious view. One might say that the
state encouraged a functionally differentiated worldview. Until the end
of the 1970s, however, GDR biology books tended to refer to religious
ideas (e.g., the idea of creation) as irrational and tried to give proof of the
supremacy of a scientific worldview. In the later period, the presentation
became more neutral, and religious perspectives were no longer addressed.

Ideological Weltanschauung and Subjective Worldviews

Regarding the process of secularization, the question is whether this Weltanschauung remained only on the level of political ideology—that is, as an
issue of political rhetoric rather than of social influence—or if it was able
to affect the actual worldviews of the population and become a subjective
motif of secularization. Survey data certainly cannot give a definite answer
to this question, but they may give some hints.

Various survey data show that East and West Germans, even today, respond differently when they are asked to give their opinion on the exclusive
relevance of rational explanations or the reliability of modern medicine. In
a survey conducted every ten years by the Protestant church in Germany
among its members and among people without church affiliation, respondents were asked to judge the following statement: "In my opinion, one
should stick to things that one can understand rationally and leave everything else as it is" (table 9.1).

Because the context in which this question was asked was different in
the two questionnaires,[56] the difference between the two surveys is difficult to interpret. Other surveys, such as ALLBUS (Die Allgemeine Be-

Table 9.1: Positive Responses to the Statement, "In My Opinion, One Should Stick to Things That One Can Understand Rationally and Leave Everything Else as It Is"

Survey	Share of survey respondents (%)			
	Nonmembers, East Germany	Nonmembers, West Germany	Protestant church members, East Germany	Protestant church members, West Germany
1992	60.0	46.0	24.0	20.0
2002	51.0	40.0	36.5	31.0

Sources: For 1992, Klaus Engelhardt, Hermann von Loewenich, and Peter Steinacker, eds., *Fremde Heimat Kirche* (Gütersloh, Germany: Gütersloher Verlagshaus, 1997), 407; for 2002, Monika Wohlrab-Sahr and Friederike Benthaus-Apel, "Weltsichten," in *Kirche in der Vielfalt der Lebenszüge: Die Vierte EKD-Erhebung über Kirchenmitgliedschaft,* ed. Johannes Friedrich, Wolfgang Huber, and Peter Steinacker (Gütersloh, Germany: Gütersloher Verlagshaus, 2006), 297.

Note: Table shows respondents who indicated 6 or 7, using a scale of 1 to 7 to indicate level of agreement with the statement.

völkerungsumfrage der Sozialwissenschaften, or the German General Social Survey), however, support this lasting difference. In 2002, regarding the statement that "[human] life is only a part of what happens in nature," 55 percent of East Germans opted for "applies completely," as opposed to 32 percent of West Germans. Regarding the statement, "In the end, our lives are determined by the laws of nature," this relationship was 50.5 percent as opposed to 27.7 percent.[57] Both surveys clearly indicate that there is still a difference between the two parts of the country, not only regarding church membership but also regarding a worldview focusing on rationalism and science as opposed to other modes of approaching life. Different from Bruce's thesis about the influence of relativism on the secularization process, the SED definitely did not support a relativistic view. The situation was, in fact, just the opposite. Science was supposed to substitute for religion and fulfill its central functions. And in line with that view, it was considered the "truth," and not—as would be the case in a relativistic view—a potentially valid perspective among others. It is not by chance that one of the books on popular science given to the participants in the Jugendweihe was introduced by Walter Ulbricht, the head of state of the GDR, with the following words: "This book is the book of truth."[58]

Obviously, in the GDR it was not the *indifference* of a pluralistic relativism that undermined the position of religion but rather the *antagonism* between religion and an ideologically framed concept of science. It was not some kind of "peaceful" functional differentiation of religion and science that was characteristic of this society; instead the characteristic feature was the direct competition of religion and science, by which an ideological concept of science as a Weltanschauung became itself a kind of religion.

But the success of this concept obviously depended on the fact that the so-called scientific worldview was not merely ideological but was ideological by means of science, aiming at the disenchantment of the world. Consequently, the relativism of developing comparative perspectives on one side and the systematic disenchantment by means of science on the other side may constitute two different types of relationships between religion and science, with a negative outcome for religion in both cases. Whereas relativism may allow for skepticism and for some kind of general religious attitude but tends to undermine a specific religious confession, disenchantment by means of science tends to devaluate a religious perspective in general—as happened in the GDR. It also puts pressure on the religious part of the population inasmuch as they have to confront the reproach of being behind the times and irrational. On top of that, Protestantism, as a confession with a great deal of internal secularization, will probably mobilize less resistance against such disenchantment and antagonism than will Catholicism.

Religion, Science, and the Worldviews of East German Families

In the following section, we will refer to findings of a research project about the religious development and secularization process in East Germany. In this project, which was undertaken between 2003 and 2006 and funded by the German Research Foundation (Deutsche Forschungsgemeinschaft), we conducted a series of biographical interviews and family interviews with three generations of family members, as well as group discussions among the youngest generation. Between three and five people of three family generations participated in the family interviews. The youngest interviewees were in their late twenties, whereas the oldest interviewees were in their seventies and eighties. These interviews were mainly about the family histories and personal biographies, with the political, ideological, social, and religious transformations during and after the GDR regime as the background. In the final part of the interviews, the family members were asked to discuss certain questions, for example: "What do you think will happen after death?"

The research, in its origin, did not hypothesize the conflicting relationship between science and religion to be an essential element of East Germans' worldviews today. The interviews made very clear, however, that the scientific worldview, with its conflictive framing of the relationship between science and religion, did not remain mere state ideology. Instead, the concept continued to play a significant role in the worldviews of ordinary people. We will give some examples to illustrate this conflicting relation.

First, we will quote a passage from an interview with a family living near Berlin. The affiliation of this family with the Protestant church was already weak during the 1950s, but the grandfather and grandmother remained church members. The mother—representing the middle generation—received some religious education from her grandmother.

> Mother: My grandmother was very pious. I remember when [Yuri Alekseyevich] Gagarin was in outer space for the first time, she said, "Child, you will see what happens. God will come and bump his head." … But, you know, she was a very simple person. At that time they didn't even have eight classes in school.… She grew up in a village and got her moral values from the Bible.… She told me about Christianity and about the Bible. And because I was somewhat opposed to the young pioneers,… I felt attached to Christianity. And I had a lot of fantasies as well. I loved myths and fairytales and stories. [Family 2]

Gagarin's statement that he had looked for God in the outer space but could not find him was spread in the Soviet Union in the 1960s as a kind of proof of God's nonexistence. In that kind of communication, religious worldviews are presented as being synonymous with irrationality, whereas science represents truth and enlightenment. Thus, the latent conflict between religion and science is transformed into a manifest one. When the grandmother's remark on Gagarin is explained by her lack of education, her religiosity is also specifically framed. The way in which the interviewee quotes her grandmother mirrors the simple and concrete form of religious thinking that the East German state ridiculed to discredit religion in general. Later, we will see that the mother finally follows this official interpretation. But during her childhood, she was still influenced by her grandmother's religious beliefs.

A few years later in school, however, the mother was more and more frequently confronted with the concept of the scientific worldview. As a result of this influence, her previous religiosity lost its plausibility:

> Mother: Later on I had the natural sciences in school. And then, you know, you become knowledgeable, and then you say, "No!" It was because I had gotten to know religious belief in this simple form. And then I thought, "This is all humbug. ... You can explain everything." Well, I didn't turn into a Communist, but rather into an Atheist at that time." [Family 2]

During her years at school, the mother disregarded the naïve and old-fashioned religious belief of her grandmother. The grandmother's religion was considered "humbug," which would obviously lose the battle against the forces of science and progress. These sequences mirror the core argument of the SED, according to which religion was part of a system of false and irrational beliefs and science represented the truth.

The example of this family also indicates a very important second point: even if Marxism–Leninism combined scientism and communism, in everyday life it was possible to just refer to the scientism aspects. This combination of "pro-science" and "contra-religion" seems especially important for the sustainability of the general (societal) secularization process. The pro-science notion could be detached from the political context and survive as a seemingly modern, enlightened position, as is the case in today's East Germany.

Later in the interview, when the family's daughter was talking with her mother, it became very clear that it was this enlightened, culturalist stance on religion that had survived the political regime:

> Mother: Well, you didn't come from a religious household with saying grace and all this. Of course, we didn't do that. Well, we talked about such things, and you knew a lot of biblical stories. I narrated them to you.

> Daughter: Well, nicely wrapped, and always with a question mark.

> Mother: Always as a story. More as cultural assets than as a matter of belief. [Family 2]

As seen in this conversation, the weak church affiliation in the older generation constitutes the foundation of the secularization process for this family. Even if the family members in the middle generation still gained some religious socialization at home, they dismissed the Christian religion as being old-fashioned and irrational during their school time. This occurrence is obviously in line with the official scientistic arguments about religion. To a certain degree, the family also represents the often-described process of the internal secularization of Protestantism. But this process is clearly enforced by the particular ideological elements that were propagated in the GDR. Religion remains relevant only as a cultural element and as a fund of myths: always narrated "as stories" and "with a question mark."

Next, we will briefly present the case of a second family. Here, the conflicting interpretations of science and religion strikingly correlate with the perspectives of different family generations. The somewhat longer sequence is taken from the last part of the interview, when the family was asked to discuss the question, "What do you think will happen after death?"

Interviewer: What do you think will happen after death?

Grandmother: Ashes and nothing else. That's what scientists think....

Mother: Well, it's different with me, well I—

Grandmother: Fifty years of medicine.

Mother: Well, we don't know.

Grandmother: I haven't seen anybody rise from the dead.

Mother: Well, I have dealt intensely with all these stories about near-death experiences. ... This is because of that experience by the ocean. I think I was three years old. I was caught by a wave, and I was actually gone. I had stopped breathing, and I was just seeing colors. It was so beautiful. And then they carried me out, and my huge father pressed on my chest—it was so terrible.

Grandmother: Reanimated.

Mother: I was so mad that they got me back.... I remember it exactly,... everything was floating, there were colors everywhere, it was really beautiful. And I read a few things about it, which had the same descriptions.

Grandmother: Well, it's not always. In neurosurgery I—

Mother: Well, OK, your brains can fool you, but—

Grandmother: I saw countless people dying. Many of them are dying with a smile on their face.

Mother: Right.…

Grandmother: Well, [asking her granddaughter] and what do you think will be then? You don't know yet, do you?

Daughter: No, I can't tell exactly.… But now I'm going to study medicine and it may be that I will have the same opinion as grandmother some day. But I can't tell now.

Grandmother: Well, you will have this opinion in fifty years.

Daughter: Well, I do think that there will be something.… I can't tell exactly what and don't know exactly if I really believe in God. But in any case I do believe in some higher power, definitely. Because there are so many mysterious things, and, I don't know, I just want it to be, because you preserve something for yourself.… But I can't tell exactly.…

Grandmother: Well, there are mysterious things, but they are just not yet explained by science, like many things in science. [Family 9]

This sequence indicates the dominance of the grandmother's scientific worldview. Mother and daughter clearly differ from that view, because the daughter attempts to reserve a certain sphere of "nonexplicability" and, thereby, keep a window open for some transcendent perspective. But with the implicit distinction of explicable versus nonexplicable, the daughter and grandmother inevitably remain within the communication code of science, only marking a larger space for inexplicable, mysterious phenomena. Clearly rejecting the possible interpretation that such phenomena may be considered signs of a completely different sphere, the grandmother insists that those things can "not yet" be explained, thus implying that in the future they certainly will be explained. None of the two other discussants is able to hold her ground against the strict scientific perspective of the grandmother.

Even the granddaughter (who became a member of a Catholic ethnic minority—the Sorbs—to which her father also belongs) concedes that her perspective might change in the future when she works as a medical doctor like her grandmother, as if she accepts that it is *normal* for a scientist not to believe.

In general, the perspective of scientistic atheism, as represented by the grandmother but also found in similar ways in a great variety of other interviews, can be summed up in the following manner:

1. All things can be scientifically proven.
2. There may be phenomena that appear miraculous today, but they will be explained by science in the future.
3. What cannot be proven does not exist.
4. Religion may be useful (for society or the community) in functional terms, but it is irrational as a belief.
5. From a personal point of view, there is nothing beyond death—only ashes or dead bodies.
6. From a universal point of view, there is something beyond death: science will move on to explain the world.

Against the background of such a worldview, religious perspectives are, indeed, as Weber argued, forced to compete with science on scientific terrain and thereby lose their specific character.

Nascent Religious-like Orientations within the Framework of a Scientific Worldview

Against the backdrop of such a predominant framework: What do nascent religious-like orientations look like?

In reference to the age group that the daughter of Family 9 belongs to, general social surveys in recent years indicate a certain opening up when it comes to religious issues—in particular, a clear increase in the belief in an afterlife. In a 2002 survey, participants in the eighteen- to twenty-nine-year-old age group reported believing in an afterlife at twice the rate as the same age group in a similar study conducted ten years earlier.[59] In 2002, 33.6 percent of participants were in favor of such a statement. If we take this finding as a measure of religiosity, the youngest age group, ranging from nineteen to twenty-nine, must be considered the most religious one in East Germany. Even if there is a growing belief in the afterlife among the youngest respondents in many parts of the world, the level of increase and the specific location of the youngest generation in East Germany are certainly noteworthy.

We will now refer to interview passages that are intended to illustrate the specific kind of religious renewal in East Germany. What we want to point out is that this renewal has a different structure than the processes of religious revitalization that have been studied in other parts of the world. Such renewals have been referred to mainly as (a) religious belief outside of churches (believing without belonging), (b) the rise of charismatic Christian groups, or (c) spirituality that is opposed to religiosity and related to New Age and other influences. Even if those tendencies certainly also exist in East Germany, our interview data show that the "religious-like" tendencies among younger East Germans—documented by a growing belief in an afterlife—are themselves related to the framework of a scientistic worldview. Referring to our concept of secularization as conflict and to Weber's notion of a competition between different societal spheres, we argue that it is part of the heritage of the GDR that an emerging religiosity has to prove itself on scientific terrain. This scientistic framework can be found in discussions among families who maintained their church ties and among those who cut church ties and consider themselves atheists.

The first passage is from an interview with a thoroughly secularized family, and the second passage is from an interview with a Catholic family that was highly integrated in a Catholic milieu throughout the GDR era. We quote a passage from the first interview during which the daughter elaborates on her idea about the reconstitution of a person's consciousness after the death of that person.

Daughter: Well,... this fact of the consciousness ... this constitution, that we are more than just a bunch of molecules, how this actually happens, I can't explain this, and maybe this cannot be explained by science at all.... I don't know. With this one exception, I think everything can be scientifically explained. And I think that it is just the same with regard to the issue of death: the molecules certainly decompose, and what may be referred to as the "soul," to be conscious of oneself, this is what I already thought as a child: that someday someone else will be me. I don't really believe in reincarnation, but I do think that there is some kind of circuit. It's obvious. I will decompose, I will be cremated, I will be eaten by maggots or thrown into the water, whatever.... I don't care what happens to my body, because it enters this circuit. But I think that someday it will happen that there will be a human being who will be me, you know....

Mother: That's what you think? [Family 18]

What is interesting here is, first of all, the idea that the consciousness is something that cannot be completely grasped by means of science. The mere existence of such a phenomenon fascinates the daughter so much that, earlier in the interview, she talks about it as a miracle. Whereas the body enters a process of unavoidable decomposition, the consciousness is considered to be excluded from this decay. The notion of reincarnation that she refers to does not seem to capture the meaning that she tries to communicate. So she comes up with a modified "circuit model" in which the consciousness has a specific position. It seems to be preserved somehow for later reconstitution. For her parents, those ideas seem to be the result of an overactive imagination.

Even if the daughter assumes that the consciousness will also decompose with the death of a person, she insists that it will later be reconstituted. Consciousness is, therefore, perceived as being independent of the physical body and possessing a unique constitution that it either maintains or regains after death. This perception gives the person a feeling of deep connectivity with the world. It is striking how the issue of the afterlife is given a very specific notion. With the idea that the consciousness may be reconstituted and settle into a new person who will say, "I am me," the daughter develops an idea of personal immortality without referring to explicit religious ideas. But, obviously, this new person is one who is able to say, "I am me" without any personal history. Molecules of consciousness will meet within this person and settle in her as in a container.

Some interviewees relied on science fiction–like notions to deal with the problem of personal finitude, thereby distancing themselves from both atheistic ideas and Christian ideas alike, whereas other interviewees used scientific theories. A Catholic family, for example, agreed after extensive debate that a "bundle of energy" remains after death—a conclusion clearly relying on the law of the conservation of energy. During the GDR period, this family had been strongly integrated into an educated, middle-class Catholic milieu. When asked what will happen after death, the family members expressed different ideas:

> Interviewer: What do you think will happen after death? [several people laughing]
>
> Father: It doesn't look very promising. [everybody laughing out loud]
>
> Son: That's the question.
>
> Daughter: Nothing...
>
> Interviewer: Nothing?
>
> Daughter: But a kind of nothing that is not scary.
>
> Interviewer: Uh-huh.
>
> Daughter: Well, I don't think that you get into some kind of garden or anything like that.
>
> Interviewer: Uh-huh.
>
> Mother: No, I wouldn't say "nothing." But as she said, not like a garden or a cloud, but maybe some kind of—this sounds silly—but some kind of power, or matter, or soul ... something like a bundle of energy or something like that [laughing] somehow is conserved [laughing].
>
> Father: Like in *Matrix*.
>
> Mother: Uh, exactly. [laughing] No matter where. [everybody laughing]
>
> Father: All that matters is to be a bundle of energy....
>
> Mother: Now you tell! What do you think?...
>
> Father: [laughing] Well, I hope that one's belief is good for something inasmuch as there still will be something. But I don't know what. One might call it a bundle of energy....

Son: Do you think that the others still will be there somewhere?...

Father: That's why the universe expands, to give space to all of us.... You could build a theory on that. [Family 1]

When approaching the issue of the afterlife, the first statements by the father and by the daughter are, respectively, "it doesn't look very promising" and "nothing." As the conversation continues, the family members do not adhere to those skeptical, even negative statements, but it becomes clear that they cannot relate to Christian doctrines and religious semantics either. Instead, they develop the abstract idea that there will be (and should be) something after death that, if it exists, will be permanent. Moreover, earthly images may not suffice to grasp the meaning of this "something" after death. But no one refers to the Christian idea of resurrection or to any similar idea. The mother's response to the daughter's "nothing" is striking: she supplies the scientific metaphor of the conservation of matter, illustrated by the phrase "a bundle of energy," which might be conserved after death. The father then relates this idea to a science fiction film (*The Matrix*) as well as to physical theories ("That's why the universe expands.... You could build a theory on that"). Though the family obviously makes fun of the metaphor, they do not completely reject it. At one point, the children offer alternative scenarios of the afterlife using biological metaphors, such as living in a tree, instead of scientific ones. However, those scenarios are rejected as well; such ideas are considered too profane and products of wishful thinking.

In the end, the result of their debate is an open question that requires further reasoning. The scientific metaphors of "conserving matter" and "a bundle of energy" are substitutes for religious semantics, yet ideas of transcendence and of eternity are still visible.

Conclusion: Modes of Relationship between Science and Religion

In conclusion, we would like to connect these empirical findings with some reflections about secularization, in general, and the role that the tension between religion and science may play in the process of secularization. Bringing Luhmann and Weber together as theoretical representatives of nonconflictive and conflictive modes of societal differentiation can help to clarify the effects of different developments in the realm of religion. The tension between science and religion is certainly one of the basic tensions accompanying the functional differentiation of societal spheres, which we consider the fundamental aspect of secularization. In this way, the example of the GDR is one in a variety of secular developments in modernity.[60] But obviously, the modes of dealing with this tension are very different, and they have different results for the position of religion in society. There are conflictive and nonconflictive modes, and the conflict may be dealt with vicariously by certain groups or may be turned into a predominant ideology by leading political or religious groups (see table 9.2).

For the GDR, a conflictive relationship between science and religion was characteristic, and it accompanied and enforced the process of secularization. The conflict was rooted in historical constellations and embedded in historical semantics, but it was reinforced by the socialist state and the state party after 1949. However, history shows very different modes of the relationship between both spheres.[61] Conflicts between science and religion obviously can occur in other forms as well, and these conflicts do not necessarily proceed according to the same logic as they did in East Germany. The political elites of the GDR propagated an interpretation of science that claimed responsibility for *absolutely all* spheres of society and personal life. Consequently, it left no space for religious institutions or beliefs, which were perceived as traditional and premodern.

The most important characteristic of the East German case is that science developed into an agent in terms of providing people salvation and

Table 9.2: Modes of Relationship between Science and Religion

	Conflict	No conflict
Religious decline	Antagonism between science and religion: enforced disenchantment (scientistic ideology)	Indifference as a result of relativism
Religious stability	Antagonism between religion and science: enforced reenchantment (fundamentalism)	Functional differentiation of religious and scientific perspectives with mutual acceptance

Source: Monika Wohlrab-Sahr, "Religion *and* Science or Religion *versus* Science? About the Social Construction of the Science-Religion-Antagonism in the German Democratic Republic and Its Lasting Consequences," in *The Role of Religion in Modern Societies*, ed. Detlef Pollack and Daniel Olson (New York: Routledge, 2008), 223–47.

meaning. Historically, this idea was not new. But in the GDR, the idea was not only propagated by small groups as before but also enforced by political state elites and spread by mass institutions, such as Urania. Hence, it is not science, as such, that is likely to collide with religion in such a fundamental way by offering a Weberian means of inner-worldly salvation, but rather a scientific worldview. Nevertheless, the possibility that the boundaries may be blurred is certainly always there.

Obviously, churches or religious movements—as the example of creationism indicates—may also gain strength from the construction of a science–religion antagonism. But in the long run, in a modern society with a highly developed system of science, such a constellation will remain precarious or stabilize itself only in a sectarian enclave. Besides this sectarian option, religious stability in modern societies depends on social support not only for functional differentiation on the societal level, but also for mental differentiation and cognitive ambiguity. This situation would imply that an important, but nevertheless limited, field is reserved for scientific explanations, whereas another similar, accepted area is reserved for religious interpretations of life events and experiences. Even if both perspectives may be partly perceived as contradictory, people may, nevertheless, have a certain tolerance for such ambiguity without trying to discuss the plausibility of religion in a scientific manner.

If the dominant perspective of a society is that religion and science are mutually exclusive, religion is in danger of being restricted to marginal institutions and sectarian perspectives. However, if the dominant perspective of a society is that religion and science do not compete in the same field but are complementary to each other, and if this perspective resonates in people's actual worldviews, the chances for religious stability or even vitality may increase. Such mental differentiation may be encouraged not only by a developed system of functional differentiation but also—in authoritarian regimes—by strong churches or religious movements that manage to uphold their opposing perspective toward the authoritarian state.

But as Weber very clearly anticipated, under such circumstances religious groups and organizations are always in danger of undermining their own religious position by trying to give a scientific foundation to the religious perspective. The issue of creation is a favorite object for such constructions.

Consequently, our general hypothesis would be that in modern societies the implications of secularization processes on religious stability, vitality, or decline depend on social and political framing, as well as on mental constructions about how religion and science relate to each other. Modernity entails a basic tension between religion and science, which constitutes a foundation for conflict. But under certain constellations, this tension may be turned into an open conflict and into a general cultural framing, as was the case in the GDR. Nevertheless, the success of this ideology depends on whether it is based on the ideas of science and, thus, could relate to a basic concept in modernity. It is this connection that enables the science–religion antagonism to be detached from the political context in which it was propagated and to create a particular type of secular habitus.

Notes

1. José Casanova, "Die religiöse Lage in Europa," in *Säkularisierung und die Weltreligionen*, ed. Hans Joas and Klaus Wiegandt (Frankfurt: Fischer Verlag, 2007), 322–57.

2. For more information, see also Monika Wohlrab-Sahr, "Religion *and* Science or Religion *versus* Science? About the Social Construction of the Science-Religion-Antagonism in the German Democratic Republic and Its Lasting Consequences," in *The Role of Religion in Modern Societies*, ed. Detlef Pollack and Daniel Olson (New York: Routledge, 2008), 223–47.

3. Monika Wohlrab-Sahr, Uta Karstein, and Thomas Schmidt-Lux, *Forcierte Säkularität: Religiöser Wandel und Generationendynamik im Osten Deutschlands* (Frankfurt: Campus, 2009); Monika Wohlrab-Sahr, Thomas Schmidt-Lux, and Uta Karstein, "Secularization as Conflict," *Social Compass* 55, no. 2 (2008): 127–39; Monika Wohlrab-Sahr, "'Forced' Secularity? On the Appropriation of Repressive Secularization," *Religion and Society in Central and Eastern Europe* 4, no. 1 (2011): 63–77.

4. Bridging the gap is obviously important in the United States. See chapter 7, by James Gilbert, in this volume.

5. Niklas Luhmann, *Funktion der Religion* (Frankfurt: Suhrkamp, 1977); Niklas Luhmann, *Die Religion der Gesellschaft* (Frankfurt: Suhrkamp, 2000).

6. Peter L. Berger, *The Sacred Canopy: Elements of a Sociological Theory of Religion* (Garden City, NY: Doubleday).

7. Thomas Luckmann, "Über die Funktion von Religion," in *Die religiöse Dimension der Gesellschaft*, ed. Peter Koslowski (Tübingen, Germany: Mohr, 1985), 26–41.

8. Detlef Pollack, *Kirche in der Organisationsgesellschaft: Zum Wandel der gesellschaftlichen Lage der evangelischen Kirchen in der DDR* (Stuttgart, Germany: Kohlhammer, 1994), 381.

9. Thomas Schmidt-Lux, *Wissenschaft als Religion: Szientismus im ostdeutschen Säkularisierungsprozess* (Würzburg, Germany: Ergon, 2008); Thomas Schmidt-Lux, "Das helle Licht der Wissenschaft: Die Urania, der organisierte Szientismus und die ostdeutsche Säkularisierung," *Geschichte und Gesellschaft* 34, no. 1 (2008): 41–72.

10. Rodney Stark and Roger Finke, *Acts of Faith: Explaining the Human Side of Religion* (Berkeley: University of California Press, 2000), 55.

11. In a comparative perspective, this approach could also imply that we look for the conditions under which the conflictive construction of the differentiation between science and religion was avoided or attempted to be reconciled. See chapter 7, by James Gilbert, in this volume.

12. Philip S. Gorski, "Historicizing the Secularisation Debate: An Agenda for Research," in *Handbook of the Sociology of Religion*, ed. Michele Dillon (Cambridge, U.K.: Cambridge University Press, 2003), 110–22; Christian Smith, *The Secular Revolution: Power, Interests, and Conflict in the Secularization of American Public Life* (Berkeley: University of California Press, 2003).

13. "Evolution, Creationism, Intelligent Design," Gallup, Washington, DC, http://www.gallup.com/poll/21814/evolution-creationism-intelligent-design.aspx.

14. Auguste Comte, *The Positive Philosophy of Auguste Comte*, trans. Harriet Martineau (Chicago: Chicago University Press, 2002).

15. Max Weber, *Economy and Society: An Outline of Interpretative Sociology* (Berkeley: University of California Press, 1978).

16. Uwe Schimank, *Theorien gesellschaftlicher Differenzierung* (Opladen, Germany: Leske & Budrich, 1996).

17. Max Weber, "Religious Rejections of the World and Their Directions," in *From Max Weber: Essays in Sociology*, ed. Hans H. Gerth and Charles W. Mills (New York: Oxford University Press, 1958), 325–59, quoted at 350–51.

18. Ibid., 357.

19. Weber, *Economy and Society*.

20. Günter Dux, *Die Logik der Weltbilder* (Frankfurt: Suhrkamp, 1982); Ulrich Oevermann, "Strukturelle Religiosität und ihre Ausprägungen unter Bedingungen der vollständigen Säkularisierung des Bewusstseins," in *Atheismus und religiöse Indifferenz*, ed. Christel Gärtner, Detlef Pollack, and Monika Wohlrab-Sahr (Opladen, Germany: Leske & Budrich, 2003), 339–87.

21. Hugh McLeod, "Secular Cities? Berlin, London, and New York in the Later Nineteenth and Early Twentieth Centuries," in *Religion and Modernization: Sociologists and Historians Debate the Secularization Thesis*, ed. Steve Bruce (Oxford, U.K.: Oxford University Press, 1992), 59–89.

22. José Casanova, "Global Trends at the Turn of the Millennium" (lecture, University of Erfurt, Germany, July 7, 2003); Casanova, "Die religiöse Lage in Europa."

23. Whereas, in the American context, the term *science* is usually used for the natural sciences, we use it here for all kinds of scientific endeavors. However, we acknowledge that in certain periods the main opposition was constructed as one between religion and natural sciences and that other sciences were conceptualized according to the model of the natural sciences.

24. Bernard Plé, *Die "Welt" aus den Wissenschaften: Der Positivismus in Frankreich, England und Italien von 1848 bis ins Zweite Jahrzehnt des 20. Jahrhunderts—Eine wissenssoziologische Studie* (Stuttgart, Germany: Klett-Cotta, 1996); Schmidt-Lux, *Wissenschaft als Religion*; Schmidt-Lux, "Das helle Licht der Wissenschaft."

25. Schmidt-Lux, *Wissenschaft als Religion*.

26. Ibid., 105.

27. The Supreme Court cases in point are *Epperson v. Arkansas*, 1968 (the ban on the teaching of evolution theory), and *Edwards v. Aguillard*, 1987 (the ban on the

teaching of Creation Science or Scientific Creationism). Recently, *Kitzmiller v. Dover Area School District*, 2005, became important. This decision prohibited the teaching of intelligent design. Although the case referred only to one district of Pennsylvania, it set a precedent.

28. "Evolution, Creationism, Intelligent Design."

29. Stark and Finke, *Acts of Faith*.

30. Ibid., 53.

31. Ibid., 55.

32. Elaine Howard Ecklund and Christopher P. Scheitle, "Religion among Academic Scientists: Distinctions, Disciplines, and Demographics," *Social Problems* 54, no. 2 (2007): 289–307. The data of this study refer to the RAAS, a survey on religion among American scientists who work at elite institutions. As a whole, the authors question the existence of fundamental differences in religiosity between natural and social scientists. Certain groups of scientists, however, indicate remarkably high numbers of nonbelief and agnosticism, especially among physicists (nonbelief, 40.8 percent; agnosticism, 29.4 percent) and biologists (nonbelief, 41 percent; agnosticism, 29.9 percent). Ibid., 296.

33. Steve Bruce, *God Is Dead: Secularization in the West* (Oxford, U.K.: Blackwell, 2002).

34. Ibid., 117.

35. Margaret S. Archer, *Culture and Agency: The Place of Culture in Social Theory* (Cambridge, U.K.: Cambridge University Press, 1996).

36. Pollack, *Kirche in der Organisationsgesellschaft*.

37. Paul M. Zulehner and Hermann Denz, *Wie Europa lebt und glaubt* (Düsseldorf, Germany: 1994); Miklós Tomka and Paul M. Zulehner, *Religion in den Reformländern Ost(Mittel)Europas* (Vienna, Austria: Schwabenverlag, 1999), 27; Miklós Tomka and Paul M. Zulehner, *Religionen im gesellschaftlichen Kontext Ost(Mittel) Europas* (Vienna, Austria: Schwabenverlag, 2000); Casanova, "Die religiöse Lage in Europa."

38. Kurt Nowak, "Staat ohne Kirche? Überlegungen zur Entkirchlichung der evangelischen Bevölkerung im Staatsgebiet der DDR," in *Christen, Staat und Gesellschaft in der DDR*, ed. Gert Kaiser and Ewald Frie (Frankfurt: Wallstein, 1996), 23–43.

39. Lucian Hölscher, ed., *Datenatlas zur religiösen Geographie im protestantischen Deutschland: Von der Mitte des 19. Jahrhunderts bis zum Zweiten Weltkrieg*, vol. 1 (Berlin: de Gruyter, 2003), 7.

40. McLeod, "Secular Cities?," 66. See also Jochen-Christoph Kaiser, "Organisierter Atheismus im 19. Jahrhundert," in *Atheismus und religiöse Indifferenz*, ed. Christel Gärtner, Detlef Pollack, and Monika Wohlrab-Sahr (Opladen, Germany: Leske & Budrich, 2003), 99–127, 120.

41. Detlef Pollack, "Der Wandel der religiös-kirchlichen Lage in Ostdeutschland nach 1989: Ein Überblick," in *Religiöser and kirchlicher Wandel in Ostdeutschland 1989–1999*, ed. Detlef Pollack and Gert Pickel (Opladen, Germany: Leske & Budrich, 2000), 18–47; Gert Pickel, "Religiosität und Kirchlichkeit in Ost- und Westeuropa: Vergleichende Betrachtungen religiöser Orientierungen nach dem Umbruch in Europa," in *Religiöser Wandel in postkommunistischen Ländern Ost- und Mitteleuropas*, ed. Detlef Pollack, Irina Borowik, and Wolfgang Jagodzinski (Würzburg, Germany: Ergon, 1998), 55–85.

42. Wohlrab-Sahr, "Säkularisierungsprozesse und kulturelle Generationen: Ähnlichkeiten und Unterschiede zwischen Westdeutschland, Ostdeutschland und den

Niederlanden," in *Lebenszeiten: Erkundungen zur Soziologie der Generationen*, ed. Günter Burkart and Jürgen Wolf (Opladen, Germany: Leske & Budrich, 2002), 209–28; Monika Wohlrab-Sahr and Friederike Benthaus-Apel, "Weltsichten," in *Kirche in der Vielfalt der Lebenszüge: Die Vierte EKD-Erhebung über Kirchenmitgliedschaft*, ed. Johannes Friedrich, Wolfgang Huber, and Peter Steinacker (Gütersloh, Germany: Gütersloher Verlagshaus, 2006), 281–329.

43. Wohlrab-Sahr and Benthaus-Apel, "Weltsichten."

44. Martin Kohli, "Die DDR als Arbeitsgesellschaft? Arbeit, Lebenslauf und soziale Differenzierung," in *Sozialgeschichte der DDR*, ed. Hartmut Kaelble, Jürgen Kocka, and Hartmut Zwar (Stuttgart, Germany: Klett, 1994), 31–61; Wolfgang Engler, *Die Ostdeutschen: Kunde von einem verlorenen Land* (Berlin: Aufbau Verlag, 1999).

45. Luhmann, *Die Religion der Gesellschaft*.

46. Robert M. Montgomery, "Social Sources of Imperialistic Science," paper presented at Society for the Scientific Study of Religion, New York, October 22–24, 2004.

47. Matthäus Klein and Götz Redlow, *Warum eine wissenschaftliche Weltanschauung?* (Berlin: Dietz, 1973), 4.

48. Matthäus Klein, "Das gesellschaftliche Bewusstsein und seine Rolle in der Entwicklung der Gesellschaft," in *Wissenschaftliche Weltanschauung*, vol. 3 (Berlin: Dietz, 1960), 71.

49. Georg Klaus, Alfred Kosing, and Götz Redlow, "Einheit und Kampf der Gegensätze," in *Wissenschaftliche Weltanschauung*, vol. 4 (Berlin: Dietz, 1959), 48.

50. Montgomery, "Social Sources of Imperialistic Science."

51. Paul Froese, "After Atheism: An Analysis of Religious Monopolies in the Post-Communist World," *Sociology of Religion* 65, no. 1 (2004): 57–75.

52. Oskar Mader, "Zu den Aufgaben und zum Inhalt des Astronomieunterrichts," in *Methodischer Brief zum Lehrplan für das Fach Astronomie*, ed. Deutsches Pädagogisches Sozialinstitut (Berlin: Dietz, 1959).

53. Schmidt-Lux, *Wissenschaft als Religion*; Schmidt-Lux, "Das helle Licht der Wissenschaft"; Igor J. Polianski, "Das Rätsel DDR und die Welträtsel: Wissenschaftlich-atheistische Aufklärung als propagandistisches Konzept der SED," *Deutschlandarchiv* 2 (2007): 265–74.

54. "Urania annual plan 1955," presented at a meeting of the Urania secretariat, December 21, 1954, and found in the Central Archives of the East German political parties and mass organizations, in the Federal Archives, Berlin; Schmidt-Lux, *Wissenschaft als Religion*, 257.

55. Torsten Morche, *Weltall ohne Gott, Erde ohne Kirche, Mensch ohne Glauben: Zur Darstellung von Religion, Kirche und "Wissenschaftlicher Weltanschauung" in "Weltall, Erde, Mensch" zwischen 1954 und 1974 in Relation zum Staat-Kirche-Verhältnis und der Entwicklung der Jugendweihe in der DDR* (Leipzig, Germany: Kirchhof & Franke, 2006).

56. In the 1992 church membership survey, the statement was put in the context of statements about belief, Christianity, and religion. In the 2002 survey, the statement was put in the context of statements about life and its meaning.

57. The results can be downloaded from the ALLBUScompact database of the Leibniz Institute for Social Science, Mannheim, Germany. See ALLBUS: ZA-Nr. 3700, variables 116 and 114 at http://www.gesis.org/dienstleistungen/daten/umfragedaten/allbus/datenzugang/download-allbuscompact.

58. Gisela Buschendorf-Otto, Horst Wolfgramm, and Irmgard Radandt, *Weltall, Erde, Mensch: Ein Sammelwerk zur Entwicklungsgeschichte von Natur und Gesellschaft* (Berlin: Verlag Neues Leben, 1957).

59. See ALLBUS: ZA-No. 3700, variable 172, and ALLBUS: ZA-No. 1900, variable 468, in the ALLBUScompact database of the Leibniz Institute for Social Science, Mannheim, Germany, http://www.gesis.org/dienstleistungen/daten/umfragedaten/allbus/datenzugang/download-allbuscompact (calculations by the author).

60. See also Shmuel N. Eisenstadt, "Multiple Modernities," *Daedalus* 129, no. 1 (2000): 1–29.

61. John Hedley Brooke, *Science and Religion: Some Historical Perspectives* (Cambridge, U.K.: Cambridge University Press, 1993).

Part IV

Identity and Politics

Chapter 10

Jewish Identity in Late Nineteenth- and Early Twentieth-Century Europe

Klaus Hödl

Throughout the nineteenth and early twentieth centuries, Jews in Central Europe strove to be accepted by society at large without having to discard their Jewishness. Accomplishing this goal was close to impossible because society's dominant culture was strongly imbued with anti-Jewish biases. Sharing this culture and asserting themselves as Germans, for example, frequently implied the adoption of Judeophobic attitudes and an abnegation of their own Jewishness. This dilemma found its telling expression in the situation of Jewish physicians, who frequently could be professionally successful only if they were acknowledged members of their "scientific community" and refrained from questioning its methodological approaches.[1] However, these "scientific tools" often served as the underpinnings for anti-Jewish stereotypes.[2] Jewish physicians were thus faced with the choice between (a) gaining a reputation as a medical expert by overlooking the

The research for this chapter was funded by the Austrian Science Fund (FWF): P22325-G18.

221

anti-Semitic implications of medical paradigms or (b) being critical of the work of many of their fellow physicians for its anti-Jewish orientation and thus risking their chances for professional advancement.

This chapter delineates various efforts made by Jews to come to terms with the hindrances to becoming full-fledged members of the larger society while retaining their particular Jewish identity. The article intends to demonstrate that in the nineteenth century, Jewish religion was understood as the crucial and indispensable moment of Jewish self-consciousness and, therefore, became the central issue of political endeavors and controversies. From the late eighteenth century onward, state authorities tried to curtail the Jewish religion's effect on Jewish everyday life to shape Jewish existence according to the standards of the non-Jewish social environment, whereas the representatives of Jewish religious orthodoxy tried to preserve the integration of religion in Jews' daily routines. A different approach was pursued by many liberal-oriented and secular-minded Jews who wanted neither to dispose of Jewish religious influence nor to secure a purely religious concept of Judaism. Instead, they aimed at reinterpreting it according to scientific standards, thus sketching the observance of Jewish rituals and laws as a rational act and rendering Jewish behavior superior to non-Jewish behavior. Jewish identity, religion, political strategies, and power relations were thus intimately bound together.

This chapter starts by depicting several examples of popular culture at the turn of the twentieth century that incited people's wish to differentiate the fake from the original. These instances were part of a development that led to so-called scientific anti-Semitism, which was bound to discover the "real Jew" and the "essence of Jewishness" that was thought to become hidden through the process of assimilation. The text places particular stress on the interactional moment of Jewish and non-Jewish relations. It intends to demonstrate that Jews and non-Jews shared in various cultural processes and worked together to shape politics and society. This sharing even happened when anti-Semitic issues had soured their relations. The public lives of both Jews and non-Jews were thus inseparably intertwined, and both parties helped mutually shape the conditions under which the other lived.

The Search for the Authentic

In early 2009, the film *Buddenbrooks*, based on the 1901 novel by Thomas Mann, was shown at movie theaters throughout Germany. Designed as a family saga, it describes the decline of a merchant family from the northern German city of Lübeck. A key scene in the film, which is also relevant to this chapter, revolves around Konsul Buddenbrook's daughter's decision to agree to an arranged marriage. She discards her original reluctance after leafing through a book on the genealogy of the Buddenbrook family that convinces her of the supposed necessity of acquiescing to the wishes of the *pater familias* to safeguard the family's perpetuity and well-being.

In highlighting genealogy as a decisive factor in the young woman's life, the movie mirrors a conspicuous development in the late nineteenth century, namely, the efforts taken by many individuals to biologically embed themselves in larger social entities and share in their collective memories.[3] Huge migratory movements to urban centers, rapid social mobility, and the blurring of accustomed social boundaries challenged the traditional sense of history and inherited identifications.[4] People tried to compensate for their increasingly belabored self-consciousness through new forms of interconnectedness that would withstand the growing fluidity of social ties. According to one of the major concepts underlying these processes, individuals were comparable to links in a chain that related people as well as generations and, thereby, the past with the future. Nations or families were seen as paradigmatic collectives that could give people a sense of belonging and a perspective of history.[5] However, being part of these groups and thereby participating in the maintenance of their traditions were thought to depend on the possession of particular somatic properties. In this way, a specific view of the past was related to biology.

Genealogy was only one among various approaches to history in the late nineteenth and early twentieth centuries that helped people anchor themselves and develop a sense of identity in a period marked by dissolving certainties. In contrast to a genealogy that connected an individual's body to a particular historical perspective, other contemporary developments spurned references to the past altogether. Among the most ferocious protagonists in the fight against historical influences on the present or future were painters, architects, and writers belonging to cultural modernism.[6] Most of them were relentless critics of former styles; they wanted to produce something new, demolishing all bridges between the past and their own present.

During the period under consideration, one phenomenon emerged that both reflected and favored contemporary cultural processes such as turning away from history: namely, the mass press. It came into being in the second half of the nineteenth century and had to compete with existing highbrow papers for readership. It doggedly tried to assert itself by focusing on sensational stories and by exaggerating banal, ordinary occurrences and presenting them as important aspects of reality.[7] The strategy of exaggeration was aimed at exciting people and winning them over as readers. This success, however, happened at the cost of explaining and contextualizing the reported incidents and of investigating their causes. The effect the articles could have on people was considered more important than analyzing single events and making them comprehensible. The majority of the mass press's newspapers thus concentrated on the immediate effect. They stressed the temporary and the present—and consequently dispensed with references to the past. They thereby contributed to undermining their readers' sense of history and concurrently to increasing the importance of the biological.

The strategy of the mass press paid off insofar as it managed to gain for itself a wide readership. The Paris-based *Le Petit Journal*, for example, could boast a readership of 1 million by 1890, whereas the *Berliner Morgenpost*, launched by Leopold Ullstein in 1898, could rely on 100,000 subscribers seven months after its introduction.[8] Many people depended on the sensational press to acquire information about their social surroundings. Their perceptions, cultural horizon, and political leanings were strongly shaped by it. The emergence of populist parties as well as the anti-Semitic movement of the 1880s and 1890s would hardly be conceivable without the cheap print media.

However, the effect of the newspapers on their readers was not unidirectional, and people were not brainwashed by them. Contrary to the thesis put forth by Theodor Adorno and Max Horkheimer, according to which newspapers serve as instruments of control and integration and strongly influence the consciousness of people,[9] readers were aware that many of the articles they consumed were based on overstatement and immoderation. People retrieved a large share of their knowledge about their immediate social world from the papers, but they also started to feel uneasy about those papers' tendency to distort everyday occurrences. The readers did not take everything they read at face value and naïvely believe every exaggerated description; instead, they increasingly put stock in the differentiation between the authentic and the fake and developed a desire for the real. This tendency among "common people," the very readership of the mass press, can paradigmatically be attested to by the effect of the Parisian wax museum, Musée Grevin, on Paris's inhabitants. The museum became extremely popular and attracted large crowds because it displayed strikingly realistic representations of well-known contemporary celebrities.[10]

Another example serving as evidence of people's wish to encounter the original or at least something close to the authentic instead of its obvious copy stems from Vienna and concerns exotic exhibitions—that is, exhibitions of indigenous people. The first display took place in 1872, on which occasion four Laplanders—purportedly the only uncivilized people within the borders of Europe—were shown to the Viennese public. The visitors doubted the authenticity of the exhibited subjects, arguing that they probably were Viennese people in disguise. Only after professional philologists were employed to examine the Laplanders and attest to the authenticity of their spoken language were the irritated audiences pacified.[11]

These examples indicate that the turn of the twentieth century was characterized by seemingly contradictory developments. On the one hand, the emerging mass culture, which found expression in new forms of entertainment such as mass papers, department stores, and the like, displayed a largely *virtual* world that served as a refuge for people who felt overstrained by their daily lives. On the other, the inclination to overdraw banal incidents incited among people a desire for the *real*. Thus, they were not passively subject to the interpretation of the world presented to them by the media or the entertainment industry but instead drew their own conclusions from these cultural offerings. Many consumers of mass culture resisted the adoption of a perspective of their social surroundings proposed to them by societal institutions and asserted themselves in the process of interacting with such institutions.

The Relations between Jews and Non-Jews

Through exaggerations, the mass press incited doubt among many of its readers regarding the authenticity of uncommon and extraordinary occurrences. The hyperbolization of common incidents was one of numerous phenomena at the turn of the twentieth century that reflected and contributed to the dissolution of clear-cut distinctions and the undermining of traditional categorizations. This effect, in turn, brought about a sense of disarray and the desire for something permanent and immutable as a means of orientation. The confusion among many people over the shattering of certainties nurtured their desire for the steady and original and their longing for that which would be able to resist the disfigurement and decomposition brought on by modernity. In contrast to contemporary artists who dealt with the disintegration of the seemingly firm and solid, the so-called

ordinary people tended to focus on the real and unchangeable — on purportedly static phenomena — to find certitude in a world of increasingly vague
standards.[12]

The latter trend characterized contemporary relationships between Jews
and non-Jews. As late as the early nineteenth century, the overwhelming
majority of Jews were discernible by their attire and religious customs.
As the opportunities for Jews to socialize with and to pursue a life similar
to that of non-Jews grew, their Jewish peculiarities began to fade away.
With the exception of a few very Orthodox Jews, by the end of the century
Jews could no longer be made out as differing from society at large. Most
Jews dressed the same way as non-Jews, largely embraced the same interests, and shared in the same or similar activities. Differentiations among
Jews or among non-Jews were bigger than those that existed between the
two groups. For this reason Jews in Vienna or Berlin vociferously pro-
tested against the westward migration of the *Ostjuden* and felt they had
more in common with non-Jews than with their coreligionists from Eastern
Europe.[13]

Still, on many occasions Jews conceived of themselves as a collective
and consciously distinguished themselves from non-Jews. At other times,
however, they transgressed religious or ethnic boundaries and identified
with certain groups of non-Jews, which indicates that a clear separation
between them no longer existed. Identifications took on a temporary character and were changeable.[14] The relations between Jews and non-Jews can
probably best be characterized as being caught in a dynamic network.

Frequently, the process of Jews discarding their cultural peculiarities
has been called *acculturation*. This concept is based on the assumption that
a minority group (largely) adapts to the majority population, in this case
Jews to larger society.[15] The narrative of acculturation tends to focus on a
unidirectional process and to ignore the togetherness and joint activities
between the various social entities. Therefore, this chapter uses instead the
different and seemingly more appropriate term *modernization*. It denotes a
development in which Jews actively took part, rather than passively adjust-
ing to a given cultural and social structure. Jews as well as non-Jews participated in the constitution of social and cultural processes. In the course of
modernization, Jews shed many — frequently most, and sometimes all — of
their "peculiarities" that were not congruent with contemporary standards
of respectability.[16] Still, this development cannot be called acculturation
because Jews did not adapt to extraneous norms. Instead, they codeter-
mined the understanding of respectability together with non-Jews, who

also underwent the process of modernization.[17] Hasidic Jews as well as non-Jewish peasants discarded many of the characteristics assumed to be incompatible with their new lives.

Efforts by both Jews and non-Jews to shape contemporary processes brought them into closer contact with each other and increased the occasions at which they could meet and socialize. Both worked on shaping social and cultural processes that brought about new meeting spaces for the two groups. Mass culture was one of the results of modernization. It gave common people the possibility to culturally assert themselves. As a largely new phenomenon, mass culture tended to ignore traditional restrictions and boundaries. Similar to the mass press, it aimed at attracting consumers and thus neglected their traditional identifications. Therefore, Jews could participate in the new cultural life. In doing so, they encountered non-Jews and both could and did establish a new sense of togetherness. The disappearance of Jewish peculiarities thus went hand in hand with a growth in interaction with non-Jews.[18]

The Jews' efforts to get rid of their peculiarities and to lose their particular social status in the course of the nineteenth century could at times be so far reaching that references to a Jewish otherness were seen as ridiculous, as debates in the Austrian parliament attest.[19] Statements about ongoing differences between Jews and non-Jews received credence only if scientific findings supported them. Similar to the Laplanders previously mentioned, whose indigenousness was stated by philologists, so it was with Jews, whose distinction from society at large was determined and purportedly proven mostly by anthropologists and physicians. Such scholars claimed to be able to point out the characteristics of Jewishness, and in so doing, they referred above all to the Jewish body. Thus, it was physical peculiarities or a certain disposition to diseases that were thought to identify Jews. Again, as was the case with genealogy, the belonging or not-belonging was tied to supposedly biological properties.

The Construction of the "Jewish Body"

Defining a body as Jewish—that is, singling out somatic properties, proclivities to specific diseases, or mental dispositions that were ascribed to Jews more often than to other ethnic or religious groups—was a means of redrawing a line between the former and society at large after Jews had discarded their religious and cultural characteristics and come to resemble non-Jews in their dress and manners. Paradigmatic markers of distinction were a specific (Jewish) mode of speaking[20] or a gaze.[21] Even if Jews could not be discerned outwardly from non-Jews, they were thought to possess a body that very likely had certain malignant taints.

If ascribed to or found to be real, whether conspicuous or latent, the respective marks of difference served the goal of restoring Jews to a disadvantaged social position—that is, of reverting the tendency to or status of (at least legal) equality. Against this background, the construction of a Jewish body must be understood as a highly political operation, and scientists doing research on Jews and their purported biologically determined otherness represented specific political interests. This is not to say that anthropologists and medical experts always intentionally advocated a particular policy. Nevertheless, the results of their research did often fall in line with and corroborate particular political concerns.[22]

The political dimension of the "Jewish body" can best be comprehended by elucidating its discursive constitution in the context of military service. In Central Europe during the late eighteenth and nineteenth centuries, carrying out one's military duty came to be regarded as a requirement for attaining full citizenship. For Jews, this link seemed to be a problem. Most Jews were very intent on achieving the status of full-fledged citizens and also wanted to serve as soldiers.[23] Yet because of their bodily constitution, a disproportionate number seemed to be unfit to join the army. Many physicians and other people dealing with the matter of Jewish emancipation claimed that Jews were not up to the exertions of soldierly life.[24] This line of thinking was proposed by Christian Wilhelm Dohm in his path-breaking book *Über die bürgerliche Verbesserung der Juden*[25] and taken up by other scholars.[26] The physiological deficiencies that were assumed to prevent an extraordinary number of Jews from participating in military service were seen in their flat feet;[27] in their particular gait, which kept them from walking long distances;[28] in their restricted chest circumference,[29] and the like. Apparently Jews had a specific physiological constitution that rendered them different from non-Jews and made them incapable of meeting a major requirement for becoming full citizens.

The image of the "Jewish body" as being frail and largely unfit to sustain the exertions of a soldierly life was widely circulated. Even though some of the designated peculiarities, such as small chest circumference, may have been more common among some Jews (particularly those in Eastern Europe) because of abject poverty,[30] their interpretation as an indicator of a physical constitution that was too weak to sustain the exertions of military life was hardly based on empirical data. Rather, it served anti-Jewish political goals. Politics, however, does not operate unilaterally, and wielding power is not a unidirectional process whereby those in the position of power use force against less privileged people.[31] The powerless also have an influence on the relationship between themselves and the powerful, even though the means used by the former in such interaction are less effective and conspicuous than those of their counterparts. The mutual influence can be illuminated easily in the realm of the Jewish body: Jews were never simply passive objects of study but were also engaged in the construction of a specific Jewish physique. Jewish as well as non-Jewish physicians examined Jews, couched their data in scientific terms, and provided results supporting the assumption of a distinct Jewish constitution.[32]

Frequently, the outcome of many studies undertaken by Jews backed extant results but were explained differently. On other occasions, the results of Jewish research deviated from or even inverted available findings. In such cases, Jews may be seen as having used their work to pursue their own interests, which stood in conflict with the aims of many non-Jews to undermine the formers' political status. Such a Jewish strategy began in the early nineteenth century with the reinterpretation of Jewish religious rituals[33] and came to be extended to the Jewish body.

Jewish Responses to Oppressive Circumstances

The writings of Abraham Geiger represent a paradigmatic example of the efforts taken by Jews to invert scientific assertions about themselves and to impugn anti-Jewish descriptions in circulation.[34] Born in Frankfurt am Main in 1810, he became one of the most prodigious Jewish intellectuals of the nineteenth century. He is widely known as a member of the Wissenschaft des Judentums (WdJ), a circle of Jewish scholars who proposed a self-assertive and secular study of Judaism, which was understood above all as an academic dedication to Jewish history and literature.[35] Judaism was no longer to be understood merely in religious terms but in its historical and concurrently its developmental dimension as well,[36] thereby allowing the WdJ to promulgate narratives of the Jewish past that contrasted with existing non-Jewish—and frequently tantamount to anti-Jewish—views.[37]

Geiger himself went much further in his writings than most of his colleagues of the WdJ in that he put forward a narrative that not only deviated from available studies but even inverted given perspectives and thus overturned central dogmas of Christian theology. He introduced a counter-discourse that transvalued prevailing Christian arguments against Judaism and shook up Christian self-understanding. Therefore, as Susannah Heschel claims, Geiger may be called a postcolonial historian,[38] even though he always saw himself as a theologian and the term *postcolonial* did not exist at his time.

Geiger's main argument was that Jesus was a Pharisee; that is, he belonged to a group described in the New Testament in very unsavory terms, and he taught nothing original but merely repeated contemporary wisdom. The beginning of Christianity started with Paul, who "took the pure monotheism of Judaism to the pagans and polluted it with polytheistic teachings, creating a religion that would be more palatable to the heathens."[39]

As can be expected, non-Jewish, that is, Christian, theologians strongly disliked Geiger's interpretation of early Christianity and launched a vicious controversy over his view. In contrast to former decades and centuries, however, they no longer had the sovereignty to dictate the historical perspective on the origins of Christianity. Geiger's research as well as the studies of his WdJ colleagues produced many new findings that could no longer be ignored by Christian scholars. In this way, Jewish writing became, although only selectively, part of the ongoing discourse. Jews thus actively contributed to a change in their position, from a group whose history was written by overwhelmingly hostile Christian theologians to a self-assertive community that claimed its place in scholarship. Jews and non-Jews argued from different perspectives,[40] were aware of their opponents' statements, and responded to them accordingly. They interacted, influenced each other, and co-constituted knowledge.

Abraham Geiger's postcolonial writing[41] was certainly not the first attempt by Jews to vindicate themselves against oppressive, anti-Jewish circumstances. Historically speaking, Jews should not be perceived as having been a solely passive community, exclusively stricken with panic over anti-Jewish attacks and remaining submissive for fear of inciting potential persecutors.[42] Admittedly, such an attitude could be observed, and at times it ensured Jewish well-being or survival. Yet Jews also frequently displayed recalcitrance. Their reactions rarely turned into violent opposition, as was displayed by the participation of Jewish revolutionaries in the bombing attacks on Alexander II, the Russian czar, in 1881 and before.[43] Instead, the Jewish strategy drew on subtle means to resist an adverse use of power. For example, Jews resorted to deriding Christian religious practices or besmirching Christian symbols such as the crucifixion of Jesus. This strategy found expression in Purim celebrations, which from the early Middle Ages onward included anti-Christian activities. Jews burned Haman[44] in effigy on a cross or chased a naked Jew through the streets and flogged him, which was meant to ridicule the Passion of Christ.[45] Jews also behaved as rogues, showing their disrespect to the Christian church,[46] or even turned to criminality, thereby in some cases aiming to take revenge for their subservient role in everyday life.

The references to these Jewish reactions to the abuse of power by non-Jews are not intended to obscure widespread anti-Jewish hostility or deny its danger, nor do they insinuate a balance of power between Jews and non-Jews. Instead, they merely indicate that the former did not always acquiesce to oppressive conditions but often used various strategies to undermine them. Jews were involved in a battle over their conditions of existence, even though the means to take part in it were distributed unequally.

With the exception of Jewish criminality,[47] these Jewish activities differ from Abraham Geiger's writing in that they hardly established interactional processes that resulted in the adoption of Jewish practices by non-Jews. They were simply reactions to anti-Jewish policies. Nevertheless, they may be taken as evidence of the fact that Jews and non-Jews never lived completely separately or estranged from each other. Rather, their relations were characterized by permanent contentions over cultural meaning.

Efforts to Retain Jewish Rituals

The WdJ introduced secular Jewish scholarship; that is, it traced historical narratives from a Jewish perspective, put forward Jewish interpretations of the origin of Christianity, and established a nonreligious version of Judaism that served as an alternative to its image as a submissive object to be examined and elucidated by non-Jews. WdJ scholars conducted serious research and painstakingly presented findings that could not be overlooked by their non-Jewish peers. The Jewish efforts to revise available studies and to provide new conceptions of Judaism belonged to a policy that was to give Judaism a new outlook and enable it to meet the challenges of modern times.

Various approaches to reforming and reinterpreting Judaism in the nineteenth and early twentieth centuries can be discerned. In this chapter, an approach that also focused on the Jewish body is elucidated. It largely attempted to mediate between the government and that part of Jewish orthodoxy that conceived of Judaism as static and was therefore reluctant to comply with the demands of official authorities. Generally speaking, the two sides of the conflict argued about the position of Jews in modern society; essentially, however, they tried to increase or safeguard their influence on Jews. The government was determined to extend its ruling power to the Jews and to bring their hitherto autonomous matters—above all religious issues[48]—into its purview, whereas Jewish religious leaders aimed at retaining as much of their sway over the Jewish community as possible.

Ensuing from this constellation was a conflict over the legitimacy of legislative interventions by the sovereign into the Jewish (religious) sphere. A very early example of this kind of controversy, which may be taken as paradigmatic and as foreshadowing similar incidents in the following decades, dates to the late eighteenth century and concerns Jewish burial practices,[49] especially the custom of burying the dead only hours after they passed away. This rite came to be interpreted by non-Jews, as well as some liberal Jews,[50] as consciously risking interring people in a state of suspended animation. The contention between them and Orthodox Jews, who opposed any changes in the accustomed procedures, was solved by a compromise that allowed Jews to largely retain their traditional burial practices if specific requirements were met. Even though early burial was not unconditionally proscribed, the Jewish religious sphere could no longer be considered an autonomous realm totally exempt from intervention.

The controversy over early burial was succeeded by a purportedly scientific discourse on brit milah, the ritual of male circumcision. By and large, the debate on the (dis)advantages of the removal of the foreskin lasted throughout the nineteenth century—and in some respects has continued to the present.[51] Non-Jewish as well as some Jewish physicians[52] claimed that the ritual of circumcision could endanger the health of the male infant and sometimes even cause his death. Although some earlier mention had been made of the supposed adverse effects of brit milah,[53] the various discursive strands of the nineteenth century were largely sparked by a physician named Johann Nepomuk Rust in 1811. Rust plied his profession in the Habsburg province of Galicia, where he was faced with the deaths of various Jewish babies. For some time, he was at pains to find the reason for their deaths, until he accidentally discovered a connection between their deaths and brit milah, especially the religious custom of *mezizah*, which is the sucking of the bleeding wound by the circumciser. Rust examined the *mohel* (circumciser) and diagnosed syphilis. He concluded that the germs of the disease were transferred from the circumciser's mouth to the infants.[54] Further reports on syphilis among circumcised babies attributable to mezizah followed[55] and backed Rust's thesis of the unhealthy effects of the ceremony. Other diseases mentioned in this context were tuberculosis and diphtheria.[56]

The findings of the medical experts indicated more than doubt of the expediency of brit milah. They represented a severe attack on the ritual of circumcision and thereby questioned an essential expression of Jewish identity.[57] Because the maintenance of health had become an essential part of Western and Central European societies' economic policies in the eighteenth century,[58] the medical references to the harmful consequences of brit milah implicitly called on state power to interfere with this practice.

For many Jews, restrictions on the performance of circumcision, let alone its abolishment, were unthinkable. The latter was an option frequently raised in the discourse and was demanded by many non-Jews as well as some Jews.[59] Even individual Jewish rabbis, such as Samuel Holdheim of Mecklenburg-Schwerin, supported it.[60] To prevent official ordinances from prohibiting brit milah, a growing number of religious Jews came to accept slight modifications of its traditional practice. This strategy was exemplarily put into practice by Hatam Sofer, a rabbi from Pressburg who was well known for his adamant orthodoxy. His stern belief in tradition notwithstanding, he concurred in the abolishment of the mezizah to safeguard the health of circumcised infants. Hatam Sofer reached his conclusion after having been informed by the Viennese rabbi Eleasar Horowitz of the death of some Jewish newborns caused by the sucking of the wound on their penis. Sofer considered the replacement of mezizah by tapping the bloody wound with a sponge permissible.[61] Thus, he brought the Jewish ritual into accord with new medical findings and safeguarded the practice of circumcision and, hence, the power of Jewish authorities to determine one's Jewishness.[62]

Jewish Religion as a Pathogenic Factor

A connection between Judaism and sickness or disease was construed not only with respect to brit milah. In a very broad sense, leading a Jewish religious life was considered to favor an existence characterized by failing health and degeneration. Being religious was widely understood as a sufficient reason to be prone to diseases. Both Jewish and non-Jewish physicians promulgated this idea. The two differed from each other, however, in how they projected the state of sickness onto Jews: whereas the former ascribed it above all to their Eastern European coreligionists, who were more religious than Jews in Western Europe,[63] non-Jews considered all Jews to be diseased.

In small towns in Poland, Romania, Russia, and other parts of Eastern Europe, where Jews in some cases represented the majority of the inhabitants, everyday life was very traditional. Children started school at the age of three or four and usually spent the whole day inside a small room, where they were taught by teachers, most of whom lacked any didactical and pedagogical proficiency. Children studied religious texts and became imbued with a sense of tradition that was to help preserve Orthodox Judaism.[64]

Many nonreligious Jews considered the Jewish schools an institution that left the children ill prepared for life in a dynamic and fast-changing world—and consequently as a causal factor for the high rate of illness among the Ostjuden. Along with nationalist economic policies that aimed at excluding Jews from many occupational spheres, Jewish religious schooling was seen as contributing to a steep increase in poverty that heightened Jews' proneness to diseases.[65] In addition, because of the obligation of male Jewish pupils to spend the whole day at school and, therefore, to dispense with playing and sports, the long hours of studying were thought to result in overstraining the nerves and the brains of children, which, in turn, accounted for the disproportionately high rate of nervous and mentally ill people among the Jewish population.[66] Other diseases that were purportedly caused by the religious schools were tuberculosis and diabetes.[67] The lack of exercise was also seen as a reason for the Jews' physical deficiencies.[68]

From this perspective, a therapy for the presumed degenerating effects of the traditional educational system could hardly be restricted to the symptoms but had to aim instead at eradicating the very cause of the Jews' misery and consequent adverse health status—namely, the sway of religious authorities over ordinary Jews. In essence, Jewish religion provided the conditions for sickness and degeneration and, thus, was to become the primary target of all activities directed at redressing the Jews' health status.

The image of the diseased Eastern European Jew was fraught with anti-Semitic references. As was the case with the issue of circumcision, it was propagated mostly by physicians. Many of them were Jewish themselves and Zionists, or at least published in Zionist papers, such as *Die Welt* or *Jüdische Turnzeitung*. They suggested a therapy to improve the conditions of the Ostjuden that was in accordance with Zionist ideology and consisted of physical exercises, gymnastics, and agricultural labor.[69] The so-called sick Jews were thus to be reformed and their mode of existence modified by replacing their religiously determined lifestyle with a peasant-like existence. Zionists intended to "normalize" the Eastern Jews and their lives and thereby release them from the tutelage of religious leaders and Hasidic miracle rabbis.[70]

The "Salubrity" of Zionism

The diagnoses made by physicians as well as the therapies thought to be conducive to mental and physical recovery were ideologically based rather than scientifically proven. This fact renders the question about the veracity of the statements on the dismal health status of Eastern European Jews unnecessary to explore.

The controversy over the sick Ostjuden had at least two dimensions. On the one hand, it was a conflict between Jewish religious authorities and secular, mostly Zionist Jews over the power to determine the appropriate mode of Jewish existence. On the other hand, it was embedded in contemporary political and cultural discourses and unfolded against the background of prevalent medical theories, policies of nationalism, anti-Semitic movements, and so on. It was as much an internal Jewish issue as a contention between Jews and non-Jews,[71] and both were closely interconnected. This can be inferred from the Zionists' adoption of the image of the diseased Jew, which was used by non-Jews for anti-Jewish reasons, and by its use in the struggle against the Jewish religious establishment in Eastern Europe.

One of the reasons for the readiness of many (mostly Western European) Zionists to embrace such anti-Jewish notions and apply them to their Eastern coreligionists lay in the fact that Zionists had attended public schools and universities, had become familiar with contemporary cultural apprehensions, and consequently had developed an unwavering belief in science and its objectivity. As physicians, they trusted available reports and statistics on the Jews' purported proclivities to certain diseases. They were reluctant, however, to rank themselves among these sick people and refused to accept the thesis that all Jews, because of their race, had a disposition to degeneration. Instead, they traced the cause of the Jews' assumed liability to diseases and physical deformation to destitute living conditions and, therefore, held mainly Eastern Jews as being prone to poor health. The medical issue of a specific Jewish diathesis thus became a social matter concerning, above all, Jews in Eastern Europe.[72]

The Zionist position undermined the monolithic view of Jews and its anti-Semitic implications. Many Jewish physicians cast doubt on the statements of non-Jewish scientists that Jews as a group suffered extraordinarily from illnesses. The former thus contributed to the ongoing discourse on Jewish diseases and proposed their own interpretations of findings. Consequently, as was the case with Abraham Geiger's postcolonial writings or the medical treatises on brit milah, the power of non-Jewish scientists to describe and determine what constituted a prototypical Jew was weakened, and their assertions were counterpoised by alternative, Jewish views.

In addition to their medical writings, Zionists advanced the notion of the brave Jew who actively warded off anti-Semitic attacks. This strategy also aimed at eroding the policy of the religious establishment that endorsed the image of the Jewish scholar who wholeheartedly dedicated himself to the study of religious texts as an ideal of Jewishness. In contrast to stories of knowledgeable rabbis, Zionists proposed historical narratives of Jewish militancy, thereby harking back to the anti-Roman revolt by Simon bar Kochba or the anti-Greek insurgency by the Maccabees. The traditional Jewish standard of learning thus came to be replaced by the supposedly non-Jewish norm of fighting.[73]

In drawing on particular symbols and negating their meaning, Zionists pursued a similar approach toward non-Jews as well. The activities of Jewish students after their ban from dueling associations or German gymnastic societies in the 1880s and the following years serve as illuminating evidence. Jewish students compensated for their exclusion from German student organizations by establishing their own institutions, which largely represented Jewish versions of German and other anti-Jewish-oriented societies. In this way, the first Jewish student fraternity, Kadimah, was founded in Vienna in 1882. It made use of all the symbols of exclusively non-Jewish German fraternities, such as *Kneipen*, *Kommers*, German songs, and dueling,[74] and thereby gave them a new, distinctly Zionist significance. Even though little changed in the use of emblems, their content became different. It expressed the yearning for Zion instead of the longing for German nationalist issues.

Zionists thus favored particular behaviors among Jews that contravened the stereotype of their weakness and degeneration. The power of constituting the meaning of symbols was taken out of the hands of anti-Semitic non-Jews. In this way, Jews and non-Jews interacted in a negative way.

They responded to each other to define themselves. Jewish and non-Jewish identifications, it is safe to say, partly resulted from attempts to set themselves apart from each other.

Summary

During the nineteenth and early twentieth centuries a growing part of European Jewry tried to redefine itself. It had to react to the challenges to the religiously determined mode of Jewish life,[75] and it did so by modernizing Judaism. Consequently, it faced new anti-Semitic accusations as well as reluctance from traditional Judaism toward changes in its religious practices. In the course of their efforts to refute anti-Jewish stereotypes and to overcome the resistance of Jewish orthodoxy, liberally oriented Jews entered contemporary discourses on so-called Jewish peculiarities and contributed their own views and findings. Together with non-Jews, they thus co-constituted cultural perspectives. At the same time, they adopted some non-Jewish—even anti-Jewish—notions and applied them to religious Jews. In this way, traditional boundaries between Jews and non-Jews increasingly became blurred. However, scientists reset and strengthened them before long.

Notes

1. Ludwig Fleck, *Entstehung und Entwicklung einer wissenschaftlichen Tatsache: Einführung in die Lehre vom Denkstil und Denkkollektiv* (Frankfurt: Suhrkamp, 1980), 52–70.

2. Klaus Hödl, *Gesunde Juden—kranke Schwarze: Körperbilder im medizinischen Diskurs* (Innsbruck, Austria: Studienverlag, 2002).

3. Benoit Massin, "From Virchow to Fischer: Physical Anthropology and 'Modern Race Theories' in Wilhelmine Germany," in Volksgeist *as Method and Ethic: Essays on Boasian Ethnography and the German Anthropological Tradition*, ed. George W. Stocking Jr. (Madison: University of Wisconsin Press, 1996), 79–154.

4. Miriam Gebhardt, *Das Familiengedächtnis: Erinnerung im deutsch-jüdischen Bürgertum 1890–1932* (Stuttgart, Germany: Franz Steiner Verlag, 1999), 9–10.

5. Claudia Castaneda, "Der Stammbaum: Zeit, Raum und Alltagstechnologie in den Vererbungswissenschaften," in *Genealogie und Genetik*, ed. Sigrid Weigel (Berlin: Akademie Verlag, 2002), 68.

6. Peter Gay, *Die Moderne* (Frankfurt: S. Fischer Verlag, 2008).

7. Daniel M. Vyleta, *Crime, Jews, and News: Vienna 1895–1914* (New York: Berghahn Books, 2007), 70–75.

8. Ernst Bollinger, *Pressegeschichte II. 1840–1930: Die goldenen Jahre der Massenpresse* (Freiburg, Germany: Universitätsverlag, 1996), 26, 39.

9. Rainer Winter, "Spielräume des Vergnügens und der Interpretation: Cultural Studies und die kritische Analyse des Populären," in *Die kleinen Unterschiede: Der Cultural Studies-Reader*, ed. Jan Engelmann (Frankfurt: zu Klampen, 1999), 35.

10. Vanessa R. Schwartz, *Spectacular Realities: Early Mass Culture in Fin-de-Siècle Paris* (Berkeley: University of California Press, 1999), 90.

11. Werner Michael Schwarz, *Anthropologische Spektakel: Zur Schaustellung "exotischer" Menschen, Wien 1870–1910* (Vienna, Austria: Turia & Kant, 2001), 25–27.

12. On these contrasting trends, see Anja Zimmermann, *Ästhetik der Objektivität: Genese und Funktion eines wissenschaftlichen und künstlerischen Stils im 19. Jahrhundert* (Bielefeld, Germany: transcript Verlag, 2009).

13. Steven E. Aschheim, *Brothers and Strangers: The East European Jew in German and German Jewish Consciousness, 1800–1923* (Madison: University of Wisconsin Press, 1982).

14. Laurence J. Silberstein, "Mapping, Not Tracing: Opening Reflection," in *Mapping Jewish Identities*, ed. Laurence J. Silberstein (New York: New York University Press, 2000), 1–36.

15. Klaus Hödl, *Wiener Juden–jüdische Wiener: Identität, Gedächtnis und Performanz im 19. Jahrhundert* (Innsbruck, Austria: Studienverlag, 2006), 30–35; Till van Rahden, "Weder Milieu noch Konfession: Die situative Ethnizität der deutschen Juden im Kaiserreich in vergleichender Perspektive," in *Religion im Kaiserreich: Milieus, Mentalitäten, Krisen*, ed. Olaf Blaschke and Frank-Michael Kuhlemann (Gütersloh, Germany: Gütersloher Verlagshaus, 1996), 409–34.

16. George L. Mosse, *Nationalismus und Sexualität: Bürgerliche Moral und sexuelle Normen* (Hamburg, Germany: Rowohlt Verlag, 1990).

17. Michael John and Albert Lichtblau, eds., *Schmelztiegel Wien: Einst und Jetzt— Zur Geschichte und Gegenwart von Zuwanderung und Minderheiten* (Vienna, Austria: Böhlau Verlag, 1990).

18. Klaus Hödl, "The Quest for Amusement: Jewish Leisure Activities in Vienna circa 1900," *Jewish Culture and History* 15 (2012): 1–17.

19. *Illustriertes Wiener Extrablatt* 33, February 8, 1896, 2.

20. Christina von Braun, "'Der Jude' und 'Das Weib': Zwei Stereotypen des 'Anderen' in der Moderne," in *Deutsch-jüdische Geschichte im 19. und 20. Jahrhundert*, ed. Ludger Heid and Joachim H. Knoll (Stuttgart, Germany: Burg-Verlag, 1992), 293.

21. Rainer Erb, "Die Wahrnehmung der Physiognomie der Juden: Die Nase," in *Das Bild der Juden in der Volks- und Jugendliteratur vom 18. Jahrhundert bis 1945*, ed. Heinrich Pleticha (Würzburg, Germany: Konigshausen & Neumann, 1985), 118; Joseph Jacobs, *Studies in Jewish Statistics: Social, Vital, and Anthropometric* (London: Nutt, 1891), xl.

22. William H. Tucker, *The Science and Politics of Racial Research* (Urbana: University of Illinois Press, 1994).

23. István Deák, *Jewish Soldiers in Austro-Hungarian Society* (New York: Leo Baeck Institute, 1990).

24. Léon Poliakov, *The History of Anti-Semitism*, vol. 3 (London: Routledge, 1975), 177.

25. Sander L. Gilman, *The Jew's Body* (New York: Routledge, 1991), 40; Dohm, Christian Wilhelm, *Über die bürgerliche Verbesserung der Juden* (Berlin: Nicolai, 1781).

26. See H. Naudh [pseud. for Heinrich Nordmann], *Israel im Heere* (Berlin: Hentze, 1879), 6.

27. Benjamin Dubovsky, *Gezund un Leben* (New York: 1920), 148.

28. Hermann Schaaffhausen, "Die Physiognomik," *Archiv für Anthropologie* 17 (1888): 336–37.

29. Ludwig Stieda, "Ein Beitrag zur Anthropologie der Juden," *Archiv für Anthropologie* 14 (1882): 71; Bernhard Blechmann, *Ein Beitrag zur Anthropologie der Juden* (Dorpat, Estonia: Just, 1882), 51.

30. John M. Efron, *Defenders of the Race: Jewish Doctors and Race Science in Fin-de-Siècle Europe* (New Haven, CT: Yale University Press, 1994), 100.

31. Winter, "Spielräume," 35–48.

32. John M. Efron, *Medicine and the German Jews: A History* (New Haven, CT: Yale University Press, 2001).

33. Hödl, *Wiener Juden*, 111–19.

34. About Abraham Geiger, see Michael A. Meyer, *Antwort auf die Moderne: Geschichte der Reformbewegung im Judentum* (Vienna, Austria: Böhlauverlag, 2000), 138–52.

35. Ismar Schorsch, *From Text to Context: The Turn to History in Modern Judaism* (Hanover, NH: Brandeis University Press, 1994), 149–254.

36. Yosef Hayim Yerushalmi, *Zachor: Erinnere Dich! Jüdische Geschichte und jüdisches Gedächtnis* (Berlin: Verlag Klaus Wagenbach, 1996), 87–110.

37. Michael A. Meyer, *Judaism within Modernity: Essays on Jewish History and Religion* (Detroit, MI: Wayne State University Press, 2001), 53–55; Michael Brenner, *Propheten des Vergangenen: Jüdische Geschichtsschreibung im 19. und 20. Jahrhundert* (Munich: Verlag C. H. Beck, 2006), 35–77.

38. Susannah Heschel, *Abraham Geiger and the Jewish Jesus* (Chicago: University of Chicago Press, 1998), 3.

39. Susannah Heschel, "Revolt of the Colonized: Abraham Geiger's 'Wissenschaft des Judentums' as a Challenge to Christian Hegemony in the Academy," in *Kulturelle Grenzräume im jüdischen Kontext*, ed. Klaus Hödl (Innsbruck, Austria: Studienverlag, 2006), 42.

40. This statement consciously overlooks the heterogeneity within the two groups and merely aims at delineating major tendencies.

41. See also Jonathan M. Hess, *Germans, Jews, and the Claims of Modernity* (New Haven, CT: Yale University Press, 2002), 51–89.

42. Such a narrative fits the Zionist perspective of history that aims at delegitimizing the Diaspora existence and concurrently serves as an argument for the Zionists' policy of "normalization."

43. Ronald Sanders, *The Downtown Jews: Portraits of an Immigrant Generation* (New York: Dover, 1987), 7–15.

44. Haman, one of the historical enemies of Jewry, almost destroyed them during their Babylonian captivity.

45. Elliott Horowitz, "The Rite to Be Reckless: On the Perpetration and Interpretation of Purim Violence," *Poetics Today* 15 (1994): 9–54.

46. Dan Miron, *The Image of the Shtetl and Other Studies of Modern Jewish Literary Imagination* (Syracuse, NY: Syracuse University Press, 2000), 2.

47. The history of Jewish criminality may be viewed as an aspect of Jewish life that shows a close interaction between Jewish and non-Jewish criminals; sometimes non-Jewish criminals joined the Jewish community to strengthen the ties with their Jewish cohorts (Vyleta, *Crime, Jews, and News*, 43). The interspersion of *Rotwelsch*, the language

frequently used by criminals, with Hebrew words gives further evidence to this kind of Jewish and non-Jewish interdependency. Robert Jütte, *Abbild und soziale Wirklichkeit des Bettler- und Gaunertums zu Beginn der Neuzeit: Sozial-, mentalitäts- und sprachgeschichtliche Studien zum Liber Vagatorum (1510)* (Vienna, Austria: Böhlau, 1988), 45ff.

48. David Sorkin, *The Transformation of German Jewry, 1780–1840* (Oxford, U.K.: Oxford University Press, 1987).

49. In February 1772, Olof Gerhard Tychsen, a scholar of Oriental studies, sent a letter to Duke Friedrich of Mecklenburg in which he instructed the duke about the Jewish custom of early sepulture and, intimately connected with it, the danger of burying seemingly dead people. In reaction to this report, the duke determined that Jews were required to let pass three days between the death of a person and the sepulture. The ordinance caused severe commotion among the local Jewish community.

50. Marcus Herz, *Über die frühe Beerdigung der Juden: An die Herausgeber des hebräischen Sammlers* (Berlin: Friedrich Voss and Son, 1788); David Friedländer, "Ueber die frühe Beerdigung der Juden," *Berlinische Monatsschrift* 9 (1787): 317–23.

51. Ephraim Tabori and Sharon Erez, "Circumscribed Circumcision: The Motivations and Identities of Israeli Parents Who Choose Not to Circumcise Their Sons," in *The Covenant of Circumcision: New Perspectives on an Ancient Jewish Rite*, ed. Elizabeth Wyner Mark (Hanover, NH: Brandeis University Press, 2003), 161–76.

52. Adolf Arnhold, *Die Beschneidung und ihre Reform, mit besonderer Rücksicht auf die Verhandlungen der dritten Rabbiner-Versammlung* (Leipzig, Germany: Hunger, 1847); J. Bergson, *Die Beschneidung vom historischen, kritischen und medicinischen Standpunkt* (Berlin: Athenaeum, 1844).

53. Eva Frojmovic, "Christian Travelers to the Circumcision: Early Modern Representations," in *The Covenant of Circumcision: New Perspectives on an Ancient Jewish Rite*, ed. Elizabeth Wyner Mark (Hanover, NH: Brandeis University Press, 2003), 128–41.

54. J. B. Friedreich, "Ueber die jüdische Beschneidung in sanitätspolizeilicher Beziehung," *Centralarchiv für die gesamte Staatsarzneikunde* 3 (1846): 684.

55. Julius Jaffe, *Die rituelle Circumcision im Lichte der antiseptischen Chirurgie mit Berücksichtigung der religiösen Vorschriften* (Leipzig, Germany: Gistav Fock, 1886), 31.

56. Leopold von Neumann, "Zur Uebertragung der Tuberculose durch die rituelle Circumcision," *Wiener medizinische Presse* 13 (1900): 569.

57. Sander L. Gilman, *Jews in Today's German Culture* (Bloomington: Indiana University Press, 1995), 71.

58. Guenter B. Risse, "Medicine in the Age of Enlightenment," in *Medicine in Society: Historical Essays*, ed. Andrew Wear (Cambridge, U.K.: Cambridge University Press, 1992), 149–95. Sick people were conceived of as a burden to the state, reducing its economic growth; see George Rosen, "The Fate of the Concept of Medical Police: 1780–1890," *Centaurus* 5, no. 2 (1957): 97.

59. Klaus Hödl, "Die deutschsprachige Beschneidungsdebatte im 19. Jahrhundert," *Aschkenas* 13, no. 1 (2003): 189–90.

60. Samuel Holdheim, *Ueber die Beschneidung zunächst in religiös-dogmatischer Beziehung* (Schwerin, Germany: Kürschner, 1844), 8.

61. Bernard Homa, *Metzitzah* (London: Initiation Society, 1960), 8; Sinai Schiffer, *Die Ausübung der Mezizoh* (Frankfurt: Golde, 1906), 4.

62. *Allgemeine Zeitung des Judenthums* 11 (1847): 497.

63. Mitchell Hart, *Social Science and the Politics of Modern Jewish Identity* (Stanford, CA: Stanford University Press, 2000), 105–7.

64. Mordechai Eliav, *Jüdische Erziehung in Deutschland im Zeitalter der Aufklärung und Emanzipation* (Münster, Germany: Waxmann, 2001), 183–207.

65. P. Berthold [pseud. for Bertha von Pappenheim], *Zur Judenfrage in Galizien* (Frankfurt: Knauer, 1900), 18–19; Charles N. Reichenberg, *Wie kann das Elend eines Teiles der Juden in Galizien und der Bukowina durch die Baron Hirsch'sche Zwölfmillionen-Stiftung gemildert werden? Eine Studie* (Vienna, Austria: Selbstverlag, 1891), 6.

66. John Duffy, "'Mental Strain' and 'Overpressure' in the Schools: A Nineteenth-Century Viewpoint," *Journal of the History of Medicine and Allied Sciences* 23, no. 1 (1968): 63–79.

67. Felix Meyer, "Der hygienische Wert des Turnens," *Jüdische Turnzeitung* 4 (1901): 48.

68. Otto Abeles, "Die jüdische Schule," *Die Welt* 38 (1912): 116.

69. Klaus Hödl, *Die Pathologisierung des jüdischen Körpers: Antisemitismus, Geschlecht und Medizin im Fin de Siècle* (Vienna, Austria: Picus, 1997), 282–88.

70. Max Nordau, *Degeneration* (Lincoln: University of Nebraska Press, 1993).

71. David Biale, *Power and Powerlessness in Jewish History* (New York: Schocken Books, 1986), 122; Veronika Lipphardt, *Biologie der Juden: Jüdische Wissenschaftler über "Rasse" und Vererbung 1900–1935* (Göttingen, Germany: Vandenhoeck & Ruprecht, 2008).

72. Hart, *Social Science*.

73. Daniel Boyarin, *Unheroic Conduct: The Rise of Heterosexuality and the Invention of the Jewish Man* (Berkeley: University of California Press, 1997), 33–80.

74. Julius H. Schoeps, "Modern Heirs of the Maccabees: The Beginning of the Vienna Kadimah, 1882–1897," *Leo Baeck Institute Yearbook* 27, no. 1 (1982): 161.

75. Among these challenges were, for example, the opportunity for greater social and occupational mobility, the new relevance assigned to secular learning, or the restructuring of time that made the observance of Shabbat difficult.

Chapter 11

Cultural and Political Images of American Jews in the Mid-Twentieth Century

Michelle Mart

In the winter of 2008, great media fanfare in the United States greeted the publication of a comprehensive report from the Pew Forum on Religion and Public Life on the state of religious affiliation in the United States.[1] The single biggest conclusion of the report was that there was great fluidity and diversity in religious life, with many Americans abandoning their childhood religions for something different, most notably an identity of "unaffiliated." Although the dramatic growth of that category—defined as atheist, agnostic, or nothing in particular—might have led observers to conclude that Americans were finally becoming less religious like other Westerners, of the 16.1 percent of respondents professing no affiliation, only 1.6 percent described themselves as atheist and 2.4 percent as agnostic.[2] Thus, most Americans had not abandoned religion to follow the atheistic prescriptions of recent best-selling books by Christopher Hitchens and Richard Dawkins.[3] In the words of sociologist and religion scholar Michael Lindsay, "If you want to understand America, you have to understand religion in America."[4]

Yet gravitation toward a more fluid religious identity perhaps indicates something powerful and long-standing in American culture, not just the doctrinal content of various faiths. Since World War II, Americans have often wrestled with the tension between universal ideals and particular identities. Recoiling at the horror of extreme particularism as manifested in the Holocaust, many Americans in the postwar era embraced so-called universal values, seeking to build a "free" world in contrast to the "slave" one of communism and closed societies. The tension between universalism and particularism was heightened further at home as Americans wrestled with the religious, ethnic, and racial diversity of the country's population. To what extent should particular identities give way to a broad national one? Or, to use the images of popular sociology, should the United States be a melting pot or a salad bowl? Do the early twenty-first century's religious trends of fluidity—which was one generation's response to the weighty questions introduced in the early postwar period—constitute a rebellion against rigid particular identities?

Whether in 2008 or in 1958, the tension between universal and particular identities was always acute for American Jews. By the mid-twentieth century, American Jews were more accepted culturally and politically in the United States than ever before. With the postwar embrace of universal ideals, anti-Semitism virtually disappeared from the *public* culture. But as Jews were more accepted and assimilated into the broader society, their particular identity was not erased. Nevertheless, American Jews had mixed feelings about assimilation. These conflicts were reflected in popular fiction and media culture in the 1950s and were seen in the American Jewish role in politics and the relationship between the United States and Israel. This chapter will consider how the image of American Jews was constructed in the 1950s—in popular and political culture—and how that image affected the American political reaction to Israel.

Intersections of Culture and Politics

Before World War II, Jews were viewed almost universally in the United States as "outsiders," who were different from other Americans. Popular images ascribed to them included being clannish, pushy, overly concerned with money, physically weak, unattractive, and urbane. One crucial aspect of the shift in postwar attitudes is that cultural narratives changed to include Jews who possessed ideologies, values, and histories in common with old-stock Americans; as a result, these "outsiders" became "insiders." The transformation of Jews and Israelis from outsiders to insiders had political as well as cultural implications. This shift in cultural narrative both reflected and helped shape the climate of political opinion in which U.S. leaders made policy and American Jews struggled for acceptance.

Changing views of Jews influenced policy makers who were subject to the same cultural messages as other Americans. At the same time, American Jews, self-conscious of their changing image, worked to carve out new areas of political influence and identity in a multicultural country. The following discussion of Jews in American culture will focus on language, written works, and artistic creations that were broadly shared in the public space, or *public culture*.[5] It traces multiple cultural narratives through fictional and nonfictional works, political memos, the press, and public opinion. Previous studies of Jews in the United States have discussed the media and public opinion polls, but such studies most often treat those data as quantifiable categories separate from the "reality" of policy making.[6] Discussion of cultural narratives must go beyond polls and narrow measures of cause and effect to examine how the narratives influenced cultural expression and national policy on many levels.[7]

The inclusion of fictional, popular culture in this discussion brings its own presuppositions. Some scholars dismiss works of popular culture as aesthetically banal and shallow and see them either as the reflection of social and economic relations imposed on the masses or as a vapid diversion without substantive meaning. Following other scholars who have taken these works seriously and analyzed them on their own terms, I argue that both fictional and nonfictional popular works provide clues about dominant cultural narratives in the mid-twentieth century. The focus in the next section, then, is on how narratives were articulated, thereby creating the language and stories that gave people a cultural framework with which to make sense of the political situations and relationships around them.

Real-Life Jews and the "Horatio Algers" of Popular Novels in the 1950s

An examination of best-selling novels and Hollywood fiction of the mid-1950s reveals that popular images of American Jews had changed greatly from the 1940s and earlier. Jewish characters moved beyond being stereotypical victims and symbols of the biblical past. They were full-fledged actors in contemporary social dramas who were distinct from other Americans but still shared much in values, goals, and loyalty. In the mid-twentieth century, Jews were accepted as full members of the nation as long as their American identity dominated their Jewish identity. This fiction drew on Cold War values of political, economic, and cultural freedoms in the West, in contrast to the closed and restricted world of the communist countries, to depict an American way of life in which a modified pluralism was celebrated. The issue of conflicting loyalties was a very real dilemma in the 1950s. Socially, the dominant culture stressed homogeneity and conformity. Politically, Americans were supposed to demonstrate unquestioned loyalty to the "free world" in a society of communist subversives and fifth columns.

The fiction about American Jews answered these dilemmas in a number of ways. First, the central theme of this fiction was the reenactment of the story of the American dream, from poor immigrant to successful, assimilated citizen. At the center of this drama, Jews stood for all Americans. Second, this fiction explored the possible costs on the road to that dream—a loss of morality, roots, family values, and a sense of identity— and provided solutions to avert those consequences. Third, it sanctioned small cultural differences that did not challenge the status quo. Finally, the fiction depicted lingering examples of anti-Semitism. But unlike the films and books of the mid-1940s, Jews were not helpless victims who were defined by discrimination. They were upright citizens who sometimes faced anachronistic thinking.

Moreover, many of the popular stories of American Jews in this period were penned by Jewish writers who were concerned with assimilation, separatism, and success in modern America. For many Jewish writers, these cultural ideologies dominated their horizons, and they wrote about themselves fitting into the American landscape. Yet Jewish writers and artists were not just telling Jewish stories. Through their now prominent roles in American film and literature, Jewish writers and artists helped to reinvent postwar American cultural ideology, and they did so in a way that shaped their own identity in the country. Thus, the Jewish characters in this fiction redefined the iconographic modern American hero to include their particular ethnic story.

It is worth pausing here to ask whether Jewish artists and the fiction they created reveal useful information about group identity and politics in the postwar period. As many historians and cultural scholars have observed in recent years, cultural productions have an interactive relationship with politics and history, helping to create meanings through which people see and understand the world and through which they make political decisions. Searching for patterns in a body of popular culture reveals how, in the words of Melani McAlister, "meanings can become naturalized by repetition" and, thus, create enduring cultural and political meaning.[8] American Jews, then, were rewriting their own story of group identification as they added to broader myths of American culture.

The popular works of fiction about American Jews drew on a long-standing cultural ideology that America was the Promised Land—a land imbued with a sense of mission in which anyone could achieve Horatio Alger's success. The material and social achievements of these characters makes them archetypal immigrants and exemplars of the American success story. By mid-century, Jews, indeed, seemed to have fulfilled the mythical dream of success. The majority of American Jews—ranging from 75 percent to 96 percent in more than a dozen sample communities across the United States—worked in nonmanual professions. In contrast, just 38 percent of the American population, as a whole, worked in nonmanual positions. And a declining proportion of Jews worked in lower-level white-collar jobs, such as clerks and salesmen. Furthermore, Jews, by mid-century, were better educated than their non-Jewish counterparts, with a higher percentage of Jews going to college than non-Jews. Those Jews who did go to college usually had incomes that exceeded those of non–college graduates, as well as those of non-Jewish graduates.[9] Thus, by many social and economic measures, Jews came to be embraced as "insiders" in American culture.

Popular fiction of the period reflected these trends of Jewish achievement. Novels and films contained a rich collection of Jewish Horatio Algers rising from new immigrants to middle-class businessmen and professionals. The stories, which told about the climb up the American ladder of success, usually began with—and celebrated—the ghetto origins of the immigrant Jews. For example, although Sholem Asch's character of Isaac Grossman in *A Passage in the Night* grew up in a cramped tenement apartment, it was transformed on Fridays "by the magic of his mother's Sabbath."[10] The "old neighborhood" in other novels, such as Gerald Green's *The Last Angry Man*, Jerome Weidman's *The Enemy Camp*, Saul Bellow's *The Adventures of Augie March*, and Herman Wouk's *Marjorie Morningstar*, is populated by colorful characters, especially parochial, older relatives.[11] In addition to embodying the image of a pure ethnic past, these older relatives are the ones who encourage their grandchildren, nieces, and nephews to reach for their dreams and to climb the American ladder to success.

Mid-century popular fiction also depicted the ghetto as a place to escape. The immigrants who were able to overcome the ghetto's disadvantages and leave its confines, such as the protagonists in *The Enemy Camp* and *A Passage in the Night*, were heroic embodiments of the Horatio Alger story. Asch's main character moves from rags to riches with just $27, which he propels into a real estate empire, asserting "This is America. Everyone has the right to get ahead."[12] Critics and others endorsed these sentiments about the possibility of mobility for all in the postwar United States, even as they noted the particular success of the Jews. One review, for example, called the Jewish Lower East Side in New York, "one of the most familiar starting points of the great American success story."[13] Jews, thus, embody *the* American story. For the characters and the authors who created them, the story of economic climbing becomes intertwined with ethnic identity. Lower class automatically signals "more ethnic."[14]

The most notable of the 1950s intergenerational immigrant stories was *Marjorie Morningstar*, a book that symbolized the dramatic changes in the images of American Jews. Wouk's book was a bestseller from September 1955 to March 1956 and was the most sold fiction book in 1955.[15] Wouk and a drawing of his character Marjorie even made the cover of *Time* magazine in November 1955. Wouk's story of coming of age, ascending to the middle class, and valuing one's heritage told Jews that they were just like other Americans. Young Jewish—and non-Jewish—girls modeled themselves on Wouk's heroine.[16] Marjorie was hailed in one review as "a classic American heroine"[17] and in another review as "a typical American girl."[18]

One reason that Wouk's novel seemed to resonate so powerfully with many Americans in the Cold War period was that, although it celebrated the ideal of success and a certain amount of assimilation, *Marjorie Morningstar* was a cautionary tale against leaving behind too much of one's history for the temptations of materialism. One of the frequent criticisms of the Soviets and the communist system was their emphasis on materialism and economic determinism. Wouk shows the danger of chasing after economic success to the exclusion of other values. Marjorie wants to assimilate and succeed in modern American society, yet she clings to her ethnic origins, as do most of the young Jewish characters in these novels.

Some of the characters seem to succeed in distancing themselves from their immigrant origins, but in so doing, they pay a heavy price. Many assimilating characters are dismayed to see that their children move away from Judaism and Jewish identity, becoming shallow and self-centered. This disappointment is seen in the novels *A Passage in the Night*, *Remem-*

ber Me to God,[19] and *Marjorie Morningstar.* In part, the parents blame their own ambition to assimilate and achieve financial success.

Although some characters are able to preserve their religious heritage, they adapt to modern America by changing the nature of their religion—with many Jews becoming Reform or Conservative Jews, as was common in the postwar United States. Many of the wealthiest Jews were Reform and ancestors of the German wave of immigrants from the mid-nineteenth century. Increasingly, the children of East European immigrants from the turn of the century abandoned orthodoxy as part of their assimilation into mainstream society. Most of the new congregations in the postwar period were Conservative, representing what many saw as a compromise between Reform and Orthodox denominations. Certainly, the denominational changes did not mean that Jews deserted organized religion. Moreover, with the general revival of civic religion in the so-called religious revival of the 1950s, Jews found that they had to demonstrate their religious values to be accepted in mainstream society.

Yet even while some Jews affirmed their civic religion and newfound Reform values under the American umbrella, many worried that Jews were in danger of losing their particular identity entirely. This possibility loomed largest in the middle-class enclaves of Cold War America—the suburbs.[20] Social commentators wrote about what had become the clichéd suburbanization of Jews in the 1950s. Nathan Glazer worried that the assimilationist pull of middle-class communities might overwhelm particular identity: "[the suburbs] simultaneously strengthened Judaism and weakened Jewishness."[21] Most of all, the suburbs posed a symbiotic danger to traditional spiritual values. Glazer and other observers believed that assimilation and material comforts could turn into shallowness and mere social climbing. One effort to counteract the loss of Jewishness was the formation of "federations" in almost every sizable Jewish community throughout the country. These organizations became the center of Jewish life for the less religious, assimilated Jews. Many suburban communities combined much of their secular and religious activities in "synagogue-centers," which were both religious houses and community centers organizing educational, social, and cultural programs.

In popular fiction, the folly of complete assimilation is also revealed in the self-hatred of some of the young Jewish characters. Wouk's Marjorie, who is embarrassed by her parents' background, finds herself disgusted by the old neighborhood and the working-class life associated with it. The life of Jerome Weidman's hero, George Hurst, is also shaped by the character's insecurity about his Jewish identity. He marries a wealthy Protestant woman and feels that he is forever an outsider in his marriage. The most extreme example of self-hatred is found in Myron Kaufmann's *Remember Me to God*, in which the young protagonist comes to believe that the wealthy Protestants whom he meets at Harvard are superior in every way to Jews. He conflates class and ethnic identity, assuming that the Jewish lower-class world from which he came is uncivilized.[22]

Kaufmann, Wouk, Weidman, Asch, and other postwar Jews affirm that the young Jews who wrestle with the feeling of what one of them terms a "split personality" between Jewish and American identities should reaffirm their Jewish heritage, values, and identity and, at the same time, should recommit to American society and the success ethic. In addition to fiction writers, many Jewish intellectuals probed the questions of Jewish identity, alienation, and assimilation.[23] The conclusion of most writers was that American Jews should recognize that their American and Jewish identities were actually compatible and that giving up their religion and Jewish heritage would mean losing something valuable for which there was no replacement.

Erasing Difference at Home, Asserting Difference in Zion

In contrast to popular novels of the 1950s that preach the importance of retaining Jewish particularity while assimilating, many 1950s Hollywood films about American Jews had a different emphasis. For the few Jewish characters who were included in films before 1958 (when adaptations from Jewish novelists were put on film), ethnic identity was minimized. The scant attention to ethnic identity was part of a continuing pattern in Hollywood that had begun in the 1930s, when films began to "de-Semitize" and "de-Judaize" images of Jews. Bland characterizations seemed even more prevalent in the 1950s, when many filmmakers and artists did their best to avoid challenges to a homogeneous view of American life. In many films, lip service was paid to a character's Jewish identity, although there was nothing distinctive that set him apart from other Americans. *Three Brave Men* tells the basically true story of a Jewish naval officer who was accused of being a security risk. The film centers on the patriotic man's attempt to clear his name and the triumph of the American system.[24] The image of the loyal Bernie Goldsmith in this film reflected the declining association in popular belief of Jews with radicalism and communism.[25]

The protagonist of the film is also just like other Americans to the extent that he shares in the Judeo–Christian heritage. When the crisis breaks, the man's rabbi is sick, so the local Presbyterian minister offers to counsel the family; the pastor becomes the Jew's greatest defender. Aside from the pastor's benign observation of difference, the only characters who mention the man's Jewish identity are anonymous crackpots who accuse him of disloyalty because he is Jewish. Anti-Semitism is also depicted as a minority position in *I Accuse!*, a film made soon after *Three Brave Men*. *I Accuse!* is a bland retelling of the Alfred Dreyfus story in which the culprits are just a few virulently anti-Semitic officers.[26]

In 1958, Irwin Shaw's and Norman Mailer's novels about World War II (*The Young Lions* and *The Naked and the Dead*, respectively) came to the screen. They, too, looked at the difficulties faced by Jewish soldiers in a sometimes hostile military establishment.[27] Yet the Hollywood versions of those novels were very different from the best-selling books that had appeared more than a decade before. The films played down the pervasiveness of anti-Semitism, focused on the abusive conduct of only a few characters, and made little distinction between Jewish and other soldiers.

In most of the popular fiction about American Jews, the mission of World War II and the Arab–Israeli War of 1948 are conflated. Yet the ties between the Jewish characters, Zionism, and the State of Israel are not always clear and are not discussed at great length. Israel forms an accepted backdrop to the lives of American Jews, but it is certainly not a dominant theme in any of these popular works. At times, Zionist work is merely a pleasant cultural activity for Jews. In *Marjorie Morningstar* and other books, the characters socialize through Zionist committees, and parents look for mates for their children among the volunteers. Admiration for Zionists is accepted as the norm in the world of these Jews.

The enthusiasm for Zionism found in the characters of fictional works mirrored the views of many contemporary Americans. Not surprisingly, the drama of Israel's story appealed to many American Jews in particular. Years earlier, Horace Kallen had pointed to Zionism as the source of his own renewed Jewish identity: "Zionism became a replacement and reevaluation of Judaism which enabled me to respect it."[28] As Arthur Hertzberg and many others have argued, the relationship between American Jews and Israel even strengthened their national identity. For example, Hertzberg writes that, in the years of the Marshall Plan and the rebuilding of Japan, "The creation of Israel was the equivalent task for American Jews." Moreover, as Israel moved to the center of Jewish community life and identity,

Hertzberg concluded, "Support for Israel, and not learning Hebrew, was the 'spiritual content' of the relationship." "Support for Israel" covered many activities as well as sentiments and eventually helped spawn a Jewish political and philanthropic network. Jewish philanthropy focused on Israel, and the new state stood as a symbol of Jewish power within the United States.[29]

For many American Jews, then, supporting Israel became one way of affirming their "Americanness." Historian Howard Sachar, writing in 1957, celebrated the importance of the "doughty and courageous little state" to American Jews:

> [The Israeli spirit] was a spirit of complete, unselfconscious, thoroughly affirmative Jewishness. Without this spirit Jewish life in America with all its wealth, security, community democracy, and pragmatic realism, would hardly signify more than the dissipation of an unprecedented opportunity for corporate self-expression. With this spirit, the American Jewish community bade fair to create a civilization of such enduring vitality as to pre-empt from medieval Spain the title of "Golden Age."[30]

For Sachar and other Jews, there was a symbiotic relationship between the United States and Israel. Even before 1948, many American Jews had envisioned the projected Jewish state as similar to the United States. Thus, observes Jonathan Sarna, American Jews could "defuse the sensitive issue of dual loyalty" and "boast of their own patriotic efforts to spread the American dream outward."[31] Importantly, American Jews were not ready to give up their nationality. From 1948 to 1967, an average of 600 to 1,200 American Jews moved to Israel each year, but most of them returned to the United States.[32] Emigration numbers notwithstanding, given the importance of Israel to American Jews, it is interesting how little the subject is mentioned in the popular fiction about the lives of American Jews. In the portraits of contemporary Jewish life, American identity was paramount; perhaps, ties to a foreign country would have threatened that image.

Although most American Jews agreed with the view put forward by historians and social observers that the story of Jews in the United States was "wholly unprecedented even in the millennial annals of the Jewish people,"[33] they could not escape from the pull of Israel—the place one critic described as the "ancestral home of the Jews."[34] At the same time, Jewish writers who were anxious to affirm their own national identity put American Jews in a different category from European Jews who were described as "always in exile."[35] In the novel *Remember Me to God*, the rabbi emphatically denies that he is not at home in the United States: "in spite of this grand concept of exile from the Promised Land, the fact is that no Jew is in exile until he's exiled from the Jews."[36] Kaufmann and many other American Jews had long before accepted Kallen's early twentieth-century ideas about pluralism as an explanation for the "multiplicity of elements" that made up America.[37]

Although some Jews accepted Kallen's explanation of pluralism as a way to understand American identity and their own role in the country, those ideas did not erase the tensions of assimilation. These tensions were revealed in the common assumption before World War II that Jews were a distinct race. Racist and racialist ideas had grown in the late nineteenth and early twentieth centuries, when Jim Crow laws became entrenched and an unprecedented wave of Southern and Eastern Europeans came to American shores. Thus, for many Americans, blacks and new European immigrants—Jews among them—were immutable biological races that were inferior to the "traditional" American group of white Anglo-Saxon Protestants. By the 1920s, notes Philip Gleason, "racialism was triumphant, both as scientific doctrine and as popular sentiment."[38] This consensus was short-lived because anthropologists and sociologists had repudiated racialist ideas by the eve of World War II, a move that led to the decline of those views among other Americans as well.

Although racialism declined before World War II, recent scholarship has shown that the cultural transition of Jews from "nonwhite" to "white" was fitful and contested by Jews and non-Jews alike.[39] In the early part of the twentieth century, Jews appeared to native whites not only as both a distinct and insular group, but also as one that was rapidly achieving success in the United States. For their part, many Jews remained ambivalent about their own racial identity, wanting both (a) to assimilate to white status in a dichotomous society that was organized around racial identities of "black" and "white" and (b) to preserve their distinctive identity. Although the decline of racialism by World War II established for Jews their identity as white Americans, efforts to assert difference shifted to a greater emphasis on religious, ethnic, and political identities.

Thus, after World War II, Jews increasingly felt—and were seen as—part of a white, pluralistic landscape. One piece of evidence of this acceptance and confidence was the widespread celebration in 1954 of the 300th anniversary of the arrival of American Jews' ancestors in New Amsterdam. Prominent politicians took the occasion to affirm a bond between Jews and other Americans. For example, Adlai Stevenson, when addressing one of the gala celebrations, told his audience, "We are all descended from immigrants and from revolutionaries. And our strength is in large part due to the multiplicity of racial, religious, and cultural strands woven together into the fabric of American liberty."[40] Other indications that Jews felt at home in America and that non-Jewish Americans were reaching out to Jews were numerous articles detailing Jewish rituals and foods. Jewish leaders seemed to take it upon themselves—with the assistance of a receptive press—to educate all Americans about the tenets of Judaism. For example, the president of the Central Council of American Rabbis, Philip Bernstein, wrote an article for *Life* in 1950 called "What Jews Believe." Bernstein emphasized the similarities between Jews and other Americans, asserting that the numerous, daily commandments that govern the lives of Orthodox Jews are really not that alien. These practices are best understood by Micah's (6:8) summary "To do justly, to love mercy and to walk humbly before God." He also notes that liberal Jews accept that Jesus was a "loving teacher."[41]

In the fictional world created by American Jews, characters were increasingly at home in America, but the tension between their Jewish and American identities was a continuing theme. Unlike Sholem Asch, who professed that there was no conflict, most of the authors grappled with how these identities fit together. Even those characters who were assimilated were drawn to Jewish culture, which cast "a spell that went back to the days of Abraham and Isaac."[42] Moreover, the religious and cultural accommodations made on the road to assimilation were seen as problematic. When the title character of Gerald Green's *The Last Angry Man* dies, there are disagreements between the religious and the nonreligious at the funeral, with the religious people asserting that they understand the man's *true* identity. In this and other novels, a tension among the religious also exists. The rise of Conservative and Reform adherents is at once ridiculed and celebrated. Reflecting their own ambivalence about assimilation, the authors imply that these denominations are less pure and, therefore, less Jewish than the Orthodox denomination.

Critics in the press also discussed the relationship between Jews and Christians, and the relationship among Jews, in a culture of assimilation. In the Jewish magazine *Commentary*, for example, one liberal Congregationalist wrote about the important connections between the Jewish and Christian traditions in a core of "ethical monotheism."[43] Such "pro-assimilationist" views were countered by others who criticized the widespread emphasis on the "Judeo–Christian" heritage as a threat to the unique tenets of Judaism. For example, British critic David Daiches said that American Jews were confused about whether to assimilate or cling to their religion; instead, they engaged in "a 'genteel' watering-down of Judaism to conform to U.S. cultural standards." He concluded that the American Jew further confused his assimilationist urge with Zionism: "He hopes that out of Zion will come forth good Rotarian Israelites and Hebrew-speaking hot-dog sellers."[44]

Others concurred that any effort to sweep away all differences between Judaism and Christianity with the Judeo–Christian broom represented a willful misunderstanding of Jewish distinctiveness.[45] Probably the most prevalent view embraced in the mainstream press was that Jews could assimilate to a certain extent but should hold on to their Jewish identity and live "a Jewish life"—however they might define it.[46] Moreover, many assumed that Jews had a common identity, no matter how much they seemed to have assimilated.[47]

Along with the celebratory images projected in popular fiction of the decade, social and political evidence also indicated that Jews were increasingly accepted as loyal Americans. In 1945, 67 percent of respondents to a public opinion poll believed that Jews held too much power. By 1962, the percentage of respondents who believed that Jews held too much power had fallen to 17 percent. Similarly, the number of survey respondents who reported that Jews represented a "menace" to the United States went from 24 percent in 1944 to 5 percent in 1950 to 1 percent in 1962.[48] The improved attitudes toward Jews were so strong that they could weather the highly publicized arrest in 1950 of suspected communists Julius and Ethel Rosenberg. Although the couple's trial went on for three years (culminating in their executions), it did not reignite the stereotypes that Jews were more likely to be communists or to be disloyal.

Politicians React to Assimilation and Achievement

Yet even if Jews were becoming normalized in cultural and political circles, some Americans, especially diplomats, continued to put American Jews in a separate category from other Americans. President Dwight D. Eisenhower's secretary of state, John Foster Dulles, was a case in point. Dulles complained about American Jews' vocal involvement in policy toward Israel. In exasperation, he told a National Security Council meeting in mid-1954 that "it was utterly impossible to make public speeches on the subject of Israeli-Arab relations.... Assistant Secretary [Henry] Byroade had recently ... written and delivered a very sensible speech. However, it had been completely misunderstood in the U.S. and Middle East." Instead of trying to navigate Jewish public opinion, Dulles recommended that the United States make its policy known only to Israel and the individual Arab states.[49]

Less than a year later, the United States collaborated with Britain to launch the Project Alpha initiative, which was designed to bring a settlement in the Arab–Israeli conflict by, among other measures, connecting Egypt and Jordan through the Negev desert, repatriating a number of Arab refugees, and providing economic aid to all participants. From the beginning of the Project Alpha proposal, Dulles remained resentful of the ability of American Jews to infringe on his delicate negotiations. He wondered how he and the other diplomats could "keep Jewish leaders ... quiet during this period of preparation."[50] Dulles was not alone in his worries. Vice President Richard M. Nixon, for example, felt "disturbed by the heavy political pressure to subsidize an Israeli economy which could never balance itself."[51] Furthermore, even with the general decline of anti-Semitism and slow dissolution of stereotypes about Jews, at least some American policy makers continued to view Israelis as "pushy." An example of these sentiments is found in a 1950 cable from Richard Ford, an American diplomat in Israel, who described Israelis as "These aggressively urgent people."[52] Whether or not such views reflected overt anti-Semitism on the part of Ford and others like him or revealed frustration with opposition to U.S. directives, the anti-Semitic resonance of the remarks cannot be missed.

While some policy makers worried about the power of American Jews, others also understood that Jewish influence could be used to the advantage of the United States in its negotiations with the Israelis. For example, in a 1955 memo prepared by the Bureau of Near Eastern, South Asian, and African Affairs that strategized Project Alpha, diplomat Francis Russell noted that the "United States Jewry could, at an appropriate time, play an important role in influencing the I.G. [Israeli Government] to cooperate."[53] American Jews were seen as potentially valuable influences on Israel to the extent that they were deemed to have real political power in the United States.

Evidence of Jewish political power, assimilation, and prosperity was found in many places. In addition to the stories of successful Jews that permeated popular fiction and the press, non-Jewish Americans could look around them and see (a) the increased number of white-collar and professional positions available to American Jews, (b) the great numbers of Jews going to college and moving to the suburbs, (c) the decrease of anti-Semitism in the public culture, and (d) the greater participation of Jews in politics. Jewish influence in politics was widely assumed to have swayed American policy toward Zionism and Israel in the late 1940s. Politicians became increasingly solicitous of Jewish-supported causes in the 1950s, appearing at banquets and rallies, such as those commemorating the Jewish tercentenary in America, and at United Jewish Appeal annual dinners.[54] Some Jews carved out an active political role in both domestic politics and policy toward Israel. For example, Abraham Feinberg was a masterful fundraiser for both Israel and the Democratic Party. Meanwhile, he lobbied presidents and secretaries of state over the years on issues concerning Israel.[55]

Feinberg was not the only Jew who had influence in the Democratic Party. Indeed, over the years, Jews had a much closer relationship with Democrats than with Republicans. Democrats such as Adlai Stevenson maintained a close relationship with Jewish organizations and pro-Israeli groups. As a partisan of Israel, Stevenson publicly agreed with Jews who argued that support for the state was above politics.[56] The Jewish relationship with the Republican Party was very different from that with the Democratic Party. Rabbi Abba Hillel Silver was the most prominent of the Republican Zionist activists. From his lonely political outpost, Silver frequently lobbied the White House on behalf of Israeli interests. Yet in the midst of the debates over the formation of Israel, Silver's bombastic manner so completely alienated President Harry Truman's White House that the outspoken activist was barred from further visits, nor did he win many friends in the Eisenhower administration.[57]

The lack of prominent Jewish Republicans contributed to a perception among American Jews that an Eisenhower administration would be less welcoming to them and less friendly to Israel. The Eisenhower campaign was well aware of these perceptions.[58] Only two months before the election of 1952, Jewish groups noted with worry that Eisenhower still had not made any position on Israel public.[59] The new administration got off on the wrong foot with Jewish groups when it proposed bringing Loy Henderson back from his ambassadorship in Iran to be the deputy under secretary of state for the Eisenhower administration. Henderson had strongly opposed the creation of Israel, and some American Jews charged that he was anti-Semitic.[60] Claims of anti-Semitism even reached the president's brother, Milton Eisenhower, and later in the 1950s, they reached Dulles.[61]

Eisenhower had no close Jewish friends, and throughout his years in the White House, he never reached out to Jewish acquaintances or other Jewish leaders. According to his biographer, Eisenhower was "uncomfortable with Jews."[62]

Assistant to the President and Secretary to the Cabinet Max Rabb, as the most prominent Jew in the Eisenhower White House, became the unofficial liaison to Jewish, ethnic, and civil rights groups. Individual Jews and Jewish organizations addressed letters and entreaties to Rabb regarding American policy toward Israel. Rabb's responses were courteous, but they made few commitments. He felt, at times, "overwhelmed from heads of Jewish organizations asking for my intervention ... relative to their pet institution."[63]

Another important Republican liaison to the Jewish community was Bernard Katzen, who became director of the Ethnic Division of the Republican National Committee and was a friend of Dulles. Publicly, Katzen defended the administration against charges that it did not care about American Jews and that it was uninterested in the welfare of Israel. He argued that the Eisenhower administration's claim to be a "fair broker" in the Arab–Israeli conflict was the only sensible course to take during the Cold War when the greatest danger to the region was from threats of Soviet encroachments. Despite Katzen's efforts, many Republican Jews worried about electoral support in the 1956 election.[64]

Although many Republicans and members of the Eisenhower administration sometimes had difficult political relationships with American Jews and found their support for Israel problematic, more Democrats seemed to embrace Jews and Israel. In particular, liberals who came of age politically during the New Deal saw in the popular image of Israel a reflection of their own values and political ideals. Eleanor Roosevelt, a leading Democrat and liberal in the mid-twentieth century, was a case in point.

Once Israel was established, Roosevelt—along with Truman and many other liberals—became a champion of the Zionist experiment. She was an ardent admirer of Israel and its people, as well as a critic of Israel's Arab neighbors. She used her political influence on Israel's behalf many times. For example, in late 1948, she lobbied Washington officials not to support a proposed peace plan that would have given the Negev desert to the Arabs instead of the Jews. In this case as in others in later years, she based her argument, in part, on what she believed to be the great drive and initiative of the Israelis. Of the Negev, she wrote to one friend, "I imagine that the Jews are the only people who would be energetic enough to develop it." Similarly, she concluded that the Israelis would soon help to develop the whole region: "The Jews in their own country are doing marvels and should, once the refugee problem is settled, help all the Arab countries."[65]

In 1952, she saw development in Israel firsthand when she toured parts of the Middle East and Asia. She drew a sharp contrast between the accomplishments of the Arabs and the Israelis, identifying strongly with the Israelis. Crossing the border between Jordan and Israel in the middle of Jerusalem was, she wrote, "like breathing the air of the United States again.... Once I was through the barrier I felt that I was among people ... dedicated to fulfilling a purpose."[66] She noted then and in subsequent years that the Israelis had many problems with development and integration of immigrants but that they were ably tackling those issues. She was impressed with the growth, development, and strength of Israelis and their country. For example, on one of her trips to Israel in 1959, she wrote home of a kibbutz that she visited: it was, she said, "literally reclaiming the desert and making it bloom."[67]

At home, in the late 1940s and 1950s, Roosevelt showed her devotion to the Jewish state by lending her considerable political clout to Israeli (and Jewish) causes. Examples are numerous.[68] In the early 1950s, she served on the advisory council for State of Israel Bonds, and she spoke at its functions. She was one of the speakers at a large "Salute to Israel Day" at Yankee Stadium in 1956. She was a patron and supporter of many pro-Israeli organizations and their events, and Roosevelt used her writing to praise the Jewish state and its liberal credentials. She was also a supporter of various American Jewish organizations, including many chapters of the B'nai B'rith service organization and Brandeis University.

Along with her institutional relationships, Roosevelt built close individual relationships—both political and personal—with American Jews. In this way, she was similar to other non-Jewish American liberal leaders. These relationships reflected the degree to which anti-Semitism had declined in the public culture. Such personal relationships helped to strengthen support for the state of Israel.

Yet regardless of the party in power and the influence of prominent Democrats or Republicans, Jewish organizations worked hard to establish political relationships in Washington that would benefit Israel. Leaders such as Jacob Blaustein of the American Jewish Committee and Philip Klutznick of B'nai B'rith remained in contact with the White House and State Department regarding policy toward Israel. The easy Jewish access to the halls of power in Washington reflected the degree to which members of this small minority group had assimilated into the American main-stream culture and become accepted as ordinary Americans. Moreover, in the public culture of the press and popular fiction, Jews were not merely accepted; they symbolized the American success narrative par excellence, embodying the story of the immigrant Horatio Alger's climb to wealth, respectability, and patriotism. With this growing idealization and the decline of negative stereotypes about them, American Jews were in, what was for them, a position of potentially unprecedented political influence. Not surprisingly, Jewish organizations tried to use this newfound power to influence American policy toward Israel.[69]

Conclusion: Becoming "Insiders"

Irrespective of the outcome of any one policy debate, during the 1950s, American Jews became more accepted not only in the halls of power but also throughout the public culture in the United States. This chapter began with the contention that the tension among ethnic, religious, and national identities was especially strong for American Jews. But while anti-Semitism declined in the United States, American Jews also found themselves to be the beneficiaries of the increased emphasis on international, multiethnic alliances in the Cold War. Such an emphasis addressed the tension between universal and particular identities. American Jews and other ethnic groups did not have to choose between these identities; they could have both, as long as the particular identity was subsumed under the universal one (now redefined by the Cold War yardstick as a Western identity).

This shift in cultural images was found throughout the public culture, including in popular fiction. But in contrast to the values espoused in the universalist fiction of the mid-1940s, a distinct ethnic identity did not threaten American identity if that ethnicity was part of a pluralistic society. Lawrence Levine concludes that the pluralism of the 1950s was actually quite shallow: "pluralist ideas were overwhelmed by the certainty that ethnic distinctions were in the process of inevitable extinction."[70] Yet despite the apparent weakness of ethnicity, many Americans in the 1950s became convinced of the value of the immigrant heritage of their country in which, as described by historian R. Laurence Moore, "outsiderhood is a characteristic way of inventing one's Americaness."[71] An apparently contradictory paradigm is at work here. In the popular fiction of this period, Jews became consummate insiders in American culture because they were posited first as outsiders and resourceful Horatio Algers. Thus, what is significant here is not whether Horace Kallen's vision of a pluralist society ever existed, but that the ideology of pluralism existed and was adapted by American Jews and others at mid-century to include their own stories of success and assimilation.

This image, of course, had a profound effect on the image of Israelis, who were intimately associated with American Jews in cultural discourse. For example, in 1951, the popular television show *The Toast of the Town* ran a special titled "The Israel Anniversary Show" to celebrate what host Ed Sullivan called "the very glorious third anniversary of the founding of the young but powerful state of Israel." The show, before an audience of 20,000 people assembled by the Zionist Organization of America, contained a mixture of American and Israeli songs, a variety of well-known performers, testimonials about Israel from politicians and American Jewish leaders, and vaudeville comedy skits playing on Yiddish expressions and accents. The message throughout was that a celebration of Israel was actually like a celebration of American Jews and that all Americans, Jewish and non-Jewish alike, could identify with Israel. Sullivan observed, "The cause of Israel is particularly close to the heart of anyone of Irish extraction, because the Irish and the Jew, their struggles were so much alike in the characteristics of their populace, their people were so much alike."[72]

In other contexts, American Jews celebrated their identification with Israel. The creation of local and national Jewish organizations in the postwar period exemplified a new Jewish confidence at home as well as loyalty to Israel. The first president of the Israel Community Center congregation in Levittown, New York, described how the founding of the Jewish state was an imperative to him and his neighbors: "we just *had* to organize a synagogue and center ... and ... we *must* call it Israel Synagogue Center in honor of the new State of Israel.... I felt that if people in Israel [were] ... saying 'We are Jews and we're going to create something worth while,' then I, too, wanted to stand up and really belong to the Jewish people."[73] Such identifications of Jewish "peoplehood" only grew stronger and more prevalent in the 1950s, helping to shape the political role of American Jews and the perception among non-Jews that Americans and Israelis had shared political interests.

The start of this chapter observed that religious identity in modern American life could best be characterized as fluid. This is true for Jews as much as for other religious groups. Yet the patterns of the mid-twentieth century demonstrated that Jews fashioned another identity that was more enduring than just a religious identification. If Jews were a "people" with ethnic, historical, political, and religious features, then this characterization sidestepped some of the tensions of assimilation and secularization. Moreover, the idea that Jews were a distinct people was reinforced by the post–World War II reinterpretation of pluralism, which allowed groups to be both separate and assimilated. Finally, unlike religious identity alone, "peoplehood" was inherently political and gave Jews a political and international role in a Cold War world.

Notes

1. Neela Banerjee, "Poll Finds a Fluid Religious Life in the U.S.," *New York Times*, February 26, 2008, http://www.nytimes.com/2008/02/26/us/26religion.html?scp=6&sq =religion+change&st=nyt&_r=0; "U.S. Religious Landscape Survey," Pew Forum on Religion and Public Life, Washington, DC, http://religions.pewforum.org.

2. Ibid.

3. Christopher Hitchens, *God Is Not Great: How Religion Poisons Everything* (New York: Twelve, 2007); Richard Dawkins, *The God Delusion* (London: Black Swan, 2007).

4. Banerjee, "Poll Finds."

5. Thomas Bender uses *public culture* to denote "a forum where power in its various forms, including meaning and aesthetics, is elaborated and made authoritative." Thomas Bender, "Wholes and Parts: The Need for Synthesis in American History," *Journal of American History* 73, no. 1 (June 1986): 126.

6. See, for example, Eytan Gilboa, *American Public Opinion toward Israel and the Arab–Israeli Conflict* (Lexington, MA: Heath, 1987); Esther Yolles Feldblum, *The American Catholic Press and the Jewish State, 1917–1959* (New York: Ktav, 1977); Issam Suleiman Mousa, *The Arab Image in the U.S. Press* (New York: Lang, 1984).

7. The study of cultural narratives is not intended to prove a direct causal link between language, images, and particular political acts. Edward Said has written extensively on the significance of cultural narratives, or the link between consciousness and material existence. See Edward Said, *Orientalism* (New York: Vintage Books, 1978) and *Culture and Imperialism* (New York: Vintage Books, 1993). Recent works by many historians, such as Gail Bederman, Emily Rosenberg, Frank Costigliola, and Melani McAlister, have followed in the footsteps of Said to use discursive analysis in many areas of history.

8. Melani McAlister, *Epic Encounters: Culture, Media, and U.S. Interests in the Middle East, 1945–2000* (Berkley: University of California Press, 2001), 8.

9. Nathan Glazer, "The American Jew and the Attainment of Middle-Class Rank: Some Trends and Explanations," in *The Jews: Social Patterns of an American Group*, ed. Marshall Sklare (Glencoe, IL: Free Press, 1958), 138–39, 140–41.

10. Sholem Asch, *A Passage in the Night* (New York: Putnam's Sons, 1953), 29.

11. Gerald Green, *The Last Angry Man* (New York: Charles Scribner's Sons, 1958); Jerome Weidman, *The Enemy Camp* (New York: Random House, 1958); Saul Bellow,

The Adventures of Augie March (New York: Penguin, 1954); Herman Wouk, *Marjorie Morningstar* (New York: Doubleday, 1955).

12. Asch, *Passage in the Night*, 87–88. Asch's book was a bestseller from December 1953 to January 1954. (This and other bestseller information is from *New York Times Book Review* bestseller lists.)

13. John Brooks, "The Education of George Hurst," *New York Times Book Review*, June 15, 1958, 5.

14. Outside of the pages of novels, the elevation of the Lower East Side as the starting point of the American success story was widespread in American Jewish memory in the postwar period. For discussion, see Hasia Diner, *Lower East Side Memories: A Jewish Place in America* (Princeton, NJ: Princeton University Press, 2000), 14, 15, 33, 59, 60, 69.

15. See *New York Times Book Review* bestseller lists. See also, "60 Years of Best Sellers," *New York Times Book Review*, October 7, 1956.

16. For more on the influence of the book, see Edward Shapiro, *A Time for Healing: American Jewry since World War II* (Baltimore: Johns Hopkins University Press, 1992), 10, 157–58.

17. Meyer Levin, "Central Park Revisited," *Saturday Review of Literature*, September 3, 1955, 9–10.

18. Florence Haxton Bullock, "Herman Wouk Spins a Tale in the Great Tradition," *New York Herald Tribune Book Review*, September 4, 1955, 1.

19. Myron S. Kaufmann, *Remember Me to God* (Philadelphia: J. B. Lippincott, 1957).

20. For further discussion, see Albert I. Gordon, *Jews in Suburbia* (Boston: Beacon Press, 1959).

21. Quoted in Paul Ramsey, "Approaches to a Faith," *New York Times Book Review*, September 1, 1957, 7.

22. Weidman, *Enemy Camp*, 85; Kaufmann, *Remember Me to God*, 458.

23. See, for example, Harold U. Ribalow, ed., *Mid-Century: An Anthology of Jewish Life and Culture in Our Times* (New York: Beechhurst Press, 1955). The publication *Commentary* was also a forum in which these issues were discussed.

24. *Three Brave Men* (Twentieth Century Fox, 1957), film copy from Motion Picture Collection, Library of Congress, Washington, DC.

25. See Charles Herbert Stember, Marshall Sklare, and American Jewish Committee, *Jews in the Mind of America* (New York: Basic Books, 1966), 160–67.

26. *I Accuse!* (MGM, 1958), film copy from Motion Picture Collection, Library of Congress, Washington, DC.

27. *The Naked and the Dead* (RKO Teleradio, 1958), film copy from Motion Picture Collection, Library of Congress, Washington, DC; *The Young Lions* (Twentieth Century Fox, 1958), film copy from Motion Picture Collection, Library of Congress, Washington, DC. *The Young Lions* was one of the top-grossing films of 1958. See Charles Aaronson, ed., *The International Motion Picture Almanac 1960* (New York: Quigley, 1960), 737.

28. Quoted in Susanne Klingenstein, *Jews in the American Academy, 1900–1940: The Dynamics of Intellectual Assimilation* (New Haven, CT: Yale University Press, 1991), 41.

29. Arthur Hertzberg, *The Jews in America: Four Centuries of an Uneasy Encounter* (New York: Simon and Schuster, 1989), 318, 342. For more on Jewish political

power and Israel, see J. J. Goldberg, *Jewish Power: Inside the American Jewish Establishment* (Reading, MA: Addison-Wesley, 1996).

30. Howard M. Sachar, *A History of Israel: From the Rise of Zionism to Our Time* (New York: Alfred A. Knopf, 1996), 118.

31. Jonathan Sarna, "A Projection of America as It Ought to Be: Zion in the Mind's Eye of American Jews," in *Envisioning Israel: The Changing Ideals and Images of North American Jews*, ed. Allon Gal (Detroit, MI: Wayne State University Press, 1996), 57.

32. Marshall Sklare, ed., *The Jews: Social Patterns of an American Group* (Glencoe, IL: Free Press, 1958), 213.

33. Richard Sullivan, "Always in Exile," *New York Times Book Review*, September 5, 1954, 6.

34. Salo W. Berson, "Three Centuries of Jewish Experience in America," *New York Times Book Review*, September 12, 1954.

35. Sullivan, "Always in Exile."

36. Kaufmann, *Remember Me to God*, 536.

37. Klingenstein, *Jews in the American Academy,* 34–35.

38. Philip Gleason, "Americans All: World War II and the Shaping of American Identity," *Review of Politics* 43, no. 4 (1981): 485.

39. For more information on the discussion of whiteness and Jews, see Eric L. Goldstein, *The Price of Whiteness: Jews, Race, and American Identity* (Princeton, NJ: Princeton University Press, 2006). See also, Karen Brodkin, *How Jews Became White Folks and What That Says about Race in America* (Piscataway, NJ: Rutgers University Press, 1998); Matthew Frye Jacobson, *Whiteness of a Different Color: European Immigrants and the Alchemy of Race* (Cambridge, MA: Harvard University Press, 1998).

40. "Address of Adlai Stevenson at the American Jewish Tercentenary," June 1, 1955, papers of Adlai E. Stevenson, series 2 speeches, box 151, folder 5, Seeley G. Mudd Library, Princeton University, Princeton, NJ.

41. Philip Bernstein, "What Jews Believe," *Life*, September 11, 1950, 160–62.

42. Weidman, *The Enemy Camp*, 524.

43. Robert Fitch, "The Bond Between Christian and Jew," *Commentary*, May 1954, 439–45.

44. "Religion: A Common Ignorance," *Time*, February 19, 1951, 59–60.

45. Jacob Taubes, "The Issue between Judaism and Christianity," *Commentary*, December 1953, 525–33.

46. See, for example, "Almost a Lutheran," *Time*, April 5, 1954, 66, 68.

47. See, for example, Herbert Mitgang, "A Lox Is a Lox," *New York Times Book Review*, March 8, 1953, 24.

48. Stember, Sklare, and American Jewish Committee, *Jews in the Mind of America*, 121–24; also cited in Goldberg, *Jewish Power*, 117.

49. "NSC Meeting #207," July 22, 1954, National Security Council series, Ann Whitman file, box 5, Dwight D. Eisenhower Library, Abilene, KS.

50. U.S. Department of State, *Foreign Relations of the United States, 1955–1957, Arab-Israeli Conflict, 1955*, vol. 14 (Washington, DC: U.S. Government Printing Office, 1989), 30.

51. "NSC Meeting #207."

52. Quoted in David Schoenbaum, *The United States and the State of Israel* (New York: Oxford University Press, 1993), 79.

53. U.S. Department of State, *Foreign Relations of the United States*, 14.

54. See, for example, "Address of Governor Averell Harriman at the United Jewish Appeal," March 21, 1957, Middle East data file, papers of David Lloyd, box 34, Harry S. Truman Library, Independence, MO.

55. See, for example, "Memo of Conversation," July 17, 1951, July 1951 file, papers of Dean Acheson, box 67, Harry S. Truman Library, Independence, MO.

56. See, for example, "Jacob Weinstein to William McCormick Blair," November 8, 1955, papers of Weinstein and Jacob, box 89, folder 1; "Material Mailed to Rabbi Weinstein, Judge Fisher, and Philip Klutznik," December 22, 1955, papers of Weinstein and Jacob, box 89, folder 1; "Address of Adlai Stevenson before American Committee for the Weizmann Institute of Science," December 2, 1954, series 2 speeches, box 150, folder 6; "John Foster Dulles to Stevenson," August 24, 1955, box 25, folder 17; "Stevenson to Irving Engel," January 23, 1956, box 374; "Jacob Weinstein to Alvin Fine," January 26, 1956, box 374; "Stevenson's Speech to Israel Bond Drive," September 11, 1956, series 2 speeches, box 158, folder 3; "Stevenson to Israel Bond Rally," November 12, 1955, series 2 speeches, box 152, folder 6; "Henry Burman to Stevenson," August 25, 1953, Stevenson papers, box 31. All papers listed are from Seeley G. Mudd Library, Princeton University, Princeton, NJ.

57. See, for example, "Silver to Dulles," June 3, 21, and 25, 1954, Silver file, Abba Hillel 1954 papers, box 87, Seeley G. Mudd Library, Princeton University, Princeton, NJ; "Silver to Dulles," September 2, 1955, box 97, Dulles papers, Seeley G. Mudd Library, Princeton University, Princeton, NJ.

58. See, for example, "C. D. Jackson to Dulles," November 10, 1953, Dwight D. Eisenhower Library, Abilene, KS; "Memo of Roderic O'Connor to C. D. Jackson," November 16, 1953, Israel Relations 5, subject series, Dulles papers, box 10, Dwight D. Eisenhower Library, Abilene, KS.

59. "Memo of Otto Schirn," August 7, 1952, Dwight D. Eisenhower Library, Abilene, KS; "Memo of Murray Chotiner to Sherman Adams," August 26, 1952, Israel Relations 1, general file, White House central file, box 817, Dwight D. Eisenhower Library, Abilene, KS.

60. "Memo from Thomas Dewey to Dulles," February 19, 1953, Dwight D. Eisenhower Library, Abilene, KS; "Memo by Nat Goldstein," strictly confidential miscellaneous reports, general correspondence, Dulles papers, box 4, Dwight D. Eisenhower Library, Abilene, KS.

61. "Henry Stupell to Eisenhower," September 6, 1956, Dwight D. Eisenhower Library, Abilene, KS; "Rabb to Stupell," October 26, 1956, Israel 118B, general file, White House central file, box 683. See also information on Eustace Seligman, who defended Dulles, "Correspondence with Eustace Seligman, Dulles, and Emanuel Celler," November 7, 1958, December 22, 1958, January 3, 1959, general correspondence, Dulles papers, box 3, Dwight D. Eisenhower Library, Abilene, KS.

62. Stephen E. Ambrose, *Eisenhower*, vol. 2 (New York: Simon and Schuster, 1984), 387.

63. "Max Rabb, OH," 2, 6; "Rabb to George Levinson," February 27, 1957, Israel Relations 4, box 817; "Rabb to Rabbi E. L. Silver," November 20, 1956; "Telegram of Silver and Meyer Cohen for the Union of Orthodox Rabbis to Eisenhower," November 14, 1956; "Memo of Rabb to Fisher Howe, Department of State," November 20, 1956; "Memo of Rabb to Dulles," December 31, 1956, Israel 122BB (3), box 881; "Memo of Rabb to Bernard Shanley," June 4, 1956; "Rabbi Blumenthal to Eisenhower," May 23, 1956; "Shanley to Blumenthal," June 6, 1956, Israel 122 (4), box 817; "Rabb to Bernard

Katzen," March 3, 1956, Israel 2, box 817; "Rabb to George Cassidy," October 14, 1957; "Rabb to Katzen," October 15, 1957, Israel (6), box 817, general file, White House central file. All papers listed are from the Dwight D. Eisenhower Library, Abilene, KS.

64. "Maxwell Abbell to Rabb," June 8, 1956, Israel 122 (4), general file, White House central file, box 817, Dwight D. Eisenhower Library, Abilene, KS.

65. Letters quoted in Joseph P. Lash, *Eleanor: The Years Alone* (New York: Norton, 1972), 135–37. See also "Eleanor Roosevelt's Address to the Nation Associates Conference, New York," May 25, 1952, which was originally printed in *Nation*, June 7, 1952, 174, 556–57, and later reprinted in Eleanor Roosevelt, *What I Hope to Leave Behind: The Essential Essays of Eleanor Roosevelt*, ed. Allida M. Black (New York: Carlson, 1995), 597–98.

66. Eleanor Roosevelt, *The Autobiography of Eleanor Roosevelt* (New York: Harper, 1958), 326–27.

67. "Eleanor Roosevelt to Edna and David Gurewitsch," March 25, 1959, letters from Eleanor Roosevelt to A. David Gurewitsch, 1947–1962, Gurewitsch papers, Franklin Delano Roosevelt Library, Hyde Park, New York.

68. These examples are taken from a survey of files in Eleanor Roosevelt, general correspondence, Franklin Delano Roosevelt Library, Hyde Park, New York.

69. For example, regarding reactions to the Kibya incident, see "Klutznick to Dulles," November 29, 1953, Seeley G. Mudd Library, Princeton University, Princeton, NJ; "Dulles to Klutznick," December 3, 1953, B'nai B'rith 1953 file, Dulles papers, box 67, Seeley G. Mudd Library, Princeton University, Princeton, NJ.

70. Lawrence Levine, *The Opening of the American Mind: Canons, Culture, and History* (Boston: Beacon Press, 1996), 118.

71. R. Laurence Moore, *Religious Outsiders and the Making of Americans* (New York: Oxford University Press, 1986), xi.

72. "The Israel Anniversary Show," *Toast of the Town*, 1951, Museum of Television and Radio, New York.

73. Gordon, *Jews in Suburbia*, 102.

Part V

Violence and World Affairs

Chapter 12

Religious Violence in Nineteenth- and Twentieth-Century American History?

Michael Hochgeschwender

At least since the tragic events of 9/11, an age-old discussion that had evolved in particular during the Age of Enlightenment in the late eighteenth century regained momentum: Does religion per se generate violence? Is there a specific relationship between religion, fanaticism, and terror?

Some authors have argued that any religion, Christianity or any other, is prone to fanaticism, highly emotionalized enthusiasm, lack of rational discretionary self-reflection, and violent fundamentalism. This general attitude was attributed to an inherent absence of intellectualism or enlightened rationalism within the sphere of religion (interpreted as the blind and purely emotional adherence to a nonexistent entity named God) as well as to the impact of priest-propagated speculations or vile machinations with the aim of reaching or safeguarding worldly powerhouses.[1] These authors not only referred to Islamist fundamentalism and its terrorist impulses but also hinted at various examples from history, such as the Crusades during the Middle Ages—which were exclusively interpreted

269

as holy wars—the witchcraft hysteria of early modernity, or the relentless activities of the holy inquisitions in both epochs.

Others defied such a radical position as far too simple because it tended to overstretch the genuinely religious impulse and overlooked purely secularist motivations such as the balance of power, the politics of ethnic or gender identity, and class interest. Although not attempting to excuse the violent excesses that were carried out in the name of religion, such authors argued that the radical position did not include a sober analysis of the contemporary sociopolitical, economic, and cultural framework within which all these actions took place.[2] More apologetic authors not only criticized the radical standpoint but also stressed the positive effects of organized religion on the individual and the social order.[3]

My primary object, however, is not to solve the question of whether religion in itself invariably generates violence. The answer to this question very much depends on the ideological outlook of the spectator, specifically on his or her personal attitude toward religion. Moreover, it depends on the methodological and notional approach taken. Whoever looks for religiously implemented violence will find it according to the concept of religion and violence that he or she accepts a priori. The methodological problem is, nevertheless, to distinguish between an intensely religious rhetoric, including emotional and violent semantics, and a real causal relation between this rhetoric and the active use of violence in a given society. One must also include an analysis of the interrelationship between possible religious causes of violence and secular causes, such as political or economic interest, class struggle, and ethnic strife.

Even in an age so deeply entangled in religious problems as the Middles Ages, it is nearly impossible to make generalizations about the degree to which religion was the central causal agent of historical processes. Fritz Stolz argues plausibly that it would be impossible to analyze the causal influence of a single-factor religion in a polytheistic society that is basically driven in all social subsystems by the influence of religious thought, which is, however, inseparable from other social subsystems.[4] With the rise of modernity and secularization, the whole matter becomes even more complicated because religion did not, as many enlightened ideologues expected, wither away more or less peacefully and because modern ideologies constructed themselves increasingly along religious lines.[5] Therefore, the relationship between religion and violence must be termed carefully within the broader framework of social, cultural, economic, and political concepts of a specific age and a specific national context.

Moreover, it is difficult, if not impossible, to precisely calculate the impact of the specific factor, or subsystem, of religion within a broader scope of other interfering sociocultural and socioeconomic causes in a given system of social interactions. In particular, with regard to modernity, we need, on the one hand, a general differentiation of social subsystems — one that includes religion both in a heuristic light and as the result of the historical process of societal fragmentation — before we can even begin to analyze religion's role in violent conflicts. Because of the functional differentiations of modern societies, this chapter focuses on this approach. On the other hand, this functional differentiation of societal subsystems must not be interpreted in a Luhmann-style monadic sense. However important the differences between the diverse systems may be, they are still intrinsically overlapping, both functionally and with regard to their reciprocal definitions.

As a result, it would seem to be impossible to present a general theory of the relationship between religion and violence beyond specific historical settings.[6] Thus, I will concentrate on several case studies regarding the violent impact of religion on social conflicts in the United States during the nineteenth and twentieth centuries — that is, under the conditions of postenlightened,[7] industrial high modernity.

The example of the United States seems to be significantly relevant, as it is perhaps the single most religious nation among the industrial countries. From the country's beginning, religion (predominantly the evangelical enthusiast and millennialist wing of Calvinist Christianity) has shaped the expectations and national identity of Americans.[8] Even the very notion of fundamentalism, which is often seen as the utter and obvious epitome of religious violence, stems from the United States. Moreover, over the two centuries of its existence, American society has been among the most violent of all modern societies. Whatever the reasons for this *Sonderweg* may have been, the fact itself is uncontested.[9] For both reasons (i.e., its specific religious and violent traditions), the United States could furnish a good basis for further case studies regarding the complexly intertwined relationship between religion and other causes of social violence.

This relative exceptionalism (relative because it was in itself regularly combined with transatlantic developments[10]) was even intensified by two further developments. First, from the eighteenth century onward, American religion became transformed into a rather pluralist patchwork of small, often grassroots-based and therefore quite "democratic" denominations instead of the traditional European early modern system of established relationships between a major church and the throne.[11] This process was a result of the increasingly revivalist structure of American religion. This revivalist, evangelical pattern, secondly and subsequently, was actively involved in another major transformational step, namely, the establishment of a competitive market beginning in the 1820s and the self-transformation of this religious market into the modern industrial and capitalist national or global market system since the 1830s by the self-commodification of predominantly evangelical-revivalist and millennialist Christianity.[12] This deep involvement of enthusiastic religion in a highly competitive and therefore rather aggressive market led to a more dramatic rhetoric and to a histrionic performative turn that stressed a perfectionistic and radical break from a world of sin and sinners more than did the older Puritan conversion narrative.[13] More and more during the nineteenth and twentieth centuries, the idea of a zealously (Protestant) missionary, millennialist-redeemer nation—sometimes framed in religious and sometimes in secular terms—evolved and became an integral, yet not necessarily aggressive or expansionistic, part of the national identity of the United States.[14]

All in all, the sum of these developments should have—according to the theoretical assumptions of those critical about the social impact of religion—led to widespread religious violence. This assumption, nevertheless, proved empirically wrong. If we consider, for instance, the existing statistical accounts regarding religious and other violence in the United States during the past two centuries, religious violence taken in the strict sense of the word[15] is, in the long run, negligible.[16] There were, nonetheless, phases of intensified outbreaks of religiously motivated violence, such as during the heydays of evangelical anti-Catholicism and social anti-Mormonism in the 1840s and 1850s, during the activities of the second Ku Klux Klan in the 1920s, and during the heated cultural wars of the 1980s and 1990s. But even during these times of intensified aggressiveness, a vast majority of religious activists in the United States—among them, a majority of the most ardent partisans of radical evangelicalism, fundamentalism, or ultramontanist Catholicism—remained in conformity with the political and social order of the Union. Both findings need an explanation. Therefore, I will formulate my central theses before I focus on a rather dense analysis of the decades with rising religious violence.

Let us start with my first basic assumption: I do not share the common conviction that religion per se, whether in its monotheistic or its polytheistic version,[17] is an efficient cause for violence. Neither is politics, society, culture, or the economy. Yet all of these abstract universals may serve as causal agents in certain combinations. They are sufficient preconditions of social violence that, under certain circumstances, can be transformed into efficient causal agents. These circumstances, however, have to be described specifically in relation to the social and cultural mode of a certain epoch. Religion will work differently under the circumstances of medieval social systems; pre- and early modern systems; and modern, industrial, and postenlightened systems.

For example, in a premodern political system, religion serves integrating purposes, whereby nearly any political action, whether based on political, dynastical, or economic assumptions, will be framed in religious terms. This mindset changes under the conditions of modernity. Economic considerations, human rights, or other secular ideological motivations become as important as (or even more important than) religious semantics in motivating the *Folgebereitschaft* of a mass society. Recent scholarship in the field of political science has, for instance, convincingly argued that economic factors by far outweigh religious implications with regard to social violence in modern civil wars.[18] In the modern era, where the nation-state serves as the central basic framework of political and social organization, the politics of ethnic identity appears to be the single most important issue in setting cultural agendas of violence.[19] Ethnic identity might include religious aspects, as with Christian Orthodoxy in Serbia, Roman Catholicism in Ireland or Poland, or Protestantism in nineteenth-century United States. Nevertheless, it focuses on a primarily functionalist, Durkheimian understanding of religion. The ethnocultural perspective on religion takes religion as an accidental matter of the nation and minimizes the inherent universalism of the religion itself.

This point leads to my second basic assumption: the transformation of religion from a sufficient precondition into an efficient causal agent for violence depends on a network of remote and proximate causes that are specified by historical circumstances. Under the conditions of industrial modernity in the North Atlantic cultural context, the most important *causa remota* seems to be the modernization process itself.[20] Primarily, the delegitimation of traditional authority and traditional institutionalization as an immediate result of the pluralization and individualization of lifestyles gave way not only to more liberal standards of rationality and tolerance but to a lack of control as well. The "fundamentalisms" of the twentieth century, for example, are predominantly a product of this break with traditional authorities and institutions, as is the apocalyptic idea of the "new man" that serves as causal agent for modern perfectionist strategies of a secular and violent millennialism.[21] Thus, pluralism and modernization have to be interpreted as ambiguous and ambivalent with regard to religious violence.

According to these assumptions, the remote cause of the transformation of religion into an active agent of social violence within the context of a specific social setting is the specific mixture of emotivism and voluntarism within postenlightened culture — specifically within postenlightened religion. Within the context of Christianity, this transformation may be called the "Schleiermacher trap." Under the pressure of the epistemic criticism of eighteenth-century philosophy, parts of Christianity withdrew from an intellectualist approach toward religion and metaphysics. Religion was no longer considered as a self-reflexive and rational *Für wahr halten* (the intellectual acceptance of the truth-value of religious statements) but as *Gefühl schlechthinniger Abhängigkeit* (religion as a *feeling* of absolute dependence), as Friedrich Schleiermacher put it. This development led to a certain further delegitimization of rationality within religious discourses.[22] Religiously inspired terrorists in the United States tend to overemphasize this emotional part of religion up to the degree of radical anti-intellectualism. Furthermore, this anti-intellectual emotivism was nevertheless in part compatible with postenlightened modernity, which was much less intellectualist and far more emotivist and voluntarist than many people may believe, partly because of the major focus of the Enlightenment on safeguarding individual liberty. Liberty is based on the will and not necessarily on rationality. In this regard, the egalitarian and voluntarist anti-intellectualism of many fundamentalisms is structurally akin to a genuinely modern way of framing the individual. Again, the results of modernization are ambivalent.[23]

Whereas the remote causes do not necessarily have an immediate effect on the transformation of religion into a causal agent for violence, the proximate causes do.

The first *causa proxima* is the crises of industrial modernity. It is not by chance that religious violence in the United States always appears in times of national or global crisis. Crises are not always purely economical; more often they are framed in terms of culture and identity. Mass immigration, the quest for a unified national culture, insecurity about rapid socioeconomic developments, and, predominantly, struggles over cultural hegemony (i.e., the discursive power to define the image of one's society according to one's own perceptions, values, and sometimes imagined past) — all these elements qualify as proximate causes. In every single case, they accompanied a climax of religious violence in the United States. Always, the most militant members of the anti-institutionalist, individualist, egalitarian, and anti-intellectualist wings of nonestablished denominations in the country felt on the defensive and felt that they were losing the ability to define socially acceptable values. The implicit and nonviolent aggressiveness of modern liberal culture and the militancy of the radical religious answers are interdependent.

As second *causa proxima*, we have to deal with personal psychological circumstances, or to be more precise, with the psychopathology of alienated and estranged individuals. No theoretical framework whatsoever will come to terms with religious violence in the modern era without somehow conceptualizing individual psychological structures, especially a dramatic, highly emotional Manichean attitude toward social problems combined with hysterical alarmism and—quite paradoxically given the egalitarian structure of the movements involved—the elitist feeling of being the last hope of and fighting the last stand for the whole of humankind. Not only is this psychological state generated by religion; it is very much akin to the elitism of juvenile terrorist movements of the late 1960s and early 1970s, which were basically secularist in their ideological outlook.[24] Furthermore, John Brown and the antiabortion terrorists of the 1990s shared this perspective. The individualist-psychopathological factor, moreover, explains the structure of violent religious movements, in which relatively few activists are really involved in violent acts, while more or less small bands of immediate sympathizers and ideologues surround them, and a large number of people share some of the ideas while rejecting the methods.

This somewhat Thomistic account of *causae remotae et proximae* is, however, still too simplistic. I will elaborate on it by introducing another median level of causal analysis, which may be called *causa media*. This level might include the effects of personal relationships, camaraderie, and group pressure on individuals. Michael Mann has, for example, introduced this aspect as *caging* (i.e., a step-by-step radicalization of peer groups bound together by common interests, grievances, and political aims).[25] This process provides the basis for dualistic and Manichean worldviews as well as radical misperceptions of social melées. One's own small and caged group becomes more and more the only mutually accepted point of social reference. The members of the group then tend to interpret everything in the outside world as dangerous, belligerent, and fiendish. Thus, their reaction becomes violent over time, even if violence was not necessarily the starting point of their process of radicalization. Frustration, isolation, and dualistic generalizations in combination with a general positive attitude toward violent solutions of perceived problems are the major agents of this radicalization. Those caged peer groups are again a result of individualist anti-institutionalism. Perhaps this median cause is the most important level of analysis with regard to modern variations of terrorist social violence. Moreover, it helps to distinguish between the core perpetrators who actually turn violent and the sympathetic bystanders who share the responsibility for a climate of violence, whether religious, ethnocultural, or economic, but are never directly involved in violent acts.

In a second step, I will now try to apply this framework to actual cases of religious violence in the United States chronologically. Having already mentioned the major background developments—especially the mixture of mass migration, transformation of a subsidiary economy into a nationalized and even globalized capitalist and industrial economy, and the search for the modern nation-state and its identity—I will now focus on the more specific details of the nineteenth-century transformational crisis of the Union. With regard to violence, two aspects are of utter importance: the slavery question and the Indian question. Either of them generated as a single issue more social violence in the United States than all other issues causing religious strife of that century taken together.[26]

The slavery question not only involved the slave masters' structural and bodily violence against their slaves but also included many harsh and gruesome attacks of proslavery lynching mobs against abolitionists and their propagandistic infrastructure. One could, however, argue that the violent implications of both the slavery question and the Indian question were basically a result of older, religious traditions.[27] And to a certain degree, this objection would be correct. There were early modern religious conceptions of the black as slave by the will of God, as well as ideas of the virgin land purified by God himself in order to present it to the saints of the Puritan community. This argument, nevertheless, overlooks the intensity with which both traditions were significantly remodeled by the implications of enlightenment and capitalism.

In the eighteenth and nineteenth centuries, the anti-Indian argument was based on the idea of efficient use of the land, and both antiblack and anti-Indian sentiments were generally confirmed by a heated and often openly nonreligious racism. The polygenetic theories of secularist Southerners, in particular, were nothing less than an open breach with the ecclesiastical traditions. In contrast, members of predominantly evangelical denominations of the North (and in the case of the Indians, Catholic missionaries) opposed the modern-secularist and eliminatory approach toward the Indians as well as the excesses of slavery. Abolitionism, in particular, included a coalition of liberal-enlightened philanthropists and ardent evangelicals. The latter were, interestingly enough and contrary to the militancy of their semantics of holiness, apocalypse, and perfectionism, much less violent and militant than the overwhelmingly nonreligious proslavery mobs.[28] Because of their religiously founded pacifism, many evangelical zealots opposed any abolitionist violence and were, until the spring of 1861, even willing to let the South go. Only after Fort Sumter did they rally around the flag of the Union and fight for the newly formed nation-state.[29]

An obvious exception to this rule was John Brown. He and his allies, most of them friends and family members, tried to trigger a revolt of the Virginian slaves at Harper's Ferry in 1859. Even before that, however, he was responsible for the Pottawatomie Massacre during Bleeding Kansas, when he overlooked the brutal slaughter of five unarmed proslavery residents. John Brown was definitely a deeply religious person, but he was not committed to radical evangelicalism. After all, he was a traditional Calvinist and very suspicious with regard to millennialist enthusiasm. Moreover, his most influential supporters were comparatively modern and secular transcendentalists in New England.[30] With all due respect to Brown's merits in the civil rights movement, so remarkably applauded by David Reynolds, Brown was the prototype of the modern psychopathological terrorist. Religion and moral fervor in combination with an elitist standpoint marked his violent tactics, a mixture that was in no way acceptable to mainstream evangelicalism. Moreover, the internal radicalization of his peer group— the most radical wing of the abolitionist movement—during and after the crisis of Bleeding Kansas and the *Dred Scott* decision of the U.S. Supreme Court destroyed all hopes for a fast and peaceful settlement of the slavery issue and accelerated the radicalization of Brown and his family. Nonetheless, the predominant form of social violence during the Jacksonian and antebellum era was antiabolitionism. Antiabolitionism, however, was a predominantly secular force based on economic and class assumptions. It was, therefore, much more comparable to anti-Indian violence than to genuinely religious strife.

Thus, although the Indian question and the slavery question were the most important sources of nonreligious violence in the United States during the nineteenth century, three types of genuine religious violence also existed:[31] anti-Judaism, anti-Mormonism,[32] and anti-Catholicism.[33] There were, however, major differences in the degree of violence and of the involvement of religious aspects in the three cases. Anti-Semitism, for example, was a widespread sentiment among many Americans in the nineteenth and early twentieth centuries and was based as much on religious intolerance and traditional anti-Judaism as on blanket racism. Despite its far-reaching implications, anti-Semitism nevertheless did not generate very much immediate violent action. The infamous lynching of Leo Frank in 1913 was the single exception.[34]

Things were different with anti-Catholicism and anti-Mormonism. Although anti-Catholicism, like anti-Semitism, was based on traditional religious and (anti-Irish) ethnocultural sentiments and on the prejudices generated by the structuring of the modern nation-state (both Catholics and Jews were seen as *vaterlandslose Gesellen*—that is, un-American—not just in the United States), anti-Catholicism generated much more violence than anti-Semitism. This increased violence was certainly due to the number of Irish and German Catholic immigrants and the traditional Anglo-Saxon position toward the Irish and toward Catholicism.[35] In 1834, 1844, and 1855, the anti-Catholic hysteria, which was frequently combined with anti-monarchist and anti-Jesuit conspiracy theories as well as by a markedly Victorian emotion against the celibate lifestyle of sisters and priests, reached its climax. Dozens of militant anti-Catholic organizations, among them the nativistic Know-Nothing movement, which even formed a partly influential third party before fusing with the newly formed Republican Party, spread all over the Northeast. Catholic churches were burned, and sometimes regular battles between Irish and anti-Catholic mobs evolved. Hundreds of people died or were wounded. Anti-Catholicism over the decades remained as an influential part of American national identity. Even today, remnants of this religious-nationalist attitude can still be found.[36] However, it never again reached the level of open violence that it had during the antebellum era. Postbellum anti-Catholicism became violent only during the 1870s, when predominantly Irish mobs (orange and green) fought each other in the streets of New York and during the 1920s when the second Ku Klux Klan evolved.[37] But as violent and aggressive as anti-Catholicism may have been in the antebellum era, it did not prevent Catholics from becoming an integral part of the U.S. citizenry. Moreover, it never became as important as the slavery issue (though it was somehow combined with this all-overarching subject matter). At the end of the day, the Civil War was not a religious struggle, and it was not primarily based on anti-Catholic sentiments. Evangelicals and Catholics fought side by side, together with secular liberals and conservatives in both armies, blue and gray. Perhaps it was the strong attachment to the Constitution and the fact that the two-party system favored political and sociocultural integration that hindered anti-Catholicism from becoming as important as the slavery matter.

The great exception to the rule was anti-Mormonism. There were no traditional religious prejudices against Mormons, and there was no fear of an antinational or supranational conspiracy. Mormonism was perhaps the most Americanized nationalist religion that stemmed from the eruptions of the Second Great Awakening of the 1820s and 1830s. Yet Mormons were persecuted at least as violently and relentlessly as the Catholics. Dozens of Mormons were lynched or killed in battle-like actions, and they answered this violence in semiregular wars and massacres, such as the Mountain Meadows Massacre of 1858. This degree of explicit hatred and violence needs further explanation, especially if one considers that during the 1840s and 1850s several utopian communities lived in similar ways and were not persecuted in such a manner. As with anti-Catholicism and anti-Semitism, this violence was not only about religion. The Mormons had, on the one hand, been aggressively missionary, but this behavior was quite normal in the religious market of the United States. On the other hand, they had two most unpleasant features that divided them from Victorian society: polygamy and a new religious revelation (i.e., the Book of Mormon). The latter aspect was a scandal in the eyes of the general public—not only the very religious. And the first was an abomination in an era when the Victorian bourgeoisie were trying to establish social control in every part of a restless society. This combination of social, cultural, and religious problems led to violence that was not always religious in nature.[38] Moreover, we have to acknowledge the specific sociocultural setting, especially in Missouri and parts of the Deep South, where most of the anti-Mormon violence occurred. These areas had already been deeply penetrated by different forms of social violence and a cultural code involving the violent solution of conflicts. Both elements had been intensely connected with slavery.[39]

Methodologically, however, the major problem is not about social developments and the psychology of individuals. We know a lot about the modernizational processes in the antebellum era, and we even know something about the psychological development of some individuals. Yet we know nearly nothing about the internal mindset of radicalized peer groups such as the Secret Six, the Order of the Star Spangled Banner,[40] or the Fenian Brotherhood. Therefore, the central steppingstone on the way from caged individualism to violence remains unintelligible. How important was, for example, modern secular nationalism among the members of the Order of the Star Spangled Banner? Or alternatively, how important was the Catholic religion among the Fenians, who were excommunicated by both the American and the Irish episcopate and still remained—or at least pretended to be—devoutly Catholic? Moreover, why was there nothing like Catholic-ultramontanist counterterrorism in the nineteenth century even among radicalized peer groups such as the Fenians or the Molly Maguires, where class was clearly more important than religion?[41] In these cases, perhaps the existence of traditional authority stressing the importance of order and stability prevented the emergence of specifically religious violence, although such authority was unable to prevent the formation of nationalistic secret societies using the semantics of cultural and thus religious identity markers.

Thus, it is nearly impossible to correctly estimate the impact of religion on social violence in the nineteenth-century United States, especially if we consider how important yet conventional the use of religious semantics used to be. Religion was a formative signifier of nationalist, universalist, or particularist identity; religious semantics were unavoidable. But there was no genuine relation between the intensity of religious belief systems and social violence. In the end, religion remained an important but not predominantly violent factor in the field of ethnocultural politics of identity in the United States during the nineteenth century.

Things changed dramatically in the late twentieth century. Although religious conflicts had lost their sociocultural relevance during the early decades of the twentieth century, they returned dramatically after the high tide of liberalism and radicalism in the 1960s and 1970s. In the early 1970s, practically no observer would have expected religion to play an important role in American culture, society, or politics anymore. By 1995, things were totally different. Moreover, religion had turned to violence again, however tiny the minority of actual terrorists may have been. It was an interesting contrast to the nineteenth century that in the 1980s and 1990s the social acceptance of religiously motivated violence was much smaller than in the 1850s, but perhaps more people than ever shared the basic convictions of the terrorists. Furthermore, in the recent decades, violence was more and more about religion and its normative impact on society. The motivations were somewhat similar to nineteenth-century violence, yet perhaps less complex.

So what had happened? A new period of socioeconomic transformation and a new and deep crisis of modernity struck the nation after the relatively quiet decades immediately after World War II, the transformation from Fordist to post-Fordist society, and globalization. Parallel to those two intertwined processes, liberal and radical reformism reached its peak in the 1960s. Without the 1960s, there would certainly have been no turn toward militant fundamentalism. In particular, the results of judicial activism gave many religious people in the United States the feeling that they were on the defensive. The new interpretation of the wall of separation, the prohibition of school prayer, the new attitudes toward abortion and same-sex marriage—all these decisions were perceived as a break with a (widely imagined) idealized past, the nineteenth century or the 1950s. In the 1980s, religious revivalism and political conservatism formed a new coalition that started the so-called culture wars in an effort to regain cultural hegemony. The heated and militant semantics of this era did serve as a catalyst for the radicalization of the fringe parts of the religious right,[42] while again a majority of evangelicals and fundamentalists remained conformists and loyal to the political system of the United States. The breaking point was the 1980s, when parts of the antiabortion movement turned violent, beginning with the bombing of abortion clinics[43] and continuing with the assassination of seven physicians in the 1990s and one further physician in the first decade of the new millennium.[44] It should, nonetheless, be noted that all mainstream denominations and churches openly condemned the use of violence. Although, for instance, Mike Bray, one of the leading ideologues of the violent antiabortion movement, stressed the Niebuhrian idea of a legitimate, immediate violent defense of the defenseless, the vast majority even of prolife activists point to the paradox of someone seeking to save a life by taking someone else's.

One aspect had become of specific importance during the violent actions of the 1980s and 1990s: individualism, anti-institutionalism, and the defiance of traditionally legitimized authority stood more than ever before in the very center of the terrorist movement. Let us, for instance, look at the three Roman Catholic antiabortionist terrorists: Father David Trosch, James Kopp, and the well-known Olympic Park bomber, Eric Robert Rudolph. Although Kopp converted from Lutheranism to schismatic Catholic traditionalism only after his violent attacks, Rudolph was raised a Catholic but had turned toward the extremely racist, anti-Semitic, and antiblack Christian Identity movement and had returned to a strange and rather incoherent Nietzschean, traditionalist Sedevacantism[45] during his time in prison. Father Trosch started as a conventional Catholic priest, but afterward also turned toward ultraradical Sedevacantism. Thus, all three defied and rejected openly the traditional authority of the Church.

One may find the same pattern with the Protestant terrorists. Yet the most interesting and formative part of their development was not the impact of traditional Christianity even in its more radicalized forms, but the caging in of the ideology and the organizational framework of both Christian identity and survivalism, an extreme form of Jeffersonian rural republicanism. *The Turner Diaries*, a radical novel published in 1978, was in all three cases more important than the Bible.[46]

Within the field of groups and splinter organizations of the survivalist–militia movement or the Christian Identity movement, we find a step-by-step radicalization based on the misperception that the government and society were ruled by well-ordered Zionist conspiracies that prevented any change in the practice of abortion. Yet the majority of these antiabortionists fought just for white fetuses; they were of the opinion that a black fetus was no human being at all. Racism and a radicalized view of white *herrenvolk* democracy remained at the very basis of their ideology.

Interestingly, the very individualism of the members of the survivalist–militia movement[47] on the one hand and of the Christian Identity movement on the other hinders them from establishing well-organized terrorist groups. Their activities are normally based on pathological individuals and are not marked by thorough organization.[48] This was again true in the recent attack on the abortionist physician George Tiller, who on May 31, 2009, was killed by another lone wolf killer named Scott Roeder. Thus, conventional teachings of Protestant and Catholic Christianity served only as the semantic framework for a terrorism that was basically modern, individualistic, and racist.

Perhaps even more interesting is the newest development in this sector, which has allegedly been initiated by the previously mentioned Mike Bray: the Army of God. This group may be called a virtual terrorist network because it predominantly exists on the Internet. The Army of God has no official leadership, no chain of command, and no clear structure at all. It thus may be compared with al-Qaeda, but up to this moment it has been much less active and, therefore, politically and socially less influential. Yet because of its very lack of organizational skill, the Army of God may be the most precise example of the underlying assumptions of antiabortionist terrorism in the United States. It is, moreover, important for two intertwining reasons. First, it is by far the most genuinely religious group among antiabortionist terrorists. Its language is that of conventional yet radicalized fundamentalism and apocalyptical Protestantism, and contrary to other hate groups, it evades open racism in the sense of the Christian Identity movement. As far as we can judge at the moment, the social structure of the Army of God's constituency seems to be more like that of traditional

Catholic and Protestant fundamentalist radicals and not that of the racist and secular lunatic fringe of American right-wing conservatism.[49] But we still lack precise data and analysis. Second, the Army of God's skilled use of the Internet suggests technological knowledge and a suburban lifestyle, as does its style of theological and political self-vindication. This utter modernity of style is quite new among the antiabortionist hate groups.

Such modernity is not found in the second major example of religiously generated violence in the contemporary United States—namely, hate crimes against homosexuals.[50] Here, we again find a similar structure in the network-like form of cooperation and mutual ideological and practical assistance in the aftermath of criminal activities. Yet the antihomosexual network has a kind of center in the Reverend Fred Phelps, the lunatic leader of the Westboro Baptist Church in Topeka, Kansas. Phelps, however, is so hateful against everybody (including the U.S. soldiers who died in Iraq) that even among right-wing Christians, counterterrorist movements have been formed that have already tried to bomb his church. Moreover, compared with the Army of God, he and his movement lack technological and intellectual skills. But he is not the one and only leader of a nationwide homophobe terror group. The wave of homophobic hate crimes that started in the 1990s and had its high tide with the cruel murder of Matthew Shepard in 1998 is the product of local, often spontaneous actions—not of a centralized organization. What makes homophobia so hard to fight is that it normally starts with hateful, militant language and then, without further organizational preparations, becomes violent.

Taken together, the violent outbreaks of the 1990s and the ongoing network-like organization of antiabortion and homophobic militants are rather impressive and frightful, but they are not significant for religious life in the United States. While right-wing, separatist Christianity may provide the ideological background for this religious violence, even conservative Protestant and Catholic hardliners oppose direct militant action. Moreover, the legal system has adapted to this new form of religious terrorism by introducing the concept of hate speech and hate crime into the law. This legislation allows law enforcement to strike back. I am, therefore, relatively sure that there is no reason to overestimate the impact of religious violence in the quite violent, overtly religious, and highly competitively structured society of the United States.[51]

Another partly religious group has to be mentioned. Contrary to the predominantly or exclusively white middle- or lower-class movements hitherto dealt with, the Death Angels stemmed from the separatist black nationalist and Black Muslim movements in the United States of the 1960s and 1970s. They were actually a covert group of radical extremists within the Nation of Islam who randomly killed 16 white or non-black persons in 1973 and 1974 in the greater San Francisco area—the so-called Zebra murders.[52] Up to a certain degree, they resembled the formerly left-wing Catholic Symbionese Liberation Army (SLA), which also operated in the early 1970s in California. In contrast to the SLA, the Death Angels had integrated cultish elements into their ideology and practice. Both groups—as well as the Jewish Defense League of Rabbi Meir Kahane, which killed four people—were part of the extreme lunatic fringe of their respective social setting. Moreover, in all these groups, religion was never the predominant factor in their activities. But they were good examples of peer group radicalization as the central element of social violence.

In conclusion, I return to my original thesis: religion taken in itself is not necessarily a causal agent for social violence, even in a highly religious society as prone to social violence as the United States. Religion might be a sociocultural subsystem that can by its specific logic contribute semantically and emotionally to a given situation and thereby intensify an already existing violent mindset that is predominantly the result of socioeconomic and political tensions. But contrary to the image coined by the liberal-enlightened tradition and contemporary talk show wisdom with their prevalent enlightenment mythology, the roots of social violence are far more complex than the reduction to religion suggests. It especially seems that, at least under the conditions of modern, industrial societies, the problem of religion and social violence cannot be answered with regard to organized religion. The major problem stems from the liberation of the individual (i.e., from the core of the modernizational process itself). Modern fundamentalist violence, for example, is in all cases connected with an opposition to traditional religious authority. Contrary to their own ideology, fundamentalists actually do not turn to tradition. They, in all their actions, despise it. As a contrasting example, during the nineteenth century Roman Catholic ultramontanism never led to religiously induced terrorism despite its stress on the importance of social order and traditional hierarchical authority. Individualized, caged peer group religious violence is a by-product of modernity, not a mere anachronism. Furthermore, without a closer look at transformational socioeconomic processes—particularly social stratification, orders of injustice and inequality, poverty, and, finally, the decline of the authoritarian system of traditional moral values—any argumentative retreat toward religion alone is nothing else than an act of self-delusion or the attempted and intentional autoimmunization of enlightened, liberal-capitalist democracy; its inherent aggressiveness; and its tendency toward social injustice and struggles over cultural hegemony.

Notes

1. See, for example, Richard Dawkins, *Der Gotteswahn* (Berlin: Ullstein, 2007); Christopher Hitchens, *Der Herr ist kein Hirte: Wie die Religion die Welt vergiftet* (Munich: Blessing, 2007); Elie Bernav, *Mörderische Religion: Eine Streitschrift* (Berlin: Ullstein, 2008); or the seminal, monumental and path-breaking work of Karlheinz Deschner, *Kriminalgeschichte des Christentums* (Reinbek, Germany: Rowohlt, 2008).

2. Karen Armstrong, *Im Kampf für Gott: Fundamentalismus in Christentum, Judentum und Islam* (Munich: Goldmann, 2007); Arnold Angenhendt, *Toleranz und Gewalt: Das Christentum zwischen Bibel und Schwert* (Münster, Germany: Aschendorff, 2007); Michael Burleigh, *Irdische Mächte, göttliches Heil: Die Geschichte des Kampfes zwischen Politik und Religion von der Französischen Revolution bis in die Gegenwart* (Munich: Deutsche Verlags-Anstalt, 2008); Hans G. Kippenberg, *Gewalt als Gottesdienst: Religionskriege im Zeitalter der Globalisierung* (Munich: Beck, 2008); Bernd Oberdorfer, *Die Ambivalenz des Religiösen: Religion als Friedensstifter und Gewalterzeuger* (Freiburg, Germany: Rombach, 2008); J. Harold Ellens, ed., *The Destructive Power of Religion: Violence in Judaism, Christianity, and Islam* (Westport, CT: Praeger, 2004); Mark Juergensmeyer, *Terror in the Mind of God: The Global Rise of Religious Violence* (Berkeley: University of California Press, 2000). Even Steven Runciman, who in his standard account of the Crusades reproachfully enumerates them among the unforgivable sins against the Holy Spirit, is much more differentiated in his historical analysis of the Crusades than most of the radical critics of Christianity; see Steven Runciman, *Geschichte der Kreuzzüge* (Munich: Beck, 1989).

3. Among them was the Anglican evangelical theologian Alister McGrath, who, above all, reiterated the argument that religion strengthens personal health. See Alister McGrath, *The Dawkins Delusion? Atheist Fundamentalism and the Denial of the Divine* (London: SPCK, 2007).

4. Fritz Stolz, *Einführung in den biblischen Monotheismus* (Darmstadt, Germany: Wissenschaftliche Buchgesellschaft, 1996), 46–48.

5. See Hans Maier, ed., *Totalitarismus und politische Religionen: Konzepte des Diktaturvergleichs* (Paderborn, Germany: Schöningh, 1996–2003), whose concept is very much based on Eric Voegelin, *Die politischen Religionen* (Paderborn, Germany: Fink, 2007). The theory of totalitarian political religions has been sharply criticized, for example, by Ernst Pieper, *Arthur Rosenberg: Hitlers Chefideologe* (Munich: Pantheon, 2007), 231–56, who focuses on the fact that National Socialism, for instance, was rigidly antireligious and only took formal elements from a religious context into the service of a genuinely secular ideology. According to Pieper, National Socialism was not a

political religion but a religious form of politics. One could, however, argue that it was neither the one nor the other, but rather a preeminent form of charismatic politics. Not everything purely emotional and irrational is through its very irrationality religious, nor is the rational in itself antireligious.

6. The hitherto most convincing and penetrating general analysis of different cultural factors of power and violence has been presented by the sociologist Michael Mann in his path-breaking book, where he presents four separate yet intertwined and overlapping general sources of power in societies based on stratified social networks, the so-called IMEP-model: ideology, military resources, economy, and political action. Within this model, religion would serve as one—and not necessarily the single most important—factor in the realm of ideology, together with secular ideologies, rational reasoning, science, and so on. Mann's general approach has, at least from the viewpoint of the historian, the major advantage of allowing a processual approach. See Michael Mann, *The Sources of Social Power*, vol. 1 (Cambridge, U.K.: Cambridge University Press, 2005), 1–34; see also William H. Sewell Jr., *Logics of History: Social Theory and Social Transformation* (Chicago: University of Chicago Press, 2005).

7. With the term *postenlightened*, I do not want to suggest that the Enlightenment as a whole has come to an end. Yet there are striking differences between the enlightened rationalist universalism of the late eighteenth century and the voluntarist and decisionist, somewhat counterenlightened subjectivism of the twentieth century. This difference stems dialectically from the inherent and conflicting potentials of the *aporiae* of enlightenment itself (i.e., the gulf between the univeralism of reason and the search for individual freedom). This dialectical gulf, moreover, helps to extend the eighteenth-century process of enlightenment and its resulting traditions into the much broader process of modernity, which includes several other traditions, such as Christian democracy, Roman Catholic ultramontanism, socialism, totalitarianism, and fundamentalism. See Michael Hochgeschwender, "Was ist der Westen? Zur Ideengeschichte eines politischen Konstrukts," *Historisch-Politische Mitteilungen* 11 (2004): 1–30; see also Wolfgang Knöbl, *Die Kontingenz der Moderne: Wege in Europa, Asien und Amerika* (Frankfurt: Campus, 2007).

8. Michael Hochgeschwender, *Amerikanische Religion: Evangelikalismus, Pfingstlertum und Fundamentalismus* (Frankfurt: Verlag der Weltreligionen, 2007); Michael Hochgeschwender, "Religion, nationale Mythologie und nationale Identität: Zu den methodischen und inhaltlichen Debatten in der amerikanischen, 'New Religious History,'" *Historisches Jahrbuch* 124 (2004): 435–520.

9. An informative discussion is found in the *AHR* Forum, "The Problems of American Homicide," *American Historical Review* 111, no. 1 (2006): 75–114. See also James Gilligan, *Violence: Reflections of a National Epidemic* (New York: Vintage Books, 1997).

10. Thomas Bender, *A Nation among Nations: America's Place in World History* (New York: Hill and Wang, 2006); Jürgen Osterhammel, *Die Verwandlung der Welt: Eine Geschichte des 19. Jahrhunderts* (Munich: Beck, 2008); Christopher A. Bayly, *Die Geburt der modernen Welt: Eine Globalgeschichte, 1780–1914* (Frankfurt: Campus, 2006).

11. Nathan O. Hatch, *The Democratization of American Christianity* (New Haven, CT: Yale University Press, 1989).

12. Roger Finke and Rodney Stark, *The Churching of America: Winners and Losers in Our Religious Economy* (New Brunswick, NJ: Rutgers University Press, 1992); R. Laurence Moore, *Selling God: American Religion and the Marketplace of Culture* (New York: Oxford University Press, 1994).

13. Douglas M. Strong, *Perfectionist Politics: Abolitionism and the Religious Tensions of American Democracy* (Syracuse, NY: Syracuse University Press, 1999); Robert H. Abzug, *Cosmos Crumbling: American Reform and the Religious Imagination* (New York: Oxford University Press, 1994).

14. Ernest Lee Tuveson, *Redeemer Nation: The Idea of America's Millennial Role* (Chicago: University of Chicago Press, 1980).

15. There is a certain notional problem with defining *religious violence*. Does it include acts of civil disobedience, such as blockading an abortion clinic? Does it include the rhetorical preparation of violence that otherwise would have been counted as ethnic, racial, or class violence? What about an enthusiastic and militant language that does not lead to immediate violence? I will use the term in a rather strict sense, applying it only to direct physical violence toward persons and things, but I will include a moderate discussion of militant language where it seems to be unavoidable.

16. Michael Newton and Judy Ann Newton, *Racial and Religious Violence in America: A Chronology* (London: Routledge, 1991); David Grimsted, *American Mobbing, 1828–1861: Toward the Civil War* (New York: Oxford University Press, 1998).

17. This view is contrary to Jan Assmann, *Die mosaische Unterscheidung oder der Preis des Monotheismus* (Munich: Hanser, 2007).

18. Paul Collier and Anne Hoeffler, "Greed and Grievance in Civil War," *Oxford Economic Papers* 56 (2004): 563–88; Elisabeth J. Wood, "Civil Wars: What We Don't Know," *Global Governance* 9 (2003): 247–66.

19. Michael Mann suggests that although monotheistic religions are often made responsible for genocide and other forms of violence, the historical reality in terms of causal agency appears to be far more complex. According to his reasoning, ethnocultural and class interests do indeed trump religion. See Michael Mann, *The Dark Side of Democracy: Explaining Ethnic Cleansing* (Cambridge, U.K.: Cambridge University Press, 2006), 6, 19. See also Thomas Meyer, *Identitätspolitik: Vom Missbrauch kultureller Unterschiede* (Frankfurt: Suhrkamp, 2002); Amartya K. Sen, *Identity and Violence: The Illusion of Destiny* (London: Penguin, 2007).

20. I am totally aware of the sharp criticisms the theories of modernization have undergone throughout the recent decades, yet I am still convinced that a modified and pluralist theory of different ways toward modernity, as discussed among social scientists, can serve as an important theoretical and methodological interpretative tool. See Wolfgang Knöbl, *Die Kontingenz der Moderne: Wege in Europa, Asien und America* (Frankfurt: Campus, 2007).

21. This view stands in contrast to the liberal-modernist account of John Gray, *Politik der Apokalypse: Wie Religion die Welt in die Krise stürzt* (Stuttgart, Germany: Klett-Cotta, 2009).

22. It would, nevertheless, be completely wrong to believe that intellectualism and rationalism will eventually lead to more peaceful forms of religion. The medieval experience teaches us the opposite. Moreover, contrary to the strange beliefs of Richard Dawkins, I do not share the opinion that even a nonreligious ratio would lead to a more peaceful humankind. Yet this topic would be part of another discussion about anthropological optimism, skepticism, or pessimism. However, under the circumstances of modern epistemology, a broader introduction of specifically rational standards could possibly help to avoid the rigid anti-intellectualism that lies at the very heart of fundamentalism. I am, nevertheless, aware that this view is a specifically Catholic way of framing the problem.

23. For a critique of modern emotivism, see Alasdair MacIntyre, *Whose Justice? Which Rationality?* (Notre Dame, IN: University of Notre Dame Press, 2003); Alasdair MacIntyre, *Three Rival Versions of Moral Inquiry: Encyclopedia, Genealogy, and Tradition* (Notre Dame, IN: University of Notre Dame Press, 1988). A coherent, concise, and quite convincing discussion of the epistemic problems of modern philosophy and the underlying voluntarism of modern thought is presented by Arbogast Schmitt, *Plato und die Moderne* (Darmstadt, Germany: Wissenschaftliche Buchgesellschaft, 2003).

24. Todd Gitlin, *The Sixties: Years of Hope, Days of Rage* (New York: Bantam Books, 1993); Ron Jacobs, *The Way the Wind Blew: A History of the Weather Underground* (London: Verso, 1997); Jeremy Varon, *Bringing the War Home: The Weather Underground, the Red Army Faction, and Revolutionary Violence in the Sixties and Seventies* (Berkeley: University of California Press, 2004).

25. Mann, *Dark Side*, 195–206.

26. Grimsted, *American Mobbing*; Newton and Newton, *Violence in America*.

27. See, for instance, with regard to the violent Indian frontier, Richard Slotkin, *Gunfighter Nation: The Myth of the Frontier in Twentieth-Century America* (Norman: University of Oklahoma Press, 1992). Slotkin points to the Puritan roots of violent anti-Indian sentiments.

28. James H. Moorhead, *American Apocalypse: Yankee Protestantism and the Civil War* (New Haven, CT: Yale University Press, 1978). It is important to note that, while the contemporaries had religious modes of description and self-description at their disposal, they were never used with regard to the antislavery mobs. This outcome is quite understandable, as a majority of the Democrats, who usually set the mob in motion, were not members of an organized religion at all. Of course, many Southern Episcopalian priests and evangelical parsons were quite zealous in defending slavery, but they were not necessarily the ones to lynch antislavery activists.

29. Randall M. Miller, Harry S. Stout, and Charles Reagan Wilson, eds., *Religion and the American Civil War* (New York: Oxford University Press, 1998); Steven E. Woodworth, *While God Is Marching On: The Religious World of Civil War Soldiers* (Lawrence: University Press of Kansas, 2001).

30. David S. Reynolds, *John Brown, Abolitionist: The Man Who Killed Slavery, Sparked the Civil War, and Seeded Civil Rights* (New York: Alfred A. Knopf, 2005).

31. See, in general, David H. Bennett, *The Party of Fear: The American Far Right from Nativism to the Militia Movement* (New York: Vintage Books, 1995); Catherine McNichol Stock, *Rural Radicals: From Bacon's Rebellion to the Oklahoma City Bombing* (New York: Penguin Books, 1996).

32. Sarah B. Gordon, *The Mormon Question: Polygamy and Constitutional Conflict in Nineteenth-Century America* (Chapel Hill: University of North Carolina Press, 2002). Basic texts include David Brion Davis, "Some Themes of Counter-subversion: An Analysis of Anti-Masonic, Anti-Catholic, and Anti-Mormon Literature," *Mississippi Valley Historical Review* 47, no. 2 (1960): 202–39; David Brion Davis, "Some Ideological Functions of Prejudice in Ante-bellum America," *American Quarterly* 15, no. 2 (1963): 98–123.

33. Jody M. Roy, *Rhetorical Campaigns of Nineteenth-Century Anti-Catholics and Catholics in America* (Lewiston, NY: Edwin Mellen, 2000).

34. Leonard Dinnerstein, *The Leo Frank Case* (Athens: University of Georgia Press, 1987). There were, nevertheless, some later incidents involving a typically Southern,

strictly racist violent anti-Semitism in the 1950s and 1960s; see Jack Nelson, *Terror in the Night: The Klan's Campaign against the Jews* (Jackson: University of Mississippi Press, 1993). One might argue that the lynching of James Chaney, Michael Schwerner, and Andrew Goodman was anti-Semitic as well, but even including those assassinations, anti-Semitic violence was dramatically less important than anti-Catholic violence.

35. Denis G. Paz, *Popular Anti-Catholicism in Mid-Victorian England* (Stanford, CA: Stanford University Press, 1992).

36. Philip Jenkins, *The New Anti-Catholicism: The Last Acceptable Prejudice* (New York: Oxford University Press, 2003).

37. See, for instance, Todd Tucker, *Notre Dame vs. The Klan: How the Fighting Irish Defeated the Ku Klux Klan* (Chicago: Loyola Press, 2004).

38. Daniel Walker Howe, *What Hath God Wrought? The Transformation of America, 1815–1848* (New York: Oxford University Press, 2007), 723–31.

39. Bertram Wyatt-Brown, *Southern Honor: Ethics and Behavior in the Old South* (Oxford, U.K.: Oxford University Press, 1982); Christopher Waldrep, "Word and Deed: The Language of Lynching," in *Lethal Imagination: Violence and Brutality in American History*, ed. Michael A. Bellesiles (New York: New York University Press, 1999), 229–60.

40. Members of the order were labeled the "Know-Nothings." With regard to the Know-Nothings, it is a well-established opinion that their primary aim was to save the Union. See Tyler Anbinder, *Nativism and Slavery: The Northern Know Nothings and the Politics of the 1850s* (New York: Oxford University Press, 1992). Consequently, religion was only one among many other factors forming the xenophobic nationalist ideology of Know-Nothingism.

41. Kevin Kenny, *Making Sense of the Molly Maguires* (New York: Oxford University Press, 1998); William S. Neidhardt, *Fenianism in North America* (University Park: Pennsylvania State University, 1975). In general, see Lawrence McCaffrey, *The Irish Catholic Diaspora in America* (Washington, DC: Catholic University of America Press, 1997).

42. One should, however, not underestimate the influence of traditional republican-revolutionary ideas, such as Jeffersonian yeoman democracy. See Stock, *Rural Radicals*.

43. From 1977 to 1987, there were 102 violent attacks against abortion clinics throughout the United States; cf. Dallas A. Blanchard and Terry J. Prewitt, *Religious Violence and Abortion: The Gideon Project* (Gainesville: University Press of Florida, 1993), 180–81; see as well Christopher Hewitt, *Political Violence and Terrorism in Modern America: A Chronology* (Westport, CT: Praeger, 2005); and Cindy C. Combs and Martin Slann, *Encyclopedia of Terrorism* (New York: Checkmark Books, 2003).

44. Mark Juergensmeyer, *Terror in the Mind of God: The Global Rise of Religious Violence* (Berkeley: University of California Press, 2000); Jessica Stern, *Terror in the Name of God: Why Religious Militants Kill* (New York: HarperCollins, 2003); Patricia Baird-Windle and Eleanor J. Bader, *Targets of Hatred: Anti-abortion Terrorism* (New York: Palgrave, 2001).

45. *Sedevacantism* is an ultratraditionalist Catholic splinter group that believes that since the death of Pope Pius XII in 1958 no real pope has been elected.

46. William Luther Pierce [pseud. Andrew Macdonald], *The Turner Diaries* (Hillsboro, WV: National Vanguard Books, 1978); Christopher Hewitt, *Understanding Terrorism in America: From the Klan to Al Qaeda* (London: Routledge, 2003), 38–43.

47. Richard Abanes, *American Militias: Rebellion, Racism, and Religion* (Downers Grove, IL: InterVarsity Press, 1996).

48. This characteristic—besides political considerations with regard to the right wing of the Republican Party—is the most important reason for the Federal Bureau of Investigation's decision to abstain from listing the antiabortion killing spree as homeland terrorism. See David A. Blanchard and Terry J. Prewitt, *Religious Violence and Abortion: The Gideon Project* (Gainesville: University Press of Florida, 1998).

49. Hewitt, *Understanding Terrorism*, 58–81; see in general John Micklethwaite and Adrian Wooldridge, *The Right Nation: Conservative Power in America* (New York: Penguin, 2004); Alan J. Lichtman, *White Protestant Nation: The Rise of the American Conservative Movement* (New York: Atlantic Monthly Press, 2008); Anatol Lieven, *America: Right or Wrong* (London: Harper Perennial, 2005).

50. Michael Corby, *God Hates Fags: The Rhetorics of Religious Violence* (New York: New York University Press, 2006).

51. I have skipped the suicidal violence, such as the Jonestown Massacre or the tragic events during the siege of the Branch Davidians in Waco, Texas, because they, more than the other events, are the result of specific psychopathological preconditions among the leaders and believers of a cult. See Ken Levi, ed., *Violence and Religious Commitment: Implications of Jim Jones's People's Temple Movement* (University Park: Pennsylvania State University Press, 1982); John R. Hall, with Philip D. Schuyler and Sylvaine Trinh, *Apocalypse Observed: Religious Movements and Violence in North America, Europe, and Japan* (London: Routledge, 2000).

52. Hewitt, *Understanding Terrorism*, 17, 61.

Chapter 13

New Wars, Old Motives? On the Role of Religion in International Relations

Gerlinde Groitl

The end of the Cold War was a clear caesura in international politics. It seemed obvious that deep-seated changes would follow, yet nobody knew what these new challenges would be. The continuing reference to the 1990s as post–Cold War era illustrates this uncertainty quite nicely. Scholars and policy makers were aware that the Cold War was a conflict of the past, yet there was no defining term for the times ahead. The *New York Times* once launched a competition to find a suitable term. And although the term *post–Cold War era* was considered "tentative, vague," and lacking "authority,"[1] none of the rival terms—Age of Anxiety, Age of Uncertainty, Age of Fragmentation, or Age of Disillusion (and Dissolution)—rose to similar prominence.[2] All of these names suggested a telling message, however: the clarity of the Cold War world was a thing of the past.

In 1993, Samuel Huntington offered a possible reading of world affairs in an article and, in 1996, a subsequent book on the "Clash of Civilizations."[3] In short, Huntington's argument was that post–Cold War conflicts would occur primarily between different civilizations—in particular, between "the

291

West and the rest." Huntington defined a civilization as "the highest cultural grouping of people and the broadest level of cultural identity people have short of that which distinguishes humans from other species. It is defined both by common objective elements, such as language, history, religion, customs, institutions, and by the subjective self-identification of people."[4] Huntington's article and book received much attention and triggered heated discussions. They did not, however, lead to a paradigm shift in the thinking about international relations, the reasons for which are manifold and are discussed elsewhere in the literature in great detail.[5]

When the transnational terrorist network al-Qaeda crashed civilian airplanes into the World Trade Center and the Pentagon on September 11, 2001, debates about the role of religion in global politics resumed. Could religion, indeed, be the defining variable for international relations in the twenty-first century and a major (new) source of international conflict? After all, those responsible for the attacks legitimized their actions on religious terms. The purpose of this chapter is to discuss the role of religion in international relations, particularly in the post-9/11 context. A constantly growing body of scholarship examines the importance of religion for our understanding of international affairs, as well as the dangerous nexus between religion and violence.[6] Even though public debates suggest that religion has returned with a vengeance, this chapter advocates caution. The seeming prominence of religion as a source of conflict cannot be viewed separately from the effects of globalization—namely, the weakening of state structures and the empowerment of nonstate actors. Although religion has long been neglected as a potential variable in international relations scholarship and theory formation, we should be careful not to fall into the other extreme and distort the causal influence of religion now. The argument will be presented in three steps. First, this chapter provides some context on the global resurgence of religion. Second, it examines the conspicuous neglect of religion in traditional international relations scholarship, as well as ways to incorporate religious belief in existing theoretical frameworks. Third, it turns to empirical data on current conflicts and wars to discuss trends and changes that have taken place.

The Importance of Religion in the World

For a long time, the social sciences took for granted that modernization would go hand in hand with secularization, as observed in Europe. Religious belief, so the common reasoning went, increasingly would be pushed from the public to the private sphere and lose importance as modernity advanced. Although explanations for the phenomenon varied, this secularization thesis was largely uncontested.[7] However, the second half of the twentieth century brought about an unexpected revitalization of religion in many parts of the world that represents more than a mere revival of one particular faith in one particular nation.[8] The resurgence of religion may even be called one of the world's recent "megatrends."[9] First, the number of adherents to major religions grew at a pace that clearly exceeds population growth. Today, roughly 64 percent of the world's population identify themselves as Catholic, Protestant, Muslim, or Hindu, compared to approximately 50 percent about a century ago. According to current projections, this number may rise to 70 percent by 2025.[10] Second, surveys captured an increase in devoutness among believers.[11] Third, traditional, conservative denominations, such as Pentecostalism, have been thriving and spreading most rapidly in recent years.[12]

The two most dynamic religious trends are the revival of Islam and the revival of evangelical Christianity.[13] The Islamic revival can be seen in virtually all Muslim nations, from North Africa to Southeast Asia. Evangelical Christianity has also spread rapidly, a development that has been particularly pronounced in the Southern half of the globe. Although evangelicalism was once considered a Western phenomenon, the majority of evangelicals today live in the global South.[14] Centers of the new evangelical revival are East Asia, Sub-Saharan Africa, and Latin America.[15] The United States, the world's leading industrial nation, also constitutes an interesting case study. Studies show that Americans are more religious than any other people in the Western world and have become increasingly so in recent decades.[16]

In light of these developments, Peter L. Berger stated quite clearly that "the assumption that we live in a secularized world is false. The world today, with some exceptions …, is as furiously religious as it ever was, and in some places more so than ever."[17] Indeed, although religion has gained importance and a greater presence in public debate over recent decades, it has always played a meaningful role in people's lives.[18] Also, as Shah and Toft point out, recent religious revivals have not been a return to "old-time religion" but, instead, represent a flourishing of "neo-orthodoxies" that have emerged along with sophisticated organizational structures, the use of modern technology, and the buildup of transnational capabilities.[19] Hence, in Berger's words: "To say the least, the relation between religion and modernity is rather complicated."[20]

Although the global vitality of religion deserves the attention of sociologists and scholars of religion, the follow-up question is whether this development has an impact on international affairs. Intuition might incline one to answer "yes," given that religion seems to play some role in a variety of recent conflicts. Be it the wars in former Yugoslavia, the genocide in Sudan, the conflict in the Middle East, or the challenge of fundamentalist terrorism—each case has a religious dimension as a common denominator. Furthermore, as scholars of domestic politics have shown, religion does at times play a meaningful role in the domestic context. The emergence and political influence of the American Christian right as well as the nexus between religious belief, political attitudes, and voting behavior serve as prominent examples.[21] Just how religion might influence international relations is a difficult question to answer and one that requires some differentiation.

Religion in International Relations Scholarship

Religion has for a long time been marginalized, both in international relations scholarship and in the policy world.[22] A U.S. Central Intelligence Agency proposal for studying the political implications of religion and culture was once dismissed as "mere sociology."[23] The U.S. support for the mujahideen in Afghanistan in the 1980s was viewed through the lens of the Cold War, without looking ahead to future developments in this area. The terror attacks of September 11, 2001, caught the U.S. government, as well as many scholars of international relations, effectively off guard. Robert O. Keohane admitted that "all mainstream theories of world politics are relentlessly secular with respect to motivation. They ignore the impact of religion, despite the fact that world-shaking political movements have so often been fueled by religious fervor."[24]

There are several reasons for this silence. International relations is a discipline with a deep-seated secular bias. As Jonathan Fox points out, one major difference between international relations and other social sciences is that "instead of explaining why religion was not important, international relations theory simply took religion's irrelevance for granted."[25] This neglect has to do with the history of the discipline, its methodological approaches, and the dominance of Western scholars and a West-centric worldview in international relations.[26] The discipline of international relations is a child of the First World War. Its self-declared goal was to examine the causes of war and find ways to secure peace. The conceptual basis for this study of war and peace was the Westphalian state system. The Peace of Westphalia codified the separation of religion and secular power after past wars of religion had devastated Europe.[27] The "privatization of religion" and the "secularization of politics," as Scott M. Thomas calls it, were intended to end religion's destructive influence on international affairs.[28] This move did not make the world a more peaceful place, considering that after the Peace of Westphalia, interreligious or interconfessional wars were replaced by interstate wars.[29] Yet the modern system of sovereign nation-states was born and became the primary level of analysis when international relations eventually emerged as an academic discipline. The international actions of sovereign nation-states and their relations became the primary objects of study, and scholars from Europe and the United States shaped the discipline. Under these circumstances, it was natural that religion was not considered a potential explanatory variable, whether understood institutionally in terms of churches or individually in terms of religious belief.

Theory formation reflects this focus.[30] The first great theoretical debate within the discipline was between idealists and realists and took place after the First World War to the 1950s. Idealists, on the one hand, argued that man was reasonable and able to learn from past mistakes. They believed that international organizations and laws could prevent future wars. Realists, on the other hand, criticized these ideas as utopian and argued that international politics was a relentless power struggle: states compete with one another in a zero-sum game and try to promote their own national interests at the expense of others. The realist school of thought eventually won the debate and dominated the field after the Second World War. Developments in the international arena were explained as power politics between nation-states.[31] In the 1960s, a methodological debate erupted. Traditionalists wanted to study international affairs with a holistic, interpretive, and historical approach, while so-called behavioralists called for the introduction of more "scientific" methods. They wanted to collect empirical data, build formal theories, validate hypotheses, and explain cause and effect. This methodological debate professionalized the field yet reinforced the neglect of "cultural" variables.[32]

In the 1970s, neorealism emerged and moved the discipline further from the context-specific analysis of individuals or their motivations. Neorealists saw states as "black boxes" and "like units"; no matter what their internal differences might be, international anarchy would force all states into a security dilemma and a struggle for survival. Neorealists looked to the structure of the international system (defined by the distribution of capabilities among states) to explain international politics.[33] Institutionalists offered a theoretical alternative in the 1970s and 1980s.[34] They identified changes in the international system, such as the emergence of complex interdependence. Under these conditions, the presence or absence of international institutions and information influenced how states pursued their interests. Despite differences, both schools were primarily interested in states, their material interests, and the structural features of the international system. Individuals, their preferences, and beliefs played little role in the theoretical debate.

In the 1980s and 1990s, liberals and constructivists criticized the assumption that states functioned like unitary actors with given interests. On the one hand, liberals emphasized that state preferences were shaped by individuals and groups within the state.[35] From this point of view, the state is nothing but a "transmission belt" for the preferences of the most influential individuals and groups. The liberal approach did not make assumptions about the motivations or specific interests of groups involved in the political process. In principle, religion might be a factor that politically motivates and guides individuals and groups, just as others participate in the political process for different reasons. In practice, it was hardly considered.

Constructivists, on the other hand, took issue with the rationalist bias of established theories.[36] Rationalists see the world in material terms, as an objective reality, in which utilitarian actors consider the costs and benefits and pursue their egoistic, externally given interests (*homo oeconomicus*). Constructivists argued that the world we live in is socially constructed and that ideas, beliefs, norms, perceptions, and culture matter. Every actor, whether an individual or a state, is embedded in a specific social context (*homo sociologicus*). According to this logic, scholars cannot give broad explanations for international relations but have to understand the specific context of developments as well as the beliefs, ideas, and perceptions of those involved. Constructivism developed into a multifaceted research program and focused on the international, national, and individual levels of analysis.[37] It admitted that factors such as culture, ideas, or identity must be considered in the analysis of international relations. Yet despite the conceptual possibilities, religious identities were not at the center of attention in constructivist debates in the past.[38]

Samuel P. Huntington's thesis on the clash of civilizations can be viewed as an explicit attempt to enrich the theoretical debate in this regard, although it did not manage to trigger a paradigm shift. According to Huntington, civilizations function as the primary source of identification and are a critical key to explaining international conflict after the Cold War: "It is my hypothesis that the fundamental source of conflict in this new world will not be primarily ideological or primarily economic. The great divisions among humankind and the dominating source of conflict will be cultural. Nation-states will remain the most powerful actors in world affairs, but the principal conflicts of global politics will occur between nations and groups of different civilizations. The clash of civilizations will dominate global politics. The fault lines between civilizations will be the battle lines of the future."[39] Interestingly, his definition of *civilization* rested largely, though not exclusively, on religious differences.[40] Fox and Sandler even suggest that Huntington meant "religion" in his thesis, but disguised it by referring to it as "civilization."[41]

The core problem that results from viewing civilizations—however they are ultimately defined—as explanatory variables is that this categorization suggests rigid causalities. Huntington's thesis on the clash of civilizations views civilizations as historically grown but essentially static, as well as objectively definable on a broad level. This conception of civilization certainly distorts reality and creates a problematic actor concept. Religions or civilizations are neither monolithic nor do they have actor quality, a fact that Huntington does take into account when he argues that civilizations interact through nation-states. Still, the question remains as to what exactly the link is between identity-conferring civilizations, states, and individuals. Bassam Tibi correctly points out that Islam, for example, is not an appropriate object of analysis.[42] According to Tibi, Islam is a religion, and maybe a civilization, but not an actor. Instead, the individual level of the "irregular warrior" must be at the center of attention.[43]

A considerable number of studies have investigated the impact of religious and cultural differences on interstate conflict in response to Huntington's publications. The claim that conflict would primarily occur among different civilizations was found empirically invalid; hence, the assumption that civilizational affiliation by itself was the dominant explanation for international conflict was wrong.[44] This argument can no doubt be attributed to the absolutist and far-reaching assumptions on which Huntington's thesis rests. Indeed, the possible impact of religion must be examined on a narrower scale. Any attempt to generalize about how religions—or in Huntington's terminology, civilizations—interact is doomed to failure because it is inherently imprecise and suggests law-like causalities. It incorrectly suggests homogeneity and views religion as a structural feature. Instead, the individual, whose views may be shaped by religion, must be taken into the equation.

One need not come up with an entirely new theoretical framework if one were to factor religion into international relations theory.[45] From a liberal–constructivist point of view, it is insufficient to model world politics as the strategic interaction of states trying to realize fixed interests under structural constraints. Although it may be analytically tempting to think of states as the only relevant actors, or as "black boxes" with similar or identical interests, such thinking obscures too much. Instead, individuals, groups, and their preferences, as well as the opportunity structures they encounter, matter. According to the liberal worldview, government action is "constrained by the underlying identities, interests, and power of individuals and groups (inside and outside the state apparatus) who constantly pressure the central decision makers to pursue policies consistent with their preferences."[46] Obviously, some individuals and groups are more powerful than others. Some may even have the means to circumvent state structures altogether and have a direct effect on world politics.

Individuals and groups have diverse preferences, and religion may loom large. It would oversimplify matters to assume that social context, culture, ideas, identities, beliefs, and perceptions of those involved in the national and international realm were unimportant. A definition of *religion* must be put forward at this point. This chapter considers religion essentially as a frame of reference that may shape the worldviews of individual believers and societies. Like Clifford Geertz, it views religion as a cultural system.[47] Religious belief may guide individuals not only in religious matters but also in social and political matters. As a system of meaning, religion offers a lens through which to perceive the world, criteria to evaluate present conditions, and guidance for future action.[48] Religion, then, is an "attempt to make sense of the world" in a very general sense.[49] Understood in this way, religion is essentially a source of identity.[50]

Such an understanding places religion within a broader cultural context. Geertz defines *culture* as follows: "Believing, with Max Weber, that man is an animal suspended in webs of significance he himself has spun, I take culture to be those webs, and the analysis of it to be therefore not an experimental science in search of law but an interpretive one in search of meaning."[51] Religious belief is essentially one of those webs, and one among many in the cultural framework of a society. As such, religious belief may constitute an interpretive framework that competes with many others. At the extreme, religion may be *the* defining belief system for specific individuals, groups, or even society as a whole. Hence, religion may have many different roles from a social science perspective. For the individual, it may be one source of identity among many, or it may constitute the sole source of identity. It may be a small subculture, or it may be the dominant national culture in a society.[52] It may have diverse effects on individuals and social systems as a whole, and it may guide human action.

Of course, such a nuanced approach forbids far-reaching if–then hypotheses about the role of religion. We cannot make broad generalizations regarding the relative significance or insignificance of religion per se in international affairs.[53] Religion may shape the way people understand the world and interact with it, and it may create vast differences in perceptions among various groups. Religion may inform the interests and attitudes of state leaders and thereby have international consequences.[54] It may spur political activism, just as other individuals and groups participate in the political process for different reasons. It may motivate interest groups to influence a state's foreign policy, as is the case with the American Christian right's international interests.[55] Religion can "create or reinvigorate collective identities, whose influence can both promote social welfare and fuel terrorism and interreligious conflict."[56] Such preferences can be channeled within or outside of state structures. All in all, this means that religion could well influence international relations in various ways, although it must not necessarily do so at all times and in all places. To exclude religion by assumption would be an oversimplification, but it would be equally flawed to expect law-like causalities. Certainly, to make sense of religion from the viewpoint of international relations, a fundamental paradigm shift is not required. However, what is required is the acknowledgment that world politics cannot be understood or explained by looking at states as black boxes and as the only relevant actors. Humans, their preferences, and their worldviews, as well as the various means at their disposal, matter.

Patterns of Conflict and War

Religion was not at the center of attention in international relations scholarship in the past, but a number of empirical studies and specific case studies have dealt with the topic. Although little evidence indicates that religious or civilizational differences offer a suitable explanation for international wars, the situation is different at the domestic level. Religious differences are involved in a considerable number of domestic conflicts today.[57] A common assumption is that religion previously played no role in conflicts but suddenly appeared as a reason for conflict after the Cold War. This view is incorrect. Studies that cover the Second World War to the present show that conflicts with a religious dimension always have existed. However, the ratio between religious and nonreligious conflicts has changed. According to one data set, about 50 percent of all civil wars that raged at the beginning of the twenty-first century had to do with religion (which does not necessarily mean they were *caused* by religion), compared with 43 percent in the 1990s, 36 percent in the 1970s, and 19 percent in the 1940s.[58] Another study that focused on the most severe internal conflicts found that although between 1960 and 1990 "nonreligious state failures" were the majority and new "nonreligious state failures" outnumbered new "religious state failures" by about two-and-a-half to one, the numbers almost balanced out between 1990 and 2001.[59] In addition, terrorist activities have increasingly reflected a "religious pattern."[60] In 2004, 46 percent of recorded international terrorist organizations had a "religious basis," whereas the figure was 33 percent in 1994 and only 4 percent in 1980.[61]

Conflicts involving religiously motivated actors possess several shared characteristics.[62] It is more likely, for example, that a conflict will escalate if religion is involved. Such conflicts are also particularly delicate in that they are more destructive and harder to resolve than other types of conflicts. Moreover, religiously inspired violence is mostly committed by individuals, without the sanction of governments.[63] Consequently, the lure of individual martyrdom draws the feasibility of successful bargaining and deterrence into doubt, because these strategies may not work when otherworldly orientation comes into play.[64] In line with such findings, religiously inspired terrorism tends to be more lethal than secular terrorism. On average, religiously inspired terrorist attacks leave seventeen people dead and thirty-nine wounded, whereas the average casualty rate for terrorist attacks of secular groups is three to four dead and eight to sixteen wounded.[65]

So religion potentially influences conflicts. But the devil is in the details. Definitions matter tremendously when we want to identify the nexus between religion and conflict. When is a conflict considered a religious conflict? Did religious wars lead to the breakup of Yugoslavia, or was nationalism at the heart of its conflict? Or were there altogether different causes? Were al-Qaeda's actions truly spurred by religion, or were they driven by some sort of political ideology? These questions defy easy answers, and depending on which definition is used, conflicts are classified differently. Hence, although some scholars identify religion as the "the single most important political-ideological default mechanism in global conflict,"[66] others find that religion is hardly ever the true source of conflict.[67]

It is inherently difficult to single out the true role of religion in many current conflicts. Just because conflicts have religious overtones does not mean that they are about religion or caused by religion. Are conflicts that involve religious differences about religion? Or are they social, economic, or, simply, interest-based conflicts that coincide with religious, cultural, or ethnic cleavages? [68] A recent study points out that the vast majority of armed intrastate identity conflicts take place in Africa and Asia, which are not only religiously and ethnically diverse but also particularly poor regions.[69] In addition, religious sentiments may merely be instrumentalized and misused as a legitimation or a mobilizer for the masses.[70] Instead of simple monocausal explanations, a complex bundle of reasons that include religious, political, social, economic, and ethnic motives provide the basis for many current conflicts. Because religious elements often may be intermingled with other elements, even in the self-conceptions of individuals, isolating individual causal factors is difficult.[71]

Because this chapter presents an overview, it allows a more promising look at the big picture instead of arguments about definitions of specific conflicts. Even though exact and correct labels may be hard to find and remain essentially disputed, it is evident that a considerable number of conflicts evolve around identity-related issues.[72] Hence, focusing on the wider concept of collective identity instead of religion seems worthwhile. Essentially, the common denominator is this: a group of people conceives of themselves as an ideational community, as opposed to others who are excluded. The sense of affiliation, whether primarily religious in nature or defined on a broader level, may, in combination with certain grievances and under specific circumstances, become a mobilizing force for political action or violence. Using this line of thought, Mary Kaldor suggests using the term *identity politics* to describe what current conflicts are often about: "movements which mobilize around ethnic, racial, or religious identity for the purpose of claiming state power. And I use the term 'identity' narrowly to mean a form of labelling. Whether we are talking about tribal conflict in Africa, religious conflict in the Middle East or South Asia, or nationalist conflict in Europe, the common feature is the way in which labels are used as a basis for political claims."[73]

The prevalence of identity politics and identity conflicts did not come about in a vacuum. Globalization processes contributed to renewed interest in local identities and reinforced cultural consciousness in the world.[74]

To look at just one example, consider a study by the Pew Research Center, which found that majorities in forty-six of forty-seven countries surveyed regarded their own traditional culture (defined as their way of life) as being lost in a rapidly changing world and demanded that it be protected.[75] These results were alike for rich and poor countries across different geographic regions and show that cultural awareness is one characteristic of a globalized world.[76] Cultural awareness alone, of course, does not necessarily lead to conflict and violence. But it may add to the explanation of why domestic identity-related conflicts have become more prominent.

The second and, from an international viewpoint, more important aspect is globalization, which has led to the empowerment of individuals and nonstate actors in politics. According to Mary Kaldor, identity politics, as it appears today, arises "out of the disintegration or erosion of modern state structures" and the fading of old loyalties and defining concepts.[77] The conditions of globalization allow movement of ideas and people in an unprecedented way, with modern communication technologies that capacitate individuals and groups. Hence, globalization changed the relation of the individual to the state and facilitated the emergence of "super-empowered individuals" who can yield great influence.[78] Thomas L. Friedman summed up these developments in a pointed remark:

> Whether by enabling people to use the Internet to communicate instantly at almost no cost over vast distances, or by enabling them to use the Web to transfer money or obtain weapons designs that normally would have been controlled by states, or by enabling them to go into a hardware store now and buy a five-hundred-dollar global positioning device, connected to a satellite, that can direct a hijacked airplane — globalization can be an incredible force-multiplier for individuals. Individuals can increasingly act on the world stage directly, unmediated by a state.[79]

Consequently, transnational networks can flourish and nonstate actors find opportunities to circumvent or challenge state power easily.[80]

Changes in the nature of armed conflicts reflect the potency of a variety of actors and the erosion or lack of stable nation-state structures in many areas. First of all, the ratio between interstate wars and intrastate wars has changed. From the 1960s, the number of armed conflicts within states has risen significantly, whereas the number of armed conflicts between states has declined.[81] Today, only in rare cases do two state-controlled military forces confront each other. Since the end of the Second World War, 246 armed conflicts have taken place in the world, 133 of which occurred between 1989 and 2010.[82] Roughly 95 percent of these conflicts were intrastate conflicts.[83] Another interesting finding is that substate wars (defined as wars between mostly nonstate actors within or across borders) have become much more frequent. Although substate wars accounted for only 5 percent of wars per year from 1971 to 1980, they constituted roughly a fourth of the wars per year in the post–Cold War era.[84] Other trends include the asymmetric nature of many current conflicts (in terms of actors and their capabilities), the demilitarization and privatization of conflict parties, the emergence of complex war economies, and the prevalence of low-intensity conflict.[85] Whether it is analytically correct to speak of "new wars" is disputable.[86] Yet there is no denying that important changes have taken place.

Such trends have international consequences and affect established notions of power. States have to deal with terrorist networks, failing and failed states, and countries plagued by instability and internal violence. The effectiveness of conventional military force is cast into doubt, and military and technological superiority do not necessarily lead to success.[87] As former U.S. President George W. Bush once remarked about difficulties in the war on terrorism, "what is the point of sending two million dollar missiles to hit a ten dollar tent that's empty?"[88] Conversely, cheap improvised explosive devices, roadside bombs, and suicide attacks pose a challenge even for the best-equipped and best-trained military in the world. In addition, scholars and policy makers question the use of deterrence after 9/11. According to the basic logic of deterrence, (military) power generates security because states will not attack a powerful rival for fear of retaliation. Yet al-Qaeda demonstrated the limits of deterrence on 9/11. The United States was unable to prevent the attacks, and subsequent responses proved difficult. The terror attacks illustrated that nonstate actors can cause considerable harm to states and that uncertainty characterizes the international system today.[89]

Globalization led to the empowerment of individuals and groups and contributed to structural changes in the international system. This is not saying that states will vanish as a category of actors but simply that they are not the only relevant actors. Reality shows that individuals and groups have the power to influence world affairs, both in domestic conflicts that often get internationalized or by direct challenges to nation-states like that of al-Qaeda. The motivations and preferences of such actors are an important field of inquiry that must not be neglected.

Conclusion

The importance of identity-related (domestic) conflict continues to demand the attention of scholars and policy makers. From an international perspective, the real challenge is not so much that the dynamics of international relations has changed, whereby civilizational or religious conflict has taken the place of other forms of conflict. Rather, the challenge is that states are increasingly only one type of actor among many in international relations. The growing consolidation of nation-state power was a defining characteristic of the international system after the Peace of Westphalia. Nation-states became the dominant actors in the international realm. The consolidation of nation-states was particularly evident in the area of warfare, where interstate wars between centrally organized, state-controlled armed forces were perceived as the typical form of warfare. The erosion of stable nation-state structures and the emergence of powerful, well-financed nonstate actors that have the potential to challenge states are two of the major changes that have taken place over the past decades and two of the most important effects of globalization.

With an eye to theory formation, one sees the neglect of religion in dominant theories as resulting from the neglect of the individual actor and his or her social context. No convincing evidence suggests that religion should be regarded as an independent variable that explains international conflict, as Samuel P. Huntington basically suggests. Instead, a more fruitful approach is to consider religion as an identity-conferring factor for both individuals and groups. The liberal and constructivist perspectives offer conceptual opportunities here. Future research will have to focus on the conceptual incorporation of nonstate actors that has already begun, and related research questions will have to revolve around nonstate actors' motivations for action, as well as the conditions that limit or enhance their opportunities to influence world affairs.

Richard N. Haass recently characterized the current period as the "Age of Nonpolarity," an age that is essentially defined by its complexity.[90] Power centers exist, many of which are not nation-states: "Indeed, one of the cardinal features of the contemporary international system is that nation-states have lost their monopoly on power and in some domains their preeminence as well."[91] Instead of the anticipated emergence of a multipolar system after the short-lived unipolar moment of the United States in the early 1990s, Haass holds that dozens of actors of different kinds influence international relations today.

This chapter argues that individuals and groups may have diverse motives for action in domestic and international politics—among these, religious identity. The specific preferences that individuals and groups pursue in the political realm cannot be generalized but must be examined, case by case. If channeled through established state structures, such preferences may not have a great impact on a state's foreign policy because they compete with other interests. Yet when preferences are channeled through powerful nonstate actors, they may have immediate effects in the international arena. In some cases, the consequences may be severe. All this being said, it turns out that the suggestions offered in the 1990s regarding how we ought to refer to present-day international relations have been all too accurate: it seems we, indeed, live in an era of uncertainty and dissolution.

Notes

1. James Atlas, as cited in Derek Chollet and James Goldgeier, *America between the Wars: From 11/9 to 9/11* (New York: Public Affairs, 2008), ix.

2. Chollet and Goldgeier, ix–x.

3. Samuel P. Huntington, "The Clash of Civilizations?," *Foreign Affairs* 72, no. 3 (1993): 22–49; Samuel P. Huntington, *The Clash of Civilizations and the Remaking of World Order* (New York: Simon & Schuster, 1996).

4. Huntington, "Clash of Civilizations?," 24.

5. See, for example, Bruce M. Russett, John R. Oneal, and Michaelene Cox, "Clash of Civilizations, or Realism and Liberalism Déjà Vu? Some Evidence," *Journal of Peace Research* 37, no. 5 (2000): 583–608; Fouad Ajami, "The Summoning," *Foreign Affairs* 72, no. 4 (1993): 2–9; Kishore Mahbubani, "The Dangers of Decadence," *Foreign Affairs* 72, no. 4 (1993): 10–14; Jonathan Fox and Shmuel Sandler, *Bringing Religion into International Relations* (New York: Palgrave Macmillan, 2004), 115–35.

6. See, as a selection, Fabio Petito and Pavlos Hatzopoulos, eds., *Religion in International Relations: The Return from Exile* (New York: Palgrave Macmillan, 2003); Scott M. Thomas, *The Global Resurgence of Religion and the Transformation of International Relations: The Struggle for the Soul of the Twenty-First Century* (New York: Palgrave Macmillan, 2005); Robert A. Seiple and Dennis R. Hoover, eds., *Religion and Security: The New Nexus in International Relations* (Lanham, MD: Rowman & Littlefield, 2004); Jeffrey Haynes, ed., *Routledge Handbook of Religion and Politics* (New York: Routledge, 2009); Jeffrey Haynes, *Religion, Politics, and International Relations: Selected Essays* (New York: Routledge, 2011).

7. Steve Bruce, "Secularisation and Politics," in *Routledge Handbook of Religion and Politics*, ed. Jeffrey Haynes (New York: Routledge, 2009), 145–58. The complexity of the issue is well captured by José Casanova, "Rethinking Secularization: A Global Comparative Perspective," in *Religion, Globalization, and Culture*, ed. Peter Beyer and Lori Beaman (Leiden, Netherlands: Brill, 2007), 101–20.

8. Peter L. Berger, "The Desecularization of the World: A Global Overview," in *The Desecularization of the World: Resurgent Religion and World Politics*, ed. Peter L. Berger (Washington, DC: Ethics and Public Policy Center, 1999), 1–18, 6–7; Scott M. Thomas, "A Globalized God," *Foreign Affairs* 89, no. 6 (2010): 93–101.

9. Thomas, *Global Resurgence of Religion*, 29.

10. Timothy Samuel Shah and Monica Duffy Toft, "Why God Is Winning," *Foreign Policy* (July–August 2006): 38–43, 40.

11. Ibid.

12. Berger, "Desecularization of the World," 4, 6; Philip Jenkins, *The Next Christendom: The Coming of Global Christianity* (Oxford, U.K.: Oxford University Press, 2002).

13. Berger, "Desecularization of the World"; Thomas, "Globalized God."

14. Asteris Huliaras, "The Evangelical Roots of U.S. Africa Policy," *Survival* 50, no. 6 (2008): 161–82, 162. In 1900, roughly 7 percent of all evangelicals lived in the developing world. The share of evangelicals in the developing world versus those in the developed world had changed to 66 percent by 1985 and remains comparably high today.

15. Berger, "Desecularization of the World," 8.

16. For a more detailed discussion of worldviews and country differences about religion, see Pew Global Attitudes Project, "World Publics Welcome Global Trade—but Not Immigration: 47-Nation Pew Global Attitudes Survey," 33–39, http://pewglobal.org/reports/pdf/258.pdf.

17. Berger, "Desecularization of the World," 2.

18. Tanja Ellingsen, "Toward a Revival of Religion and Religious Clashes?," *Terrorism and Political Violence* 17, no. 3 (2005): 305–32, 312.

19. Shah and Toft, "Why God Is Winning," 42.

20. Berger, "Desecularization of the World," 3.

21. Manfred Brocker, *Protest–Anpassung–Etablierung: Die Christliche Rechte im politischen System der USA* (Frankfurt: Campus, 2004); Andrew Kohut, John C. Green, Scott Keeter, and Robert C. Toth, *The Diminishing Divide: Religion's Changing Role in American Politics* (Washington, DC: Brookings Institution, 2000).

22. For a discussion, see Thomas, *Global Resurgence of Religion*; Jonathan Fox, "Religion as an Overlooked Element of International Relations," *International Studies Review* 3, no. 3 (2001): 53–73.

23. "In God's Name: A Special Report on Religion and Public Life," *Economist*, November 3, 2007, 5.

24. Robert O. Keohane, "The Globalization of Informal Violence, Theories of World Politics, and the 'Liberalism of Fear,'" *Dialogue IO* 1, no. 1 (2002): 29–43, 29.

25. Jonathan Fox, "Integrating Religion into International Relations Theory," in *Routledge Handbook of Religion and Politics*, ed. Jeffrey Haynes (New York: Routledge, 2009), 273–92, 275.

26. For an overview, see Fox and Sandler, *Bringing Religion into International Relations*.

27. Thomas, *Global Resurgence of Religion*, 54–55.

28. Scott M. Thomas, "Taking Religious and Cultural Pluralism Seriously: The Global Resurgence of Religion and the Transformation of International Society," in *Religion in International Relations: The Return from Exile*, ed. Fabio Petito and Pavlos Hatzopoulos (New York: Palgrave Macmillan, 2003), 21–53, 24.

29. Michèle Schmiegelow, "Religionen und Werte: Kennzeichen des internationalen Systems?," *Internationale Politik* (February 2000): 19–26, 19.

30. Fox, "Integrating Religion," 273–92, 275–76; Siegmar Schmidt, "Ursachen und Konsequenzen des Aufstiegs religiöser Orientierungen in der internationalen Politik," in *Religion–Staat–Politik: Zur Rolle der Religion in der nationalen und internationalen Politik*, ed. Manfred Brocker, Hartmut Behr, and Mathias Hildebrandt (Wiesbaden, Germany: Westdeutscher Verlag, 2003), 295–318, 309–12.

31. Hans Morgenthau, *Politics among Nations: The Struggle for Power and Peace* (New York: Alfred A. Knopf, 1948).

32. For an overview, see Robert Jackson and Georg Sørensen, *Introduction to International Relations: Theories and Approaches* (New York: Oxford University Press, 2010), 28–57.

33. Kenneth N. Waltz, *Theory of International Politics* (New York: McGraw-Hill, 1979).

34. Robert O. Keohane and Joseph S. Nye, *Power and Interdependence: World Politics in Transition* (Boston: Little, Brown, 1977); Robert O. Keohane, *International Institutions and State Power: Essays in International Relations Theory* (Boulder, CO: Westview Press, 1989); Michael Brecher and Frank P. Harvey, eds., *Realism and Institutionalism in International Studies* (Ann Arbor: University of Michigan Press, 2002).

35. Andrew Moravcsik, "Taking Preferences Seriously: A Liberal Theory of International Politics," *International Organization* 51, no. 4 (1997): 513–53.

36. Alexander Wendt, "Anarchy Is What States Make of It: The Social Construction of Power Politics," *International Organization* 46, no. 2 (1992): 391–425; Alexander Wendt, *Social Theory of International Politics* (Cambridge, U.K.: Cambridge University Press, 1999).

37. Thomas Risse summarizes this view concisely. He argues that the mere insight that ideas matter is not enough. Constructivism leaves open what ideas, actors, and level of analysis matter in international relations. See Thomas Risse, "Konstruktivismus, Rationalismus und Theorien Internationaler Beziehungen," in *Die neuen Internationalen Beziehungen: Forschungsstand und Perspektiven in Deutschland*, ed. Gunther Hellmann, Klaus Dieter Wolf, and Michael Zürn (Baden-Baden, Germany: Nomos, 2003), 99–132, 101.

38. Claudia Baumgart-Ochse, "Religiöse Akteure und die Opportunitätsstruktur der internationalen Beziehungen," *Zeitschrift für Internationale Beziehungen* 17, no. 1 (2010): 101–17, 102–5; Fox, "Integrating Religion," 273–92, 276.

39. Huntington, "Clash of Civilizations?," 22.

40. Huntington identifies seven or eight civilizations: Western, Confucian, Japanese, Islamic, Hindu, Slavic-Orthodox, Latin American, and (possibly) African. See Huntington, "Clash of Civilizations?," 25.

41. Fox and Sandler, *Bringing Religion into International Relations*, 115–36.

42. Bassam Tibi, "Politisierung der Religion: Sicherheitspolitik im Zeichen des islamischen Fundamentalismus," *Internationale Politik* (February 2000): 27–34, 27.

43. Ibid., 28. On the importance of individuals and leaders, see also the discussion in Andreas Hasenclever and Volker Rittberger, "Does Religion Make a Difference? Theoretical Approaches to the Impact of Faith on Political Conflict," in *Religion in International Relations: The Return from Exile*, ed. Fabio Petito and Pavlos Hatzopoulos (New York: Palgrave Macmillan, 2003), 107–45.

44. Russett, Oneal, and Cox, "Clash of Civilizations, or Realism and Liberalism Déjà Vu?"; Jonathan Fox, "Religion and State Failure: An Examination of the Extent and Magnitude of Religious Conflict from 1950 to 1996," *International Political Science Review* 25, no. 1 (2004): 55–76; Giacomo Chiozza, "Is There a Clash of Civi-

lizations? Evidence from Patterns of International Conflict Involvement, 1946–97," *Journal of Peace Research* 39, no. 6 (2002): 711–34.

45. Several authors have recently reflected about ways to incorporate religion into theoretical frameworks. See, as a selection, Fox, "Integrating Religion"; Baumgart-Ochse, "Religiöse Akteure"; Carolyn M. Warner and Stephen G. Walker, "Thinking about the Role of Religion in Foreign Policy: A Framework for Analysis," *Foreign Policy Analysis* 7, no. 1 (2011): 113–35; Nukhet A. Sandal and Patrick James, "Religion and International Relations Theory: Towards a Mutual Understanding," *European Journal of International Relations* 17, no. 1 (2011): 3–25.

46. Moravcsik, "Taking Preferences Seriously," 518.

47. Clifford Geertz, *The Interpretation of Cultures* (New York: Basic Books, 1973), 87–125.

48. Ibid., 123–25.

49. Lester Kurtz, *Gods in the Global Village: The World's Religions in Sociological Perspective* (Thousand Oaks, CA: Pine Forge, 1995), 10.

50. This view seems to be the most common interpretation. See also Jonathan Fox and Shmuel Sandler, "The Question of Religion and World Politics," *Terrorism and Political Violence* 17, no. 3 (2005): 293–303.

51. Geertz, *Interpretation of Cultures*, 5.

52. Kurtz, *Gods in the Global Village*, 10; Fox, "Integrating Religion into International Relations Theory," 279–80.

53. A differentiated overview is offered in Haynes, *Religion, Politics, and International Relations*.

54. See, as an example, Brian Lai, "An Empirical Examination of Religion and Conflict in the Middle East, 1950–1992," *Foreign Policy Analysis* 2, no. 1 (2006): 21–36.

55. Huliaras, "Evangelical Roots"; Gerlinde Groitl, *Evangelical Internationalism: The American Christian Right and Global Human Rights* (Hamburg, Germany: Kovač, 2007); Jeffrey Haynes, "Transnational Religious Actors and International Order," *Perspectives* 17, no. 2 (2009): 43–69.

56. Thomas, "Globalized God," 101.

57. Aurel Croissant, Uwe Wagschal, Nicolas Schwank, and Christoph Trinh, *Kultur und Konflikt in globaler Perspektive: Die kulturellen Dimensionen des Konfliktgeschehens 1945–2007* (Gütersloh, Germany: Bertelsmann Stiftung, 2009).

58. Monica Duffy Toft, "Religion, Civil War, and International Order," BCSIA Discussion Paper 2006-03, Belfer Center for Science and International Affairs, Kennedy School of Government, Harvard University, July 2006, 9, http://belfercenter.ksg.harvard.edu/files/toft_2006_03_updated_web.pdf.

59. Jonathan Fox, "The Increasing Role of Religion in State Failure: 1960 to 2004," *Terrorism and Political Violence* 19, no. 3 (2007): 395–414, 403–4; see also Ellingsen, "Toward a Revival of Religion and Religious Clashes?"; Fox, "Religion and State Failure."

60. Fox and Sandler, *Bringing Religion into International Relations*, 104.

61. Timothy Shah, Daniel Philpott, and Monica Duffy Toft, "God and Terror," *Public Discourse*, May 20, 2011, http://www.thepublicdiscourse.com/2011/05/3316.

62. Conflict characteristics are discussed, for example, in Hasenclever and Rittberger, "Does Religion Make a Difference?"; Andreas Hasenclever, "Getting Religion Right: Zur Rolle von Religionen in politischen Konflikten," in *Religion und Globale*

Entwicklung: Der Einfluss der Religionen auf die soziale, politische und wirtschaftliche Entwicklung, ed. Jürgen Wilhelm and Hartmut Ihne (Berlin: Berlin University Press, 2009), 170–86; Toft, "Religion, Civil War, and International Order"; Monica Duffy Toft, "Getting Religion? The Puzzling Case of Islam and Civil War," *International Security* 31, no. 4 (2007): 99–131; Pauletta Otis, "Religion and War in the Twenty-First Century," in *Religion and Security: The New Nexus in International Relations*, ed. Robert A. Seiple and Dennis R. Hoover (Lanham, MD: Rowman & Littlefield, 2004), 11–24; Michael C. Horowitz, "Long Time Going: Religion and the Duration of Crusading," *International Security* 34, no. 2 (2009): 162–93; Schmidt, "Ursachen und Konsequenzen," 308–9.

63. Harold H. Saunders, "Relational Realism: Toward a New Political Paradigm for Security," in *Religion and Security: The New Nexus in International Relations*, ed. Robert A. Seiple and Dennis R. Hoover (Lanham, MD: Rowman & Littlefield, 2004), 163–74, 164.

64. Toft, "Getting Religion?," 100–1.

65. Shah, Philpott, and Toft, "God and Terror."

66. Otis, "Religion and War in the Twenty-First Century," 11.

67. For summaries, see, for example, Fox, "Religion and State Failure," 60–61, 70; Hasenclever and Rittberger, "Does Religion Make a Difference?"; Andreas Hasenclever and Alexander De Juan, "Religionen in Konflikten: Eine Herausforderung für die Friedenspolitik," *Aus Politik und Zeitgeschichte* 6 (February 2007): 10–16; Hasenclever, "Getting Religion Right."

68. Hasenclever and De Juan, "Religionen in Konflikten,"11.

69. Ellingsen, "Toward a Revival of Religion and Religious Clashes?," 314.

70. Hasenclever and Rittberger, "Does Religion Make a Difference?"; Hasenclever and De Juan, "Religionen in Konflikten," 11–12; Hasenclever, "Getting Religion Right."

71. Mathias Hildebrandt, "Krieg der Religionen?" *Aus Politik und Zeitgeschichte* 6 (February 2007): 3–9, 7.

72. Croissant et al., *Kultur und Konflikt*. For a detailed list of current conflicts, see, for example, "Conflict Barometer 2010: Crises–Wars–Coups d'État–Negotiations–Mediations–Peace Settlements," Heidelberg Institute for International Conflict Research, Heidelberg, Germany, 2010, http://www.hiik.de/de/konfliktbarometer/pdf/ConflictBarometer_2010.pdf.

73. Mary Kaldor, *New and Old Wars: Organized Violence in a Global Era* (Stanford, CA: Stanford University Press, 2007), 80.

74. For a discussion, see, for example, Schmidt, "Ursachen und Konsequenzen," 298–304; Giorgio Shani, "Transnational Religious Actors and International Relations," in *Routledge Handbook of Religion and Politics*, ed. Jeffrey Haynes (New York: Routledge, 2009), 308–22.

75. Sweden was the only exception. There, 49 percent responded that they feared that their traditional culture was being lost.

76. Pew Global Attitudes Project, "World Publics Welcome Global Trade," 21.

77. Kaldor, *New and Old Wars*, 81.

78. Thomas L. Friedman, *Longitudes and Attitudes: Exploring the World after September 11* (New York: Farrar, Straus and Giroux, 2002), 6.

79. Ibid., 5.

80. See, in particular, Kaldor, *New and Old Wars*, chapters 4 and 5; Audrey Kurth Cronin, "Behind the Curve: Globalization and International Terrorism," *International*

Security 27, no. 3 (2002–03): 30–58; Keohane, "Globalization of Informal Violence." For a discussion of state sovereignty, see, for example, Thomas Risse, "Paradoxien der Souveränität," *Internationale Politik* (July–August 2007): 40–47.

81. Sven Chojnacki, "Anything New or More of the Same? Wars and Military Interventions in the International System, 1946–2003," *Global Society* 20, no. 1 (2006): 25–46, 39–43.

82. Data are from the Uppsala Conflict Data Program. See Lotta Themnér and Peter Wallensteen, "Armed Conflict, 1946–2010," *Journal of Peace Research* 48, no. 4 (2011): 525–36, 525–27.

83. Lotta Harbom and Peter Wallensteen, "Armed Conflict, 1989–2006," *Journal of Peace Research* 44, no. 5 (2007): 623–34, especially at 624; Andrew Heywood, *Global Politics* (New York: Palgrave Macmillan, 2011), 247. The percentage refers to conflicts after the Cold War.

84. Chojnacki, "Anything New or More of the Same?," 34, 39–40.

85. See, for example, Martin van Creveld, *The Transformation of War* (New York: Free Press, 1991); Kaldor, *New and Old Wars*; Herfried Münkler, *Die neuen Kriege* (Reinbek, Germany: Rowohlt, 2002); Herfried Münkler, *Der Wandel des Krieges: Von der Symmetrie zur Asymmetrie* (Weilerswist, Germany: Velbrück Wissenschaft, 2006). *Wars* are commonly defined as conflicts with more than 1,000 battle-related deaths per year.

86. For a detailed analysis, see Sven Chojnacki, *Wandel der Gewaltformen im internationalen System 1946–2006* (Osnabrück, Germany: Deutsche Stiftung Friedensforschung, 2008). For an overview of the debate on new wars, see Patrick A. Mello, "In Search of New Wars: The Debate about a Transformation of War," *European Journal of International Relations* 16, no. 2 (2010): 297–309. For a critique, see Errol A. Henderson and J. David Singer, "'New Wars' and Rumors of 'New Wars,'" *International Interactions* 28, no. 2 (2002): 165–90.

87. Implications for military planning are discussed in Keith W. Mines, "Force Size for the Post-Westphalian World," *Orbis* 49, no. 4 (2005): 649–62.

88. George W. Bush, as cited in Fraser Cameron, *U.S. Foreign Policy after the Cold War: Global Hegemon or Reluctant Sheriff?* (New York: Routledge, 2005), 139.

89. Oliver Kessler and Christopher Daase, "From Insecurity to Uncertainty: Risk and the Paradox of Security Politics," *Alternatives: Global, Local, Political* 33, no. 2 (2008): 211–32.

90. Richard N. Haass, "The Age of Nonpolarity," *Foreign Affairs* 87, no. 3 (2008): 44–56.

91. Ibid., 44.

Chapter 14

"Heaven Is under Our Feet": Contextualizing Faith, Religion, and Politics in the Post-9/11 Era

Volker Depkat and Jürgen Martschukat

The tenth anniversary of 9/11 coincided with both the violent death of Osama bin Laden, the mastermind of the terrorist attacks on the World Trade Center and the Pentagon, and a series of peoples' revolutions shaking the political landscape in North Africa and the Middle East. From Tunisia to Egypt, one authoritarian regime after another fell to freedom movements composed predominantly of Muslims, shaking a region of the world that, until recently, appeared to be one of the major breeding grounds of Islamic fundamentalism. These changes open a possible future for Islamic democratization. In this context, Elias Khoury, one of the best-known Arab intellectuals, has interpreted the Maghrebian revolutions as the Arab response to 9/11, marking the end of the decade of terror ushered in by the jihadists of al-Qaeda in 2001.[1]

At the same time, the historicization of 9/11 has gained significant momentum in recent years and currently appears to be in full swing, fueled yet again by the event's tenth anniversary in 2011.[2] This momentous event, initially understood to mark a new epoch, is currently being contextualized and embedded into the course of post-1945 history. Although the debate in newspapers, in magazines, and on television is still very much informed by the idea that 9/11 changed the world, historians, cultural critics, political scientists, economists, sociologists, and scholars from all walks of academic life have begun to carefully assess the balance of change and continuity in the post-9/11 world.

Indisputably, 9/11 marks a pivotal event whose consequences still remain with us. The war in Afghanistan continues unabated. Whether the war in Iraq has ended remains far from clear. Meanwhile, the Bush Doctrine, claiming the right to preemptive strikes whenever American security seems threatened, has rightly been interpreted as a major break with U.S. foreign policy traditions.[3] Furthermore, as the extensive recent media coverage of the tenth anniversary of the terrorist attacks on the World Trade Center and the Pentagon demonstrates, 9/11 continues to be represented as an "interruption of the deep rhythms of cultural time."[4] Jeffrey Melnick additionally argues that "'9/11' has become the most important question and answer shaping American cultural discussions" since 2001.[5]

This focus on the changes and ruptures brought about by 9/11, however, should not blind us to the multiple continuities that scholars have unearthed from various disciplines working to critically relate the pre- and post-9/11 worlds. In this context, one of the most important insights gained in the course of this discussion appears to be that American experiences with terrorism originating in the Middle East did not start ten years ago. Rather, as Melani McAlister writes, the emotional engagement of the U.S. public with Middle Eastern terrorism and the fight against it began as early as September 1972, when Palestinian terrorists broke into the Israeli compound at the Munich Olympic Games, killing two members of the Israeli team and taking nine other athletes hostage.[6] What started out as emotional engagement soon turned into direct involvement, as hundreds of U.S. citizens were killed or injured in terrorist attacks in the course of the 1970s and 1980s. From late 1979 to early 1981, fifty-two Americans were held hostage by Iranian revolutionaries within the U.S. embassy in Tehran for a grueling 444 days. In April 1983, a car bomb destroyed the grounds of the U.S. embassy in Beirut; later that October, a series of truck bombs detonated outside the barracks of U.S. Marines and French paratrooper peacekeeping forces in the Lebanese capital, killing hundreds. Three years later, in April 1986, the bombing of the discothèque La Belle in West Berlin occurred, targeting U.S. servicemen. On December 21, 1988, 270 people from twenty-one different nations—including 190 U.S. citizens—died when Pan

Am Flight 103 exploded in midair over Lockerbie, Scotland, from a bomb planted in its cargo space by Libyan terrorists. In February 1993, Muslim terrorists attempted a strike at the World Trade Center by detonating a car bomb in the complex's underground garage, killing 6 people and injuring 1,000. Not all of these acts were perpetrated by Muslim extremist groups — many were acts of state-sponsored terrorism — yet Muslim activists from militant groups such as Hezbollah, Islamic Jihad, and Hamas played a major role in these events.

The current American "War on Terrorism," triggered by the 9/11 attacks, must be embedded into this thirty-year history of encounters with Middle Eastern terrorism. Already in 1981, President Ronald Reagan announced in his inaugural address — delivered on January 20, the day the American hostages were released in Tehran — that terrorism would replace Jimmy Carter's focus on human rights as America's primary foreign policy concern.[7] This concern survived the Cold War. In 1993, National Security Adviser Anthony Lake, in one of the few programmatic statements of the Clinton administration, argued that global terrorism was one of the prime threats that confronted the United States after the collapse of the Soviet Union.[8] Inextricably linked to this threat perception was the call for quick, clean military responses to terrorist offenses, which was also well established in pre-9/11 America.[9]

Although these and other continuities are important, they cannot negate the notion of a distinct change in era, ushering in a clash of cultures between the secular and enlightened West (identified with modernity as such) and a backward region peopled by preenlightened religious fanatics living in the Middle Ages, who lacked the emancipatory achievements of the Enlightenment, as a large part of the cultural and political history of 9/11. The terrorist attacks of September 11 have been described, as David Simpson argues, as "the result of a clash of civilizations, ours and theirs, signaling the existence of an implacably different culture that does not march to the same beat as ours, one that is messianic, vengeful, unenlightened, premodern, other: the culture of terror," with many willingly inclined to identify this "culture of terror" with Islam and a genuine anti-Americanism in the Arab world.[10] What may actually be a secular political conflict was thus interpreted as a religious struggle, touching off a "search for the 'nature of Islam' as the source of the problem."[11]

Hand in hand with this notion went the construction of a new enemy image in the post–Cold War West: the Muslim with terrorist inclinations from the Middle East, who hated America and modernity. In the immediate wake of the 9/11 attacks, a number of rumors revolving around Arabs or Middle Eastern–looking protagonists acting as an enemy within surfaced throughout the United States. They included tales of Arab Americans allegedly cheering on the 9/11 attacks in a Detroit restaurant or folklore about Middle Eastern–looking individuals distributing poisoned candy to American children trick-or-treating on Halloween.[12] Although these rumors did not originate from nowhere—stereotypes of Middle Eastern–looking villains and terrorists have circulated widely through U.S. popular culture since the 1970s—their dimensions now took on a clear religious dynamic, driven by a diffuse fear of Islam as the source of violence and terrorism.[13] This Islamophobia emerged on both sides of the Atlantic, apparently taking on a life of its own over the past ten years.

Despite the fact that in the immediate aftermath of 9/11, Chancellor Gerhard Schröder and other political leaders in Germany and elsewhere in Europe keenly insisted that the attacks in New York and Washington had nothing to do with religion, many Europeans were inclined to see every pious Muslim as a potential terrorist and a threat to their pluralistic and open societies.[14] In 2003, a fierce debate about Muslim women wanting to be hired as teachers in public schools erupted in Germany, triggering legislation in several German states prohibiting instructors from wearing headscarves, an event viewed by many as an act of cultural dissociation and a violation of the separation of church and state.[15] Seven years later, on October 3, 2010, Bundespräsident Christian Wulff remarked in a speech celebrating the anniversary of Germany's reunification that Islam was an integral part of Germany and its culture. This statement caused a major uproar that only amplified and prolonged a heated debate that had already begun with the publication of Deutsche Bundesbank executive board member Thilo Sarrazin's book *Deutschland schafft sich ab* (Germany abolishes itself) some weeks before.[16] In it, Sarrazin argues head-on that Germans in their own society are becoming marginalized by the huge influx of immigrants from Muslim countries who are unwilling to assimilate into the core values of Germany's democracy and Western lifestyle. Sarrazin's theses met with violent criticism, forcing him to resign from his Deutsche Bundesbank post in October 2010. Such criticism, however, did not stop *Deutschland schafft sich ab* from becoming one of the best-selling books in twenty-first-century Germany, garnering many adamant defenders of Sarrazin and his views. Among them, Hans-Ulrich Wehler, the doyen of social history in Germany, has labeled Islamic fundamentalism as "the political plague" of the post–Cold War world.[17] The potential political consequences of this Islamophobia are far reaching: in a 2010 study regarding right-wing extremism and xenophobia in Germany, the renowned Friedrich Ebert Foundation discovered that 55 percent of all Germans felt uncomfortable with Arabs and 58 percent favored restricting freedom of religion for Muslims.[18]

This diffuse fear of Islam is not confined to Germany, a country that is still coming to grips with its new status as an immigrant society, with its enormous cultural transformation wrought by the huge influx of immigrants from Italy, Turkey, Greece, and other countries from the eastern Mediterranean beginning in the 1950s. Rather, Islamophobic anxiety is something that post-9/11 Europe appears to share equally. The German *Kopftuchstreit* (headscarf dispute) is part of a larger European debate about Islamic religious symbols in the public sphere.[19] On September 30, 2005, the Danish newspaper *Jyllands-Posten* published a set of twelve editorial cartoons originally meant to be a contribution to the ongoing debate on Islam and free speech. Most of the cartoons depicted the Islamic prophet Muhammad, with some cartoons establishing a direct link between Islam and terrorism. Their publication caused an intensely fierce international controversy, driving new wedges between the Islamic world and the West.[20] The most violent and extreme expression of Islamophobia to date occurred on July 22, 2011, in Norway, when right-wing extremist Anders Behring Breivik bombed government buildings in central Oslo, leaving eight people dead, and then went on to slaughter sixty-nine people, mostly teenagers, at the Labor Party's Workers' Youth League camp on the island of Utøya. In confessing his deeds, Breivik described his actions as serving to preserve a Christian Europe by annihilating Islam and "cultural Marxism."[21] Ironically, the fear of Islamic fundamentalism was also a tool in the hands of the now deposed authoritarian regimes in North Africa, which until recently found support in Western democracies as long as they promised to keep the floodgates closed for Islamic fundamentalism and intrusion.[22]

A diffuse fear of Islam appears to have steadily grown stronger in Germany, other European countries, and the United States over the past decade, only reinforcing the predominance of binary oppositions in the political controversies about the meaning of 9/11 and its adequate political responses. All too often, the "Muslim world" is perceived and presented as a monolithic entity, acting and thinking alike in its entirety. This, of course, suggests absolute simplicity, whereas in reality complexity and diversity exist. By identifying Islam with fundamentalism and Islamic politics with militancy and terrorism, as Michael H. Hunt argues, we conflate a wide va-

riety of religiously inspired political movements in various Muslim countries. "In a sweep of territory running from northern Africa to Southeast
Asia," Hunt writes, "there are at least as many public, political expressions
of Islam as there are countries, each with its own linguistic, ethnic, and historical profile."[23] This leaves us with the challenge "to understand Islam, as
among other things, a source of political ideas that have taken quite distinct
national forms, that are also transnational in their reach, and that thus resist
easy categorization or generalization."[24] The recent upheavals in Northern
Africa seem to have validated Hunt's argument yet again.

Still, the 9/11 attacks have not only provoked debates about the terrorist
potential of Islamic religion. They have also revived debates about identity
within the Western world, which is currently grappling to define both its
own position vis-à-vis Islam and Islam's place in Western culture. In this
context, the Enlightenment has experienced an astonishing rebirth as one of
the defining elements of Western identity, supposedly taming the destructive powers of religious irrationalism and turning religion into a private
affair. At the beginning of the twenty-first century, in a recent piece for the
American Historical Review, Karen O'Brien argued a highly positive view
of the Enlightenment, which "as an intellectual clustering, as a method of
experimental inquiry, and as an ideal, even, of rationality and toleration to
be pitted against the world's zones of intolerance ... is back in circulation
and generating new historical work."[25] Recent studies by Jonathan Israel
and Tzvetan Todorov featuring the primacy of ideas have also celebrated
the Enlightenment unabashedly as "a repository of good political intentions," so that the Enlightenment currently "suffers from an embarrassment
of admiration," as characterized by Karen O'Brien in her article.[26] "Gone,"
O'Brien argues, "is the sense of a need to readdress the Marxist postwar
critique of the Enlightenment as the precursor of the murderously techno-
cratic state mounted by [Theodor] Adorno and [Max] Horkheimer in their
Dialectic of Enlightenment (1944), or to resist the philosophical assaults
on its foundational universalism and rationalism by poststructuralists."[27]

Furthermore, the focus on Islamic fundamentalism as a threat to open
and pluralistic societies blinds us to the (religious) fundamentalisms existing within the Western world, particularly in the United States, where religion and morality are major driving factors in a series of culture wars that
have transformed U.S. political culture substantially since the 1970s. In
the course of these transformations, particularly because of the rise of the
so-called religious right as a politicized form of conservative evangelical
Protestantism in the United States, an increasingly deep divide has opened

up within the Atlantic world. Hugh McLeod has argued that despite important and interesting differences, the shape of American religious history has not been so very different from that of many European countries over the centuries. Only in the 1970s did Europe and the United States really begin to diverge, "when the trend towards rapid secularisation continued in most European countries, while in the United States levels of religious practice stabilised, and religion began to play an increasingly conspicuous role in politics."[28] Although Great Britain, West Germany, and other European countries all experienced a move to the right in the 1980s, a "significant link between conservative politics and conservative religion" materialized only in the United States.[29] This cultural gap became visible once more in the crusader rhetoric that the Bush administration used to frame America's military response to the 9/11 attacks.[30] Thus, if the supposed "clash of civilizations" evolving in the wake of September 11 has indeed something to do with fundamentalism, then one should look at the fundamentalism on both sides of the conflict and the roles that religion plays in it.[31]

Because we are still working to define the meaning of 9/11 and its place in the history of the twentieth and twenty-first centuries, the nature of the conflict sparked by the terrorist attacks on the World Trade Center and the Pentagon remains rather ill defined historically.[32] Jacques Derrida's statement of 2003 that we do not yet know what we are talking about when we talk about 9/11 has lost none of its validity.[33] Although binaries pitting monolithic entities against each other along the lines of an "us versus them" continue to structure the debate on the meaning of 9/11, it is still altogether unclear who the "us" and "them" are, and—maybe even more importantly—what religion has to do with it.[34]

Historians of the modern world generally seem to be at a loss to deal with this issue sufficiently because they have marginalized religion in their historiographical analyses and narratives. On the American side, Jon Butler has pointed out that while the religion problem is an integral part of all major historiographical narratives related to U.S. history before the Civil War, "religion has not fared well in the historiography of modern America."[35] So focused were historians of modern America on secular politics and modernization, Butler argues, that they were unable to come up with narratives that systematically integrate religion as a factor shaping the course of American history since 1865. Like a jack-in-the-box, religion pops up every once in a while, to be sure, yet no systematic treatment exists of the religion problem in modern America and its historical impact. The only exceptions to this rule occurred, Butler acknowledges, "in treatments of the 1928 and 1960 presidential elections, the post–World War II civil rights movement, though even there specifically religious foundations are sometimes oddly ignored, and the rise of the new Christian Right."[36] This historiographical marginalization of religion stands in stark contrast to the continued and even heightened importance of religion in twentieth- and twenty-first-century America: religious affiliation rates have been "robust," Butler argues, suggesting that "Americans not only have continued to be individually religious throughout the twentieth century but may have also attached themselves to religious institutions at rates higher than at any time since the Puritans commanded Massachusetts in the 1630s, 1640s, and 1650s."[37] Hartmut Lehmann argues along just these lines when he points to rich statistical evidence proving that the United States and Europe have taken different paths with regard to religion in the last quarter or so of the twentieth century. Although much of the evidence published since the 1980s "underlined the ongoing secularization, even the dechristianization of Western Europe, even more data were made available that demonstrated a remarkable christianization," maybe even "rechristianization or desecularization of many segments of public and private life in the United States."[38] The evidence produced by political scientist Gerlinde Groitl in this volume suggests that Americans are more religious than any other people in the West and have become increasingly so in recent decades.

In the historiography of modern Europe, religion has not fared better. In a recent review essay on the latest literature regarding religion in the Federal Republic of Germany, Mark Edward Ruff speaks of a "seeming alienation of religious history from the historical mainstream," with Uta Balbier wholeheartedly seconding, arguing that the religion problem has not systematically been tackled by scholars of post-1945 German history.[39] Although systematic research into contemporary church history exists, the findings of this historiographical subdiscipline do not explicitly radiate into the field of political, social, or cultural history.[40] Not only historians, however, have neglected the presence of religion in modern life. Political scientists—especially those in the field of international relations scholarship—have equally marginalized religion as a factor of the foreign policy process, which is why they have a hard time defining the nature of the conflict provoked by the September 11 terrorist attacks and the role religion played as a causal factor in it, as Groitl demonstrates in chapter 13 of this volume.

The contributions to this book must be viewed in this context. The few existing comparative studies on religion and politics in Europe and the United States are mostly limited to contemporary history, with the bulk of the relevant data, such as church attendance and membership, the frequency of prayer, and other indicators of religiosity, being collected by experts in the field of religious sociology. By contrast, most of the essays in this volume take a much broader chronological approach as they deal with problems from the eighteenth through the twentieth centuries, highlighting some new aspects of the role of religion in modern politics from a transatlantic perspective, such as capital punishment, conflicts between science and theology, and the problem of how to measure acts of violence as "religious violence." If one tries to assess the balance between divergence and convergence in the relationship between religion and politics in Europe and the United States in light of the contributions collected in this volume, some striking similarities appear noteworthy.

On both sides of the Atlantic, purely secular states emerged between 1750 and 1850—as shown in this volume by Frank Kelleter, Michael Broers, Daniel A. Cohen, and André Krischer (in chapters 2 through 5)—but the paths taken differed greatly. In America, the secular state was the product of a democratic revolution; in Europe, the secularization of statehood was driven by the bureaucracies of monarchic states—sometimes with the consent of the monarch, sometimes without it. The emergence of the secular state increasingly separated the political and the religious spheres, yet religion neither vanished from the public arena nor ceased to be politically relevant. In the United States, the formal separation of church and state brought about by the American Revolution initially applied to the national level only. The states, especially those in New England, where the process of disestablishing churches lasted well into the first third of the nineteenth century, tell quite a different story. Even after it had been completed formally around 1830, the separation of church and state in the United States was never as strict in practice as it appeared to be in principle. Children continued to pray in schools, American churches enjoyed tax benefits granted by authorities, and religious language remained ubiquitous in nineteenth- and twentieth-century political and legal discourses. Only in 1954 did Congress add "under God" to the Pledge of Allegiance, and a year later, President Dwight D. Eisenhower, in keeping with Public Law 140, ordered the words "In God We Trust" to be stamped on all American coins and dollar bills. Since 1956, "In God We Trust" has been the officially designated national motto.[41] In this context, the contribution of Anthony Santoro to this volume (chapter 6) provides ample evidence of the continuing omnipresence of religious motifs and values in the contemporary debates on capital punishment.

Nineteenth- and twentieth-century Europe offers a similar picture. Europe also experienced a movement toward the formal separation of church and state, yet regional variations are immense and the practical disentanglement was more a question of degree than principle. A spectrum of broad possibilities exists, ranging from laical France to the Scandinavian monarchies, where the alliance of throne and altar continues to be strong in the framework of the modern secular state. Only in the socialist states emerging in Central and Eastern Europe after World War II did the severing of all ties between the churches and the state proceed rigorously, as Monika Wohlrab-Sahr and Thomas Schmidt-Lux argue in chapter 9 of this volume—but then, the communist system had no place for religion at all. The communist politics of atheism was an outright war against all religious beliefs, institutions, and cultural practices, becoming an integral part of the Marxist–Leninist fight against all forms of aristocratic and bourgeois cultures. If we follow Wohlrab-Sahr and Schmidt-Lux's findings, the communist policy of atheism was quite successful and of lasting impact, because the still visible cultural gap between East and West in today's Germany to a very large extent rests on the very different role religion and religious cultures played in both German states during the Cold War.

Thus, although the Enlightenment and the age of the bourgeois revolutions of the eighteenth and nineteenth centuries put legitimate political rule on a new secular basis, they did not relegate religion to the private sphere after all. Quite to the contrary, religion remained highly visible and publicly relevant in modern Europe and America, mostly because it continued to be a powerful source of morality in a secular state, acting as an important social cement for societies based on natural rights, individualism, and pluralism. A connection also appears to exist between the multiple ruptures, uncertainties, and market-driven economic insecurities that form part of life in the modern age and religion's continuing attractiveness and impact. In their widely read book *Sacred and Secular: Religion and Politics Worldwide*, Pippa Norris and Ronald Inglehart trace this connection between "security" and "religiosity," arguing that "human security encourages secularization," whereas "social vulnerability, insecurity, and risk" drive religiosity.[42] Accordingly, Americans faced greater economic insecurities than citizens in other advanced industrial countries, which may explain why Americans are more inclined than Europeans, who enjoy the benefits of firmly established welfare states, to embrace religion as a source of certainty, solace, and orientation.

Although Norris and Inglehart's thought-provoking theses give the reader ideas to build on, their approach needs further qualification, mostly because Norris and Inglehart too monolithically pit America and Europe against each other without applying the necessary degree of differentiation in terms of region and sociopolitical milieus. The contributions by Monika Wohlrab-Sahr and Thomas Schmidt-Lux, Klaus Hödl, Michelle Mart, and Michael Hochgeschwender in chapters 9 through 12 of this volume demonstrate the gains of taking a closer look at the function of religion in specific milieus interconnecting ideological, social, ethnic, and cultural factors to produce notions of identity and a political outlook connected to them. From an international relations perspective, Groitl also cautions against far-sweeping and undifferentiated theoretical models analyzing religion as a source of international conflicts, because the causal influence of religion on current foreign policy processes cannot be viewed separately from the effects of globalization, the weakening of state structures, and the empowerment of nonstate actors. Although religion is a source of identity—and as such can fuel identity-related international and intrastate conflicts—religion always is only one factor among many.

All in all, the contributions to this volume suggest that both the religious history in Europe and the United States and the history of the relationship between religion and politics were strongly shaped by the social upheavals associated with urbanization, industrialization, and the intellectual earthquakes brought about by the scientific knowledge revolution of the nineteenth century. Darwinism and biblical criticism questioned the very foundations of religious certainties, while the socioeconomic transformations of the industrial world severed social ties and reconfigured social milieus. These changes only accelerated the politics of secularization, climaxing in the Soviet Union and its Eastern European satellites, where the promotion of atheism became an integral part of the *raison d'état* for a period of forty years. However, as the contributions of James Gilbert (chapter 7), Ronald Doel (chapter 8), and Michelle Mart (chapter 11) show, religious groups and milieus in the United States were highly able to adapt to the challenges of modernity, using mass media and covering its values, institutions, and practices to spread the gospel and generate a larger following. The result is the proximity of religious life to a thoroughly commercialized popular culture that is in many ways specific to the United States, as Gilbert and Mart demonstrate. This blending of religiosity and entertainment in the modern mass media context turned religion into an integral part of popular culture. In the course of this process, religious symbols such as the crucifix or Buddha in many cases became icons of popular culture, completely divorced from all religious contexts. Still, one could argue that the very means of the modern age and its thoroughly commercialized popular culture reinvigorated religious life in America, whereas religion's vitality dwindled in Europe, particularly after 1945, when many European social milieus that previously supported religious culture eroded rapidly under the onslaught of the enormous transformations wrought by the accelerating modernization of the continent after World War II.

The reasons for this transatlantic divergence are multiple, yet in light of the contributions collected in this volume, two reasons appear to be fundamental: first, the principle of voluntarism, which has shaped America's religious history from its colonial beginnings onward, and second, the lack of socialism in the United States.

America's religious life is based on voluntary membership and choice, whereas Europeans generally are nominal members of institutional churches. Whereas Americans over the centuries were in a position to choose their religion from an array of churches and religious organizations competing in a vibrant marketplace of ideas (see chapter 7 by Gilbert and chapter 11 by Mart), most Europeans to this day are, as Hartmut Lehmann argues, "born into a church and they remain members of this church as long as they live unless they decide to leave. By contrast, Americans decide to join a church or a special religious organization, and if they take that step they are convinced that this matters to them."[43] Voluntarism and choice are also the reason religious life in the United States is predominantly local, with ethnic traditions in many cases reinforcing social bonding in churches on the local level. Religious life in the United States has always been and continues to be organized bottom up—not top down—giving laypersons multiple opportunities to participate in the life and government of their churches.[44] In a variety of Europe's states, by contrast, the opposite exists. Church life is organized top down, regulated by central bodies that are highly suspicious of local initiatives.[45] This is, ironically enough, the heritage of the European secularization of the state in the nineteenth and twentieth centuries, in the course of which, as Michael Broers shows in chapter 3 of this volume, the churches were subordinated to aggressively secular states, thereby becoming integral parts of the state bureaucracy.

A second political factor shaping the difference in transatlantic religious history is most certainly the lack of a strong, antireligious socialist labor movement in the United States. The predominant ideology of individualism in combination with significantly higher degrees of social mobility, leading to a smaller number of "hereditary proletarians" in the United States, is the main reason for the relative weakness of the American labor movement, as Werner Sombart argued in his famous elaborations on the question, "Why is there no socialism in the United States?"[46] On the other side of the Atlantic, the petrified class structures in Europe's industrial societies produced strong socialist movements and working-class identities that, among other things, were ostentatiously antireligious. Evidence shows that in nineteenth-century Europe, churchgoing was lower in the working class than in the middle and upper classes, and it was lowest among the poor.[47] The twentieth century then saw the labor movement being voted into positions of political power, and in some states—most importantly the Soviet Union and its Eastern European satellites—the socialist labor movement even was in a position to make its values and norms the basis for the organization of freshly engineered socialist societies. The impact of the twentieth-century totalitarian dictatorships, which also include the Third Reich, on the process of European dechristianization, still remains to be investigated more fully and systematically. It is, however, not the only problem in the field of religion and politics in the modern world that calls for further investigation from a historical perspective.

Notes

1. Elias Khoury, "Die Chance, das Terror-Jahrzehnt zu beenden," *Süddeutsche Zeitung*, September 5, 2011.

2. Among the plethora of works dealing with 9/11, several titles stand out: Jeffrey Melnick, *9/11 Culture: America under Construction* (Chichester, U.K.: Wiley-Blackwell, 2009); Joanne Meyerowitz, ed., *History and September 11th* (Philadelphia: Temple University Press, 2003); David Simpson, *9/11: The Culture of Commemoration* (Chicago: University of Chicago Press, 2006); Derek Rubin and Jaap Verheul, eds., *American Multiculturalism after 9/11* (Amsterdam: Amsterdam University Press, 2009); Andrew S. Gross and Maryann Snyder-Körber, eds., *Trauma's Continuum: September 11 Reconsidered*, Special Issue, *Amerikastudien/American Studies* 55, no. 3 (2010).

3. Jürgen Wilzewski, "Lessons to Be Learned: Die Bush-Doktrin, der Irakkrieg und die präventive Weltordnungspolitik der USA," *Amerikastudien/American Studies* 53, no. 3 (2008): 355–73; Jochen Hils and Jürgen Wilzewski, eds., *Defekte Demokratie–Crusader State? Die Weltpolitik in der Ära Bush* (Trier, Germany: Wissenschaftlicher Verlag Trier, 2006); Ivo H. Daalder and James M. Lindsay, *America Unbound: The Bush Revolution in Foreign Policy* (Washington, DC: Brookings Institution, 2003); John Lewis Gaddis, "A Grand Strategy," *Foreign Policy* 133 (2002): 50–57; G. John Ikenberry, "America's Imperial Ambition," *Foreign Affairs* 81, no. 5 (2002): 44–60; Peter Rudolf, *George W. Bushs aussenpolitische Strategie* (Berlin: Stiftung Wissenschaft und

324   VOLKER DEPKAT AND JÜRGEN MARTSCHUKAT

Politik, 2005); Werner Kremp and Jürgen Wilzewski, eds., *Weltmacht vor neuer Bedro-hung: Die Bush-Administration und die US-Aussenpolitik nach dem Angriff auf Amerika* (Trier, Germany: Wissenschaftlicher Verlag Trier, 2003).

4. Simpson, *9/11: The Culture of Commemoration*, 4.

5. Melnick, *9/11 Culture*, 3.

6. Melani McAlister, "A Cultural History of the War without End," in *History and September 11th*, ed. Joanne Meyerowitz (Philadelphia: Temple University Press, 2003), 94–116.

7. Ronald Reagan, "Inaugural Address," January 20, 1981, http://www.reagan.utexas.edu/archives/speeches/1981/12081a.htm.

8. Anthony Lake, "From Containment to Enlargement," *Dispatch Magazine* 4, no. 39, September 27, 1993, http://dosfan.lib.uic.edu/ERC/briefing/dispatch/1993/html/Dispatchv4no39.html. On the continuities of U.S. foreign policy in the transition from the Cold War to the post–Cold War world, see Volker Depkat, "Die Ausbreitung von Demokratie als Friedensprogramm unter den US-Präsidenten William J. Clinton und George W. Bush," in *Frieden durch Demokratie? Genese, Wirkung und Kritik eines Deutungsmusters*, ed. Jost Dülffer and Gottfried Niedhart (Essen, Germany: Klartext, 2011), 209–26.

9. McAlister, "A Cultural History," 102–3.

10. Simpson, *9/11: The Culture of Commemoration*, 5–6. See also Ussama Makdisi, "'Anti-Americanism' in the Arab World: An Interpretation of a Brief History," *Journal of American History* 89, no. 2 (2002): 538–57.

11. McAlister, "A Cultural History," 107.

12. Melnick, *9/11 Culture*, 25–49.

13. On the presence of Middle Eastern terrorists in American popular culture since the 1970s, see McAlister, "A Cultural History," 106–13.

14. On September 19, 2001, in an official statement of the German government, Schröder declared, "Die Anschläge von New York und Washington haben—das wis-sen wir alle—nichts, aber auch gar nichts mit Religion zu tun" (The attacks on New York and Washington have—as we all know—nothing, but nothing to do with religion). Gerhard Schröder, "Regierungserklärung: Terroranschläge in den USA und Beschlüsse des Sicherheitsrates der Vereinten Nationen sowie der NATO," Deutscher Bunde-stag: Stenographischer Bericht 187, Sitzung, September 19, 2001, 18303, http://dipbt.bundestag.de/dip21/btp/14/14187.pdf. On the Islamophobia that has developed over the recent years in Germany, see Patrick Bahners, *Die Panikmacher: Die deutsche Angst vor dem Islam: Eine Streitschrift* (Munich: Beck, 2011).

15. Heide Oestreich, *Der Kopftuch-Streit: Das Abendland und ein Quadratmeter Islam* (Frankfurt: Brandes und Apsel, 2004); Christine Kinzinger-Büchel, *Der Kopftuchstreit in der deutschen Rechtsprechung und Gesetzgebung: Eine verfassungsrechtliche Analyse* (Bonn, Germany: Deutscher Anwalt-Verlag, 2009); Julia von Blumenthal, *Das Kopftuch in der Landesgesetzgebung: Governance im Bundesstaat zwischen Unitarisierung und Föderalisierung* (Baden-Baden, Germany: Nomos, 2009); Kirsten Wiese, *Lehrerinnen mit Kopftuch: Zur Zulässigkeit eines religiösen und geschlechtsspezifischen Symbols im Staatsdienst* (Berlin: Duncker & Humblot, 2008); Bahners, *Die Panikmacher*, 92–130.

16. Bahners, *Die Panikmacher*, 6–45; Thilo Sarrazin, *Deutschland schafft sich ab: Wie wir unser Land aufs Spiel setzen* (Munich: Deutsche Verlags-Anstalt, 2010).

17. Hans-Ulrich Wehler, *Deutsche Gesellschaftsgeschichte: Fünfter Band: Bundes-republik und die DDR, 1949–1990* (Munich: Beck, 2008), xiv.

18. Nora Langenbacher and Oliver Decker, eds., *Die Mitte in der Krise: Rechtsextreme Einstellungen in Deutschland 2010* (Berlin: Friedrich-Ebert-Stiftung, 2010), 134.

19. Sabine Berghahn and Petra Rostock, eds., *Der Stoff, aus dem Konflikte sind: Debatten um das Kopftuch in Deutschland, Österreich und der Schweiz* (Bielefeld, Germany: Transcript, 2009); Schirin Amir-Moazami, *Politisierte Religion: Der Kopftuchstreit in Deutschland und Frankreich* (Bielefeld, Germany: Transcript, 2007).

20. Jytte Klausen, *The Cartoons That Shook the World* (New Haven, CT: Yale University Press, 2009); Elisabeth Eide, Risto Kunelius, and Angela Phillips, eds., *Transnational Media Events: The Mohammed Cartoons and the Imagined Clash of Civilizations* (Göteborg, Sweden: Nordicum, 2008); Stefan Piasecki, *Das Schaufenster des Schreckens in den Tagen des Zorns: Eine inhaltliche Analyse der Darstellung von Islam, Islamismus und islamischer Religiosität in der Berichterstattung über den Karikaturenstreit in Spiegel, Stern und Focus sowie ihre Wirkung auf eine säkularisierte Gesellschaft und ihre Tradition von christlicher bzw. islamischer Religiosität* (Marburg, Germany: Tectum-Verlag, 2008).

21. Sebastian Balzter and Christoph Erhardt, "Kreuzzug gegen den Kulturmarxismus," *Frankfurter Allgemeine*, FAZ.Net, July 25, 2011, http://www.faz.net/artikel/C32742/attentaeter-anders-breivik-kreuzzug-gegen-den-kulturmarxismus-30472288.html.

22. See Khoury, "Die Chance."

23. Michael H. Hunt, "In the Wake of September 11: The Clash of What?," in *History and September 11th*, ed. Joanne Meyerowitz (Philadelphia: Temple University Press, 2003), 16.

24. Ibid., 16.

25. Karen O'Brien, "The Return of the Enlightenment," *American Historical Review* 115, no. 5 (2010), 1426.

26. Quotations are from O'Brien, "Return of the Enlightenment," 1427. See also Jonathan Israel, *Radical Enlightenment: Philosophy and the Making of Modernity, 1650–1750* (Oxford, U.K.: Oxford University Press, 2001); Jonathan Israel, *Enlightenment Contested: Philosophy, Modernity and the Emancipation of Man, 1670–1752* (Oxford, U.K.: Oxford University Press, 2006); Tzvetan Todorov, *In Defence of the Enlightenment* (London: Atlantic Books, 2009).

27. O'Brien, "Return of the Enlightenment," 1427.

28. Hugh McLeod, "Religion in the United States and Europe: The Twentieth Century," in *Transatlantische Religionsgeschichte: 18. bis 20. Jahrhundert*, ed. Hartmut Lehmann (Göttingen, Germany: Wallstein, 2006), 131.

29. McLeod, "Religion in the United States and Europe," 141.

30. Assessments of the Bush administration's foreign policy to a considerable extent revolve around the notion of a "crusader state." See Hils and Wilzewski, *Defekte Demokratie*.

31. See Hunt, "In the Wake of September 11," 18.

32. Ibid., 8.

33. Giovanna Borradori, Jacques Derrida, and Jürgen Habermas, *Philosophy in a Time of Terror: Dialogues with Jürgen Habermas and Jacques Derrida* (Chicago: University of Chicago Press, 2003), 86. See also Simpson, *9/11: The Culture of Commemoration*, 9–10.

34. Jürgen Martschukat, "'Lebensgefährlich für Vorurteile, Bigotterie und Engherzigkeit': Einige Überlegungen zur Geschichtsschreibung nach 9/11," *Comparativ* 11, no. 5–6 (2004): 163–72.

35. Jon Butler, "Jack-in-the-Box Faith: The Religion Problem in Modern American History," *Journal of American History* 90, no. 4 (2004): 1358.

36. Ibid., 1369.

37. Ibid., 1362.

38. Hartmut Lehmann, "Secular Europe versus Christian America? Re-examination of the Secularizations Thesis," *Transatlantische Religionsgeschichte*, ed. Hartmut Lehmann (Göttingen, Germany: Wallstein, 2006), 146–47.

39. Mark Edward Ruff, "Integrating Religion into the Historical Mainstream: Recent Literature on Religion in the Federal Republic of Germany," *Central European History* 42, no. 2 (2009): 307–37, 308; Uta Andrea Balbier, "'Sag: Wie hast Du's mit der Religion?' Das Verhältnis von Religion und Politik als Gretchenfrage der Zeitgeschichte," *H-Soz-u-Kult*, November 10, 2009, http://hsozkult.geschichte.hu-berlin.de/forum/2009-11-001. A recent exception is a special issue of *Zeithistorische Forschungen/Studies in Contemporary History* 3 (2010) on "Religion in der Bundesrepublik Deutschland/Religion in the Federal Republic of Germany." See also Benjamin Ziemann, *Sozialgeschichte der Religion: Von der Reformation bis zur Gegenwart* (Frankfurt: Campus, 2009).

40. Martin Greschat, *Kirchliche Zeitgeschichte: Versuch einer Orientierung* (Leipzig, Germany: Evangelische Verlagsanstalt, 2005).

41. Frank Lambert, *Religion in American Politics: A Short History* (Princeton, NJ: Princeton University Press, 2008), 157.

42. Pippa Norris and Ronald Inglehart, *Sacred and Secular: Religion and Politics Worldwide* (New York: Cambridge University Press, 2004), 13–14, 132, 106.

43. Lehmann, "Secular Europe versus Christian America?," 157.

44. See Roger Finke and Rodney Stark, *The Churching of America, 1776–2005: Winners and Losers in Our Religious Economy*, 2nd ed. (New Brunswick, NJ: Rutgers University Press, 2005); Philip Schaff, *America: A Sketch of Its Political, Social, and Religious Character*, ed. Perry Miller (1854; reprint Cambridge, MA: Belknap of Harvard University Press, 1961), 71–81.

45. Lehmann, "Secular Europe versus Christian America?," 157.

46. Werner Sombart, *Warum gibt es in den Vereinigten Staaten keinen Sozialismus?* (Tübingen, Germany: J. C. B. Mohr, 1906).

47. McLeod, "Religion in the United States and Europe," 136–37.

Contributors

Volker Depkat is professor of American studies at Regensburg University. His most recent major publications are *Visual Cultures: Transatlantic Perspectives* (Heidelberg, Germany: Universitätsverlag, 2012), with Meike Zwingenberger; "American History/ies in Germany: Assessments, Transformations, Perspectives," Special Issue of *Amerikastudien/American Studies* 54, no. 3 (2009); and *Geschichte Nordamerikas: Eine Einführung* (Cologne: Böhlau/UTB, 2008).

Jürgen Martschukat is professor of North American history at Erfurt University. His most recent major publications are *Die Ordnung des Sozialen: Väter und Familien in der amerikanischen Geschichte seit 1770* (Frankfurt: Campus, 2013); *Is the Death Penalty Dying? European and American Perspectives* (Cambridge, U.K.: Cambridge University Press, 2011), with Austin Sarat; and *Geschichte der Männlichkeiten* (Frankfurt: Campus, 2008), with Olaf Stieglitz.

Michael Broers is professor of Western European history at the University of Oxford and a fellow of Lady Margaret Hall. His book *The Napoleonic Empire in Italy, 1796–1814: Cultural Imperialism in a European Context?* (Basingstoke, U.K.: Palgrave, 2005) won the Prix Napoléon of the Fondation Napoléon. He has been a visiting member of the Institute for Advanced Study, Princeton. His most recent book is *Napoleon's Other War: Bandits, Rebels, and Their Pursuers in the Age of Revolutions* (Witney, U.K.: Peter Lang, 2010).

Daniel A. Cohen, associate professor of history at Case Western Reserve University, is the author of *Pillars of Salt, Monuments of Grace: New England Crime Literature and the Origins of American Popular Culture, 1674–1860* (New York: Oxford University Press, 1993); *The Female Marine and Related Works: Narratives of Cross-Dressing and Urban Vice in America's Early Republic* (Amherst: University of Massachusetts Press, 1997); and most recently, "Winnie Woodfern Comes Out in Print: Story-Paper Authorship and Protolesbian Self-Representation in Antebellum America," *Journal of the History of Sexuality* 21, no. 3 (2012): 367–408.

Ronald E. Doel, associate professor of history at Florida State University, is the author of *Solar System Astronomy in America: Communities, Patronage, and Interdisciplinary Science, 1920–1960* (reissued in paperback by Cambridge University Press, 2009). His recent publications include *The Historiography of Contemporary Science, Technology, and Medicine: Writing Recent Science* (New York: Routledge, 2006), coedited with Thomas Söderqvist, and "Quelle place pour les sciences d'environnement dans l'histoire environnementale?" *Revue d'histoire moderne et contemporaine* 56, no. 4 (2009): 137–64.

James Gilbert is distinguished university professor emeritus at the University of Maryland. He is the author of *Redeeming Culture: American Religion in an Age of Science* (Chicago: University of Chicago Press, 1998) and, most recently, *Whose Fair? Experience, Memory, and the History of the Great St. Louis Exposition* (Chicago: University of Chicago Press, 2009) and *Secrets and Strangers*—a book of short stories—in 2012.

Gerlinde Groitl is assistant professor of international and transatlantic relations at Regensburg University. She is the author of *Evangelical Internationalism: The American Christian Right and Global Human Rights* (Hamburg, Germany: Verlag Dr. Kovač, 2007).

Michael Hochgeschwender is professor for North American cultural history and cultural anthropology at the Ludwig-Maximilians-University at Munich. Recent publications include *Amerikanische Religion: Evangelikalismus, Pfingstlertum und Fundamentalismus* (Frankfurt: Verlag der Weltreligionen, 2007) and *Der Amerikanische Bürgerkrieg* (Munich: Beck, 2010).

Klaus Hödl is historian at the Center for Jewish Studies at the University of Graz. Among his most recent publications are *Wiener Juden-Jüdische Wiener* (Innsbruck, Austria: Studienverlag 2006); *Kultur und Gedächtnis* (Paderborn, Germany: Schöningh 2012); and *Nicht nur Bildung, nicht nur Bürger: Juden in der Populärkultur* (Innsbruck, Germany: Studienverlag, 2013), which he edited.

Frank Kelleter is professor of American studies at Göttingen University. He recently published *Populäre Serialität: Narration–Evolution–Distinktion* (Bielefeld, Germany: Transcript, 2012). He has written chapters in *The Wire: Race, Class, Genre*, ed. Liam Kennedy and Stephen Shapiro (Ann Arbor: University of Michigan Press, 2012), and *Film Remakes, Adaptations, and Fan Productions: Remake/Remodel*, ed. Kathleen Loock and Constantine Verevis (Basingstoke, U.K.: Palgrave, 2012).

André Krischer is assistant professor of British and Commonwealth History at WWU Muenster. His most recent publication is *Herstellung und Darstellung von Entscheidungen: Verwalten, Verfahren und Verhandeln in der Vormoderne* (Berlin: Duncker & Humblot, 2010), with Barbara Stollberg-Rilinger.

Michelle Mart is associate professor of history at Penn State University, Berks Campus. She is the author of *Eye on Israel: How America Came to View Israel as an Ally* (Albany, NY: SUNY Press, 2006) and, most recently, "U.S.–Israeli Relations and the Quest for Peace in the Middle East," in *A Guide to U.S. Foreign Policy: A Diplomatic History*, ed. Robert McMahon and Thomas Zeiler, 563–78 (Washington, DC: Congressional Quarterly Press, 2012) and "Rhetoric and Response: The Cultural Impact of Rachel Carson's *Silent Spring*," *Left History* 14, no. 2 (2010): 31–57.

Anthony Santoro, postdoctoral fellow in American history at Heidelberg University, is the author of *Exile and Embrace: Contemporary Religious*

Discourse on the Death Penalty (Boston: Northeastern University Press, 2013) and "Hermeneutical Communities in Conflict: The Bible and the Capital Jury," in *Religion and State: From Separation to Cooperation? Legal–Philosophical Reflections for a De-secularized World*, ed. Bart C. Labuschagne and Ari M. Solon, 87–109 (Stuttgart, Germany: Franz Steiner Verlag, 2009).

Thomas Schmidt-Lux is assistant professor of cultural sociology at Leipzig University. His most recent publications are "Vigilantismus: Ein Phänomen der Grenze?," *Kriminologisches Journal* 44, no. 2 (2010): 118–32; *Forcierte Säkularität: Religiöser Wandel und Generationendynamik im Osten Deutschlands* (Frankfurt: Campus, 2009), with Monika Wohlrab-Sahr and Uta Karstein; and "Das helle Licht der Wissenschaft: Die Urania, der organisierte Szientismus und der ostdeutsche Säkularisierungsprozess," *Geschichte und Gesellschaft* 34, no. 1 (2008): 41–72.

Monika Wohlrab-Sahr is professor of cultural sociology at Leipzig University. Her most recent publications are *Forcierte Säkularität: Religiöser Wandel und Generationendynamik im Osten Deutschlands* (Frankfurt: Campus, 2009), with Uta Karstein and Thomas Schmidt-Lux; "Multiple Secularities: Towards a Cultural Sociology of Secular Modernities," *Comparative Sociology* 11, no. 6 (2012): 875–909, with Marian Burchardt; and "Contested Secularities: Religious Minorities and Secular Progressivism in the Netherlands," *Journal of Religion in Europe* 5, no. 3 (2012) 349–83, with Cora Schuh and Marian Burchardt.

Index

Information in figures, tables, and footnotes is indicated by *f, t,* and n respectively.